MARK 9–16

BHGNT

Baylor Handbook on the Greek New Testament
Martin M. Culy
General Editor

MARK 9–16
A Handbook on the Greek Text

Rodney J. Decker

BAYLOR UNIVERSITY PRESS

Scripture translations are the author's.

Cover Design by Pamela Poll Graphic Design

Library of Congress Cataloging-in-Publication Data

Decker, Rodney J., 1952–2014
 Mark : a handbook on the Greek text / Rodney J. Decker.
 pages cm. — (Baylor handbook on the Greek New Testament)
 Includes bibliographical references and index.
 ISBN 978-1-4813-0238-8 (v. 1 : pbk. : alk. paper)
 ISBN 978-1-4813-0239-5 (v. 2 : pbk. : alk. paper)
1. Bible. Mark—Criticism, Textual. 2. Bible. Mark Greek—
Versions. I. Title.
 BS2585.52.D425 2014
 226.3'0486—dc23
                                        2014011308

*To the Northmoreland Baptist Church
and Pastor Kurt Sebo*

CONTENTS

Contents

SERIES INTRODUCTION

The Baylor Handbook on the Greek New Testament (BHGNT) is designed to guide new readers and seasoned scholars alike through the intricacies of the Greek text. Each handbook provides a verse-by-verse treatment of the biblical text. Unlike traditional commentaries, however, the BHGNT makes little attempt to expound on the theological meaning or significance of the document under consideration. Instead, the handbooks serve as "prequels" to commentary proper. They provide readers of the New Testament with a foundational analysis of the Greek text upon which interpretation may then be established. Readers of traditional commentaries are sometimes dismayed by the fact that even those that are labeled "exegetical" or "critical" frequently have little to say about the mechanics of the Greek text and all too often completely ignore the more perplexing grammatical issues. In contrast, the BHGNT offers an accessible and comprehensive, though not exhaustive, treatment of the Greek New Testament, with particular attention given to the grammar of the text. In order to make the handbooks more user-friendly, authors have only selectively interacted with secondary literature. Where there is significant debate on an issue, the handbooks provide a representative sample of scholars espousing each position; when authors adopt a less known stance on the text, they generally list any other scholars who have embraced that position.

The BHGNT, however, is more than a reliable guide to the Greek text of the New Testament. Each author brings unique strengths to the task of preparing the handbook. As a result, students and scholars alike will at times be introduced to ways of looking at the Greek language that they have not encountered before. This feature makes the handbooks valuable not only for intermediate and advanced Greek courses but also for students and scholars who no longer have the luxury of increasing their Greek proficiency within a classroom context. While handbook authors do not consider modern linguistic theory to be a panacea for all questions exegetical, the BHGNT does aim both to help move linguistic insights into the mainstream of New Testament reference works and, at the same time, to help weed out some of the myths about the Greek language that continue to appear in both scholarly and popular treatments of the New Testament.

Using the Baylor Handbook on the Greek New Testament

Each handbook consists of the following features. The introduction draws readers' attention to some of the distinctive features of the biblical text and treats some of the broader issues relating to the text as a whole in a more thorough fashion. In the handbook proper, the biblical text is divided into sections, each of which is introduced with a translation that illustrates how the insights gleaned from the analysis that follows may be expressed in modern English. Following the translation is the heart of the handbook, an extensive analysis of the Greek text. Here, the Greek text of each verse is followed by comments on grammatical, lexical, and text-critical issues. Handbook authors may also make use of other features, such as passage overviews between the translation and notes.

Each page of the handbook includes a header to direct readers to the beginning of the section where the translation is found (left page header) or to identify the range of verses covered on the two facing pages (right-hand header). Terminology used in the comments that is potentially unfamiliar is included in a glossary in the back of the handbook and/or cross-referenced with the first occurrence of the expression, where an explanation may be found. Each volume also includes an index that provides a list of grammatical phenomena occurring in the biblical text. This feature provides a valuable resource for students of Greek wanting to study a particular construction more carefully or Greek instructors needing to develop illustrations, exercises, or exams. The handbooks conclude with a bibliography of works cited, providing helpful guidance in identifying resources for further research on the Greek text.

The handbooks assume that users will possess a minimal level of competence with Greek morphology and syntax. Series authors generally utilize traditional labels such as those found in Daniel Wallace's *Greek Grammar Beyond the Basics*. Labels that are drawn from the broader field of modern linguistics are explained at their first occurrence and included in the glossary. Common labels that users may be unfamiliar with are also included in the glossary.

The primary exception to the broad adoption of traditional syntactic labels relates to verb tenses. Most New Testament Greek grammars describe the tense system as being formally fairly simple (only 6 tenses) but functionally complex. The aorist tense, it is frequently said, can function in a wide variety of ways that are associated with labels such as "ingressive," "gnomic," "constative," "epistolary," "proleptic," and so forth. Similar functional complexity is posited for the other tenses. Positing such "functions," however, typically stems not from a careful analysis of Greek syntax but rather from grappling with the challenges of translating Greek verbs into English. When we carefully examine the Greek verb tenses themselves, we find that the tense forms do not themselves denote semantic features such as ingressive, iterative, or conative; they certainly do not emphasize such notions; at best they may allow for ingressive, iterative, or conative translations. Although many of the other traditional labels are susceptible to similar critique, the tense labels have frequently led to exegetical claims that go beyond the syntax, e.g., that a particular aorist verb *emphasizes* the beginning of an action. For this reason, we have chosen not to utilize these labels. Instead, where the context points to an ingressive nuance for the action of the verb, this will be incorporated into the translation.

Deponency

Although series authors will vary in the theoretical approaches they bring to the text, the BHGNT has adopted the same general approach on one important issue: deponency. Traditionally, the label "deponent" has been applied to verbs with middle, passive, or middle/passive morphology that are thought to be "active" in meaning. Introductory grammars tend to put a significant number of middle verbs in the New Testament in this category, despite the fact that some of the standard reference grammars have questioned the validity of the label. Robertson (332), for example, argues that the label "should not be used at all."

In recent years, a number of scholars have taken up Robertson's quiet call to abandon this label. Carl Conrad's posts on the B-Greek Internet discussion list (beginning in 1997) and his subsequent formalization of those concerns in unpublished papers available on his website have helped flesh out the concerns raised by earlier scholars. In a recent article, Jonathan Pennington (61–64) helpfully summarizes the rationale for dispensing with the label, maintaining that widespread use of the term "deponent" stems from two key factors: (1) the tendency to attempt to analyze Greek syntax through reference to English translation—if a workable translation of a middle form appears "active" in English, we conclude that the verb must be active in meaning even though it is middle in form; and (2) the imposition of Latin categories on Greek grammar. Pennington (61) concludes that "most if not all verbs that are considered 'deponent' are in fact truly middle in meaning." The questions that have been raised regarding deponency as a syntactic category, then, are not simply issues that interest a few Greek scholars and linguists but have no bearing on how one understands the text. Rather, if these scholars are correct, the notion of deponency has, at least in some cases, effectively obscured the semantic significance of the middle voice, leading to imprecise readings of the text (see also Bakker and Taylor).

It is not only middle voice verbs, however, that are the focus of attention in this debate. Conrad, Pennington, and others also maintain that deponency is an invalid category for passive verbs that have traditionally been placed in this category. To account for putative passive deponent verbs, these scholars have turned to the evolution of voice morphology in the Greek language. They draw attention to the fact that middle morphology was being replaced by passive morphology (the θη morpheme) during the Koine period (see esp. Conrad, 3, 5–6; cf. Pennington, 68; Taylor, 175; Caragounis, 153). Consequently, in the Common Era we find "an increasing number of passive forms without a distinctive passive idea . . . replacing older middle forms" (Pennington, 68). This diachronic argument leads Conrad (5) to conclude that the θη morpheme should be treated as a middle/passive rather than a passive morpheme. Such arguments have a sound linguistic foundation and raise serious questions about the legitimacy of the notion "passive deponent."

Should, then, the label "deponent" be abandoned altogether? While more research needs to be done to account for middle/passive morphology in Koine Greek fully, the arguments, which are very briefly summarized above, are both compelling and exegetically significant. "The middle voice needs to be understood in its own status and function as indicating that the subject of a verb is the focus of the verb's action or state" (Conrad, 3; cf. Taylor, 174). Consequently, users of the BHGNT will discover that verbs that are typically labeled "deponent," including some with θη morphology, tend to be listed as "middle."

In recognizing that so-called deponent verbs should be viewed as true middles, users of the BHGNT should not fall into the trap of concluding that the middle form emphasizes the subject's involvement in the action of the verb. At times, the middle voice appears simply to be a morphological flag indicating that the verb is intransitive. More frequently, the middle morphology tends to be driven by the "middle" semantics of the verb itself. In other words, the middle voice is sometimes used with the verb not in order to place a focus on the subject's involvement in the action but precisely because the sense of the lexical form itself involves subject focus.

It is the hope of Baylor University Press, the series editor, and each of the authors that these handbooks will help advance our understanding of the Greek New Testament, be used to further equip the saints for the work of ministry, and fan into flame a love for the Greek New Testament among a new generation of students and scholars.

Martin M. Culy

PREFACE

I have written this handbook over the past years (the editor might say "too many years"!) in a variety of settings and locations across the country: squeezed into airplane seats, traveling the Interstates, in motels, remote cabins and cottages, homes of friends and family, as well as in the more conventional settings of my study at home or the seminary. The process has been interrupted by a variety of other writing deadlines, teaching loads, and health issues. The time it has taken to complete this work has likely introduced a variety of inconsistencies that I have not noticed in the final editing. I have learned a lot in the course of writing and editing: a lot about Greek and a lot about Mark. Although Mark has the reputation of being some of the simplest Greek in the NT, only by having to grapple with every word in the text at the grammatical level does one discover that even "simple Greek" has its challenges.

I owe a great deal to many people who have contributed to this book in one way or another. My students from multiple Exegesis of Mark classes over the past years have worked through various parts of this material with me. Mark Mills, one of my Ph.D. students who has served as my TA since 2010, has been an invaluable help in proofing, asking hard grammatical questions which required me to justify (or sometimes change) my analysis, and especially in wrestling a large, unwieldy manuscript into submission to create the indices with his skill in complex Word searches and VBA code in Excel. Ronoldo Ghenov, an M.Div. grad, carefully proofed a large portion of the manuscript while preaching through Mark in his pastoral ministry. I am greatly indebted to Carl Conrad for a great deal of interaction on the grammar of Mark over the years that this volume has been in preparation. He has been generous with his time both in personal email and interacting on my blog, saving me from more than one mistake and helping me untangle various grammatical knots (some of which were my own creation). My dean, Mike Stallard, and provost, Jim Lytle, have been more than helpful in making it possible for me to both teach and write. I have had the privilege of working with an editor who knows Greek better than I do—and who has not been hesitant to challenge some of my analyses and point out mistakes, all the while pruning and compressing my comments in an attempt to keep the manuscript somewhere near the verbal budget. The series is well served by Martin Culy's guiding hand. My wife compiled the long list of abbreviations and helped me wrestle the references and bibliography into some measure of consistency as she proofed the manuscript. Any remaining discrepancies are certainly my fault, not hers. She also deserves a large measure of thanks for creating a home environment where I can write, especially in the last few years as life has gradually become more complicated.

I have dedicated this book to my church family and pastor, the Northmoreland Baptist Church and Pastor Kurt Seboe. One could not ask for a better family of friends who have prayed for me and encouraged me in the years we have worshipped and ministered together. They also studied the Gospel of Mark with me for several years. Pastor Seboe, one of my students of twenty years ago, has recently come to minister at Northmoreland. His faithful exposition of the Word, his pastoral wisdom, his prayers with and for me, and his friendship have meant a great deal. His ministry to me began several years ago when I was first diagnosed with cancer; he called from Iowa every month without fail and always prayed with me on the phone. To be able to now call him pastor is my privilege. God has provided a good and healthy church home for my wife and me at Northmoreland and for that we are grateful.

Editor's note: Rod Decker was a master of the Greek language who was intent on helping others gain a fuller understanding of the New Testament so that they could "rightly handle the word of truth." Even as he was suffering from the debilitating effects of cancer treatments Rod never stopped pushing forward to complete his final literary offerings to the Lord and final gifts to God's people. Rod's two handbooks on the Gospel of Mark serve as testaments of Rod's meticulous commitment to teaching God's Word, a commitment that flowed out of his exemplary devotion to his Lord. All of us who knew him will not only miss him but also owe him a debt of gratitude. In the final two months of his life, when it became apparent that he would not have the strength to review the proofs of his manuscript personally before it went to publication, Rod and his wife Linda were very grateful when Will Varner graciously stepped in and filled that gap.

ABBREVIATIONS

Note: References to ancient sources use the standard SBL abbreviations.

1st	first person
2nd	second person
3rd	third person
||	(in the) parallel passage
*	verb root (when prefixed to Greek text)
acc	accusative
act	active
adj	adjective
ad loc.	*ad locum*, "at *or* to the place"
ad sensum	*ad sensum*, "according to the sense"
AF	Apostolic Fathers
aor	aorist
ASV	American Standard Version
BAG	Bauer, *A Greek-English Lexicon of the NT*, 1st ed., 1957
BDAG	Danker, *A Greek-English Lexicon of the NT*, 3rd ed., 2000
BDB	Brown, Driver, and Briggs, *A Hebrew and English Lexicon of the OT*
BDF	Blass, Debrunner, Funk, *A Greek Grammar of the NT*
BGU	*Aegyptische Urkunden aus den Königlichen Staatlichen Museen zu Berlin, Griechische Urkunden*
CEB	Common English Bible
CEV	Contemporary English Version
ch(s).	chapter(s)
CL	Danker, *The Concise Greek-English Lexicon of the New Testament*
dat	dative

EDNT	Balz and Schneider, *Exegetical Dictionary of the New Testament*
Eng.	English
ESV	English Standard Version
fem	feminine
frag.	fragment
fr.	from
fut	future
gen	genitive
GNB	Good News Bible
GW	God's Word (version)
HALOT	*Hebrew and Aramaic Lexicon of the Old Testament*, ed. Koehler and Baumgartner
HCSB	Holman Christian Standard Bible
impf	imperfect
impv	imperative
ind	indicative
inf	infinitive
ISV	International Standard Version
KJV	King James Version
l.	line
LEH	Lust, Eynikel, and Hauspie, *A Greek-English Lexicon of the Septuagint*
LN	Louw and Nida, *Greek-English Lexicon*
LSJ	Liddell, Scott, and Jones, *A Greek-English Lexicon*
LXX	the Septuagint and/or Old Greek translations of the OT
masc	masculine
MBG	Mounce, *Morphology of Biblical Greek*
mg.	marginal translation
MHT	Moulton, Howard, Turner, *Grammar of NT Greek*
mid	middle
MM	Moulton and Milligan, *Vocabulary of the Greek NT*
MT	Masoretic Text
ms(s)	manuscript(s)
n(n).	note(s)
NA	Nestle-Aland, *Novum Testamentum Graece*
NAB	New American Bible
NASB	New American Standard Bible
New Docs	*New Documents Illustrating Early Christianity*
NCV	New Century Version
NEB	New English Bible
NET	New English Translation

neut	neuter
NIV	New International Version (1984 and 2011)
NIV84	New International Version, 1984
NIV11	New International Version, 2011
NJB	New Jerusalem Bible
NLT	New Living Translation (2nd ed.)
nom	nominative
NRSV	New Revised Standard Version
NT	New Testament
opt	optative
OT	Old Testament
pass	passive
pl	plural
plprf	pluperfect
pres	present
prf	perfect
ptc	participle
REB	Revised English Bible
RSV	Revised Standard Version
RV	Revised Version
sg	singular
subj	subjunctive
s.v.	*sub voce*, "under the word"
TDM	Decker, *Temporal Deixis of the Greek Verb in the Gospel of Mark*
TEV	Today's English Version
TLG	*Thesaurus Linguae Graecae*
UBS[4]	United Bible Society, The Greek New Testament, 4th ed.
v.l.(l.)	*varia lectio*, "variant reading(s)"
w.	with
WH	Westcott and Hort, *The NT in the Original Greek; Introduction to the NT*

INTRODUCTION

Mark has a reputation of being a simple book. I am not so sure that status is deserved. True, there are far fewer stylistic niceties and syntactical developments than one reads in, say, Hebrews (to pick an example from the opposite end of the NT's literary range). Mark's Greek is more on the plain side and at times even rough when compared with more polished writers, yet he communicates his message clearly and effectively. That message is simple only at a surface level. This is a Gospel that, if read seriously and attentively, will challenge any reader.

Mark's purpose is related to discipleship. He works it out, paragraph by paragraph, by challenging his readers to answer two intertwined questions: Who is Jesus? and What does he expect from those who follow him? Mark's answers are not stated in a formal way as an argued thesis. Rather they are demonstrated in narrative form. The included stories have been selected and arranged to prompt both questions in a reader's mind and to marshal the evidence that leads to the intended answer: Jesus is a powerful Savior who is worth obeying.

But this is a grammatical handbook, not a full commentary. Though I would greatly enjoy unpacking Mark's portrait of Jesus in an expository fashion, that is not the task of this book. As a grammatical handbook it forms the first step that ought to be taken before anyone sits down at the keyboard to write a commentary or who prepares to expound the message of Mark to a congregation. I suspect that both tasks are too often undertaken without this first step. If I can encourage and facilitate other writers and preachers to grapple seriously with the text of this Gospel as they prepare their own exposition, I will count the years of work I have invested in this handbook to have been worth the time spent.

As to "Mark," I refer to the book, formally anonymous, which we have come to know by that name, or to its author, whomever that may have been. My comments are upon the book as it stands (the Greek text of NA^{27}/UBS^4), not on presumed or theoretical sources or composition methods that may have been involved in its creation. Some fascinating theories have been proposed by scholars more brilliant than I as to the background of this literary work. I am not as confident as they are as to the degree of certainty these theories hold. We can only seek with any degree of certainty to understand what we have in the text before us. Although my tentative working assumptions include Markan priority and even authorship by the John Mark of the NT who wrote as Peter's "homiletic biographer" (I am inclined to give some credence to the testimony of Papias), I freely acknowledge that I might be wrong on either score. But even if that were the case, the same text would be before us and would still demand our study and explanation.

One of the challenges of a grammatical handbook is making too much of the grammar. I have resisted the lure of grammatical maximalism, whether the older "golden nuggets" approach of writers like Wuest, or the much more sophisticated approach of Gundry, whose valuable commentary—and it is that—explicitly claims to be "an attempt to make interpretative capital out of Mark's grammar and style" (24). Despite his overplaying the significance of particular grammatical features, his comments are almost always worth considering carefully since they force a careful reading of the text. Though I frequently disagree, I often find that Gundry has put his finger on something that has not been considered previously and at times he makes brilliant observations. Balancing what should and can be said with some confidence against what might be said or what might be allowed on the basis of grammar is not always easy. Doubtless some will think I have strayed to one side of that path or the other.

As the years go by I grow increasingly unsatisfied with claims of "emphasis," etc. on the basis of grammatical features. Silva's brilliant parody of exegetical maximalism in his valuable *God, Language and Scripture* rings all too true, not only at the popular level where preachers "mine" the text (or rather, the commentaries, software-generated summaries, and such "tools" as Wuest) to find nuggets that support an emphasis that they want to make in the text, but even in some commentaries that attempt to focus only on the Greek text. We do not understand our own language in this way even though a grammarian can dissect such texts and assign appropriate taxonomical labels to the individual elements. Grammatical study of ancient texts in "dead" languages (i.e., those no longer spoken by a community of native speakers) is of value. It helps us understand what is being said and enables us to grasp the alternative possibilities in a written text. More often it facilitates *eliminating* invalid possibilities of meaning. But when all is said and done, all the grammatical and syntactical data are important only in that they enable us to grasp the meaning of the statements in their context. Claims of emphasis rarely (note that I do not say "never") come from individual words or constructions. When, for example, I read claims by a commentator that a particular word is emphatic because "it is the only finite verb expressed anywhere in the parable" (Gundry, 748, commenting on ἐνετείλατο in Mark 13:34), I throw up my hands in dismay since the parable in question is only one sentence long and has only one main clause.

Some currently popular approaches to evaluating the contribution of grammar leave me a bit skeptical. These include not only the significance of word order, but also some claims in the name of discourse analysis. Though there is probably some truth in these avenues, I do not sense sufficient consensus to commend unreserved dependence on any one such tool. I have even attempted to avoid relying too heavily on the discourse function of verbal aspect—an area in which I have done more work than in some other areas (see further on this below).

I have tried to remember that I was writing a grammatical handbook, not a full-fledged commentary, a biblical theology, a text-critical handbook, a discourse-analysis handbook, or a study of verbal aspect, though doubtless some readers may think that I have strayed further across the line into some of those areas from time to time than I should. Others will be disappointed that I have not done so more often in their area of interest or specialty. The focus is therefore on what has traditionally been viewed as the purview of grammar, though informed by more recent discussion in a number of areas. I have tried to keep the terminology manageable. Though any area of study has its own vocabulary of specialized terms, I have eschewed jargon, especially terminology that my students have found to be obtuse. There is therefore plenty of discussion about the basic grammatical categories (case, tense, voice, etc.) and a careful selection of some newer terms that seem to me to be useful and necessary (e.g., in the discussion of aspect), but no mention of right (or left) dislocation, rheme, frames, or equipollent binary opposition. These terms (and many others like them) have their place, but not in material designed for students and practitioners. I am writing primarily for those who are not professional grammarians, linguists, or theoreticians.

After completing the first draft of my comments I then turned, section by section, to a selection of commentaries. My conversation partners at this level were Gould, Swete, Bruce, Cranfield, V. Taylor, Lane, Gundry, Guelich, Edwards, Evans, France, Collins, and Stein. Occasional gleanings from other commentators will be found along the way, but not consistently. My choice to engage these writers beginning with the old ICC volume by Gould (1896) to the most recently published work by Stein (2008) is an attempt to give writers their due. Sometimes more recent commentators are simply a collection of snippets from older works, with or without credit. Although this could obviously be pushed back much further, I have limited my efforts in this regard to a century's worth of major critical commentaries which, for the most part (Lane and Edwards are exceptions), make a deliberate effort to engage the Greek text systematically and explicitly.

For purposes of this handbook, "Koine Greek texts related to the Bible" refers to the LXX, the Pseudepigrapha, Josephus, Philo, and the Apostolic Fathers. Various grammatical, syntactical, and semantic notes from these works, accessed via the grammatically tagged texts in Accordance, have been cited to provide examples that may help to elucidate Markan usage and meaning.

The English translation given is intended as a study tool, not a literary work. It is fairly formal in most parts to show the grammatical analysis and decisions reflected in the handbook sections that follow, though there are some noticeable instances of functional equivalents when it is necessary to communicate the meaning with greater clarity and accuracy in English. (I deliberately use the terms *formal* and *functional* in the handbook in place of such terms as *literal* or *dynamic* as more accurate descriptions of the issues involved; *literal* in particular is too often assumed to mean "more accurate" when it typically refers only to a gloss-based rendering.) Translation choices in individual passages have not been compared with other similar choices elsewhere in the book, even if that may have resulted in some variations of choice over the years. One convention in the translation should be noted: parenthetical comments in the text included by Mark (something fairly common in his gospel, see, e.g., 3:30; 7:19; 13:14) are not punctuated with parentheses in the English translation, but with spaced em-dashes (—). The BHGNT series conventions use parentheses only for supplied English words and square brackets for textual variants marked with single square brackets in the UBS[4] text. Regular punctuation dashes are also used in normal English fashion, but these are not spaced.

The sections into which I have broken the text for comment are not intended to have any interpretive function. Though the break is always at a transitional point of some sort, I have broken some long paragraphs and combined other short ones. The primary criteria is simply length. I have often supplied the antecedent of a pronoun (explicit or as part of a verb form) when the reference is not immediately clear, particularly at the beginning of a pericope. In such instances I have not marked the supplied reference with parentheses. In Mark's Gospel the referent in such cases is most often Jesus.

All OT references are to the versification of Rahlfs' LXX unless noted otherwise. This handbook uses the term "the Septuagint" (LXX) somewhat loosely. Unless it is helpful to be more specific it may refer to any of the text forms of the OT in Greek, recognizing that there is not one such text (see Jobes and Silva, 30; and with several detailed examples, Steyn, 697–707).

Given the frequency in typical narrative of αὐτοῦ as a term of relationship (especially variations of οἱ μαθηταὶ αὐτοῦ, more than 60 times in Mark), I have not commented each time this expression is found. It may refer to familial relations ("his brother," τὸν ἀδελφὸν αὐτοῦ, 1:19), other personal relationships ("his disciples," τοῖς μαθηταῖς αὐτοῦ, 2:16; "his elect," τοὺς ἐκλεκτοὺς αὐτοῦ, 13:27), intangibles of various sorts ("his teaching," τῇ διδαχῇ αὐτοῦ, 1:22; "his reputation," ἡ ἀκοὴ αὐτοῦ, 1:28; "his heart" [not the body part], τῇ καρδίᾳ αὐτοῦ, 11:23), bodily parts ("his hand," τὴν χεῖρα αὐτοῦ, 1:41; "his ear," αὐτοῦ τὸ ὠτάριον, 14:47), or other related objects (which may be "owned" or not: "his house," τῇ οἰκίᾳ αὐτοῦ, 2:15; "its shade," τὴν σκιὰν αὐτοῦ, 4:32; possibly of a donkey: "his master," ὁ κύριος αὐτοῦ, 11:3). Labeling all such uses as genitives of possession, though perhaps convenient shorthand, is not an accurate description of the various relationships involved.

Some grammatical specifics of Mark's Gospel are worth noting. The following notes in that regard are selective; they do not comprise a full Markan grammar, something which neither time nor space allow.

Indefinite Plurals

A feature of Mark's Greek that is distinctive, though not entirely unique (it occurs less frequently elsewhere), is the use of a third person plural verb in the indefinite sense of "people" where other Greek writers would often use τινες. This construction refers to an unspecified group that has no grammatical antecedent or other identification in its clause or the preceding context. Mark's more frequent use of this feature than other NT writers may be due to Aramaic influence. Maloney (2008, 138–62) has explored such uses in detail and generally offers a good account of the evidence. (I am not persuaded that the tense distinctions that he finds are relevant since they appear to confuse tense with *Aktionsart* values.) He lists the following references as those containing an impersonal plural form: 1:22 (ἐξεπλήσσοντο), 32 (ἔφερον), 45 (ἤρχοντο); 2:3 (ἔρχονται), 18 (ἔρχονται, λέγουσιν); 3:2 (παρετήρουν); 5:14 (ἦλθον), 35 (ἔρχονται); 6:14 (ἔλεγον), 33 (εἶδον), 55 (περιέδραμον); 7:32 (φέρουσιν); 8:22 (φέρουσιν); 10:13 (προσέφερον); 13:9 (παραδώσουσιν), 26 (ὄψονται). I disagree on his listing of 3:2, consider 3:32 (λέγουσιν) possible (Maloney considers but rejects this example), and would add 6:12 (μετανοῶσιν). Although it is possible to distinguish among this list those that refer to specific, though unnamed, people who do specific things on the one hand, and more generic references to people in general, these are not categories inherent in the indefinite plural or in the tense used (Maloney does make such distinctions); they come rather from the context of the statements. That some tenses show up frequently in such statements (e.g., imperfects) is not due to some particularity of the imperfect, but because the sort of contexts in which imperfects are often used (e.g., summary statements) frequently overlap with the contexts in which indefinite verbs are used. (The list above includes present, imperfect, future, and aorist tenses.) For more on this phenomenon, see MHT (3:292–93); C.H. Turner (4–12), who designates such use "impersonal"; Wallace (1996, 402–3); and Zerwick (§§1–6).

The Use of καί and δέ

About 64 percent of the sentences in Mark begin with καί (376 of 583); this compares with 30 percent in Matthew (Ellingworth, 125; S. Black, 108). The usual explanation for Mark's usage is a Semitic background, with Aramaic being his probable heart language. Though this has been challenged (S. Black, 109–10), I think the essence of the explanation is valid, though I would prefer to speak of a Semitic enhancement rather than a pure Semitism. Black may be correct that this is not a complete explanation for such usage, but it should begin here. The value of Black's study of καί in Matthew is that she goes beyond the question of origin to ask *how* καί is used at a discourse level. Her proposal appears to be correct and also to be valid for Markan usage. She explains that "καί, as the unmarked or default sentence conjunction in Matthew, is a procedural, non-truth-conditional signal of continuity, normally found in contexts where there is—or is presented as being—continuity of time, action, or (especially) actor" (112). She goes on to note that "When the audience encounters καί they recognize it as a signal that what follows is to be integrated into the current mental representation of the discourse without significant adjustment to that representation, that new material is to be processed within the model they have currently constructed" (113). By contrast, δέ indicates some shift or development in the narrative. It guides "the audience to modify the mental representation they construct of the discourse" (166). This is typically a subject switch which is "a change in the notional subject from the previous independent coordinate clause in the narrative framework—a change in the grammaticalized subject if any, or in 'who or what the sentence is about' as understood from surrounding text if there is no explicit subject" (166).

I have consistently commented in the handbook on the use of δέ rather than καί. Although Mark overwhelmingly prefers καί as his clausal connective, δέ is used consistently to indicate some shift in the narrative (157 times). Often this is a shift of speakers in dialogue, but other times it may be a shift of grammatical subject, of topic, a turning point in the argument, or a contrast between two concepts. By contrast, καί joins equal items that continue with no shift, whether that is a subsequent element in the storyline, the same speaker, etc. There are only a very few instances where δέ does not fit this pattern (e.g., the "additive" use in 7:7). The relative frequency of καί over δέ is consistent in narrative genre in the NT (5,775 vs. 1,976 in the Gospels and Acts), but Mark's proportion shows both a higher frequency of καί and a lower frequency of δέ, making his use of the less common δέ more noteworthy. In the translation provided, I have often not translated καί when it is clause-initial, not because it is not significant, but because in English narrative (the closest equivalent in most instances) it has a different function and "feel," often appearing as clumsy and redundant to an English reader despite that probably not being the case for an original reader of Mark in Greek.

Verbal Aspect

The last quarter century has seen the fruition of much earlier work on the Greek verb. Although dissatisfaction was voiced at the end of the nineteenth century and in the early twentieth century, it was not until the end of the twentieth that workable solutions were proposed to the problems sensed by Curtius, Brugmann, Burton, and Robertson. The earlier attempts had begun to speak of *Aktionsart* and questioned the dominance of temporal explanations of the Greek verb system. The modern phase of the discussion likely owes its inception to K. L. McKay beginning in the 1960s, but the formal statements of a theory of verbal aspect (in distinction from *Aktionsart*) are credited to the works of Porter (1989, 2nd ed., 1993) and Fanning (1990). These published dissertations provoked an extended period of discussion and debate. My first exposure to the issues was at the famous "Porter-Fanning Debate" at SBL in 1992. I well remember telling my Greek students the next day (the debate was held in Kansas City where I was teaching at the time) that if I understood even half of what I had heard, I had a lot of reading to do—and both books were in the $120 range at the time! My own subsequent doctoral study and dissertation research convinced me that the distinction between aspect and *Aktionsart* (argued and defined by both Porter and Fanning in very similar terms) was valid as was Porter's further thesis that the semantic value of Greek tense was aspect in *distinction from* time. (The discussion is documented in Decker 2001, 1–28; the following summary is from pp. 26, 128–29.)

I define *verbal aspect* as the semantic category by which a speaker or writer grammaticalizes a view of the situation by the selection of a particular verb form in the verbal system. This is a grammatical category expressed by the form of the verb. The view is either perfective, imperfective, or stative and is expressed by the aorist, present/imperfect, and perfect/pluperfect forms respectively. Perfective aspect views the situation in summary as a complete event without regard for its progress (or lack thereof). Imperfective aspect views the situation as in progress without regard for its beginning or end. Stative aspect depicts a state of affairs that exists with no reference to any progress and which involves no change. All of these aspects are the speaker's view of the situation. They are sometimes determined by various factors (lexis, grammatical construction, context, etc.) and other times are the speaker's reasoned choice of a viewpoint that best expresses the nuance he desires to communicate. The same situation may often be described by two or even three such viewpoints. *Aktionsart*, by contrast, is a description of the actional features ascribed to the verbal referent as to the way in which it happens or exists. It is not a grammatical category based on the form of the verb, but is a pragmatic category based on the meaning of the word (lexis) as it is used in a particular context.

Verb forms only grammaticalize aspect at the level of code; temporal reference is not coded, but comes from interaction with contextual features (deixis), genre, and background knowledge as the forms are found in specific utterances. The temporal reference that can be determined on this basis is not expressed grammatically, but is an implicature. To use a specific example, although the aorist form does not grammaticalize past time, it can be (and often is) used to describe events in the past. This is clearly the dominant usage of the aorist form in Mark. This past reference, however, need not be explained as part of the tense-form. Just because a form is aorist neither means nor implies that the situation so described is past in time. The temporal reference comes from a host of other contextual factors. Given an aorist form in a specific utterance, it may be possible to say, on the basis of temporal implicature (and not on the basis of the aorist form alone), that it does, indeed, refer to a past time situation.

There are some natural affinities between the aspects and certain temporal references. Perfective indicative forms (i.e., aorist) most frequently do refer to past time, especially in narrative texts such as Mark. It is inherently logical, however, that one would use perfective aspect for such a description since it views the action as a complete event. In actual occurrence, the frequent use of a string of aorist forms in narrative to carry the storyline is quite evident. This is not to say that imperfective aspect is not feasible in such instances. Indeed, the imperfect form can and does make reference to events in the past (even the same events), but it views them as processes rather than as complete events. Use of the imperfective aspect for this purpose is not as common because the usual point of referring to past events is simply to note what happened, for which the perfective aspect is well suited. Imperfective references in this situation tend to be more marked and suggest that the speaker is often making a specific point of describing the action as a process by his choice of aspects.

Verbal aspect also plays a role in structuring texts. This structure is readily apparent in narrative texts, though it should not be viewed as a mechanical system; there are too many other factors which may influence or constrain a writer's choice of tense in some instances. The general pattern is, however, fairly clear. The aorist (perfective aspect) is the storyline form—the choice a writer most commonly makes when describing a series of events. These statements are what moves the story forward informing the reader of what happens next. This is consistent with the semantic meaning of the aorist: it describes events in summary, which is the usual point of narrating past happenings. Within this storyline a writer often uses the imperfective forms to highlight or expound particular parts of the story. Most commonly this is the primary imperfective form, the present tense. It is noticeable, for example, that in an aorist narrative framework, dialogue that is included shifts to the present tense. The other imperfective form, the imperfect, typically functions in summary statements or in providing background information helpful to the reader (see further Decker 2013a). The third aspect, the stative (perfect and pluperfect tenses), is much less commonly used. When the perfect tense is used it often functions to highlight specific events or statements that are particularly important in the narrative. The more remote stative form, the pluperfect, is used to describe "the background of the background," often occurring in γάρ clauses.

I have not attempted to expound each and every instance of such patterns in Mark. To do so would require a handbook in its own right. There are a multitude of factors involved here that must be weighed as to their interworkings. As a result I have sometimes commented where I thought such matters clear and helpful, or where they serve to counter popular, but unreliable criteria or classifications. Other times such comments have seemed to be either overconfident or banal, so I have passed them by silently.

Voice

The Series Introduction has already summarized the recent study of the Greek voice system as it relates to "deponency," the middle voice, and θη middles, so that will not be repeated here. Suffice it to say that I concur with that summary and the fundamental research by Conrad, Pennington, and Taylor that is referenced there. It is reflected not only in this handbook, but also in my recently released grammar, *Reading Koine Greek* (Decker 2014). I have tried to work out the implications of this model consistently throughout Mark's Gospel.

Periphrastics

A periphrastic is the combination of a linking verb and an anarthrous nominative participle, which together express a single idea. This construction is used in place of a single verb. The linking verb is usually a form of εἰμί, though sometimes γίνομαι (possible instances in Mark are 9:3, 7), ὑπάρχω, and possibly ἔχω are used. (Some scholars prefer to describe instances using a verb other than εἰμί as a catenative construction; see Porter 1993, 487–92.)

Periphrastics are common in Mark—much more so than Matthew (25 vs. 3). This is perhaps a reflection of Mark's mother-tongue being Aramaic. (Matthew, though also a native speaker of Aramaic, writes more polished Greek.) The Aramaic influence in Mark is debated by various scholars, though the general consensus seems to point to some Semitic influence, if only as mediated through the LXX (i.e., the frequent use of periphrasis in Mark may be viewed as a Septuagintalism). Periphrasis is much more common in Aramaic than in Hebrew. It begins to appear in later Hebrew, perhaps through Aramaic influence. For Hebrew examples and discussion, see Waltke and O'Connor (629–30, §37.7.1.c; e.g., Esth 6:1, נִקְרָאִים וַיִּהְיוּ, "and they were read"); for Aramaic, see Rosenthal (55 §177; e.g., Dan 2:31, where the participle precedes the verb [word order is very loose in the Aramaic sections of Daniel]: הֲוַיְתָ חָזֵה, "you were seeing").

Periphrastics are best cataloged according to verbal aspect. Thus in Mark there are imperfective periphrastics) imperfect of εἰμί with a present participle, e.g., 1:22, ἦν διδάσκων), stative periphrastics (imperfect of εἰμί with a perfect participle, e.g., 15:46, ἦν λελατομημένον), and future imperfective periphrastics (future of εἰμί with a present participle, e.g., 13:13, ἔσεσθε μισούμενοι). There is only one perfective periphrastic in Mark (9:7, ἐγένετο . . . ἐπισκιάζουσα; they are very rare elsewhere). All seventeen imperfective periphrastics in Mark (see the grammar index) are formed with the imperfect of εἰμί and a present participle (and are thus functionally equivalent to an imperfect finite form), though elsewhere the present form of εἰμί may also be used (equivalent to a present). Likewise all of Mark's six stative periphrastics use the imperfect of εἰμί and a perfect participle (functionally equivalent to a pluperfect finite form), though present forms of εἰμί may be found elsewhere (equivalent to a perfect). Mark's periphrastics are all equivalent to indicative forms, though a periphrastic may also substitute for other moods.

The future imperfective periphrastic is the only way to express imperfective aspect in a context of expectation (i.e., future time). The time value comes in part from the future form of εἰμί, whereas the imperfective aspect comes from the participle. None of the periphrastics in Mark carry any special emphasis; almost all are simply substitute, equivalent forms used for stylistic variation. A few are formulaic uses (5:41; 15:22, 34) and two have a distinctive form that cannot be expressed by an existing monolectic form (13:13, 25, both future periphrastics).

Not every instance of a linking verb with an adverbial participle is a periphrastic. Scholars differ as to how this is determined and how any given instance is to be evaluated. Some suggest that the only basis is "appropriateness in the context" (e.g., Fanning, 311). Others argue that periphrastic constructions cannot have any words between the verb and the participle except conjunctions or words that explicitly modify the participle (e.g., Porter 1994, 45–46;

1993, 441–86). One general principle that is often helpful is the presence of a phrase indicating location between the two elements. In such cases it is less likely that a legitimate periphrastic occurs, though there are a few apparent exceptions. Each instance will need to be evaluated in light of its context. A decision one way or the other can sometimes make an interpretive difference in a passage (see, e.g., Mark 1:13, which is probably not a periphrastic). All instances in Mark in which εἰμί and the participle are immediately adjacent are, indeed, periphrastics.

Prepositions with Verbs of Movement

As a narrative corpus recording the ministry of Jesus, Mark often uses verbs of movement, the most common of which is ἔρχομαι (particularly the aorist ἦλθεν) and its compounds. There is a general consistency in the prepositions used with these verbs. When someone goes (ἔρχομαι) to some place, whether a specific city (Capernaum, 9:33), an unnamed city (10:46), a region (Galilee, 1:14), a named place (Gethsemane, 14:32), or a house (5:38), Mark always uses εἰς, never πρός. When the preposition's object is personal, Mark consistently uses πρός ("to him," 1:45). When movement within an area is described, the choice is ἐν ("in the crowd," 5:27, but this use is not common) or διά (through a region, 7:31); ἐν is used more commonly in a metaphorical way to describe manner ("come with power," 9:1). Mark never uses ἔρχομαι with ἐκ to describe leaving a place. In these cases it is sometimes ἔρχομαι ἀπό (from a town, 1:9), but more commonly a compound form such as ἐξέρχομαι, either absolutely (1:35—this is the norm), with ἀπό (11:12), or in good Greek style with a matching preposition (ἐξέρχομαι ἐκ, 1:25). Leaving is also described with ἀπέρχομαι either absolutely (5:20) or with εἰς to identify the destination (1:35), less commonly with ἀπό (5:17) or πρός (a "personal" destination, 14:10). Entrance is depicted with εἰσέρχομαι, almost always with εἰς (1:21), but sometimes absolutely (6:22), or with πρός (6:25, personal). Infrequently used compounds include διέρχομαι, παρέρχομαι, προέρχομαι, and προσέρχομαι. (Mark uses no double compounds of ἔρχομαι.)

Imperfect Tense

The use of the imperfect tense in Mark is worthy of more attention. It has often been abused and used to substantiate some questionable exegesis of Mark's text. In this regard I must settle for a reference to a published paper that I presented at SBL in 2009 that was based on my work for this handbook (see Decker 2013a).

A HANDBOOK ON THE GREEK TEXT
OF MARK 9–16

Mark 9:2-8

²After six days Jesus took Peter, James, and John and led them to a high mountain by themselves. He was transformed before them ³and his clothes became radiantly white, whiter than an earthly cloth refiner could whiten them. ⁴Now Elijah along with Moses appeared to them and they were talking with Jesus. ⁵Peter said to Jesus, "Rabbi, it is good for us to be here. Let us build three shelters, one for you, one for Moses, and one for Elijah." — ⁶He did not know what to say for they were terrified. — ⁷Then a cloud enveloped them and a voice came from the cloud, "This is my beloved Son; listen to him." ⁸Suddenly, looking around, they no longer saw anyone except Jesus alone with them.

9:2 Καὶ μετὰ ἡμέρας ἓξ παραλαμβάνει ὁ Ἰησοῦς τὸν Πέτρον καὶ τὸν Ἰάκωβον καὶ τὸν Ἰωάννην καὶ ἀναφέρει αὐτοὺς εἰς ὄρος ὑψηλὸν κατ᾽ ἰδίαν μόνους. καὶ μετεμορφώθη ἔμπροσθεν αὐτῶν,

μετὰ ἡμέρας ἓξ. Temporal. The explicit temporal reference (the most precise in Mark) is probably intended to tie this pericope to the preceding one, which just referred to events soon to transpire (9:1).

παραλαμβάνει. Pres act ind 3rd sg παραλαμβάνω. The two present tense verbs (παραλαμβάνει and ἀναφέρει) along with the temporal reference and the geographical marker together serve to indicate the beginning of a new paragraph (see 1:21).

ὁ Ἰησοῦς. Nominative subject of παραλαμβάνει.

τὸν Πέτρον καὶ τὸν Ἰάκωβον καὶ τὸν Ἰωάννην. Accusative direct object of παραλαμβάνει.

ἀναφέρει. Pres act ind 3rd sg ἀναφέρω. In this context the active voice of ἀναφέρω expresses a causative idea, "to cause to move from a lower position to a higher" (BDAG, 75.1); thus, "he led."

αὐτοὺς. Accusative direct object of ἀναφέρει.

1

εἰς ὄρος ὑψηλὸν. Locative. The adjective ὑψηλόν is added to clarify the reference to a mountain, since ὄρος can also refer to a hill (Evans 2001, 35).

κατ᾽ ἰδίαν μόνους. For κατ᾽ ἰδίαν, see 4:34; μόνους adds emphasis to the prepositional phrase "and expresses the passion for solitude" (Bruce, 399).

μετεμορφώθη. Aor pass ind 3rd sg μεταμορφόω ("to be changed in form"; BDAG, 639). The following description makes it evident here (and in ‖ Matt 17:2) that this transformation in form was an outward one. Elsewhere the change is inward without visible change of form (Rom 12:2; 2 Cor 3:18). The agent of the passive verb is not indicated, though God may be implied.

ἔμπροσθεν αὐτῶν. Spatial.

9:3 καὶ τὰ ἱμάτια αὐτοῦ ἐγένετο στίλβοντα λευκὰ λίαν, οἷα γναφεὺς ἐπὶ τῆς γῆς οὐ δύναται οὕτως λευκᾶναι.

τὰ ἱμάτια. Nominative subject of ἐγένετο.

ἐγένετο. Aor mid ind 3rd sg γίνομαι. The singular verb is used with a neuter plural subject (see 4:4).

στίλβοντα λευκὰ λίαν. Formally, "very shining white."

στίλβοντα. Pres act ptc neut nom pl στίλβω (attributive; "to cast rays of light," BDAG, 945). In its eight occurrences in the LXX, this word typically refers to the glittering or shining effect produced by light reflecting off polished metal (e.g., Ezek 40:3; 1 Macc 6:39). Alternatively, Fanning (310 n. 255), BDF (§354), and *New Docs* (4.66 §17) take ἐγένετο στίλβοντα as a periphrastic (thus, "his garments were shining").

λευκά. Predicate adjective.

οἷα γναφεὺς ἐπὶ τῆς γῆς οὐ δύναται οὕτως λευκᾶναι. Formally, "such as a cloth refiner on earth is not able thus to whiten."

οἷα. Correlative pronoun that describes something as similar (BDAG, 701, s.v. οἷος).

γναφεύς. Nominative subject of δύναται. "A specialist in one or more of the processes in the treatment of cloth, incl. fulling, carding, cleaning, bleaching. Since the Eng. term 'fuller' refers to one who shrinks and thickens cloth, a more general rendering such as cloth refiner is required to cover the various components. In our lit. (only Mk 9:3) ref. is to the bleaching aspect, without suggesting that the term applies only to one engaged in that particular feature. Hence such glosses as 'bleacher' or 'fuller' would overly limit the professional niche" (BDAG, 202; see also LN 48.7). Only here in the NT.

ἐπὶ τῆς γῆς. Spatial, modifying γναφεύς. Less likely, the prepositional phrase could be taken to modify the following verb, i.e., "no one is able to whiten them on earth," or perhaps, "on the ground," if bleaching clothes on the ground was a common practice in first-century Palestine (as several scholars have argued; see, e.g., Gundry, 458).

δύναται. Pres mid ind 3rd sg δύναμαι.

λευκᾶναι. Aor act inf λευκαίνω (complementary; "to make white," BDAG, 593).

9:4 καὶ ὤφθη αὐτοῖς Ἠλίας σὺν Μωϋσεῖ καὶ ἦσαν συλλαλοῦντες τῷ Ἰησοῦ.

ὤφθη. Aor mid ind 3rd sg ὁράω. This is a "θη middle" form, not passive (see 2:2). The use of ὤφθη alone (without ὅραμα) need not indicate a vision rather than the actual presence of the persons referenced. "The language is of actual changes (μετεμορφώθη, ἐγένετο, ἐγένετο, ἐγένετο), and Peter's suggestion of building τρεῖς σκηνάς suggests that he did not regard Elijah and Moses, any more than Jesus, as merely figures in a 'vision'" (France, 348).

αὐτοῖς. Dative complement of ὤφθη.

Ἠλίας. Nominative subject of ὤφθη.

σὺν Μωϋσεῖ. Accompaniment. It has been argued that Moses is the central character, accompanied by Elijah (e.g., Edwards 2002, 265, "the Greek has Elijah appearing *with* Moses"), but if that were so, it is based on something other than grammar, since Elijah is the subject of the verb and Moses appears only in a prepositional phrase; the main statement is that Elijah appeared. "In view of the changed order in the next verse it is unlikely that Mark chose the phrase to indicate precedence either way" (France, 351).

ἦσαν. Impf act ind 3rd pl εἰμί.

συλλαλοῦντες. Pres act ptc masc nom pl συλλαλέω (imperfective periphrastic). On the possibility that this periphrastic functions as an inceptive imperfect as in the NLT, see 1:21.

τῷ Ἰησοῦ. Dative complement of συλλαλοῦντες.

9:5 καὶ ἀποκριθεὶς ὁ Πέτρος λέγει τῷ Ἰησοῦ, Ῥαββί, καλόν ἐστιν ἡμᾶς ὧδε εἶναι, καὶ ποιήσωμεν τρεῖς σκηνάς, σοὶ μίαν καὶ Μωϋσεῖ μίαν καὶ Ἠλίᾳ μίαν.

ἀποκριθεὶς. Aor mid ptc masc nom sg ἀποκρίνομαι (means; redundant adverbial participle of speaking. See 3:33 for a discussion of this intransitive, "θη middle" form.

ὁ Πέτρος. Nominative subject of λέγει.

λέγει. Pres act ind 3rd sg λέγω.

τῷ Ἰησοῦ. Dative indirect object of λέγει.

Ῥαββί . . . Ἠλίᾳ μίαν. Clausal complement (direct discourse) of λέγει.

Ῥαββί. Vocative (indeclinable). This Aramaic term has been explained either as "an honorary title for outstanding teachers of the law" (BDAG, 902) or as an informal designation of "prominent citizens," most of whom were not ordained (Evans 2001, 50; see also 14:45). In the parallel accounts Matthew translates it as κύριε (17:4) and Luke as ἐπιστάτα (9:33).

καλόν. Predicate adjective.

ἐστιν. Pres act ind 3rd sg εἰμί.

ἡμᾶς. Accusative subject of εἶναι.

εἶναι. Pres act inf εἰμί. The infinitive clause (ἡμᾶς ὧδε εἶναι) functions as the subject of ἐστιν.

ποιήσωμεν. Aor act subj 1st pl ποιέω (hortatory). Interestingly, the Matthean parallel has the fut act ind 1st sg ποιήσω (Matt 17:4).

τρεῖς σκηνάς. Accusative direct object of ποιήσωμεν.

σοὶ . . . Μωϋσεῖ . . . Ἠλίᾳ. Datives of advantage.

μίαν . . . μίαν . . . μίαν. The three feminine accusative forms are in apposition to σκηνάς.

9:6 οὐ γὰρ ᾔδει τί ἀποκριθῇ, ἔκφοβοι γὰρ ἐγένοντο.

οὐ γὰρ ᾔδει τί ἀποκριθῇ. Note the similar statement in 14:40, οὐκ ᾔδεισαν τί ἀποκριθῶσιν αὐτῷ.

γὰρ. This verse is parenthetical (introduced by γάρ), explaining Peter's impulsive proposal in the previous verse—an explanation that may originate with Peter's own retrospective account of the event.

ᾔδει. Plprf act ind 3rd sg οἶδα. The rare pluperfect form grammaticalizes remoteness (C. Campbell, 213–23, 229–33) and stative aspect (I disagree with Campbell in assigning the tense imperfective aspect), recording an offline explanatory comment.

τί ἀποκριθῇ. Clausal complement (indirect question/discourse) of ᾔδει.

τί. Accusative direct object of ἀποκριθῇ.

ἀποκριθῇ. Aor mid subj 3rd sg ἀποκρίνομαι. Subjunctive in an indirect question.

ἔκφοβοι. Predicate adjective ("terrified"). Bruce translates, "they were frightened out of their wits" (400).

γὰρ. The γάρ clause explains why Peter did not know what to say. On two successive γάρ clauses, see 11:18.

ἐγένοντο. Aor mid ind 3rd pl γίνομαι. The number shifts to plural here, referring not just to Peter, but to James and John as well.

9:7 καὶ ἐγένετο νεφέλη ἐπισκιάζουσα αὐτοῖς, καὶ ἐγένετο φωνὴ ἐκ τῆς νεφέλης, Οὗτός ἐστιν ὁ υἱός μου ὁ ἀγαπητός, ἀκούετε αὐτοῦ.

καὶ ἐγένετο. This phrase (both occurrences in the verse) indicates an immediate sequence of events in the narrative (see 1:9; *TDM*, 85).

ἐγένετο. Aor mid ind 3rd sg γίνομαι.

νεφέλη. Nominative subject of the periphrastic ἐγένετο ἐπισκιάζουσα.

ἐπισκιάζουσα. Pres act ptc fem nom sg ἐπισκιάζω (perfective periphrastic, the only such construction in Mark; see BDF §354; *New Docs*, 4.66 §17). Fanning (310 n. 255; cf. Porter 1993, 491) rejects this instance as a periphrastic, suggesting that it may be adjectival (thus perhaps, "an enveloping cloud came upon them"?). Lane suggests that the use here "has the nuance of enveloping or concealing, rather than 'overshadowing'" (315 n. 12). In the NT, the verb is usually used to refer to the presence of God (|| Matt 17:5; Luke 9:34; see also Luke 1:35). This probably reflects the terminology (or at least the concept) of LXX Exod 40:35, where ἐπεσκίαζεν refers to the Shekinah connected with the tabernacle (see also Edwards 2002, 267).

αὐτοῖς. Dative complement of ἐπισκιάζουσα.

ἐγένετο. Aor mid ind 3rd sg γίνομαι.

φωνὴ. Nominative subject of ἐγένετο.

ἐκ τῆς νεφέλης. Source.

Οὗτός ἐστιν ... ἀκούετε αὐτοῦ. Clausal complement (direct discourse) of ἐγένετο. One might have expected the clause to be introduced with λέγων or λέγει, especially since ἐγένετο is intransitive, but the meaning is clear enough.

Οὗτός. Nominative subject of ἐστιν. On the pronoun as the subject with two nominatives and a linking verb, see 3:11.

ἐστιν. Pres act ind 3rd sg εἰμί.

ὁ υἱός ... ὁ ἀγαπητός. Predicate nominative.

ἀκούετε. Pres act impv 2nd pl ἀκούω. Swete points out that ἀκούετε αὐτοῦ may be a deliberate reference to LXX Deut 18:15, 19, which use the same wording with reference to Moses, suggesting that "the allegiance due to Moses is now with Moses' concurrence transferred to Jesus" (191). The Deuteronomic text, however, does not describe Moses, but "the prophet" who will come after Moses: προφήτην ἐκ τῶν ἀδελφῶν σου ὡς ἐμὲ ἀναστήσει σοι κύριος ὁ θεός σου, αὐτοῦ ἀκούσεσθε (v. 15).

αὐτοῦ. Genitive direct object of ἀκούετε.

9:8 καὶ ἐξάπινα περιβλεψάμενοι οὐκέτι οὐδένα εἶδον ἀλλὰ τὸν Ἰησοῦν μόνον μεθ᾽ ἑαυτῶν.

ἐξάπινα. Although ἐξάπινα can also mean "unexpectedly," the meaning here is "suddenly" (note the explicitly temporal οὐκέτι later in the clause) The word occurs fifteen times in the LXX and in many instances either meaning is possible. In Sir 11:21 it is parallel with διὰ τάχους, "quickly."

περιβλεψάμενοι. Aor mid ptc masc nom pl περιβλέπω (temporal).

οὐκέτι. The use of the adverb ("no longer") suggests that a fair bit of time passed before the disciples suddenly realized that they were once again alone with Jesus.

οὐδένα. Accusative direct object of εἶδον. The double negative is emphatic.

εἶδον. Aor act ind 3rd pl ὁράω.

ἀλλὰ. The coordinating conjunction introduces a contrasting, elliptical statement that assumes the same verb as the previous clause: "but (they saw) only Jesus."

μεθ᾽ ἑαυτῶν. Accompaniment.

Mark 9:9-13

⁹Now as they were going down the mountain he commanded them that they should not relate what they had seen to anyone until the Son of Man should rise from the dead. ¹⁰So they kept this matter to themselves, discussing what was the "rising from the dead." ¹¹They asked him, saying, "Why do the scribes say that Elijah must come first?" ¹²He said to them, "To be sure, Elijah comes first and he restores all things. (Why then is it written about the Son of Man that he should suffer greatly and be rejected?) ¹³But I tell you both that Elijah has come and that they did to him whatever they wished, just as it is written about him."

9:9 Καὶ καταβαινόντων αὐτῶν ἐκ τοῦ ὄρους διεστείλατο αὐτοῖς ἵνα μηδενὶ ἃ εἶδον διηγήσωνται, εἰ μὴ ὅταν ὁ υἱὸς τοῦ ἀνθρώπου ἐκ νεκρῶν ἀναστῇ.

καταβαινόντων. Pres act ptc masc gen pl καταβαίνω. Genitive absolute (see 1:32), temporal.

αὐτῶν. Genitive subject of καταβαινόντων. On the overlap of reference with αὐτοῖς in the main clause, see 5:2 and 14:3.

ἐκ τοῦ ὄρους. Separation.

διεστείλατο. Aor mid ind 3rd sg διαστέλλω. On the meaning and usage of διαστέλλω, see 5:43.

αὐτοῖς. Dative indirect object of διεστείλατο.

ἵνα. Introduces indirect discourse giving the content of the command (cf. 3:9). BDAG notes that "in this case the ἵνα-constr. serves as a substitute for an inf. that supplements a verb" (476.2; cf. Wallace 1996, 476).

μηδενί. Dative indirect object of διηγήσωνται.

ἃ εἶδον. The relative clause functions as the direct object of διηγήσωνται.

ἅ. Accusative direct object of εἶδον.

εἶδον. Aor act ind 3rd pl ὁράω. Stein translates εἶδον as "witnessed" because it functions as "an abbreviation for 'seen and heard'" (2008, 428).

διηγήσωνται. Aor mid subj 3rd pl διηγέομαι.

εἰ μὴ ὅταν. Formally, "except when." See 2:7 on εἰ μή.

ὁ υἱὸς. Nominative subject of ἀναστῇ. On the title ὁ υἱὸς τοῦ ἀνθρώπου, see 2:10.

ἐκ νεκρῶν. Separation. On the lack of an article, see 6:14.

ἀναστῇ. Aor act subj 3rd sg ἀνίστημι. Subjunctive with ὅταν.

9:10 καὶ τὸν λόγον ἐκράτησαν πρὸς ἑαυτοὺς συζητοῦντες τί ἐστιν τὸ ἐκ νεκρῶν ἀναστῆναι.

τὸν λόγον. Accusative direct object of ἐκράτησαν. Here λόγος refers to "a happening to which one may refer" (LN 13.115; cf. BDAG, 600.1.a.ε). Swete argues that λόγος "is not the fact of the Transfiguration, but the Lord's saying, especially what He had said about rising from the dead" (192), but that is probably too limited. The referent of λόγος seems, rather, to be ἃ εἶδον (v. 9).

ἐκράτησαν. Aor act ind 3rd pl κρατέω. For κρατέω meaning "to keep information to oneself," rather than the more common "to seize or hold," see BDAG (565.6.c).

πρὸς ἑαυτούς. Association, modifying ἐκράτησαν (see also BDAG, 565.6.c, s.v. κρατέω; the semantic range of κρατέω is quite broad, even in Mark, something that Bolt, 61, understates). It is far less likely that this prepositional phrase modifies συζητοῦντες: "They seized upon that statement, discussing with one another ..." (NASB; see also France, 356–57; Bolt, 60–62). Elsewhere in

Mark (1:27; 11:31), when verb + πρὸς ἑαυτούς + participle occurs, the prepositional phrase always modifies the preceding verb (Stein 2008, 424; see also Luke 20:5). More important, πρὸς ἑαυτούς almost always follows the verb it modifies (Mark 10:26; 14:4; Luke 20:5; 22:23; John 7:35; 12:19; LXX Gen 19:10; Exod 28:43; 1 Sam 6:21; Neh 3:35; 1 Macc 11:9; Ep Jer 1:48). The only counter-example is Mark 12:7.

συζητοῦντες. Pres act ptc masc nom pl συζητέω (likely temporal).

τί ἐστιν τὸ ἐκ νεκρῶν ἀναστῆναι. Clausal complement (indirect discourse) of συζητοῦντες.

τί. Predicate nominative.

ἐστιν. Pres act ind 3rd sg εἰμί.

ἐκ νεκρῶν. Separation. On the lack of an article with νεκρῶν, see 6:14.

τὸ ... ἀναστῆναι. Aor act inf ἀνίστημι. The nominative article marks the infinitive as the subject of ἐστιν (Burk, 133–34). Burk argues that it is not anaphoric (contra BDF §399.1.1; Gundry, 463), but his thesis regarding the use of the article (that it indicates case) does not, I think, preclude anaphoric reference. BDF (§§398–99) also affirms that case is only significant *with genitive and dative* articles and following prepositions, but allows both case and anaphoric reference with nominative and accusative. These issues become exegetically significant when the question of referent is raised. Does Mark refer to the disciples discussing among themselves *Jesus' resurrection*? Or were they debating some broader question about *their* future resurrection? An anaphoric article would point toward the first option, a nonanaphoric use would allow for either.

9:11 καὶ ἐπηρώτων αὐτὸν λέγοντες, ὅτι λέγουσιν οἱ γραμματεῖς ὅτι Ἠλίαν δεῖ ἐλθεῖν πρῶτον;

ἐπηρώτων. Impf act ind 3rd pl ἐπερωτάω. On ἐπερωτάω versus the simple form ἐρωτάω, see 4:10. On the possibility that this is an inceptive imperfect as in HCSB, see 1:21.

αὐτὸν. Accusative direct object of ἐπηρώτων.

λέγοντες. Pres act ptc masc nom pl λέγω (means; redundant participle of speaking; see also 1:7; 3:33).

ὅτι. Interrogative ὅτι: "why?" (see 2:16). The Matthean parallel (17:10) makes the statement unambiguously a question: τί οὖν οἱ γραμματεῖς λέγουσιν. This is not a quotation formula as, e.g., in the RV, "And they asked him, saying, 'The scribes say that Elijah must first come,'" a translation that Field finds "simply intolerable" (33).

λέγουσιν. Pres act ind 3rd pl λέγω.

οἱ γραμματεῖς. Nominative subject of λέγουσιν.

ὅτι. Introduces the clausal complement (indirect discourse) of λέγουσιν (see 1:15).

Ἠλίαν. Accusative subject of ἐλθεῖν.

δεῖ. Pres act ind 3rd sg δεῖ.

ἐλθεῖν. Aor act inf ἔρχομαι. The infinitive clause, Ἠλίαν . . . ἐλθεῖν πρῶτον, is the subject of δεῖ.

9:12 ὁ δὲ ἔφη αὐτοῖς, Ἠλίας μὲν ἐλθὼν πρῶτον ἀποκαθιστάνει πάντα· καὶ πῶς γέγραπται ἐπὶ τὸν υἱὸν τοῦ ἀνθρώπου ἵνα πολλὰ πάθῃ καὶ ἐξουδενηθῇ;

The complex issues of meaning raised in verses 12-13 cannot be resolved in a grammatical handbook. The notes here record one basic way of understanding the grammar and syntax, but exegetical judgments affect a number of factors here, not least the OT background and the reference of ἐλθών and ἀποκαθιστάνει (the traditional renderings have been retained for these two forms despite the fact that one is an aorist participle and the other a present indicative). For more, see esp. Stein (2008, 425–27).

ὁ. Nominative subject of ἔφη. On the use of ὁ δέ to change subjects, see 1:45.

ἔφη. Aor act ind 3rd sg φημί.

αὐτοῖς. Dative indirect object of ἔφη.

Ἠλίας μὲν . . . ἐπ' αὐτόν (v. 13). Clausal complement (direct discourse) of ἔφη.

Ἠλίας. Nominative subject of ἀποκαθιστάνει.

μὲν. The μέν suggests a correlative construction, but the second part of the construction is not grammatically parallel. It may consist of the question introduced with καὶ πῶς γέγραπται (so France, 358). Alternatively (and perhaps most plausibly), the adversative clause may be verse 13, introduced with ἀλλά (so Gould, 164; BDAG, 629.1.a.β, s.v. μέν; Lee, 5 n. 18); in this case μέν would be translated as "indeed, to be sure." If the second alternative is followed, then the question at the end of verse 12 must be either part of the concessive clause introduced with μέν, or perhaps it is parenthetical. France concludes that "the sequence of clauses is clumsy, and the effect much more cryptic than in Matthew's 'tidied-up' parallel. If verse 12b had *followed* verse 13, the whole train of thought would have been much easier to follow" (359). Another alternative, suggested by Bruce, is to shorten the question and provide the answer via the ἵνα clause: "Elias, indeed, coming first, restoreth all things (so teach the scribes)—and how stands it written about the Son of Man?—that He should suffer many things and be set at nought!" (401). On the use of μέν as a "prestige feature," see the discussion at 4:4.

ἐλθὼν. Aor act ptc masc nom sg ἔρχομαι (attendant circumstance, though perhaps temporal is adequate). Alternatively, Duckwitz (154) classes it as "modal," i.e., means). The exegesis of verses 12-13 will determine this classification as much as a grammatical specification.

ἀποκαθιστάνει. Pres act ind 3rd sg ἀποκαθιστάνω ("to change to a previous good state," LN 13.65). This verb is usually a –μι verb form in the NT (ἀποκαθίστημι; see 3:5; 8:25), but sometimes (as here) the newer –ω form appears.

πάντα. Accusative direct object of ἀποκαθιστάνει.

γέγραπται. Prf pass ind 3rd sg γράφω.

ἐπὶ τὸν υἱὸν. Respect. On this use of ἐπί with the accusative, see 6:34. Literary references about someone or something that use γέγραπται, i.e., "it is written about X," usually use περί + genitive (e.g., Matt 26:24; Mark 14:21; Heb 10:7 || Ps 39:8). The only other use parallel to this passage related to the NT is *Barn.* 11:1.

τὸν υἱὸν τοῦ ἀνθρώπου. On this title, see 2:10.

ἵνα. Introduces the clausal complement of γέγραπται (indirect discourse). BDAG notes that "in this case the ἵνα-constr. serves as a substitute for an inf. that supplements a verb" (476.2; cf. Wallace 1996, 476).

πολλὰ. Adverbial, see 1:45. If viewed as adjectival ("many things"), πολλά would be the accusative direct object of πάθη.

πάθῃ. Aor act subj 3rd sg πάσχω. Subjunctive with ἵνα.

ἐξουδενηθῇ. Aor pass subj 3rd sg ἐξουδενέω ("to ill-treat, to ill-treat and look down upon," [LN 88.133; BDAG, 352]). Subjunctive with ἵνα.

9:13 ἀλλὰ λέγω ὑμῖν ὅτι καὶ Ἡλίας ἐλήλυθεν, καὶ ἐποίησαν αὐτῷ ὅσα ἤθελον, καθὼς γέγραπται ἐπ' αὐτόν.

λέγω. Pres act ind 1st sg λέγω.

ὅτι. Introduces the clausal complement of λέγω.

καὶ . . . καὶ. The paired conjunctions function as correlatives to connect two clauses: *both* this *and* this.

ἐλήλυθεν. Prf act ind 3rd sg ἔρχομαι.

ἐποίησαν αὐτῷ ὅσα ἤθελον. Swete points out that "the phrase ποιεῖν ὅσα (ἃ) θέλω (τινί) [is] frequently used in the OT to represent irresponsible or arbitrary action," citing 1 Kgs 9:1; 10:13; Ps 113:11 (Eng. 115:3); Dan 8:4; and 2 Macc 7:16. He further suggests that this phrase "points with sufficient distinction to the murder of John by Antipas" (194). The first three OT texts cited are positive descriptions of autonomous actions, but Daniel and 2 Maccabees are close parallels.

ἐποίησαν. Aor act ind 3rd pl ποιέω.

αὐτῷ. Dative indirect object of ἐποίησαν (or dative of disadvantage).

ὅσα ἤθελον. The relative clause functions as the direct object of ἐποίησαν.

ὅσα. Accusative direct object of ἤθελον. On ὅσος, see 3:8.

ἤθελον. Impf act ind 3rd pl θέλω.

καθὼς. Introduces a comparative clause.

γέγραπται. Prf pass ind 3rd sg γράφω.

ἐπ' αὐτόν. Respect. On this use of ἐπί with the accusative, see 6:34. On γέγραπται ἐπί, see verse 12.

Mark 9:14-24

¹⁴When they came to the disciples, they saw a large crowd around them and scribes who were arguing with them. ¹⁵Then all the crowd, when they saw him, were very excited and running up they greeted him. ¹⁶He asked them, "What were you arguing about with them?" ¹⁷One out of the crowd answered him, "Teacher, I brought to you my son who has a mute spirit. ¹⁸Whenever it seizes him it throws him down and he foams at the mouth and gnashes his teeth and becomes rigid. I asked your disciples to exorcize it, but they were not able. ¹⁹But Jesus said to them, "O unbelieving generation, how long will I be with you? How long will I put up with you? Bring him to me." ²⁰So they brought the boy to Jesus. Now when the spirit saw Jesus he immediately convulsed the boy; having fallen to the ground he was rolling around, foaming at the mouth. ²¹Jesus asked his father, "How long has it been since this has happened to him?" He said, "From childhood. ²²Often it has even thrown him into the fire or water to destroy him, but if you are able, help us, having compassion on us." ²³Jesus said to him, "'If you are able' indeed!' All things are possible for the one who believes." ²⁴Immediately crying out, the father of the child said, "I believe; help my unbelief!"

9:14 Καὶ ἐλθόντες πρὸς τοὺς μαθητὰς εἶδον ὄχλον πολὺν περὶ αὐτοὺς καὶ γραμματεῖς συζητοῦντας πρὸς αὐτούς.

ἐλθόντες. Aor act ptc masc nom pl ἔρχομαι (temporal).

πρὸς τοὺς μαθητάς. Spatial.

εἶδον. Aor act ind 3rd pl ὁράω.

ὄχλον πολὺν . . . καὶ γραμματεῖς. Accusative direct object of εἶδον. This is the only anarthrous instance of γραμματεύς in Mark (it is more common in Matthew).

περὶ αὐτούς. Spatial.

συζητοῦντας. Pres act ptc masc acc pl συζητέω (attributive, modifying γραμματεῖς). This verb can have a hostile connotation, especially when followed by πρός. Gundry (487) suggests that this plural participle may modify not just γραμματεῖς, but the entire compound direct object (ὄχλον . . . καὶ γραμματεῖς), with the scribes leading the discussion.

πρὸς αὐτούς. Opposition, given its use with συζητοῦντας. The use of πρός with the accusative instead of a simple dative (i.e., αὐτοῖς) may be better suited to express the hostility of the scribes (so Gould, 166).

9:15 καὶ εὐθὺς πᾶς ὁ ὄχλος ἰδόντες αὐτὸν ἐξεθαμβήθησαν καὶ προστρέχοντες ἠσπάζοντο αὐτόν.

καὶ εὐθύς. See 1:10.

πᾶς ὁ ὄχλος. Nominative subject of ἐξεθαμβήθησαν.

ἰδόντες. Aor act ptc masc nom pl ὁράω (temporal).

αὐτόν. Accusative direct object of ἰδόντες.

ἐξεθαμβήθησαν. Aor mid ind 3rd pl ἐκθαμβέω. This is a "θη middle" form. The word ἐκθαμβέω (see also 1:22) is a general term meaning "to be moved to a relatively intense emotional state because of someth. causing great surprise or perplexity" (BDAG, 303; cf. LN 25.210). The context must determine the sort of strong emotion (the ἐκ prefix is probably intensive) in view. Here, BDAG translates it "to be very excited," and argues that "the presence of Jesus suggests possible resolution of a dispute; but consideration of Mark's larger narrative structure leads some scholars to prefer the sense *be amazed* . . . which lacks immediate motivation in the scene at hand" (303). Gundry (488) supplies a motive by suggesting that Jesus' transfigured appearance, including his radiant garments, was still visible, but the text does not say that this is the case, and as France points out, "verse 8 suggests an immediate return to normality, and the secrecy demanded in verse 9 would be strange if the 'transfiguration' of Jesus remained visible for all to see" (364). The other NT uses of ἐκθαμβέω, all of which are found in Mark, suggest either distress (14:33, parallel with ἀδημονέω) or alarm (16:5, 6). The lone use in the LXX (Sir 30:9) is parallel with λυπέω and perhaps best understood in the sense "to distress" ("terrorize" in NETS seems overdone). On the use of plural forms with ὄχλος in Mark, see 5:21.

προστρέχοντες. Pres act ptc masc nom pl προστρέχω (temporal; "to run to," BDAG, 886). The two verbs, ἐξεθαμβήθησαν and ἠσπάζοντο, may suggest that people were shouting their greetings, etc., as they ran toward Jesus.

ἠσπάζοντο. Impf mid ind 3rd pl ἀσπάζομαι. The imperfect appears to be used to recount background information that sets the scene for the discussion that follows. This is the only imperfect form of ἀσπάζομαι in the NT. It does not occur at all in the LXX or AF, and is found only twice in Philo and once in the Pseudepigrapha, though Josephus has sixteen instances.

αὐτόν. Accusative direct object of ἠσπάζοντο.

9:16 καὶ ἐπηρώτησεν αὐτούς, Τί συζητεῖτε πρὸς αὐτούς;

ἐπηρώτησεν. Aor act ind 3rd sg ἐπερωτάω. On ἐπερωτάω versus the simple form ἐρωτάω, see 4:10.

αὐτούς. Accusative direct object of ἐπηρώτησεν. The referent is apparently the crowd (Stein 2008, 432), the subject of the preceding verb, since it is someone from the crowd who answers. It could be limited to the scribes in light of verse 14 (so France, 364; a textual variant, found as early as A and C, replaces αὐτούς with τοὺς γραμματεῖς). It could also be an inclusive reference to both scribes and the crowd since at least the scribes are the ones already identified as disputing with the disciples (v. 14). Although it could conceivably refer to the disciples, in which case the second αὐτούς in the verse refers to the crowd (or the scribes), since the answer does not come from the disciples, this is highly unlikely.

Τί συζητεῖτε πρὸς αὐτούς. Clausal complement (direct discourse) of ἐπηρώτησεν.

Τί. Accusative direct object of συζητεῖτε. Although Gundry (488) contends Τί must be understood as "why?" here because a "what" question would require περί rather than πρός, the evidence for that is very slim (Gundry cites none; BDAG cites one instance of συζητέω with περί in AF, though with a different meaning).

συζητεῖτε. Pres act ind 2nd pl συζητέω.

πρὸς αὐτούς. Opposition, given its use with συζητεῖτε (see v. 14). The referent is apparently to the group of disciples who had not been with Jesus on the mountain.

9:17 καὶ ἀπεκρίθη αὐτῷ εἷς ἐκ τοῦ ὄχλου, Διδάσκαλε, ἤνεγκα τὸν υἱόν μου πρός σέ, ἔχοντα πνεῦμα ἄλαλον·

ἀπεκρίθη. Aor mid ind 3rd sg ἀποκρίνομαι. See the discussion of this intransitive, "θη middle" form at 3:33. This is one of the few uses in Mark of ἀποκρίνομαι without an associated participle of speaking to introduce direct discourse (see also 8:4 and 12:29).

αὐτῷ. Dative indirect object of ἀπεκρίθη.

εἷς. Nominative subject of ἀπεκρίθη. On the use of εἷς, see 10:17.

ἐκ τοῦ ὄχλου. Partitive (cf 14:18); the use of ἐκ is an alternative in Koine to the partitive genitive (see, e.g., 8:28, εἷς τῶν προφητῶν; 14:20, εἷς τῶν δώδεκα). It is more common when used with εἷς. By contrast when a partitive genitive is used with τίς, a preposition is rarely used (though see 13:15, τι ἐκ τῆς οἰκίας αὐτοῦ).

Διδάσκαλε . . . οὐκ ἴσχυσαν (v. 18). Clausal complement (direct discourse) of ἀπεκρίθη.

Διδάσκαλε. Vocative. Mark records the use of διδάσκαλε as a title for Jesus much more frequently than the other gospels (see 4:38).

ἤνεγκα. Aor act ind 1st sg φέρω.

τὸν υἱόν. Accusative direct object of ἤνεγκα.

πρὸς σέ. Spatial.

ἔχοντα. Pres act ptc masc acc sg ἔχω (attributive, modifying υἱόν). On the use of ἔχω to refer to demon possession, see 3:22.

πνεῦμα ἄλαλον. Accusative direct object of ἔχοντα. In the NT ἄλαλος ("mute," BDAG, 41) is used only in Mark (7:37; 9:25). "Either the adjective ἄλαλον has a causal sense [i.e., "a spirit who causes muteness"] or it is a transferred epithet in which the adjective shifts from the word to which it strictly belongs; i.e., τὸν υἱόν, to a word closely collocated; i.e., πνεῦμα" (Duckwitz, 155). The first alternative seems preferable and is what BDAG implies, "*a mute spirit*, which robs pers. of their speech" (41).

9:18 καὶ ὅπου ἐὰν αὐτὸν καταλάβῃ ῥήσσει αὐτόν, καὶ ἀφρίζει καὶ τρίζει τοὺς ὀδόντας καὶ ξηραίνεται· καὶ εἶπα τοῖς μαθηταῖς σου ἵνα αὐτὸ ἐκβάλωσιν, καὶ οὐκ ἴσχυσαν.

ὅπου ἐάν. Here, an indefinite temporal expression ("whenever,"

BDAG, 717.1.a.δ), though it could also be spatial ("wherever"; see also 6:10). Gundry suggests that it "indicates that the dominion is so complete that the spirit can strike him down at will" (488).

αὐτὸν. Accusative direct object of καταλάβῃ.

καταλάβῃ. Aor act subj 3rd sg καταλαμβάνω. Subjunctive with ὅπου ἐάν. Beyer (196) suggests that this expresses an iterative idea in this context.

ῥήσσει. Pres act ind 3rd sg ῥήσσω ("to cause to fall down"). This word is probably not the by-form of ῥήγνυμι ("to tear or break," BDAG, 904, s.v. ῥήγνυμι; 905.1, s.v. ῥήσσω) but a less common poetic homonym (BDAG, 905.2, s.v. ῥήσσω). Including the idea of convulsions in this word (so LN 23.168, "to cause to fall to the ground in convulsions") is probably to read more into the word than can be justified, though in some contexts convulsions do follow.

αὐτόν. Accusative direct object of ῥήσσει.

ἀφρίζει. Pres act ind 3rd sg ἀφρίζω ("to foam [at the mouth]").

τρίζει. Pres act ind 3rd sg τρίζω ("to gnash, grind," BDAG, 1015; only here in the NT).

τοὺς ὀδόντας. Accusative direct object of τρίζει.

ξηραίνεται. Pres mid ind 3rd sg ξηραίνω. Here, "to become dry to the point of being immobilized, *be paralyzed*" (BDAG, 684.2).

εἶπα. Aor act ind 1st sg λέγω. Here λέγω functions as a verb of entreaty: "I asked."

τοῖς μαθηταῖς. Dative indirect object of εἶπα.

ἵνα. Introduces indirect discourse. Following a verb of entreaty the ἵνα clause gives the content of the request (see Burton §200; Wallace 1996, 476; BDAG, 476.2)

αὐτὸ. Accusative direct object of ἐκβάλωσιν.

ἐκβάλωσιν. Aor act subj 3rd pl ἐκβάλλω. Subjunctive with ἵνα.

ἴσχυσαν. Aor act ind 3rd pl ἰσχύω. This expression is not the more typical οὐ + δύναμαι ("they were not able," e.g., 6:5), but rather "they were not strong enough."

9:19 ὁ δὲ ἀποκριθεὶς αὐτοῖς λέγει, Ὦ γενεὰ ἄπιστος, ἕως πότε πρὸς ὑμᾶς ἔσομαι; ἕως πότε ἀνέξομαι ὑμῶν; φέρετε αὐτὸν πρός με.

ὁ. Nominative subject of λέγει. On the use of ὁ δέ to change subjects, see 1:45.

ἀποκριθεὶς. Aor mid ptc masc nom sg ἀποκρίνομαι (means; redundant participle of speaking). On this intransitive, "θη middle" form, see 3:33.

αὐτοῖς. Dative indirect object of λέγει. The antecedent is more likely the crowd (ὄχλου, v. 17; so Gundry, 489; Edwards 2002, 278) than the disciples (μαθηταῖς, v. 18; contra Gould, 168; Lane, 332), despite the grammatical difference in number, since ὄχλος is often treated as a plural and the disciples hardly constitute a γενεά. It is also possible that the reference is to the scribes (cf. Collins, 437), or to Jesus' "whole human environment" (France, 365; cf. Swete, 198). The reading αὐτῷ (𝔐, see Legg, ad loc) shifts Jesus' reply explicitly to the man, though it is unclear why the man would be described as a γενεά.

λέγει. Pres act ind 3rd sg λέγω.

Ὦ γενεὰ ἄπιστος. . . πρός με. Clausal complement (direct discourse) of λέγω. The tone of this statement is clearly one of exasperation: "a rare diatribe . . . Jesus has had enough of unbelief" (France, 365–66).

Ὦ γενεὰ ἄπιστος. Interjection followed by a vocative. By form, γενεά could be either nominative or vocative. The interjection strongly suggests the vocative, though this results in a nominative adjective in apposition to a vocative. The use of ὦ is probably best explained as "a feature of higher style," which gives a "formal and elevated tone" that is appropriate to the speaker (Lee, 17; see also 11:14; 14:7).

ἕως πότε. Formally, "until when?"

πρὸς ὑμᾶς. Association.

ἔσομαι. Fut mid ind 1st sg εἰμί.

ἀνέξομαι. Fut mid ind 1st sg ἀνέχω. Although this form only occurs in the middle voice in the NT (and thus some lexicons list it as ἀνέχομαι; e.g., LN 25.171), it does occur in the active in the LXX (e.g., ἀνέξει, Hag 1:10) and should thus not be treated as a middle-only verb.

ὑμῶν. Genitive direct object of ἀνέξομαι.

φέρετε. Pres act impv 2nd pl φέρω.

αὐτὸν. Accusative direct object of φέρετε.

πρός με. Spatial.

9:20 καὶ ἤνεγκαν αὐτὸν πρὸς αὐτόν. καὶ ἰδὼν αὐτὸν τὸ πνεῦμα εὐθὺς συνεσπάραξεν αὐτόν, καὶ πεσὼν ἐπὶ τῆς γῆς ἐκυλίετο ἀφρίζων.

ἤνεγκαν. Aor act ind 3rd pl φέρω.

αὐτὸν. Accusative direct object of ἤνεγκαν.

πρὸς αὐτόν. Spatial.

ἰδὼν. Aor act ptc masc nom sg ὁράω (temporal, modifying

συνεσπάραξεν). As an adverbial participle ἰδών should agree with the subject of the main verb in gender (πνεῦμα), but this is a *constructio ad sensum* (BDF §134.3). Gould suggests that the gender of ἰδών comes from the fact that the demon "sees" through the eyes of the boy (τὸν υἱόν in v. 17), and notes that "in all these stories, the man and the evil spirit get mixed up in this way. The outward acts belong to the man, but the informing spirit is sometimes that of the man, and sometimes the evil spirit" (168–69).

αὐτὸν. Accusative direct object of ἰδών.

τὸ πνεῦμα. Nominative subject of συνεσπάραξεν.

εὐθὺς. Adverbial, modifying συνεσπάραξεν: "as soon as" (see 1:28; Decker 1997, 109).

συνεσπάραξεν. Aor act ind 3rd sg συσπαράσσω ("to convulse," BDAG, 978). This compound form (σύν + σπαράσσω) is not found in the LXX, Pseudepigrapha, Josephus, Philo, or the AF. The simple form, σπαράσσω, is used in similar contexts with the same meaning (e.g., Mark 1:26; 9:26; Luke 9:39); it could be used as a medical term for retching or convulsion (France, 366).

αὐτόν. Accusative direct object of συνεσπάραξεν.

πεσὼν. Aor act ptc masc nom sg πίπτω (temporal).

ἐπὶ τῆς γῆς. Spatial.

ἐκυλίετο. Impf mid ind 3rd sg κυλίω ("to roll," BDAG, 574). On the possibility that this is an inceptive imperfect as in NAB, see 1:21.

ἀφρίζων. Pres act ptc masc nom sg ἀφρίζω (temporal; "to foam [at the mouth]"; see v. 20).

9:21 καὶ ἐπηρώτησεν τὸν πατέρα αὐτοῦ, Πόσος χρόνος ἐστὶν ὡς τοῦτο γέγονεν αὐτῷ; ὁ δὲ εἶπεν, Ἐκ παιδιόθεν·

ἐπηρώτησεν. Aor act ind 3rd sg ἐπερωτάω. On ἐπερωτάω versus the simple form ἐρωτάω, see 4:10.

τὸν πατέρα. Accusative direct object of ἐπηρώτησεν.

Πόσος χρόνος ἐστὶν ὡς τοῦτο γέγονεν αὐτῷ. Clausal complement (direct discourse) of ἐπηρώτησεν.

Πόσος χρόνος. Nominative subject of ἐστίν. Formally, "how much time?" The word πόσος is a correlative pronoun often used in direct questions.

ἐστὶν. Pres act ind 3rd sg εἰμί.

ὡς. Here, a temporal conjunction: "since" (BDAG, 1105.8.b) introducing the subordinate temporal clause, ὡς τοῦτο γέγονεν αὐτῷ, which serves as the second half of the correlative statement introduced by πόσος.

τοῦτο. Nominative subject of γέγονεν.

γέγονεν. Prf act ind 3rd sg γίνομαι.

αὐτῷ. Dative of disadvantage.

ὁ. Nominative subject of εἶπεν. On the use of ὁ δέ to change subjects, see 1:45.

εἶπεν. Aor act ind 3rd sg λέγω.

Ἐκ παιδιόθεν. Clausal complement (direct discourse) of εἶπεν. The prepositional phrase is temporal, and marks the beginning of the time period involved.

παιδιόθεν. Adverb: "from childhood." The classical expression would have used a genitive noun (ἐκ παιδός) rather than the adverb (MM, 474).

9:22 καὶ πολλάκις καὶ εἰς πῦρ αὐτὸν ἔβαλεν καὶ εἰς ὕδατα ἵνα ἀπολέσῃ αὐτόν· ἀλλ᾽ εἴ τι δύνῃ, βοήθησον ἡμῖν σπλαγχνισθεὶς ἐφ᾽ ἡμᾶς.

καὶ . . . καὶ. The first καί is Mark's frequent connective; the second is adverbial modifying ἔβαλεν, along with the adverb πολλάκις.

εἰς πῦρ . . . καὶ εἰς ὕδατα. Spatial. The reference to water is plural, which may be due to Semitic influence, or perhaps more likely to the multiple times the demon has caused the boy to fall into water (Stein 2008, 437).

αὐτὸν. Accusative direct object of ἔβαλεν.

ἔβαλεν. Aor act ind 3rd sg βάλλω.

ἵνα. Introduces a purpose clause. "Such injury or death is not just a collateral hazard, but the malevolent intention of the demon" (France, 366–67).

ἀπολέσῃ. Aor act subj 3rd sg ἀπόλλυμι. Subjunctive with ἵνα.

αὐτὸν. Accusative direct object of ἀπολέσῃ.

ἀλλ᾽. This conjunction is most commonly used in conjunction with a negative clause, but here there is no explicit negative, though there is clear contrast between the two clauses.

εἴ τι δύνῃ, βοήθησον ἡμῖν σπλαγχνισθεὶς ἐφ᾽ ἡμᾶς. A first-class conditional statement. The boy's father is not assuming that Jesus is able (i.e., one should not read a "since" into the statement), but is desperately hoping that it is possible.

τι. Accusative direct object of an understood ποιεῖν (see below). Omitted in the translation to suggest the same abrupt plea. The indefinite pronoun might suggest that "even a little help is better than none" (France, 367).

δύνῃ. Pres mid ind 2nd sg δύναμαι. The contracted form of the second singular is used here (cf. the uncontracted form, δύνασαι, in 1:40). This verb is typically accompanied by a complementary infinitive; here, ποιεῖν is to be supplied (contra Gould, 169). BDAG (262.c) lists only three NT examples of an accusative with δύναμαι that assume the presence of ποιεῖν.

βοήθησον ... σπλαγχνισθείς. This combination of verbal forms may use a figure of speech called *hysteron proteron* (ὕστερον πρότερον, i.e., "later first"). This "reverses the logical sequence of events to emphasize what is most important in the mind of the speaker or writer. The feelings of compassion precede the act of helping" (Duckwitz, 158). On the figure, see Robertson (423.g) who is cautious about its validity in the NT, referring to Winer who rejects it (see Winer 1874, 563; Winer 1882, 692, "nor can we admit this figure of speech in other N.T. passages"). Neither Robertson nor Winer discuss the present passage, which would appear to justify Duckwitz's analysis.

βοήθησον. Aor act impv 2nd sg βοηθέω.

ἡμῖν. Dative complement of βοήθησον.

σπλαγχνισθείς. Aor mid ptc masc nom sg σπλαγχνίζομαι (means). This is a "θη middle" intransitive form (see 2:2), not passive. On σπλαγχνίζομαι, see 1:41.

ἐφ' ἡμᾶς. Respect. On this use of ἐπί with the accusative, see 6:34.

9:23 ὁ δὲ Ἰησοῦς εἶπεν αὐτῷ, Τὸ Εἰ δύνῃ, πάντα δυνατὰ τῷ πιστεύοντι.

ὁ ... Ἰησοῦς. Nominative subject of εἶπεν.

δὲ. The use of δέ rather than καί marks the change of speaker from the boy's father in verse 22 to Jesus in verse 23.

εἶπεν. Aor act ind 3rd sg λέγω.

αὐτῷ. Dative indirect object of εἶπεν.

Τὸ Εἰ δύνῃ ... πιστεύοντι. Clausal complement (direct discourse) of εἶπεν.

Τὸ Εἰ δύνῃ. The article τό is a nominalizer, turning the clause Εἰ δύνῃ (a partial restatement [aposiopesis] of the protasis from the preceding statement by the boy's father) into a nominative substantive (probably used as a nominative of exclamation; see Wallace 1996, 59–60). "The article τό is used as in classical before quoted words, sentences and sentence fragments" (BDF §267.1; see also Robertson, 766—both reference this text; cf. Eph 4:9, τὸ δὲ ἀνέβη τί ἐστιν). Here, both Τό and Εἰ are capitalized, since Τό begins Jesus' statement and Εἰ is the first word of the man's statement quoted by

Jesus. The result is "an idiomatic exclamation . . . echoing the man's tentative request in a tone of ironical rebuke: '"If you can" indeed!' How dare he express any doubt about the matter? Grammatically it is rough but effective" (France, 367).

δύνῃ. Pres mid ind 2nd sg δύναμαι. See also verse 22.

πάντα δυνατὰ τῷ πιστεύοντι. A nominal statement with ἐστίν (with a neuter plural subject) omitted as is common in exclamations (BDF §127.4). The same basic statement, πάντα δυνατά, appears three other times in the NT: Matt 19:26; Mark 10:27; 14:36, in each case without an expressed verb.

πάντα. Nominative subject of an understood ἐστίν.

δυνατὰ. Predicate adjective of an understood ἐστίν.

τῷ πιστεύοντι. Pres act ptc masc dat sg πιστεύω (substantival). Dative of advantage.

9:24 εὐθὺς κράξας ὁ πατὴρ τοῦ παιδίου ἔλεγεν, Πιστεύω· βοήθει μου τῇ ἀπιστίᾳ.

εὐθὺς. Adverbial, modifying κράξας: "immediately" (see 1:28; Decker 1997, 109). This instance illustrates the importance of the context in determining the meaning of εὐθύς. The man's immediate declaration of faith upon being questioned by Jesus is a necessary component of Mark's theme at this point in his narrative. It is not that the man spoke quickly (though he may have), but that he responded promptly and without hesitation.

κράξας. Aor act ptc masc nom sg κράζω (temporal).

ὁ πατὴρ. Nominative subject of ἔλεγεν.

τοῦ παιδίου. On the meaning of a παιδίον, see 7:28.

ἔλεγεν. Impf act ind 3rd sg λέγω.

Πιστεύω. Pres act ind 1st sg πιστεύω. See 1:15.

βοήθει. Pres act impv 2nd sg βοηθέω.

τῇ ἀπιστίᾳ. Dative complement of βοήθει.

Mark 9:25-32

[25]But Jesus, seeing that a crowd was quickly gathering, commanded the unclean spirit, saying to it, "You dumb and mute spirit, I command you, come out of him and no longer enter him." [26](The spirit) cried out and convulsed (him) violently and came out; and (the boy) became corpse-like so that most of them said that he died. [27]But Jesus, taking hold of his hand, lifted him and he stood up. [28]After he went into a house his disciples asked him privately, "Why

were we not able to cast it out?" ²⁹He answered them, "This kind is able to come out by nothing except prayer."

³⁰Having left from there they traveled through Galilee; now Jesus did not want anyone to know (where they were going), ³¹for he was teaching his disciples and he said to them, "The Son of Man will be delivered into human hands, and they will kill him, and having been killed, after three days he will rise." ³²But they did not understand this saying and they were afraid to ask him (what it meant).

9:25 ἰδὼν δὲ ὁ Ἰησοῦς ὅτι ἐπισυντρέχει ὄχλος, ἐπετίμησεν τῷ πνεύματι τῷ ἀκαθάρτῳ λέγων αὐτῷ, Τὸ ἄλαλον καὶ κωφὸν πνεῦμα, ἐγὼ ἐπιτάσσω σοι, ἔξελθε ἐξ αὐτοῦ καὶ μηκέτι εἰσέλθῃς εἰς αὐτόν.

ἰδών. Aor act ptc masc nom sg ὁράω (causal or perhaps temporal—the difference is minimal since one implies the other).

δέ. The use of δέ rather than καί marks the change of speaker from the boy's father in verse 24 to Jesus in verse 25.

ὁ Ἰησοῦς. Nominative subject of ἐπετίμησεν.

ὅτι. Introduces the clausal complement of ἰδών.

ἐπισυντρέχει. Pres act ind 3rd sg ἐπισυντρέχω ("to come together hurriedly to, toward, or at a particular location, 'to rush together to a place, to throng to,'" LN 15.134). Only here in the NT. Since the crowd began running toward Jesus in verse 15 (though there described with προστρέχω), perhaps the idea here is that the crowd was quickly assembling where he was (so NET, HCSB, NASB), rather than simply "running together" (contra NRSV, NIV, ESV).

ὄχλος. Nominative subject of ἐπισυντρέχει.

ἐπετίμησεν. Aor act ind 3rd sg ἐπιτιμάω.

τῷ πνεύματι τῷ ἀκαθάρτῳ. Dative complement of ἐπετίμησεν.

λέγων. Pres act ptc masc nom sg λέγω (means; redundant adverbial participle of speaking; see 1:7).

αὐτῷ. Dative indirect object of λέγων.

Τὸ ἄλαλον . . . εἰς αὐτόν. Clausal complement (direct discourse) of λέγων.

Τὸ ἄλαλον καὶ κωφὸν πνεῦμα. Nominative of address instead of a vocative (see 5:8). On the semantics of the two adjectives, see 7:37. The collocation with ἄλαλος suggests that κωφός here means "deaf."

ἐγώ. Nominative subject of ἐπιτάσσω.

ἐπιτάσσω. Pres act ind 1st sg ἐπιτάσσω.

σοι. Dative complement of ἐπιτάσσω.

ἔξελθε ἐξ αὐτοῦ . . . εἰς αὐτόν. Clausal complement of ἐπιτάσσω.

ἔξελθε. Aor act impv 2nd sg ἐξέρχομαι.

ἐξ αὐτοῦ. Separation.

εἰσέλθῃς. Aor act subj 2nd sg εἰσέρχομαι (prohibitive subjunctive).

εἰς αὐτόν. Spatial.

9:26 καὶ κράξας καὶ πολλὰ σπαράξας ἐξῆλθεν· καὶ ἐγένετο ὡσεὶ νεκρός, ὥστε τοὺς πολλοὺς λέγειν ὅτι ἀπέθανεν.

κράξας. Aor act ptc masc nom sg κράζω (attendant circumstance).

πολλά. Adverbial use of πολύς (see 1:45).

σπαράξας. Aor act ptc masc nom sg σπαράσσω (attendant circumstance; "to shake to and fro, convulse," BDAG, 936, "acc. of person to be supplied"; see also 1:26).

ἐξῆλθεν. Aor act ind 3rd sg ἐξέρχομαι.

ἐγένετο. Aor mid ind 3rd sg γίνομαι. Here, καὶ ἐγένετο is not an introductory formula, as is sometimes the case in Mark (see 1:9). When καὶ ἐγένετο occurs within a pericope (as here), it marks an immediate sequence of events (*TDM*, 85).

ὡσεὶ νεκρός. The comparative ὡσεί with νεκρός ("dead," or substantivally, "dead body, corpse," BDAG, 667.B.1) is formally "as a corpse."

τοὺς πολλούς. Accusative subject of λέγειν, "the many," in the sense of a majority (BDAG, 849.2.a.β.‎ℵ), though perhaps "many of them" is adequate.

λέγειν. Pres act inf λέγω. Used with ὥστε to introduce a result clause.

ὅτι. Introduces the clausal complement (indirect discourse) of λέγειν.

ἀπέθανεν. Aor act ind 3rd sg ἀποθνήσκω.

9:27 ὁ δὲ Ἰησοῦς κρατήσας τῆς χειρὸς αὐτοῦ ἤγειρεν αὐτόν, καὶ ἀνέστη.

ὁ . . . Ἰησοῦς. Nominative subject of ἤγειρεν.

δέ. The use of δέ rather than καί marks the change of subject from the onlookers in verse 26 to Jesus in verse 27.

κρατήσας. Aor act ptc masc nom sg κρατέω (means).

τῆς χειρός. Genitive direct object of κρατήσας.

ἤγειρεν. Aor act ind 3rd sg ἐγείρω.

αὐτόν. Accusative direct object of ἤγειρεν.

ἀνέστη. Aor act ind 3rd sg ἀνίστημι. It is overstating the text to assert that this is a reference to resurrection (contra Edwards 2002,

280). The previous verse used a comparative phrase, ὡσεὶ νεκρός, which is not an appropriate description of someone who actually is dead. The word ἀνίστημι can be used in reference to resurrection (e.g., 10:30; 12:25), but here is probably simply means to stand up (cf. 14:57, 60).

9:28 καὶ εἰσελθόντος αὐτοῦ εἰς οἶκον οἱ μαθηταὶ αὐτοῦ κατ᾽ ἰδίαν ἐπηρώτων αὐτόν, Ὅτι ἡμεῖς οὐκ ἠδυνήθημεν ἐκβαλεῖν αὐτό;

εἰσελθόντος. Aor act ptc masc gen sg εἰσέρχομαι. Genitive absolute (see 1:32), temporal.

αὐτοῦ. Genitive subject of εἰσελθόντος. On the overlap of reference with αὐτόν in the main clause, see 5:2 and 14:3.

εἰς οἶκον. Spatial. On the repeated preposition, see 1:21.

οἱ μαθηταὶ. Nominative subject of ἐπηρώτων.

κατ᾽ ἰδίαν. "Privately" (see 4:34).

ἐπηρώτων. Impf act ind 3rd pl ἐπερωτάω. On ἐπερωτάω versus the simple form ἐρωτάω, see 4:10.

αὐτόν. Accusative direct object of ἐπηρώτων.

Ὅτι. Interrogative ὅτι: "Why?" (see 2:16).

ἡμεῖς. Nominative subject of ἠδυνήθημεν.

ἠδυνήθημεν. Aor mid ind 1st pl δύναμαι. This is an intransitive, "θη middle" form (see 2:2).

ἐκβαλεῖν. Aor act inf ἐκβάλλω (complementary).

αὐτό. Accusative direct object of ἐκβαλεῖν.

9:29 καὶ εἶπεν αὐτοῖς, Τοῦτο τὸ γένος ἐν οὐδενὶ δύναται ἐξελθεῖν εἰ μὴ ἐν προσευχῇ.

εἶπεν. Aor act ind 3rd sg λέγω.

αὐτοῖς. Dative indirect object of εἶπεν.

Τοῦτο τὸ γένος ... ἐν προσευχῇ. Clausal complement (direct discourse) of εἶπεν.

Τοῦτο τὸ γένος. Nominative subject of δύναται. In the NT, γένος is most commonly a reference to people who are related, whether as descendant, family, nation, or people. It can, however, also refer to any sort of entity "united by common traits," thus "class, kind" (BDAG, 194–95.4). Gould argues that γένος should be understood as "*this kind of thing, i.e.,* the genus evil spirit; not this kind of spirit, as if this was a specially vicious kind of spirit, that it took a good deal to exorcise" (171; so also France, 370; contra Swete, 202, "spirits of such malignity," and many recent commentators).

ἐν οὐδενί. Instrumental.

δύναται. Pres mid ind 3rd sg δύναμαι.

ἐξελθεῖν. Aor act inf ἐξέρχομαι (complementary). Swete (202; so also V. Taylor, 401) proposes that this active infinitive be understood as equivalent to a passive.

εἰ μή. Idiom: "except."

ἐν προσευχῇ. Instrumental. The textual variant at this point, ἐν προσευχῇ καὶ νηστείᾳ, reflects a common association in the minds of many early Christians. Although apparently originating fairly early in the transmission of the text (𝔓⁴⁵ᵛⁱᵈ אᵇ A etc.), the shorter reading, ἐν προσευχῇ, is supported by early external evidence (א* B etc.), and is also most consistent with internal evidence (viz., Jesus' attitude toward fasting as expressed in 2:18-22). That it should be favored by later Byzantine scribes, for whom the association of prayer and fasting was a given in monastic practice, is not surprising.

9:30 Κἀκεῖθεν ἐξελθόντες παρεπορεύοντο διὰ τῆς Γαλιλαίας, καὶ οὐκ ἤθελεν ἵνα τις γνοῖ·

Κἀκεῖθεν. This is a crasis form: καὶ + ἐκεῖθεν.

ἐξελθόντες. Aor act ptc masc nom pl ἐξέρχομαι (temporal).

παρεπορεύοντο. Impf mid ind 3rd pl παραπορεύομαι ("to make a trip, 'go through' with διά + gen.," BDAG, 770). On the possibility that this is an inceptive imperfect as in NASB and NLT, see 1:21.

διὰ τῆς Γαλιλαίας. Spatial.

ἤθελεν. Impf act ind 3rd sg θέλω. The imperfect sketches background information explaining the travels of the group.

ἵνα. The verb θέλω usually takes an infinitive as its complement, but its complement can sometimes be a ἵνα clause (see Wallace 1996, 476; BDAG, 476.2.a).

γνοῖ. Aor act subj 3rd sg γινώσκω. Subjunctive with ἵνα. On the form, see 5:43.

9:31 ἐδίδασκεν γὰρ τοὺς μαθητὰς αὐτοῦ καὶ ἔλεγεν αὐτοῖς ὅτι Ὁ υἱὸς τοῦ ἀνθρώπου παραδίδοται εἰς χεῖρας ἀνθρώπων, καὶ ἀποκτενοῦσιν αὐτόν, καὶ ἀποκτανθεὶς μετὰ τρεῖς ἡμέρας ἀναστήσεται.

ἐδίδασκεν. Impf act ind 3rd sg διδάσκω. The imperfect provides explanatory, background information.

γάρ. Explanatory.

τοὺς μαθητάς. Accusative direct object of ἐδίδασκεν.

ἔλεγεν. Impf act ind 3rd sg λέγω.

ὅτι. Introduces the clausal complement (direct discourse) of ἔλεγεν (see 1:15).

Ὁ υἱὸς τοῦ ἀνθρώπου. On this title, see 2:10.

Ὁ υἱὸς. Nominative subject of παραδίδοται.

παραδίδοται. Pres pass ind 3rd sg παραδίδωμι. The verb has future time reference in parallel with the two future verbs that follow. The present tense is not used to reflect "the certainty of the future event" (contra Gould, 172), but rather to enable the speaker to use imperfective aspect in a future time reference, a temporal reference that is within the normal range for the present tense. On the meaning and use of παραδίδωμι in Mark, see 1:14 and 3:19.

εἰς χεῖρας ἀνθρώπων. A metaphorical expression used with παραδίδωμι to indicate that the betrayal would result in Jesus' arrest by human authorities.

ἀποκτενοῦσιν. Fut act ind 3rd pl ἀποκτείνω.

αὐτόν. Accusative direct object of ἀποκτενοῦσιν.

ἀποκτανθεὶς. Aor pass ptc masc nom sg ἀποκτείνω (temporal).

μετὰ τρεῖς ἡμέρας. Temporal.

ἀναστήσεται. Fut mid ind 3rd sg ἀνίστημι. The ησ is *not* the second future passive form marker –θησ– with the *theta* elided, but rather is the form marker for future middle with a lengthened stem vowel: στα + σ > στησ.

9:32 οἱ δὲ ἠγνόουν τὸ ῥῆμα, καὶ ἐφοβοῦντο αὐτὸν ἐπερωτῆσαι.

οἱ. Nominative subject of ἠγνόουν.

δὲ. On the use of οἱ δέ to change subjects, see 1:45.

ἠγνόουν. Impf act ind 3rd pl ἀγνοέω. The nuance of ἀγνοέω may not relate to understanding *what* Jesus had just said; more likely it refers to not accepting what his words *implied* (cf. Stein 2008, 440).

ἐφοβοῦντο. Impf mid ind 3rd pl φοβέομαι.

αὐτὸν. Accusative direct object of ἐπερωτῆσαι.

ἐπερωτῆσαι. Aor act inf ἐπερωτάω (complementary). On ἐπερωτάω versus the simple form ἐρωτάω, see 4:10.

Mark 9:33-41

³³Then they came to Capernaum, and when he was in the house he asked them, "What were you arguing about on the road?" ³⁴But they were silent, for on the road they had been disputing who was the greatest. ³⁵So sitting down he summoned the Twelve and said to them, "If anyone desires to be first, he must be last of all and servant

of all." ³⁶Taking a child he stood him in their midst and giving him a hug he said to them, ³⁷"Whoever welcomes one of these little children in my name welcomes me, and whoever welcomes me, welcomes the one who sent me."

³⁸John said to him, "Teacher, we saw someone casting out demons in your name and we forbid him because he was not following us." ³⁹But Jesus said, "Do not forbid him, for there is no one who will do an act of power in my name and soon after be capable of speaking evil of me; ⁴⁰for the one who is not against us is for us. ⁴¹For whoever gives you a cup of water to drink because of my name, that is, because you belong to Christ, truly I say to you that he will certainly not lose his reward.

On the significance (or lack thereof) of the numerous "catchwords" in verses 33-50, see Gundry's perceptive analysis (507–8).

9:33 Καὶ ἦλθον εἰς Καφαρναούμ. καὶ ἐν τῇ οἰκίᾳ γενόμενος ἐπηρώτα αὐτούς, Τί ἐν τῇ ὁδῷ διελογίζεσθε;

ἦλθον. Aor act ind 3rd pl ἔρχομαι.

εἰς Καφαρναούμ. Spatial.

ἐν τῇ οἰκίᾳ. Locative.

γενόμενος. Aor mid ptc masc nom sg γίνομαι (temporal).

ἐπηρώτα. Impf act ind 3rd sg ἐπερωτάω. On ἐπερωτάω versus the simple form ἐρωτάω, see 4:10. On the possibility that this is an inceptive imperfect as in NASB and NLT, see 1:21.

αὐτούς. Accusative direct object of ἐπηρώτα.

Τί. Accusative direct object of διελογίζεσθε.

ἐν τῇ ὁδῷ. Temporal (see similar uses in 8:27; 10:32; and possibly 8:3; see also *TDM*, 79, 211 n. 111).

διελογίζεσθε. Impf mid ind 2nd pl διαλογίζομαι. Although διαλογίζομαι can mean simply "discuss," the reaction of the disciples (v. 34) suggests that Jesus' question has more of an edge to it (note also the explanatory πρὸς ἀλλήλους γὰρ διελέχθησαν in the next verse). The words διαλογίζομαι and διαλέγομαι (v. 34) are used interchangeably in this context (the second occurs in a γάρ clause explaining the first). On Mark's other uses of διαλογίζομαι, see 11:31.

9:34 οἱ δὲ ἐσιώπων· πρὸς ἀλλήλους γὰρ διελέχθησαν ἐν τῇ ὁδῷ τίς μείζων.

οἱ δὲ ἐσιώπων. The same phrase is used to describe the Pharisees in 3:4-5 (see Edwards 2002, 285). There is "an almost comical incongruity in the picture of these grown men acting like guilty schoolboys before the teacher" (France, 373).

οἱ. Nominative subject of ἐσιώπων. On the use of οἱ δέ to change subjects, see 1:45.

ἐσιώπων. Impf act ind 3rd pl σιωπάω.

πρὸς ἀλλήλους. Opposition.

γὰρ. Introduces an explanation of the previous statement.

διελέχθησαν. Aor mid ind 3rd pl διαλέγομαι. This is an intransitive, "θη middle" form (see 2:2). With this verb a prepositional phrase using πρός identifies the parties of the dispute/discussion in contrast to περί, which identifies the subject matter (e.g., Acts 24:25).

ἐν τῇ ὁδῷ. Temporal.

τίς μείζων. An indirect question with εἰμί omitted as is common in questions (BDF §127.3), especially indirect ones (Doudna, 4).

τίς. Nominative subject in a verbless clause.

μείζων. Predicate adjective in a verbless clause. The form is comparative, but the sense of the context makes it clear that it is used as a superlative. This is common in Koine.

9:35 καὶ καθίσας ἐφώνησεν τοὺς δώδεκα καὶ λέγει αὐτοῖς, Εἴ τις θέλει πρῶτος εἶναι, ἔσται πάντων ἔσχατος καὶ πάντων διάκονος.

καθίσας. Aor act ptc masc nom sg καθίζω (temporal, or perhaps attendant circumstance).

ἐφώνησεν. Aor act ind 3rd sg φωνέω. Here, the context makes it clear that φωνέω has the sense of "summon, call, invite" (see also 10:49 [2×]; 15:35) rather than "cry out" (e.g., 1:26; 14:30). There is no justification for insisting on a "certain degree of loudness that this verb does connote . . . [which] displays the vigor with which Jesus exercises authority over his disciples" (Gundry, 509).

τοὺς δώδεκα. Accusative direct object of ἐφώνησεν. On the use and referent of δώδεκα, see 4:10.

λέγει. Pres act ind 3rd sg λέγω. The narrative present is simply the use of a present tense to introduce discourse (see also 1:21 on εἰσπορεύονται).

Εἴ τις . . . πάντων διάκονος. Clausal complement (direct discourse) of λέγει. The statement takes the form of a first-class condition.

τις. Nominative subject of θέλει.

θέλει. Pres act ind 3rd sg θέλω.

πρῶτος. Predicate nominative of εἶναι.

εἶναι. Pres act inf εἰμί (complementary).
ἔσται. Fut mid ind 3rd sg εἰμί. Imperatival use of the future.
πάντων. Partitive genitive (both occurrences; see 8:8).
ἔσχατος καὶ ... διάκονος. Predicate nominative.

9:36 καὶ λαβὼν παιδίον ἔστησεν αὐτὸ ἐν μέσῳ αὐτῶν καὶ ἐναγκαλισάμενος αὐτὸ εἶπεν αὐτοῖς,

λαβών. Aor act ptc masc nom sg λαμβάνω (temporal).
παιδίον. Accusative direct object of λαβών.
ἔστησεν. Aor act ind 3rd sg ἵστημι.
αὐτό. Accusative direct object of ἔστησεν.
ἐναγκαλισάμενος. Aor mid ptc masc nom sg ἐναγκαλίζομαι (temporal; "to take in one's arms, hug").
αὐτό. Accusative direct object of ἐναγκαλισάμενος.
εἶπεν. Aor act ind 3rd sg λέγω.
αὐτοῖς. Dative indirect object of εἶπεν.

9:37 Ὃς ἂν ἓν τῶν τοιούτων παιδίων δέξηται ἐπὶ τῷ ὀνόματί μου, ἐμὲ δέχεται· καὶ ὃς ἂν ἐμὲ δέχηται, οὐκ ἐμὲ δέχεται ἀλλὰ τὸν ἀποστείλαντά με.

This entire verse is a clausal complement (direct discourse) of εἶπεν (v. 36). The verse contains two main clauses (ἐμὲ δέχεται and οὐκ ἐμὲ δέχεται), each with an indefinite relative clause introduced with ὃς ἄν that functions as the subject of the main verb.

Ὃς ἄν. Indefinite relative pronoun ("whoever") functioning as the nominative subject of δέξηται.
ἕν. Accusative direct object of δέξηται. The gender is neuter to agree with the antecedent (technically, "postcedent"), παιδίων.
τῶν τοιούτων παιδίων. Partitive genitive (see 8:8).
δέξηται. Aor mid subj 3rd sg δέχομαι. Subjunctive with ὃς ἄν.
ἐπὶ τῷ ὀνόματί μου. This idiom "focuses on the authorizing function of the one named in the gen." (BDAG, 366.17, s.v. ἐπί; see also 9:39; 13:6). France, however, suggests that "perhaps the sense is more broadly of 'doing as I would do' " (374).
δέχεται. Pres mid ind 3rd sg δέχομαι.
ὃς ἄν. Indefinite relative pronoun ("whoever") functioning as the nominative subject of δέξηται.
ἐμέ. Accusative direct object of δέχηται.
δέχηται. Pres mid subj 3rd sg δέχομαι. Subjunctive with ὃς ἄν. In the first part of the verse the parallel verb is aorist subjunctive (δέξηται). As France observes, this is "probably no more than

natural linguistic variation" (375 n. 66); he also warns of overexegesis at this point. It is possible, however, that there is some slight aspectual shift involved, the initial statement referring to human relationships being phrased with the default aorist subjunctive, but the (ultimately) more significant relationship to Jesus receiving the more heavily marked present subjunctive (so Porter 1993, 326).

οὐκ . . . ἀλλά. Two contrasting propositions are given, the negative statement being "corrected" by the coordinating, contrasting conjunction ἀλλά.

δέχεται. Pres mid ind 3rd sg δέχομαι.

ἀλλὰ τὸν ἀποστείλαντά με. In this elliptical statement the verb is assumed from the preceding clause: δέχεται.

τὸν ἀποστείλαντά. Aor act ptc masc acc sg ἀποστέλλω (substantival). Accusative direct object of the implied δέχεται.

με. Accusative direct object of ἀποστείλαντά.

9:38 Ἔφη αὐτῷ ὁ Ἰωάννης, Διδάσκαλε, εἴδομέν τινα ἐν τῷ ὀνόματί σου ἐκβάλλοντα δαιμόνια καὶ ἐκωλύομεν αὐτόν, ὅτι οὐκ ἠκολούθει ἡμῖν.

Ἔφη. Aor act ind 3rd sg φημί.

αὐτῷ. Dative indirect object of ἔφη.

ὁ Ἰωάννης. Nominative subject of ἔφη.

Διδάσκαλε. Vocative. Mark records the use of διδάσκαλε as a title for Jesus much more frequently than the other Gospels (see 4:38).

εἴδομέν. Aor act ind 1st pl ὁράω.

τινα. Accusative direct object of εἴδομέν.

ἐν τῷ ὀνόματί σου. Instrumental.

ἐκβάλλοντα. Pres act ptc masc acc sg ἐκβάλλω (attributive modifying τινα).

δαιμόνια. Accusative direct object of ἐκβάλλοντα.

ἐκωλύομεν. Impf act ind 1st pl κωλύω. The imperfect may be conative, "we tried to stop him," but there is no way to know if they only attempted the action or if they actually stopped him (the imperfect requires neither conclusion).

αὐτόν. Accusative direct object of ἐκωλύομεν.

ὅτι. Introduces a causal clause.

ἠκολούθει. Impf act ind 3rd sg ἀκολουθέω.

ἡμῖν. Dative complement of ἠκολούθει. The use of the plural here is unexpected. We might have expected John to refer to not following *Jesus* (σέ). Jesus' reply first refers to himself (μου, με, v. 39), but then broadens the reference to include his disciples (ἡμῶν, v. 40).

9:39 ὁ δὲ Ἰησοῦς εἶπεν, Μὴ κωλύετε αὐτόν. οὐδεὶς γάρ ἐστιν ὃς ποιήσει δύναμιν ἐπὶ τῷ ὀνόματί μου καὶ δυνήσεται ταχὺ κακολογῆσαί με·

ὁ . . . Ἰησοῦς. Nominative subject of εἶπεν.

δὲ. The use of δέ rather than καί marks the change of subject from John in verse 38 to Jesus in verse 39.

εἶπεν. Aor act ind 3rd sg λέγω.

Μὴ κωλύετε . . . ἐν ἀλλήλοις (v. 50). Clausal complement (direct discourse) of εἶπεν.

κωλύετε. Pres act impv 2nd pl κωλύω.

αὐτόν. Accusative direct object of κωλύετε.

οὐδεὶς. Predicate nominative.

γάρ. Introduces a clause that explains why Jesus countermands his followers' interdiction.

ἐστιν. Pres act ind 3rd sg εἰμί.

ὃς. Nominative subject of ποιήσει.

ποιήσει. Fut act ind 3rd sg ποιέω.

δύναμιν. Accusative direct object of ποιήσει. On δύναμις as a word for "miracle," see 6:2.

ἐπὶ τῷ ὀνόματί μου. See 9:37; 13:6.

δυνήσεται. Fut mid ind 3rd sg δύναμαι. This is an intransitive, "θη middle" form (see 2:2).

ταχὺ. Temporal adverb: "soon afterward."

κακολογῆσαί. Aor act inf κακολογέω (complementary; "speak evil of, revile, insult").

9:40 ὃς γὰρ οὐκ ἔστιν καθ᾽ ἡμῶν, ὑπὲρ ἡμῶν ἐστιν.

ὃς. Nominative subject of ἔστιν. A relative pronoun may introduce an informal condition: "if anyone is not . . ."

γὰρ. Introduces an explanatory clause.

ἔστιν. Pres act ind 3rd sg εἰμί. On the accent, see 12:32.

καθ᾽ ἡμῶν. Opposition.

ὑπὲρ ἡμῶν. Advantage.

ἐστιν. Pres act ind 3rd sg εἰμί.

9:41 Ὃς γὰρ ἂν ποτίσῃ ὑμᾶς ποτήριον ὕδατος ἐν ὀνόματι ὅτι Χριστοῦ ἐστε, ἀμὴν λέγω ὑμῖν ὅτι οὐ μὴ ἀπολέσῃ τὸν μισθὸν αὐτοῦ.

Ὃς . . . ἂν ποτίσῃ ὑμᾶς ποτήριον ὕδατος. Formally, "whoever gives you to drink a cup of water."

Ὅς . . . ἄν. Indefinite relative pronoun ("whoever") functioning as the nominative subject of ποτίσῃ.

γὰρ. Introduces a statement that introduces a further explanation of Jesus' statement in verse 39, though also picking up the train of thought from verse 37 prior to John's interruption in verse 38. This clause ties Jesus' response to John's concern back to Jesus' original statement in verse 37. Syntactically, the γάρ clause is parallel with the γάρ clause in verse 40.

ποτίσῃ. Aor act subj 3rd sg ποτίζω. Subjunctive with ἄν.

ὑμᾶς. Accusative direct object of ποτίσῃ.

ποτήριον. Complement in an object-complement double accusative construction.

ἐν ὀνόματι ὅτι Χριστοῦ ἐστε. Formally, "because of [the] name that you are of Christ." The use of "my" in the translation is supplied for clarity, not because of the textual variant found in some manuscripts (א D Θ W f¹³ 𝔐).

ἐν ὀνόματι. Causal. Swete points out that "ἐν ὀνόματι ὅτι κτλ. is nearly equivalent to διὰ τὸ Χριστοῦ εἶναι, on the score of your being Christ's" (208). There are "titular" or "categorical" connotations to the use of ὄνομα here. Note BDAG's translation: "*whoever gives you a drink under the category that you belong to Christ,* i.e., *in your capacity as a follower of Christ*" (BDAG, 714.3, s.v. ὄνομα; see also BDF §397.3).

ὅτι Χριστοῦ ἐστε. The ὅτι clause is in apposition to the dative ὀνόματι (Robertson, 1034; cf. 2 Cor 10:7; Rom 8:9; 1 Cor 1:12; 3:23).

Χριστοῦ. Possessive genitive. It is unusual for Jesus to refer to himself as Χριστός; this is the only such instance in the Synoptics. It does occur in Jesus' words in 12:35 and 13:21, but in neither case does he refer directly to himself; it is also articular in both cases (for more, see France, 378).

ἐστε. Pres act ind 2nd pl εἰμί.

ἀμὴν λέγω ὑμῖν. See 3:28.

λέγω. Pres act ind 1st sg λέγω.

ὅτι. Introduces the clausal complement (direct discourse) of λέγω.

οὐ μὴ. The double negative with ἀπολέσῃ in this context expresses an emphatic denial (see 9:41).

ἀπολέσῃ. Aor act subj 3rd sg ἀπόλλυμι. Subjunctive with οὐ μὴ.

τὸν μισθὸν. Accusative direct object of ἀπολέσῃ.

Mark 9:42-50

⁴²If anyone should cause one of these little ones who believe in me to sin, it would be better for him rather that a large millstone were hung around his neck and he were thrown into the lake. ⁴³If your hand causes you to sin, cut it off; it is better to enter into life crippled than for you to depart into Gehenna—into unquenchable fire—having your two hands. ⁴⁵If your foot causes you to sin, cut it off; it is better to enter into life maimed than to be thrown into Gehenna having two feet. ⁴⁷If your eye causes you to sin, gouge it out; it is better to enter the kingdom of God with one eye than to be thrown into Gehenna with two eyes, ⁴⁸where the worm does not die and the fire is not quenched; ⁴⁹for everyone will be salted with fire. ⁵⁰Salt is good, but if the salt has become unsalty, with what will it be made salty? Have salt among yourselves; then you will be able to live at peace with one another.

9:42 Καὶ ὃς ἂν σκανδαλίσῃ ἕνα τῶν μικρῶν τούτων τῶν πιστευόντων [εἰς ἐμέ], καλόν ἐστιν αὐτῷ μᾶλλον εἰ περίκειται μύλος ὀνικὸς περὶ τὸν τράχηλον αὐτοῦ καὶ βέβληται εἰς τὴν θάλασσαν.

This statement is recorded in all the Synoptics, but is worded differently in each. Luke 17:2 retains the first-class condition, but in place of καλόν ἐστιν has λυσιτελέω and for βάλλω has ἔρριπται, appending the comparison with ἢ ἵνα and a subjunctive verb at the end of the sentence. Matthew's sentence structure (18:6) is closer to Mark's, but uses συμφέρω instead of καλόν ἐστιν, a ἵνα clause instead of the first-class condition, and κρεμάννυμι rather than περίκειμαι.

ὃς ἂν σκανδαλίσῃ ἕνα τῶν μικρῶν τούτων τῶν πιστευόντων [εἰς ἐμέ]. This indefinite relative clause is used to introduce the subject to be discussed (a topic construction in the terms of discourse analysis) which is resumed with the pronoun αὐτῷ in the main clause that follows. It expresses a conditional idea, "if anyone should. . . ." For this function see Young (231–32) and Informal Conditions in the Glossary.

ὃς ἂν. The indefinite relative pronoun ("whoever") functions as the nominative subject of σκανδαλίσῃ.

σκανδαλίσῃ. Aor act subj 3rd sg σκανδαλίζω. Subjunctive with ἂν. The nonmetaphorical meaning of σκανδαλίζω is "to stumble," but it is used in the NT metaphorically in relation to sin. Just as I may stick out my foot to cause someone to stumble physically, I may also act in such a way as to cause that person to stumble spiritually, i.e., to sin.

ἕνα. Accusative direct object of σκανδαλίσῃ.

τῶν μικρῶν τούτων. Partitive genitive (see 8:8). On the adjectival use of demonstratives in Mark, see 4:11.

πιστευόντων. Pres act ptc masc gen pl πιστεύω (attributive).

[εἰς ἐμέ]. The normal expression of faith in Jesus (or his name, or God, or the message, etc.) in the NT uses πιστεύω εἰς (about 40×) rather than πιστεύω ἐν (only 1:15; John 3:15). Mark uses both expressions with no difference in meaning, though only once each. Bracketing εἰς ἐμέ appears unnecessary. This choice is probably due primarily to the absence of the phrase in ℵ, which likely reflects an accidental omission. The phrase is present in a wide range of mss (A B C² L W Θ Ψ ƒ¹,¹³ 𝔐).

καλόν ἐστιν αὐτῷ μᾶλλον. Apodosis of a conditional statement.

καλόν. Predicate adjective. The positive form of the adjective is being used in a comparative sense ("better"), as is clarified by the adverb μᾶλλον (see also v. 43). This is the normal way to express the comparative of καλός. The lack of an explicit comparison likely lends force to the statement: "whatever it is that makes drowning with an upper millstone around your neck better must be horrible beyond description" (Gundry, 512).

ἐστιν. Pres act ind 3rd sg εἰμί.

αὐτῷ. Dative of "advantage"—though here it is the lesser of two disadvantages.

εἰ. Introduces the protasis of a first-class condition (so BDAG, 277.1.a.β, s.v. εἰ).

περίκειται. Pres mid ind 3rd sg περίκειμαι ("to be around, be placed around," BDAG, 801; LN 85.54). Matthew 18:6 uses κρεμάννυμι ("to hang").

μύλος ὀνικὸς. "A great (lit. 'donkey') millstone, i.e. not a stone fr. the small handmill, but one fr. the large mill, worked by donkey-power" (BDAG, 661.2, s.v. μύλος).

μύλος. Nominative subject of περίκειται.

περὶ τὸν τράχηλον. Spatial.

βέβληται. Prf pass ind 3rd sg βάλλω. The stative aspect refers to the (very disadvantageous) state in which the offender would find himself.

εἰς τὴν θάλασσαν. Spatial.

9:43 Καὶ ἐὰν σκανδαλίζῃ σε ἡ χείρ σου, ἀπόκοψον αὐτήν· καλόν ἐστίν σε κυλλὸν εἰσελθεῖν εἰς τὴν ζωὴν ἢ τὰς δύο χεῖρας ἔχοντα ἀπελθεῖν εἰς τὴν γέενναν, εἰς τὸ πῦρ τὸ ἄσβεστον.

ἐάν. Introduces the protasis of a third-class condition. In ‖ Matt 18:8 and 5:29 a first-class condition is used, suggesting that first and third-class conditions are nearly identical in meaning, though first-class conditions are more versatile and third-class conditions are largely restricted to future situations due to the subjunctive verb used. Both conditions present a simple logical connection between the two parts of the statement, which the writer assumes to be true, either an actual assumption/belief, or simply for purposes of argument.

σκανδαλίζῃ. Pres act subj 3rd sg σκανδαλίζω. Subjunctive with ἐάν.

σε. Accusative direct object of σκανδαλίζῃ.

ἡ χείρ. Nominative subject of σκανδαλίζῃ.

ἀπόκοψον. Aor act impv 2nd sg ἀποκόπτω. All three uses of ἀποκόπτω in this context are aorist, the simple, unmarked imperative. For a critique of some older views of the imperative in this regard, see Wallace (1996, 714–17).

αὐτήν. Accusative direct object of ἀπόκοψον.

καλόν. The positive adjective is here (as in vv. 42, 45, 47) used in a comparative sense, i.e., "better" rather than "good." The second half of the comparison is introduced by ἤ. This is not a common use of the positive adjective, but is attested elsewhere in the NT (e.g., Matt 24:12; Luke 16:10; 18:14; John 2:10; 1 Cor 10:33). See the discussion in Wallace (1996, 297). An alternative evaluation is proposed by Doudna who takes the adjective as a positive and the following ἤ as adversative rather than comparative, translating "it is well to enter into life, even though maimed" (90–92). As Wallace points out, however, "the idea of the positive adj. is insufficient, i.e., it is not good in and of itself to enter life crippled" (1996, 297, in relation to ‖ Matt 18:8).

ἐστίν. Pres act ind 3rd sg εἰμί.

σε. Accusative subject of εἰσελθεῖν.

κυλλὸν. Adverbial accusative ("crippled").

εἰσελθεῖν. Aor act inf εἰσέρχομαι. The infinitival clause (σε κυλλὸν εἰσελθεῖν εἰς τὴν ζωὴν) functions as the subject of ἐστίν.

εἰς τὴν ζωὴν. Spatial.

ἤ. Compartive particle following the comparative καλόν to introduce the second half of the comparison.

τὰς δύο χεῖρας. Accusative direct object of ἔχοντα.

ἔχοντα. Pres act ptc masc acc sg ἔχω (manner). The entire participial phrase (τοὺς δύο πόδας ἔχοντα) functions parallel with κυλλόν in the previous phrase and modifies ἀπελθεῖν.

ἀπελθεῖν. Aor act inf ἀπέρχομαι. The infinitival clause (τὰς δύο χεῖρας ἔχοντα ἀπελθεῖν εἰς τὴν γέενναν) functions as the subject of an implied ἐστίν.

εἰς τὴν γέενναν. Spatial. The noun γέεννα is a Greek transliteration of the Aramaic *gê hinnôm* ("Valley of Hinnom"), though it was probably well removed from that etymology by Mark's time, since he does not explain it as he does other Aramaic words.

εἰς τὸ πῦρ τὸ ἄσβεστον. Spatial. The adjective ἄσβεστος refers to "something whose state of being cannot be nullified or stopped; hence of fire, 'inextinguishable'" (BDAG, 141). The figurative language probably comes from LXX Isa 66:24, which negates the cognate verb (τὸ πῦρ αὐτῶν οὐ σβεσθήσεται), as does the more extensive figure in verse 48.

9:44, 46

These two verses, though appearing in the textual tradition fairly early (A D) and consistently in the later text (Θ *f*[13] 𝔐), are not likely original. They are lacking in ℵ B C L W Δ Ψ 0274 *f*[1] 28 etc. The text of these verses is identical with verse 48.

9:45 καὶ ἐὰν ὁ πούς σου σκανδαλίζῃ σε, ἀπόκοψον αὐτόν· καλόν ἐστίν σε εἰσελθεῖν εἰς τὴν ζωὴν χωλὸν ἢ τοὺς δύο πόδας ἔχοντα βληθῆναι εἰς τὴν γέενναν.

For more on the analysis of this verse, see the discussion of verse 43.

ἐάν. Introduces the protasis of a third-class condition.

ὁ πούς. Nominative subject of σκανδαλίζῃ.

σκανδαλίζῃ. Pres act subj 3rd sg σκανδαλίζω.

σε. Accusative direct object of σκανδαλίζῃ.

ἀπόκοψον. Aor act impv 2nd sg ἀποκόπτω.

αὐτόν. Accusative direct object of ἀπόκοψον.

καλόν. The positive adjective is used in a comparative sense.

ἐστίν. Pres act ind 3rd sg εἰμί.

σε. Accusative subject of εἰσελθεῖν.

εἰσελθεῖν. Aor act inf εἰσέρχομαι. The infinitival phrase (σε εἰσελθεῖν εἰς τὴν ζωὴν χωλὸν) functions as the subject of ἐστίν.

εἰς τὴν ζωήν. Spatial.

χωλόν. Adverbial accusative.

ἤ. Comparative particle following the comparative καλόν to introduce the second half of the comparison.

τοὺς δύο πόδας. Accusative direct object of ἔχοντα.

ἔχοντα. Pres act ptc masc acc sg ἔχω (manner). The entire participial phrase (τοὺς δύο πόδας ἔχοντα) functions parallel with χωλόν in the previous phrase and modifies βληθῆναι.

βληθῆναι. Aor pass inf βάλλω. The infinitival clause (τοὺς δύο πόδας ἔχοντα βληθῆναι εἰς τὴν γέενναν) functions as the subject of an implied ἐστίν.

εἰς τὴν γέενναν. Spatial.

9:47 καὶ ἐὰν ὁ ὀφθαλμός σου σκανδαλίζῃ σε, ἔκβαλε αὐτόν· καλόν σέ ἐστιν μονόφθαλμον εἰσελθεῖν εἰς τὴν βασιλείαν τοῦ θεοῦ ἢ δύο ὀφθαλμοὺς ἔχοντα βληθῆναι εἰς τὴν γέενναν,

ἐὰν. Introduces the protasis of a third-class condition (see v. 43).

ὁ ὀφθαλμός. Nominative subject of σκανδαλίζῃ.

σκανδαλίζῃ. Pres act subj 3rd sg σκανδαλίζω.

σε. Accusative direct object of σκανδαλίζῃ.

ἔκβαλε. Aor act impv 2nd sg ἐκβάλλω. With reference to an eye the imperative of ἐκβάλλω means "gouge out" (BDAG, 299.3, "tear out and throw away").

αὐτόν. Accusative direct object of ἔκβαλε.

καλόν. Predicate adjective. The positive adjective is used in a comparative sense (see 9:43).

ἐστιν. Pres act ind 3rd sg εἰμί.

μονόφθαλμον. Adverbial accusative modifying εἰσελθεῖν. This was a colloquial form in Koine: "one-eyed" (BDAG, 659).

εἰσελθεῖν. Aor act inf εἰσέρχομαι. The infinitival phrase (μονόφθαλμον εἰσελθεῖν εἰς τὴν βασιλείαν τοῦ θεοῦ) functions as the subject of ἐστιν.

εἰς τὴν βασιλείαν. Spatial.

τοῦ θεοῦ. Subjective genitive indicating the regent of the kingdom: the kingdom over which God reigns.

ἤ. Comparative particle following the comparative καλόν to introduce the second half of the comparison.

δύο ὀφθαλμοὺς. Accusative direct object of ἔχοντα.

ἔχοντα. Pres act ptc masc acc sg ἔχω (manner). The entire participial phrase (δύο ὀφθαλμοὺς ἔχοντα) functions parallel with μονόφθαλμον in the previous phrase and modifies βληθῆναι.

βληθῆναι. Aor pass inf βάλλω. The infinitival phrase (δύο

ὀφθαλμοὺς ἔχοντα βληθῆναι εἰς τὴν γέενναν) functions as the subject of an implied ἐστιν.

εἰς τὴν γέενναν. Spatial.

9:48 ὅπου ὁ σκώληξ αὐτῶν οὐ τελευτᾷ καὶ τὸ πῦρ οὐ σβέννυται.

This verse is a close paraphrase or adaptation of LXX Isa 66:24b—ὁ γὰρ σκώληξ αὐτῶν οὐ τελευτήσει, καὶ τὸ πῦρ αὐτῶν οὐ σβεσθήσεται.

σκώληξ. Nominative subject of τελευτᾷ. This NT *hapax legomenon* ("worm") occurs eighteen times in the LXX.

τελευτᾷ. Pres act ind 3rd sg τελευτάω.

τὸ πῦρ. Nominative subject of σβέννυται.

σβέννυται. Pres pass ind 3rd sg σβέννυμι.

9:49 πᾶς γὰρ πυρὶ ἁλισθήσεται.

"This enigmatic verse was apparently as impenetrable to ancient scribes as to modern commentators" (France, 379). The explanatory gloss in the "Western" text (D it) and in 𝔐 suggests one early understanding of this enigmatic verse: πᾶσα γὰρ θυσία ἁλὶ ἁλισθήσεται (quoted from Lev 2:13, πᾶν δῶρον θυσίας ὑμῶν ἁλὶ ἁλισθήσεται).

πᾶς. Nominative subject of ἁλισθήσεται.

γὰρ. This conjunction introduces an explanation of the preceding statement, though a very cryptic one.

πυρὶ. Probably a dative of material (a rare usage of the dative; see Wallace 1996, 169–70), though such a description is tenuous given the obscurity of the statement.

ἁλισθήσεται. Fut pass ind 3rd sg ἁλίζω ("to salt"). This word is "a causative derivative of ἅλς 'salt' ... to cause something to taste salty—'to apply salt to something, to restore the flavor to salt'" (LN 5.28).

9:50 Καλὸν τὸ ἅλας· ἐὰν δὲ τὸ ἅλας ἄναλον γένηται, ἐν τίνι αὐτὸ ἀρτύσετε; ἔχετε ἐν ἑαυτοῖς ἅλα καὶ εἰρηνεύετε ἐν ἀλλήλοις.

Καλὸν. Predicate nominative in a verbless clause. A nominal sentence with εἰμί omitted is common in proverbial statements (BDF §127.1).

τὸ ἅλας. Nominative subject in a verbless clause.

ἐὰν. Introduces the protasis of a third-class condition.

δέ. The use of δέ helps set up the contrast between good salt in the previous clause and the worthless salt following.

τὸ ἅλας. Nominative subject of γένηται.

ἄναλον. Predicate adjective ("without salt, saltless").

γένηται. Aor mid subj 3rd sg γίνομαι. Subjunctive with ἐάν.

ἐν τίνι. Instrumental.

αὐτὸ. Accusative direct object of ἀρτύσετε.

ἀρτύσετε. Fut act ind 2nd pl ἀρτύω ("to season," i.e., add condiments such as salt; BDAG, 137).

ἔχετε . . . καὶ εἰρηνεύετε. "An instance in Greek of two imperatives in conditional parataxis joined by the consecutive καί; translate 'have salt in yourselves, then you will be able to maintain peace with one another'" (Lane, 347 n. 77, with reference to BDF §442.2).

ἔχετε. Pres act impv 2nd pl ἔχω.

ἐν ἑαυτοῖς. Association.

ἅλα. Accusative direct object of ἔχετε. An alternative spelling of ἅλας, -ατος, τό "salt." The alternative spelling given in the NA²⁷/ UBS⁴ is found here in ℵ A B D L W Δ Ψ, in some minuscules, and Old Latin. Earlier instances in this verse have the more common spelling, ἅλας, though the mss vary in each instance.

εἰρηνεύετε. Pres act impv 2nd pl εἰρηνεύω ("live in peace, be at peace, keep the peace," BDAG, 287; cf. 1 Thess 5:13, εἰρηνεύετε ἐν ἑαυτοῖς).

ἐν ἀλλήλοις. Association.

Mark 10:1-12

¹Setting out from there he went into the regions of Judea [and] across the Jordan, and again crowds flocked to him; and again, as was his custom, he taught them. ²Now Pharisees came and asked him if it was legal for a husband to divorce a wife, in order to test him. ³He answered, "What did Moses command you?" ⁴They replied, "Moses permitted (a husband) to write a divorce notice and to send (his wife) away." ⁵Jesus said to them, "Because of your hardheartedness he wrote this command for you. ⁶But from the beginning of creation (God) 'made them male and female'; ⁷'for this reason a man will leave his father and mother [and cling to his wife], ⁸and the two will be one flesh.' So then, they are no longer two, but one flesh. ⁹Therefore, what God has joined, let no one separate."

¹⁰In the house again, the disciples asked him about this. ¹¹He said to them, "Whoever divorces his wife and marries another woman commits adultery against her, ¹²and if she, having divorced her husband, marries another man, she commits adultery."

10:1 Καὶ ἐκεῖθεν ἀναστὰς ἔρχεται εἰς τὰ ὅρια τῆς Ἰουδαίας [καὶ] πέραν τοῦ Ἰορδάνου, καὶ συμπορεύονται πάλιν ὄχλοι πρὸς αὐτόν, καὶ ὡς εἰώθει πάλιν ἐδίδασκεν αὐτούς.

ἀναστὰς. Aor act ptc masc nom sg ἀνίστημι (temporal). The participle is somewhat superfluous, but this usage is not uncommon in the Koine (see 12:12).

ἔρχεται. Pres mid ind 3rd sg ἔρχομαι. The two present tenses (ἔρχεται and συμπορεύονται) introduce a new paragraph (see 1:21).

εἰς τὰ ὅρια. Spatial. The plural of ὅριον ("boundaries") communicates the idea of "region, area, vicinity," i.e., an area encompassed by boundaries.

[καὶ]. The bracketed conjunction in the UBS[4], which seems secure textually on external grounds (א B etc.), indicates two locations: the regions of Judea and beyond the Jordan (i.e., Perea). NA[27] suggests (with the notation "*p*" at the beginning of the textual note) that the omission is an assimilation with Matt 19:1, ἦλθεν εἰς τὰ ὅρια τῆς Ἰουδαίας πέραν τοῦ Ἰορδάνου. The conjunction is omitted in C[2] D W Δ Θ *f* [1, 13] etc.; καὶ πέραν is replaced with διά in 𝔐 (see V. Taylor, 416–17).

πέραν τοῦ Ἰορδάνου. Technically πέραν is an adverb of place, but here (as in 3:8; 5:1) it is used as a spatial preposition with the genitive (more often πέραν is used as a substantive in Mark; see 4:35).

συμπορεύονται. Pres mid ind 3rd pl συμπορεύομαι ("to gather, come together, flock," BDAG, 959.2; LN 15.123). This is the only NT occurrence of συμπορεύομαι outside of Luke (where it means not "to gather," but "to travel with," 7:11; 14:25; 24:15; the meaning also found in Josephus, Philo, and the Pseudepigrapha). Mark's usage is paralleled in the LXX; though it usually means "to travel with" (21 times, e.g., Gen 13:5), it sometimes means "to gather" (Deut 31:11; Job 1:4; Ezek 33:31; Dan 11:6).

ὄχλοι. Nominative subject of συμπορεύονται. Of thirty-eight occurrences of ὄχλος in Mark, this is the only instance of the plural form. This may reflect the fact that it is the only reference to a crowd in Mark in the context of multiple geographical locations (so Gundry, 529).

πρὸς αὐτόν. Spatial.

εἰώθει. Plprf act ind 3rd sg εἴωθα/ἔθω ("to be accustomed," BDAG, 295). The present tense ἔθω is obsolete in Koine; only the perfect occurs. The association with the perfect tense is a logical one given the lexical meaning of the word: one's custom is readily expressed with a stative form.

ἐδίδασκεν. Impf act ind 3rd sg διδάσκω. On the possibility that this is an inceptive imperfect as in NASB, HCSB, ISV, note that his custom (εἰώθει) was not to begin teaching, but to teach (see also 1:21). The imperfect is used in a summary statement that is best represented in English as "he taught" (NIV) rather than "he was teaching."

αὐτούς. Accusative direct object of ἐδίδασκεν. On the use of plural forms with ὄχλος in Mark, see 5:21.

10:2 καὶ προσελθόντες Φαρισαῖοι ἐπηρώτων αὐτὸν εἰ ἔξεστιν ἀνδρὶ γυναῖκα ἀπολῦσαι, πειράζοντες αὐτόν.

προσελθόντες. Aor act ptc masc nom pl προσέρχομαι. The participle could be read several ways. Most translations take it as attendant circumstance, though temporal is possible. It could also be attributive modifying Φαρισαῖοι ("the Pharisees who came"), as some scribes may have understood it (W Θ have οἱ δὲ Φαρισαῖοι προσελθόντες).

Φαρισαῖοι. Nominative subject of ἐπηρώτων.

ἐπηρώτων. Impf act ind 3rd pl ἐπερωτάω. On ἐπερωτάω versus the simple form ἐρωτάω, see 4:10. V. Taylor (417) describes this as an impersonal plural, "people asked him," but this is only because he rejects προσελθόντες Φαρισαῖοι on questionable textual grounds (it is a reading found only in the "Western" text). See the extended textual note in NET. On the possibility that this is an inceptive imperfect as in NASB, see 1:21.

αὐτὸν. Accusative direct object of ἐπηρώτων.

εἰ. Introduces indirect discourse. Most translations make this a direct question, but that may be due more to English style than Greek grammar. The use of εἰ is more likely in indirect than direct questions.

ἔξεστιν. Pres act ind 3rd sg ἔξεστιν. This verb is typically followed by a dative indicating the person involved and an infinitive identifying the action (BDAG, 349.1.b): here, ἀνδρί and ἀπολῦσαι.

ἀνδρὶ γυναῖκα. Both ἀνδρί and γυναῖκα are anarthrous, probably intending a qualitative nuance (so Robertson, 794.j): "husbands and (their respective) wives."

γυναῖκα. Accusative direct object of ἀπολῦσαι.

ἀπολῦσαι. Aor act inf ἀπολύω. The infinitival clause (γυναῖκα ἀπολῦσαι) functions as the subject of ἔξεστιν.

πειράζοντες. Pres act ptc masc nom pl πειράζω (purpose).

10:3 ὁ δὲ ἀποκριθεὶς εἶπεν αὐτοῖς, Τί ὑμῖν ἐνετείλατο Μωϋσῆς;

ὁ. Nominative subject of εἶπεν. On the use of ὁ δέ to change subjects, see 1:45.

ἀποκριθεὶς. Aor mid ptc masc nom sg ἀποκρίνομαι (means; redundant adverbial participle of speaking). On the intransitive, "θη middle" form, see 3:33.

εἶπεν. Aor act ind 3rd sg λέγω.

αὐτοῖς. Dative indirect object of εἶπεν.

Τί ὑμῖν ἐνετείλατο Μωϋσῆς. Clausal complement (direct discourse) of εἶπεν.

Τί. Accusative direct object of ἐνετείλατο.

ὑμῖν. Dative indirect object of ἐνετείλατο.

ἐνετείλατο. Aor mid ind 3rd sg ἐντέλλω.

Μωϋσῆς. Nominative subject of ἐνετείλατο.

10:4 οἱ δὲ εἶπαν, Ἐπέτρεψεν Μωϋσῆς βιβλίον ἀποστασίου γράψαι καὶ ἀπολῦσαι.

οἱ δὲ. Nominative subject of εἶπαν. On the use of οἱ δέ to change subjects, see 1:45.

εἶπαν. Aor act ind 3rd pl λέγω.

Ἐπέτρεψεν Μωϋσῆς … ἀπολῦσαι. Clausal complement (direct discourse) of εἶπαν.

Ἐπέτρεψεν. Aor act ind 3rd sg ἐπιτρέπω.

Μωϋσῆς. Nominative subject of ἐπέτρεψεν.

βιβλίον ἀποστασίου γράψαι καὶ ἀπολῦσαι. The infinitive clause functions as the direct object of ἐπέτρεψεν. The subject of both infinitives is to be inferred from the preceding context: "a husband." Likewise, the object of the second infinitive must be supplied: "his wife."

βιβλίον. Accusative direct object of γράψαι.

ἀποστασίου. The noun ἀποστάσιον is a legal term that designated the legal relinquishment of property; in Jewish use it came to be used as the technical term for divorce (BDAG, 120). The use of βιβλίον ἀποστασίου ("notice of divorce" or "divorce papers") in this regard comes from LXX Deut 24:1.

γράψαι. Aor act inf γράφω (see above).

ἀπολῦσαι. Aor act inf ἀπολύω (see above).

10:5 ὁ δὲ Ἰησοῦς εἶπεν αὐτοῖς, Πρὸς τὴν σκληροκαρδίαν ὑμῶν ἔγραψεν ὑμῖν τὴν ἐντολὴν ταύτην.

ὁ . . . Ἰησοῦς. Nominative subject of εἶπεν.

δὲ. The use of δέ rather than καί marks the change of speaker from the Pharisees in verse 4 to Jesus in verse 5.

εἶπεν. Aor act ind 3rd sg λέγω.

αὐτοῖς. Dative indirect object of εἶπεν.

Πρὸς τὴν σκληροκαρδίαν . . . μὴ χωριζέτω (v. 9). Clausal complement (direct discourse) of εἶπεν.

Πρὸς τὴν σκληροκαρδίαν. Reference, *"with reference to hard-heartedness, (i.e., because of) your perversity"* (BDAG, 875.3.e.α, s.v. πρός; contra Gundry, 538, who argues for purpose [to incite them to disobey], though Gundry thinks that Jesus is applying this statement to the Pharisees, "at least specifically and probably exclusively," rather than a historical reference at the time of Moses). The noun σκληροκαρδία refers to "an unyielding frame of mind, *hardness of heart, coldness, obstinacy, stubbornness*" (BDAG, 930).

ἔγραψεν. Aor act ind 3rd sg γράφω.

ὑμῖν. Dative indirect object of ἔγραψεν.

τὴν ἐντολὴν ταύτην. Accusative direct object of ἔγραψεν.

10:6 ἀπὸ δὲ ἀρχῆς κτίσεως ἄρσεν καὶ θῆλυ ἐποίησεν αὐτούς·

The OT quotation is from LXX Gen 1:27: καὶ ἐποίησεν ὁ θεὸς τὸν ἄνθρωπον κατ᾽ εἰκόνα θεοῦ ἐποίησεν αὐτόν ἄρσεν καὶ θῆλυ ἐποίησεν αὐτούς.

ἀπὸ . . . ἀρχῆς κτίσεως. Temporal. The same phrase occurs in 2 Pet 3:4, ἀπ᾽ ἀρχῆς κτίσεως (cf. Rom 1:20, ἀπὸ κτίσεως κόσμου). The reference is to the time when God created the world, i.e., from the very beginning.

δὲ. The use of δέ marks the contrast between the proposition of verse 5 and the OT precept of verse 6—between the regulation of divorce due to sin and the creation model of lifelong commitment.

ἄρσεν καὶ θῆλυ. Complement in an object-complement double accusative construction. The use of two neuter adjectives ("male and female") may seem unusual, but "the neuter is sometimes used with reference to persons if it is not the individuals but a general quality that is to be emphasized" (BDF §138.1).

ἐποίησεν. Aor act ind 3rd sg ποιέω. "Western" (D it) and Byzantine (A 𝔐) mss make the subject explicit by adding ὁ θεός.

αὐτούς. Accusative direct object of ἐποίησεν.

10:7 ἕνεκεν τούτου καταλείψει ἄνθρωπος τὸν πατέρα αὐτοῦ καὶ τὴν μητέρα [καὶ προσκολληθήσεται πρὸς τὴν γυναῖκα αὐτοῦ],

The OT quotation in verses 7-8a is from LXX Gen 2:24: ἕνεκεν τούτου καταλείψει ἄνθρωπος τὸν πατέρα αὐτοῦ καὶ τὴν μητέρα αὐτοῦ καὶ προσκολληθήσεται πρὸς τὴν γυναῖκα αὐτοῦ καὶ ἔσονται οἱ δύο εἰς σάρκα μίαν. The bracketed text in verse 7b may not be original; it is omitted in ℵ and B, but included in D W Θ *f*¹³ 𝔐 etc. Jesus quotes selected statements from two chapters, so he may not have included this clause; the sense of his argument is not affected one way or the other.

ἕνεκεν τούτου. Causal. The referent of τούτου is the OT quotation in verse 6.

καταλείψει. Fut act ind 3rd sg καταλείπω. The future tense has an imperatival sense, reflecting the force of the OT quote.

ἄνθρωπος. Nominative subject of καταλείψει.

τὸν πατέρα ... καὶ τὴν μητέρα. Accusative direct object of καταλείψει.

προσκολληθήσεται. Fut mid ind 3rd sg προσκολλάω ("to adhere to closely, *be faithfully devoted to, join*," BDAG, 882). This is a metaphorical use of a word with a transparent etymology: πρός + κολλάω ("to glue, join"; cf. κόλλα, "glue"). This is an intransitive, "θη middle" form, not passive (see 2:2); the force is semantically parallel to the active voice of καταλείψει. The future tense has an imperatival sense, reflecting the force of the OT quote.

πρὸς τὴν γυναῖκα. Association.

10:8 καὶ ἔσονται οἱ δύο εἰς σάρκα μίαν· ὥστε οὐκέτι εἰσὶν δύο ἀλλὰ μία σάρξ.

ἔσονται. Fut mid ind 3rd pl εἰμί.

οἱ δύο. Nominative subject of ἔσονται. The article οἱ is a nominalizer, changing the adjective δύο into a substantive.

εἰς σάρκα μίαν. The prepositional phrase functions as the predicate of ἔσονται. This citation from the LXX employs a very formal translation of the Hebrew text (V. Taylor, 419; see also MHT 1:71–72; Wallace 1996, 47).

ὥστε. Introduces a result clause that reflects the conclusion Jesus draws from the OT passage he cites.

εἰσὶν. Pres act ind 3rd pl εἰμί.

δύο. Predicate nominative of εἰσίν.

ἀλλὰ μία σάρξ. The contrasting conjunction introduces an elliptical statement, where the verb from the previous statement is implied: εἰσὶν μία σάρξ.

10:9 ὃ οὖν ὁ θεὸς συνέζευξεν ἄνθρωπος μὴ χωριζέτω.

ὃ ... ὁ θεὸς συνέζευξεν. The relative clause serves as the direct object of χωριζέτω.

ὅ. Accusative direct object of συνέζευξεν.

οὖν. Inferential conjunction drawing a conclusion from the OT quotation and Jesus' explanation of the results of the God-ordained marriage relationship. This conjunction is relatively rare in Mark, occurring only five times (4 in the words of Jesus, once by Pilate, but always in discourse; contrast the non-Markan use in 16:19 where it occurs in narrative).

ὁ θεὸς. Nominative subject of συνέζευξεν.

συνέζευξεν. Aor act ind 3rd sg συζεύγνυμι ("to join together," BDAG, 954).

ἄνθρωπος. Nominative subject of χωριζέτω.

χωριζέτω. Pres act impv 3rd sg χωρίζω.

10:10 Καὶ εἰς τὴν οἰκίαν πάλιν οἱ μαθηταὶ περὶ τούτου ἐπηρώτων αὐτόν.

εἰς τὴν οἰκίαν. Spatial. This phrase can be understood as either a verbless clause ("When they were in the house again," NIV), or as an adverbial modifier of ἐπηρώτων ("in the house the disciples asked him again," ESV).

οἱ μαθηταὶ. Nominative subject of ἐπηρώτων.

περὶ τούτου. Reference. The antecedent of the demonstrative pronoun τούτου is either the entire dialogue between Jesus and the Pharisees (vv. 2-9), or perhaps just Jesus' conclusion in verse 9 (which implies the entire discussion).

ἐπηρώτων. Impf act ind 3rd pl ἐπερωτάω. On the possibility that this is an inceptive imperfect as in NASB, see 1:21. On ἐπερωτάω versus the simple form ἐρωτάω, see 4:10.

αὐτόν. Accusative direct object of ἐπηρώτων.

10:11 καὶ λέγει αὐτοῖς, Ὃς ἂν ἀπολύσῃ τὴν γυναῖκα αὐτοῦ καὶ γαμήσῃ ἄλλην μοιχᾶται ἐπ᾽ αὐτήν·

λέγει. Pres act ind 3rd sg λέγω.

αὐτοῖς. Dative indirect object of λέγει.

ὃς ἂν ἀπολύσῃ ... μοιχᾶται (v. 12). Clausal complement (direct discourse) of λέγει.

Ὃς ἂν. Indefinite relative pronoun ("whoever") functioning as the nominative subject of ἀπολύσῃ.

ἀπολύσῃ. Aor act subj 3rd sg ἀπολύω. Subjunctive with ὃς ἂν.

τὴν γυναῖκα. Accusative direct object of ἀπολύσῃ.

γαμήσῃ. Aor act subj 3rd sg γαμέω. Subjunctive with ὃς ἂν.

ἄλλην. Accusative direct object of γαμήσῃ.

μοιχᾶται. Pres mid ind 3rd sg μοιχάω ("to commit adultery"). To insist that the present tense means that the new marriage is one of continual adultery is to press grammar beyond what it can bear.

ἐπ' αὐτήν. Respect. The antecedent of αὐτήν is most likely the first wife ("against her"), particularly since the reference to the same person likely continues in verse 12 (αὐτή), but a reference to the second wife is possible ("with her"; see BDAG, 656.1.b, s.v. μοιχάω).

10:12 καὶ ἐὰν αὐτὴ ἀπολύσασα τὸν ἄνδρα αὐτῆς γαμήσῃ ἄλλον μοιχᾶται.

ἐάν. Introduces the protasis of a third-class condition.

αὐτὴ. Nominative subject of γαμήσῃ. The pronoun is neither emphatic nor intensive (see 6:17).

ἀπολύσασα. Aor act ptc fem nom sg ἀπολύω (temporal, though attendant circumstance is possible).

τὸν ἄνδρα. Accustive diret object of ἀπολύσασα.

γαμήσῃ. Aor act subj 3rd sg γαμέω. Subjunctive with ἐάν.

ἄλλον. Accusative direct object of γαμήσῃ.

μοιχᾶται. Pres mid ind 3rd sg μοιχάω (see v. 11).

Mark 10:13-16

[13]People were bringing little children to him in order that he might touch them, but the disciples rebuked them. [14]But seeing (this), Jesus was indignant and said to them, "Permit the little children to come to me, do not prevent them, for the kingdom of heaven belongs to such ones. [15]Truly I say to you, whoever does not welcome the kingdom of God as a little child will never enter it. [16]Having taken (the children) into his arms, he blessed (them), placing his hands on them.

10:13 Καὶ προσέφερον αὐτῷ παιδία ἵνα αὐτῶν ἅψηται· οἱ δὲ μαθηταὶ ἐπετίμησαν αὐτοῖς.

προσέφερον. Impf act ind 3rd pl προσφέρω. This is an "indefinite plural" (see 1:22), which shifts subjects from the preceding context (either husbands and wives, vv. 11-12, or the disciples, v. 11) without specifying who it is that is doing the bringing.

αὐτῷ. Dative indirect object of προσέφερον.

παιδία. Accusative direct object of προσέφερον. On the meaning of παιδίον, see 7:27-28.

ἵνα. Introduces a purpose clause.

αὐτῶν. Genitive direct object of ἅψηται. Verbs of sense perception often take genitive objects.

ἅψηται. Aor mid subj 3rd sg ἅπτω. Subjunctive with ἵνα.

οἱ . . . μαθηταὶ. Nominative subject of ἐπετίμησαν.

δὲ. The use of δέ marks a deliberate contrast between those bringing children to Jesus (v. 13a) and the disciples' prohibition (v. 13b).

ἐπετίμησαν. Aor act ind 3rd pl ἐπιτιμάω.

αὐτοῖς. Dative complement of ἐπετίμησαν. Presumably this refers to those who were bringing the children (προσέφερον), not to the children themselves.

10:14 ἰδὼν δὲ ὁ Ἰησοῦς ἠγανάκτησεν καὶ εἶπεν αὐτοῖς, Ἄφετε τὰ παιδία ἔρχεσθαι πρός με, μὴ κωλύετε αὐτά, τῶν γὰρ τοιούτων ἐστὶν ἡ βασιλεία τοῦ θεοῦ.

ἰδών. Aor act ptc masc nom sg ὁράω (temporal).

δὲ. Following the contrast in verse 13 (also with δέ), there is another contrast, this time between the disciple's prohibition and Jesus' permission.

ὁ Ἰησοῦς. Nominative subject of ἠγανάκτησεν.

ἠγανάκτησεν. Aor act ind 3rd sg ἀγανακτέω ("be indignant against what is assumed to be wrong," BDAG, 5). This is the only time in the NT that this attitude is attributed to Jesus. Bruce suggests that "indignation" is too strong, preferring "was annoyed" (409).

εἶπεν. Aor act ind 3rd sg λέγω.

αὐτοῖς. Dative indirect object of εἶπεν.

Ἄφετε τὰ παιδία . . . εἰς αὐτήν (v. 15). Clausal complement (direct discourse) of εἶπεν.

Ἄφετε. Aor act impv 2nd pl ἀφίημι.

τὰ παιδία. Accusative subject of ἔρχεσθαι.

ἔρχεσθαι. Pres mid inf ἔρχομαι. The infinitival clause, τὰ παιδία ἔρχεσθαι πρός με, functions as the direct object of ἄφετε.

πρός με. Spatial.

μὴ κωλύετε αὐτά. The asyndeton between this phrase and the preceding with the resulting abruptness of the command may reflect Jesus' indignation (so V. Taylor, 423).

κωλύετε. Pres act impv 2nd pl κωλύω. The context makes it clear that the negated present imperative is an injunction to halt an action, though many wrongly assume that the use of μή + present imperative alone indicates this. In Mark this construction sometimes refers to stopping an action in progress or terminating an existing state (as here, see also 5:36; 6:50; 9:39), but in other instances it would be presumptuous to assume this to be the case (e.g., 10:9; 13:5, 7, 11, 21). For more, see Wallace (1996, 714–17). It is possible in the context that a conative sense is in view: "do not try to stop them" (NET).

αὐτά. Accusative direct object of κωλύετε.

γὰρ. Introduces a clause that explains the basis of Jesus' two preceding commands.

τῶν . . . τοιούτων. Genitive of quality functioning as the predicate of ἐστίν. The correlative semantics of τοιοῦτος implies degree ("of persons ὁ τοιοῦτος *such a person*; either in such a way that a definite individual with special characteristics is thought of, or that any bearer of certain definite qualities is meant," BDAG, 1010.c.α.‎א). Alternatively, some commentators describe this as a possessive genitive (e.g., V. Taylor, 423), but that terminology seems too strong for the categories used here unless the definition of possession is softened to the point of "have a rightful share in" (as does France, 396).

ἐστὶν. Pres act ind 3rd sg εἰμί. This use of εἰμί means "to belong to" (see BDAG, 285.9, "to belong to someone or someth. through association or genetic affiliation, *be, belong* w. simple gen.").

ἡ βασιλεία. Nominative subject of ἐστίν.

τοῦ θεοῦ. Subjective genitive indicating the regent of the kingdom: the kingdom over which God reigns.

10:15 ἀμὴν λέγω ὑμῖν, ὃς ἂν μὴ δέξηται τὴν βασιλείαν τοῦ θεοῦ ὡς παιδίον, οὐ μὴ εἰσέλθῃ εἰς αὐτήν.

ἀμὴν λέγω ὑμῖν. See 3:28.

λέγω. Pres act ind 1st sg λέγω.

ὑμῖν. Dative indirect object of λέγω.

ὃς ἄν. Indefinite relative pronoun ("whoever") functioning as the nominative subject of δέξηται.

δέξηται. Aor mid subj 3rd sg δέχομαι. Subjunctive with ὃς ἄν.

τὴν βασιλείαν. Accusative direct object of δέξηται.

τοῦ θεοῦ. Subjective genitive indicating the regent of the kingdom: the kingdom over which God reigns.

ὡς. Introduces a comparative clause that assumes the same verb and object as the preceding clause: "as a young child (would welcome the kingdom)."

παιδίον. Nominative subject of an implied δέξηται. This could also be taken as the accusative direct object of the implied verb ("as one would welcome a little child"), but "the context must decide between the two options, and the sequence from verse 14b supports the nominative" (France, 398).

οὐ μή. Emphatic negation (see 9:1; on double negatives in general, see 1:44).

εἰσέλθῃ. Aor act subj 3rd sg εἰσέρχομαι. Subjunctive with ἄν.

εἰς αὐτήν. Spatial.

10:16 καὶ ἐναγκαλισάμενος αὐτὰ κατευλόγει τιθεὶς τὰς χεῖρας ἐπ᾽ αὐτά.

ἐναγκαλισάμενος. Aor mid ptc masc nom sg ἐναγκαλίζομαι (temporal; "take in one's arms, hug," BDAG, 330).

αὐτά. Accusative direct object of ἐναγκαλισάμενος.

κατευλόγει. Impf act ind 3rd sg κατευλογέω. If accented κατευλογεῖ this could also be a present tense form. The compound form κατευλογέω ("to bless") could be a "strengthened form of εὐλογέω" (V. Taylor, 424), but more likely is not different in meaning from the simple form, εὐλογέω (cf. LN 33.470). This NT *hapax legomenon* is also extremely rare elsewhere (though it occurs in LXX Tob 10:14; 11:17). The imperfective form allows for the possibility that this describes an iterative situation (i.e., he was blessing them "one after another"; so Gundry, 545). It could also simply refer to the process of a collective blessing.

τιθεὶς. Pres act ptc masc nom sg τίθημι (temporal, contemporaneous time). Means is not a viable classification since the laying on of hands does not, in itself, produce a blessing. Nor is this a participle of manner (contra Stein 2008, 464) since that would describe an emotional feature of the action (Wallace 1996, 627).

τὰς χεῖρας. Accusative direct object of τιθείς.

ἐπ᾽ αὐτά. Spatial.

Mark 10:17-22

¹⁷Now as he was leaving on a journey, a man, having run up and knelt before him, asked him, "Good Teacher, what should I do in order that I may inherit eternal life?" ¹⁸Jesus said to him, "Why do you call me good? No one is good except one—God. ¹⁹You know the commandments: Do not murder. Do not commit adultery. Do not steal. Do not give false testimony. Do not defraud. Honor your father and mother." ²⁰But he said to him, "Teacher, all these things I have kept from my youth." ²¹Jesus, having looked at him, loved him and said to him, "One thing you are lacking; go, sell whatever you have and give (the proceeds) to the poor so you will have treasure in heaven; then come, follow me." ²²But he, shocked at the require-ment, went away in distress, for he had many possessions.

10:17 Καὶ ἐκπορευομένου αὐτοῦ εἰς ὁδὸν προσδραμὼν εἷς καὶ γονυπετήσας αὐτὸν ἐπηρώτα αὐτόν, Διδάσκαλε ἀγαθέ, τί ποιήσω ἵνα ζωὴν αἰώνιον κληρονομήσω;

ἐκπορευομένου. Pres mid ptc masc gen sg ἐκπορεύομαι. Genitive absolute (see 1:32), temporal. This word is not used frequently in the NT with reference to travel, though most commonly so in Mark (see 1:5; 6:11; 10:46; 11:19; elsewhere only Luke 3:7; Acts 25:4; perhaps Acts 9:28), and only here with ὁδός.

αὐτοῦ. Genitive subject of ἐκπορευομένου. On the overlap of reference with αὐτόν in the main claus, see 5:2 and 14:3.

εἰς ὁδὸν. Reference. Mark appears to use this phrase in the sense of "on/for a journey" (see 6:8).

προσδραμὼν. Aor act ptc masc nom sg προστρέχω (temporal; or perhaps attendant circumstance, but that would be unusual with an imperfect verb; "to run towards," BDAG, 886).

εἷς. The word εἷς can be used synonymously with the indefinite pronoun τις (BDAG, 292.3, s.v. εἷς; see also Wackernagel, 587). This use of εἷς is similar to the use of εἷς with a partitive genitive (see 8:8) to identify one member of a larger group (only here in Mark without a modifier). In 9:17 εἷς is followed by a prepositional phrase (also nonstandard). For the usual use with a partitive genitive, see 5:22; 6:15; 8:28; 12:28; 13:1; 14:10, 20, 43, 66. A related use is εἷς as equiva-lent to the (English) indefinite article (see 12:42; Matt 8:19; 9:18; 21:19; 26:9; Rev 8:13; 18:21; 19:17). Collins (475–76) thinks that this usage is typical of nonliterary writers in the Koine, but BDAG lists the same usage in numerous literary classical writers (BDAG, 292.3, s.v. εἷς). For a discussion of the possible Semitic influence on this expression, see Maloney 1981, 130–31. Here, εἷς means "someone, a person" without further identification.

γονυπετήσας. Aor act ptc masc nom sg γονυπετέω (temporal; "to kneel down").

αὐτόν. Accusative direct object of γονυπετήσας. With γονυπετέω the accusative indicates before whom one kneels.

ἐπηρώτα. Impf act ind 3rd sg ἐπερωτάω. On ἐπερωτάω versus the simple form ἐρωτάω, see 4:10.

αὐτόν. Accusative direct object of ἐπηρώτα.

Διδάσκαλε ἀγαθέ . . . κληρονομήσω. Clausal complement (direct discourse) of ἐπηρώτα.

Διδάσκαλε ἀγαθέ. Vocative (see also 4:38). This is the only instance (other than ‖ Luke 18:18) in which this title is qualified with a vocative adjective. For the designation διδάσκαλε ἀγαθέ, "there are no examples from the first century or earlier of anyone being called 'good teacher' as we have it here," though one instance can be found much later in the Talmud (Evans 2001, 95). TLG lists this text as the earliest occurrence of the phrase διδάσκαλε ἀγαθέ and later instances (through the 5th cent. AD) are all Christian writers. BDAG (3.2.a.α) understands ἀγαθέ in this context to mean "beneficent."

τί. Accusative direct object of ποιήσω.

ποιήσω. Aor act subj 1st sg ποιέω (deliberative subjunctive).

ἵνα. Introduces a purpose clause.

ζωὴν αἰώνιον. Accusative direct object of κληρονομήσω.

κληρονομήσω. Aor act subj 1st sg κληρονομέω. Subjunctive with ἵνα.

10:18 ὁ δὲ Ἰησοῦς εἶπεν αὐτῷ, Τί με λέγεις ἀγαθόν; οὐδεὶς ἀγαθὸς εἰ μὴ εἷς ὁ θεός.

ὁ . . . Ἰησοῦς. Nominative subject of εἶπεν.

δὲ. The conjunction δέ is used instead of καί due to the change of speakers: the man in verse 17 and Jesus in verse 18.

εἶπεν. Aor act ind 3rd sg λέγω.

αὐτῷ. Dative direct object of εἶπεν.

Τί με λέγεις . . . τὴν μητέρα (v. 19). Clausal complement (direct discourse) of εἶπεν.

Τί. Interrogative pronoun: "Why?"

με. Accusative direct object of λέγεις.

λέγεις. Pres act ind 2nd sg λέγω.

ἀγαθόν. Complement in an object-complement double accusative construction.

οὐδεὶς. Nominative subject in a verbless clause.
ἀγαθὸς. Predicate nominative in a verbless clause.
εἰ μὴ. Idiom: "except" (see 2:7).
εἷς. Nominative subject of an elliptical statement: "One is good."
ὁ θεός. Nominative in apposition to εἷς.

10:19 τὰς ἐντολὰς οἶδας· Μὴ φονεύσῃς, Μὴ μοιχεύσῃς, Μὴ κλέψῃς, Μὴ ψευδομαρτυρήσῃς, Μὴ ἀποστερήσῃς, Τίμα τὸν πατέρα σου καὶ τὴν μητέρα.

τὰς ἐντολὰς. Accusative direct object of οἶδας.
οἶδας. Prf act ind 2nd sg οἶδα.
Μὴ φονεύσῃς . . . τὴν μητέρα. This series of six clauses is in apposition to τὰς ἐντολάς. Except for the final command, Mark uses all aorist subjunctives with μή (as does Luke), but the LXX and Matthew have future indicatives with οὐ. There is no difference in meaning.
φονεύσῃς. Aor act subj 2nd sg φονεύω (prohibitive subjunctive).
μοιχεύσῃς. Aor act subj 2nd sg μοιχεύω (prohibitive subjunctive).
κλέψῃς. Aor act subj 2nd sg κλέπτω (prohibitive subjunctive).
ψευδομαρτυρήσῃς. Aor act subj 2nd sg ψευδομαρτυρέω (prohibitive subjunctive; "to give false testimony").
ἀποστερήσῃς. Aor act subj 2nd sg ἀποστερέω (prohibitive subjunctive).
τίμα. Pres act impv 2nd sg τιμάω.
τὸν πατέρα . . . καὶ τὴν μητέρα. Accusative direct object of τίμα.

10:20 ὁ δὲ ἔφη αὐτῷ, Διδάσκαλε, ταῦτα πάντα ἐφυλαξάμην ἐκ νεότητός μου.

ὁ. Nominative subject of ἔφη. On the use of ὁ δέ to change speakers, see 1:45.
ἔφη. Aor act ind 3rd sg φημί.
αὐτῷ. Dative indirect object of ἔφη.
Διδάσκαλε . . . νεότητός μου. Clausal complement (direct discourse) of ἔφη.
Διδάσκαλε. Vocative (see also 4:38).
ταῦτα πάντα. Accusative direct object of ἐφυλαξάμην.
ἐφυλαξάμην. Aor mid ind 1st sg φυλάσσω. This verb is almost always active voice in the NT (out of 13 aorists it is middle voice only here; 10 of 16 present forms are active voice; cf. 69 of 173 aorist middle forms in the LXX, and 32 of 173 present middle forms). Matthew uses the active ἐφύλαξα (19:20), as does Luke (18:21). Although

Moulton (MHT 1:159) views the middle voice here as an error that is corrected by the other Synoptic writers, that is too prescriptive a judgment. Mark likely chose the middle to make a subject-focused statement. The middle need not be reflexive ("I kept for myself"), as the objection might imply (V. Taylor, 428), but could as well be, "I myself have kept."

ἐκ νεότητός μου. Temporal. The noun νεότης refers to "youth."

10:21 ὁ δὲ Ἰησοῦς ἐμβλέψας αὐτῷ ἠγάπησεν αὐτὸν καὶ εἶπεν αὐτῷ, Ἕν σε ὑστερεῖ· ὕπαγε, ὅσα ἔχεις πώλησον καὶ δὸς [τοῖς] πτωχοῖς, καὶ ἕξεις θησαυρὸν ἐν οὐρανῷ, καὶ δεῦρο ἀκολούθει μοι.

ὁ . . . Ἰησοῦς. Nominative subject of ἠγάπησεν.

δὲ. The conjunction δέ is used rather than καί due to the change of subjects.

ἐμβλέψας αὐτῷ ἠγάπησεν. Bruce (410) suggests "lovingly regarded him," which may catch the tone despite not following the grammar very closely.

ἐμβλέψας. Aor act ptc masc nom sg ἐμβλέπω (temporal). In general ἐμβλέπω means "to direct one's vision and attention to a particular object" (LN 24.9), and is not appreciably different from many instances of βλέπω. The difference may not be more than our English "he saw" (βλέπω) versus "he looked at" (ἐμβλέπω), with the compound form adding a slight volitional twinge.

αὐτῷ. Dative complement of ἐμβλέψας.

ἠγάπησεν. Aor act ind 3rd sg ἀγαπάω.

αὐτὸν. Accusative direct object of ἠγάπησεν.

εἶπεν. Aor act ind 3rd sg λέγω.

αὐτῷ. Dative indirect object of εἶπεν.

Ἕν σε ὑστερεῖ . . . ἀκολούθει μοι. Clausal complement (direct discourse) of εἶπεν.

Ἕν σε ὑστερεῖ. This is quite unusual usage. Normally ὑστερέω "has the subject of the deficiency in the nominative and the thing in respect of which there is a deficiency in the genitive" (Doudna, 20), but here it is reversed: the person who is deficient is in the accusative (σε) and that which is lacking is the nominative (ἕν; cf. LXX Ps 22:1, οὐδέν με ὑστερήσει).

Ἕν. Nominative subject of ὑστερεῖ.

σε. Accusative of respect.

ὑστερεῖ. Pres act ind 3rd sg ὑστερέω.

ὕπαγε. Pres act impv 2nd sg ὑπάγω.

ὅσα ἔχεις. This phrase functions as the direct object of πώλησον.

ὅσα. Accusative direct object of ἔχεις. On ὅσος, see 3:8.

ἔχεις. Pres act ind 2nd sg ἔχω.

πώλησον. Aor act impv 2nd sg πωλέω.

καὶ ... καὶ ... καὶ. The string of three coordinating conjunctions is not coordinating a string of commensurate ideas (even though the linked elements, all verbs, are grammatically comparable). Though the first and third do join three imperatives, the second introduces a result of the second imperative (cf. Gundry, 554). The translation reflects this by using "so" for the second καί.

δός. Aor act impv 2nd sg δίδωμι.

[τοῖς] πτωχοῖς. Dative indirect object of δός.

ἕξεις. Fut act ind 2nd sg ἔχω. With the verb ἔχω, the initial σ of the root (σεχ) drops out, being replaced by a smooth breathing mark in most tense-forms, but with a rough breathing mark in the future due to the ξ (χ + future morpheme σ; see *MBG*, 260 n. 10).

θησαυρὸν. Accusative direct object of ἕξεις.

ἐν οὐρανῷ. Locative.

δεῦρο. An adverb of place, but in the NT it usually functions as an interjection ("over here, [come] here, come!") and is often followed by an imperative. When the following verb is singular, δεῦρο is used; with a plural verb, the form is δεῦτε. Here, it is "almost a verb" (Robertson, 302).

ἀκολούθει. Pres act impv 2nd sg ἀκολουθέω. The string of imperatives in this verse consists of three aorist forms followed by one present. Though the actions referenced by all four will take some time (one does not sell and distribute a large estate quickly; see v. 22), the perfective aspect of the aorist imperatives simply refers to the necessary actions. By contrast, the present imperative portrays a process—appropriate for a description of following Jesus which is, presumably, to be a long-term commitment.

10:22 ὁ δὲ στυγνάσας ἐπὶ τῷ λόγῳ ἀπῆλθεν λυπούμενος· ἦν γὰρ ἔχων κτήματα πολλά.

ὁ. Nominative subject of ἀπῆλθεν. On the use of ὁ δέ to change subjects, see 1:45.

στυγνάσας. Aor act ptc masc nom sg στυγνάζω (manner; "to be in state of intense dismay, *be shocked*," BDAG, 949.1). Louw and Nida translate the sentence: "he was appalled at what was said and went away sad" (25.222).

ἐπὶ τῷ λόγῳ. Causal: "shocked at the prescription" (BDAG, 949.1, s.v. στυγνάζω). The word λόγος is quite flexible and "may take on a variety of formulations or topical nuances" (BDAG, 599.1.β, s.v. λόγος). "Requirement" may be a better choice here than BDAG's proposed "prescription."

ἀπῆλθεν. Aor act ind 3rd sg ἀπέρχομαι.

λυπούμενος. Pres mid ptc masc nom sg λυπέω (manner). The description of man's departure with a second participle with similar meaning reinforces the dismay that he felt.

ἦν. Impf act ind 3rd sg εἰμί.

ἔχων. Pres act ptc masc nom sg ἔχω (imperfective periphrastic; contra the NASB, AV, and RSV, all of which imply it is substantival).

κτήματα. Accusative direct object of ἦν ἔχων. The noun κτῆμα refers to "that which is acquired or possessed" (BDAG, 572.1). It commonly refers to "a piece of landed property," or in the plural, "lands or estates" (V. Taylor, 430), but can refer to other possessions as well (cf. χρῆμα in v. 23).

Mark 10:23-31

[23]Jesus, having looked around, said to his disciples, "With what difficulty will those who have wealth enter the kingdom of God!" [24]Now the disciples were astounded at his words. But Jesus, responding (to their astonishment), said to them again, "Children, how difficult it is to enter the kingdom of God." [25]It is easier for a camel to go through the eye of a sewing needle than for a rich person to enter the kingdom of God. [26]So they were even more amazed and were saying to each other, "Who then is able to be saved?" [27]Jesus looked at them and said, "With humans it is impossible, but not with God; for all things are possible with God." [28]Peter began to say to him, "Look, we left everything and we follow you." [29]Jesus said, "Truly I say to you, there is no one who has left house or brothers or sisters or mother or father or children or fields for my sake or for the sake of the good news [30]who will not receive a hundredfold now in this age, houses and brothers and sisters and mothers and children and fields with persecutions, and in the coming age, eternal life. [31]But many who are first will be last, and the last (will be) first.

10:23 Καὶ περιβλεψάμενος ὁ Ἰησοῦς λέγει τοῖς μαθηταῖς αὐτοῦ, Πῶς δυσκόλως οἱ τὰ χρήματα ἔχοντες εἰς τὴν βασιλείαν τοῦ θεοῦ εἰσελεύσονται.

περιβλεψάμενος. Aor mid ptc masc nom sg περιβλέπω (temporal).

ὁ Ἰησοῦς. Nominative subject of λέγει.

λέγει. Pres act ind 3rd sg λέγω. The use of the narrative present marks the transition from the discussion with the wealthy man to Jesus' discussion of the significance of that dialogue with his disciples (see also 1:21 on εἰσπορεύονται).

τοῖς μαθηταῖς. Dative indirect object of λέγω.

Πῶς δυσκόλως ... εἰσελεύσονται. Clausal complement (direct discourse) of λέγω. This statement is normally understood as an exclamation (formally, "How difficultly will the ones who have wealth enter the kingdom of God"; see below), but it could be taken as a question, e.g., "With what difficulty will those having wealth enter into the kingdom of God?" (Gould, 192), with πῶς functioning as an interrogative (BDAG, 901.1).

Πῶς. Exclamatory use of the adverb, modifying δυσκόλως (BDAG, 901.2). In comparing this statement with the illustration of the camel in verse 25, Gundry observes that "the exclamatory πῶς, 'how!' shows that the difficulty is not mere, and the severity of a difficulty may make the difficulty equal to an impossibility" (565).

δυσκόλως. Adverb modifying εἰσελεύσονται ("difficultly, with difficulty," BDAG, 265).

οἱ ... ἔχοντες. Pres act ptc masc nom pl ἔχω (substantival).

τὰ χρήματα. Accusative direct object of ἔχοντες. This is the only NT usage in which the generalized sense of "wealth" is in view (|| Luke 18:24; cf. Herm. Sim. 2.5), including "all property whether in coin or convertible into it" (Swete, 228). More commonly χρῆμα means simply "money" (Acts 4:37; 8:18, 20; 24:26). It likely has a broader reference than κτῆμα (v. 22), which refers to property rather than to money or monetary value (for more on the difference between κτῆμα and χρῆμα, see Gundry, 555, 564; contrast France, 404, who concludes that "there seems no significant difference between the various terms used for affluence: ἔχων κτήματα πολλά [v. 22], τὰ χρήματα ἔχοντες [v. 23], πλούσιος [v. 25]"; so also Stein 2008, 471).

εἰς τὴν βασιλείαν. Spatial.

τοῦ θεοῦ. Subjective genitive indicating the regent of the kingdom: the kingdom over which God reigns.

εἰσελεύσονται. Fut mid ind 3rd pl εἰσέρχομαι.

10:24 οἱ δὲ μαθηταὶ ἐθαμβοῦντο ἐπὶ τοῖς λόγοις αὐτοῦ. ὁ δὲ Ἰησοῦς πάλιν ἀποκριθεὶς λέγει αὐτοῖς, Τέκνα, πῶς δύσκολόν ἐστιν εἰς τὴν βασιλείαν τοῦ θεοῦ εἰσελθεῖν·

οἱ ... μαθηταὶ. Nominative subject of ἐθαμβοῦντο.

δέ. The use of δέ rather than καί at the beginning of a sentence both here and in verse 24b is due to the change in speakers.

ἐθαμβοῦντο. Impf mid ind 3rd pl θαμβέω ("be astounded, amazed," only in Mark in the NT; also 1:27; 10:32). The middle voice is often used with verbs of strong emotion (see also 1:22 on ἐκπλήσσω).

ἐπὶ τοῖς λόγοις. Causal, but it is the *content* of the words that causes the amazement, not simply that he spoke.

ὁ . . . Ἰησοῦς. Nominative subject of λέγει.

δέ. See above.

πάλιν. The adverb probably modifies the main verb, λέγει, rather than ἀποκριθείς.

ἀποκριθεὶς. Aor mid ptc masc nom sg ἀποκρίνομαι (means; redundant participle of speaking). On this intransitive, "θη middle" form, see 3:33.

λέγει. Pres act ind 3rd sg λέγω.

αὐτοῖς. Dative indirect object of λέγει.

Τέκνα, πῶς δύσκολόν . . . εἰσελθεῖν (v. 25). Clausal complement (direct discourse) of λέγει.

Τέκνα. Vocative. This is the only time in the Gospels that Jesus refers to the Twelve as τέκνα. It is not clear if this is significant or not; it could stress his authority as a father to them, or perhaps it is an affectionate term (Gundry, 556, suggests both possibilities, but prefers the first, while France, 404, prefers the second: "affectionate epithet for his close companions").

πῶς. Exclamatory use of the adverb modifying δύσκολον (BDAG, 901.2; see also v. 23).

δύσκολόν. Predicate adjective ("difficult"; see also the adverb form, δυσκόλως, in v. 23).

ἐστιν. Pres act ind 3rd sg εἰμί.

εἰσελθεῖν. Aor act inf εἰσέρχομαι (subject). The infinitival clause, εἰς τὴν βασιλείαν τοῦ θεοῦ εἰσελθεῖν, functions as the subject of ἐστιν.

10:25 εὐκοπώτερόν ἐστιν κάμηλον διὰ [τῆς] τρυμαλιᾶς [τῆς] ῥαφίδος διελθεῖν ἢ πλούσιον εἰς τὴν βασιλείαν τοῦ θεοῦ εἰσελθεῖν.

Gundry rightly describes Jesus' statement as one of "humorously ironic hyperbole" (556). For an evaluation of some of the fanciful interpretations of this verse (e.g., making the camel into a cable [Gould, 194], or the needle's eye into a city gate), see, e.g., Swete, 229; Evans 2001, 101.

εὐκοπώτερόν. Predicate (comparative) adjective (see also 2:9).

ἐστιν. Pres act ind 3rd sg εἰμί.

κάμηλον. Accusative subject of διελθεῖν.

διὰ [τῆς] τρυμαλιᾶς [τῆς] ῥαφίδος. Spatial. The noun τρυμαλιά can refer to a "hole" of any kind), but here with ῥαφίς ("[sewing] needle") refers to the "eye (of a needle)." It is synonymous with τρῆμα (‖ Luke 18:25), as the textual variants in both passages suggest. Luke uses a different word for needle (βελόνη), which BDAG (904, s.v. ῥαφίς) suggests "may reflect a higher style"; it was also the Atticistic preference (Cadbury 1920, 46, with reference to Phrynichus).

διελθεῖν. Aor act inf διέρχομαι. The infinitival clause, κάμηλον διὰ [τῆς] τρυμαλιᾶς [τῆς] ῥαφίδος διελθεῖν, is the subject of ἐστιν.

ἤ. Comparative particle used with εὐκοπώτερόν ἐστιν.

πλούσιον. Accusative subject of εἰσελθεῖν.

εἰς τὴν βασιλείαν τοῦ θεοῦ. Spatial.

εἰσελθεῖν. Aor act inf εἰσέρχομαι. The infinitival clause, πλούσιον εἰς τὴν βασιλείαν τοῦ θεοῦ εἰσελθεῖν, is the subject of an elliptical clause (εὐκοπώτερόν ἐστιν is assumed from v. 25a).

10:26 οἱ δὲ περισσῶς ἐξεπλήσσοντο λέγοντες πρὸς ἑαυτούς, Καὶ τίς δύναται σωθῆναι;

οἱ. Nominative subject of ἐξεπλήσσοντο. On the use of οἱ δέ to change subjects, see 1:45.

περισσῶς. Comparative adverb: "even more."

ἐξεπλήσσοντο. Impf mid ind 3rd pl ἐκπλήσσω (see also 1:22).

λέγοντες. Pres act ptc masc nom pl λέγω (attendant circumstance, or possibly result).

πρὸς ἑαυτούς. Spatial. The preposition indicates to whom they speak (BDAG, 3.a.ε, s.v. πρός): "to one another, among themselves." More than half the NT uses of πρὸς ἑαυτούς are found in Mark (Mark 1:27; 9:10; 10:26; 11:31; 12:7; 14:4; see also Luke 20:5; 22:23; John 7:35; 12:19). All the NT uses modify a verb of speaking (except perhaps Mark 14:4, though even that may imply indignant speech), but this pattern does not hold in the LXX where only one of the six instances involves a verb of speaking (Neh 3:35; cf. Gen 19:10; Exod 28:43; 1 Sam 6:21; 1 Macc 11:9; Ep Jer 1:48).

Καὶ τίς δύναται σωθῆναι, Clausal complement (direct discourse) of λέγοντες. The introduction of a question with καί and an interrogative pronoun (τίς) may convey the tone of "an abrupt rejoinder": "Who then . . . ?" (Gould, 194).

τίς. Nominative subject of δύναται.

δύναται. Pres mid ind 3rd sg δύναμαι.

σωθῆναι. Aor pass inf σῴζω (complementary).

10:27 ἐμβλέψας αὐτοῖς ὁ Ἰησοῦς λέγει, Παρὰ ἀνθρώποις ἀδύνατον, ἀλλ᾽ οὐ παρὰ θεῷ· πάντα γὰρ δυνατὰ παρὰ τῷ θεῷ.

ἐμβλέψας. Aor act ptc masc nom sg ἐμβλέπω (temporal). Since
the aorist participle preceding the main verb probably implies
"having looked," it is possible that the use of ἐμβλέπω carries the
connotation "looking intently." See the similar use in 14:67 and
BDAG (321.1).

αὐτοῖς. Dative complement of ἐμβλέψας.

ὁ Ἰησοῦς. Nominative subject of λέγει.

λέγει. Pres act ind 3rd sg λέγω.

Παρὰ ἀνθρώποις . . . τῷ θεῷ. Clausal complement (direct discourse) of λέγει, consisting of three verbless clauses, which is common in proverbial statements (BDF §127.1).

Παρὰ ἀνθρώποις. Sphere: "with/in the sight of men."

ἀδύνατον. Predicate adjective in a verbless clause.

ἀλλ᾽ οὐ. Introduces a contrasting, negative statement.

παρὰ θεῷ. Sphere: "with/in the sight of God."

πάντα. Nominative subject in a verbless clause.

γὰρ. The conjunction introduces a clause that explains the reason
for the preceding statement.

δυνατὰ. Predicate adjective in a verbless clause.

παρὰ τῷ θεῷ. Sphere: "with/in the sight of God."

10:28 Ἤρξατο λέγειν ὁ Πέτρος αὐτῷ, Ἰδοὺ ἡμεῖς ἀφήκαμεν πάντα
καὶ ἠκολουθήκαμέν σοι.

Ἤρξατο. Aor mid ind 3rd sg ἄρχω.

λέγειν. Pres act inf λέγω (complementary).

ὁ Πέτρος. Nominative subject of ἤρξατο.

αὐτῷ. Dative indirect object of λέγειν.

Ἰδοὺ ἡμεῖς . . . ἠκολουθήκαμέν σοι. Clausal complement (direct
discourse) of λέγειν.

Ἰδοὺ. See 1:2 (see also 3:34 on ἴδε).

ἀφήκαμεν. Aor act ind 1st pl ἀφίημι.

πάντα. Accusative direct object of ἀφήκαμεν.

ἠκολουθήκαμέν. Prf act ind 1st pl ἀκολουθέω. The stative aspect
does not focus on the action of following ("we are following you
around" or "we have been following you"), but on the fact that they

are presently his followers ("we follow you" or "we are your followers"). The preceding action that has produced this state is not a prior following, but is expressed by the previous clause, ἀφήκαμεν πάντα. This would suggest a result relationship, though that relationship is not grammaticalized here. By contrast, the NET suggests that a paratactic καί in this context should likely be taken to imply a hypotactic relationship, which from their translation is understood to be purpose: "we have left everything to follow you!"

σοι. Dative complement of ἠκολουθήκαμεν.

10:29 ἔφη ὁ Ἰησοῦς, Ἀμὴν λέγω ὑμῖν, οὐδείς ἐστιν ὃς ἀφῆκεν οἰκίαν ἢ ἀδελφοὺς ἢ ἀδελφὰς ἢ μητέρα ἢ πατέρα ἢ τέκνα ἢ ἀγροὺς ἕνεκεν ἐμοῦ καὶ ἕνεκεν τοῦ εὐαγγελίου,

ἔφη. Aor act ind 3rd sg φημί.

ὁ Ἰησοῦς. Nominative subject of ἔφη.

Ἀμὴν λέγω ὑμῖν. See 3:28.

λέγω. Pres act ind 1st sg λέγω.

ὑμῖν. Dative indirect object of λέγω.

οὐδείς ἐστιν ὃς ἀφῆκεν. See verse 30 on ἐὰν μὴ λάβῃ.

οὐδείς. Nominative subject of ἐστιν.

ἐστιν. Pres act ind 3rd sg εἰμί.

ὅς. Nominative subject of ἀφῆκεν. The antecedent is οὐδείς.

ἀφῆκεν. Aor act ind 3rd sg ἀφίημι.

οἰκίαν ἢ ἀδελφοὺς ... ἢ ἀγρούς. Accusative direct object of ἀφῆκεν.

ἕνεκεν ἐμοῦ καὶ ἕνεκεν τοῦ εὐαγγελίου. The improper prepositions with the genitive give the reason for the previous action. Hengel suggests that this expression should be taken as a hendiadys: "'for Jesus' sake' at the same time means 'for the gospel's sake', and vice versa. Jesus is the content of the gospel" (1985, 54). Here, εὐαγγέλιον refers to good news regarding the kingdom of God (see vv. 23, 24, 25; Gould, 195).

10:30 ἐὰν μὴ λάβῃ ἑκατονταπλασίονα νῦν ἐν τῷ καιρῷ τούτῳ οἰκίας καὶ ἀδελφοὺς καὶ ἀδελφὰς καὶ μητέρας καὶ τέκνα καὶ ἀγροὺς μετὰ διωγμῶν, καὶ ἐν τῷ αἰῶνι τῷ ἐρχομένῳ ζωὴν αἰώνιον.

ἐὰν μὴ λάβῃ. The phrase ²⁹οὐδείς ἐστιν ὃς ἀφῆκεν ... ³⁰ἐὰν μὴ λάβῃ is judged by Swete to be "rough but forcible" (231). Matthew states it positively: πᾶς ὅστις ἀφῆκεν ... λήμψεται (19:29), with no difference in meaning.

ἐὰν. Introduces the protasis of a third-class condition; the apodosis consists of Jesus' words in verse 29.

λάβῃ. Aor act subj 3rd sg λαμβάνω. Subjunctive with ἐάν.

ἑκατονταπλασίονα. Accusative direct object of λάβῃ ("hundredfold").

νῦν ἐν τῷ καιρῷ τούτῳ. The temporal adverb νῦν, which modifies λάβῃ, is reinforced and defined by the prepositional phrase ἐν τῷ καιρῷ τούτῳ, and subsequently contrasted with ἐν τῷ αἰῶνι τῷ ἐρχομένῳ.

οἰκίας καὶ ἀδελφοὺς ... καὶ ἀγροὺς. Accusative in apposition to ἑκατονταπλασίονα. The use of ἤ (v. 29) and καί here may be intended to contrast the forfeit of only one item on the list (few people would leave all these things) with receiving *all* the items on the replacement list (cf. Gundry, 558). Such a reading, however, may well overexegete simple stylistic differences (so France, 407, who observes that the reward outweighing the loss is explicitly stated by ἑκατονταπλασίονα).

μετὰ διωγμῶν. Accompaniment.

ἐν τῷ αἰῶνι. Temporal.

ἐρχομένῳ. Pres mid ptc masc dat sg ἔρχομαι (attributive).

ζωὴν αἰώνιον. The accusative may be understood either as a continuation of the previous appositional string of accusatives, or as the direct object of a new clause with λάβῃ assumed. Since a separate temporal modifier qualifies this last accusative it is likely that two separate clauses are intended.

10:31 πολλοὶ δὲ ἔσονται πρῶτοι ἔσχατοι καὶ [οἱ] ἔσχατοι πρῶτοι.

πολλοὶ ... πρῶτοι. Nominative subject of ἔσονται. The word order is unusual with the verb intervening between the modifier and its head noun. The noun may have been held until later in the clause in order to juxtapose it for effect with the contrasting predicate adjective, ἔσχατοι.

δὲ. The use of δέ transitions from Jesus' detailed discussion of the losses and rewards of obedience to a proverbial summary statement.

ἔσονται. Fut mid ind 3rd pl εἰμί.

ἔσχατοι. Predicate adjective.

[οἱ] ἔσχατοι. Nominative subject of an elided ἔσονται, assumed from the previous clause.

πρῶτοι. Predicate adjective of an elided ἔσονται.

Mark 10:32-34

³²Now they were on the road going up to Jerusalem and Jesus was going before them, and they were amazed; but those who followed were afraid. Then having taken the Twelve aside again, he began to tell them the things that were about to happen to him: ³³"We are going up to Jerusalem and the Son of Man will be handed over into the custody of the chief priests and the scribes, and they will sentence him to death, and then they will hand him over to the custody of the Gentiles, ³⁴and they will mock him and flog him and kill him, and after three days he will rise."

10:32 Ἦσαν δὲ ἐν τῇ ὁδῷ ἀναβαίνοντες εἰς Ἱεροσόλυμα, καὶ ἦν προάγων αὐτοὺς ὁ Ἰησοῦς, καὶ ἐθαμβοῦντο, οἱ δὲ ἀκολουθοῦντες ἐφοβοῦντο. καὶ παραλαβὼν πάλιν τοὺς δώδεκα ἤρξατο αὐτοῖς λέγειν τὰ μέλλοντα αὐτῷ συμβαίνειν

Ἦσαν. Impf act ind 3rd pl εἰμί. This is not an indefinite plural (contra Stein 2008, 479) since there is a clear antecedent in the preceding paragraph (ἡμεῖς in v. 28 and ὑμῖν in v. 29) with no indication of a shift in reference until a new group is identified in the next clause (οἱ δὲ ἀκολουθοῦντες). On the use of the plural verb here, see 5:38.

δὲ. The conjunction δέ is used rather than καί since there is development in the storyline and a new pericope is introduced.

ἐν τῇ ὁδῷ. Locative.

ἀναβαίνοντες. Pres act ptc masc nom pl ἀναβαίνω (probably purpose; a periphrastic use with ἦσαν would not normally have an intervening locative phrase; see Green, 129–32).

εἰς Ἱεροσόλυμα. Spatial, indicating their destination. On the form of Ἱεροσόλυμα, see 3:8.

ἦν. Impf act ind 3rd sg εἰμί.

προάγων. Pres act ptc masc nom sg προάγω (imperfective periphrastic).

αὐτοὺς. Accusative direct object of ἦν προάγων.

ὁ Ἰησοῦς. Nominative subject of ἦν προάγων.

ἐθαμβοῦντο. Impf mid ind 3rd pl θαμβέω ("to be amazed, astounded"; a unique Markan word in the NT; see also 1:27; 10:24; cf. 1:22 on ἐκπλήσσω).

οἱ . . . ἀκολουθοῦντες. Pres act ptc masc nom pl ἀκολουθέω (substantival; for another example of article + δέ + participle + finite verb in which the participle is substantival, see 13:13). This is probably the third party identified. Initially we meet Jesus and (presumably) the Twelve (note the plurals ἦσαν, ἐθαμβοῦντο and the later reference to τοὺς δώδεκα) who are taken aside (παραλαβών) from a larger group. The third group is likely the larger group that often traveled with Jesus (οἱ ἀκολουθοῦντες), whose reaction is described separately (ἐφοβοῦντο). This also accounts for the use of δέ here instead of καί, which would be expected if the same group were in view. Some mss (D K f^{13} 28 700 𝔐, thus the KJV) omit the article, enabling the participle to be read adverbially as a further description of the same group referenced in ἦσαν and ἐθαμβοῦντο.

ἐφοβοῦντο. Impf mid ind 3rd pl φοβέομαι.

παραλαβών. Aor act ptc masc nom sg παραλαμβάνω (temporal). In this context παραλαμβάνω means "to take aside," rather than simply "to take with," as is evident by the contrast with the larger group (οἱ ἀκολουθοῦντες; cf. Matthew's more explicit παρέλαβεν τοὺς δώδεκα μαθητὰς κατ᾽ ἰδίαν [20:17]).

τοὺς δώδεκα. Accusative direct object of παραλαβών. On the use and referent of δώδεκα, see 4:10.

ἤρξατο. Aor mid ind 3rd sg ἄρχω.

αὐτοῖς. Dative indirect object of λέγειν.

λέγειν. Pres act inf λέγω (complementary).

τὰ μέλλοντα. Pres act ptc neut acc pl μέλλω (substantival). Accusative direct object of λέγειν.

αὐτῷ. Dative of reference.

συμβαίνειν. Pres act inf συμβαίνω (complementary to μέλλοντα).

10:33 ὅτι Ἰδοὺ ἀναβαίνομεν εἰς Ἱεροσόλυμα, καὶ ὁ υἱὸς τοῦ ἀνθρώπου παραδοθήσεται τοῖς ἀρχιερεῦσιν καὶ τοῖς γραμματεῦσιν, καὶ κατακρινοῦσιν αὐτὸν θανάτῳ καὶ παραδώσουσιν αὐτὸν τοῖς ἔθνεσιν

ὅτι. Introduces direct discourse (note the capitalization of Ἰδού in the UBS[4]) that explains τὰ μέλλοντα.

Ἰδού. See 1:2 (see also 3:34 on ἴδε).

ἀναβαίνομεν. Pres act ind 1st pl ἀναβαίνω.

εἰς Ἱεροσόλυμα. Spatial. On the form ο Ἱεροσόλυμα, see 3:8.

ὁ υἱὸς. Nominative subject of παραδοθήσεται. On ὁ υἱὸς τοῦ ἀνθρώπου, see 2:10.

παραδοθήσεται. Fut pass ind 3rd sg παραδίδωμι (a technical term: "of police and courts 'hand over into [the] custody [of],'" BDAG, 762.1.b; for more on the use of παραδίδωμι in Mark, see 1:14; 3:19).

τοῖς ἀρχιερεῦσιν καὶ τοῖς γραμματεῦσιν. Dative indirect object of παραδοθήσεται.

κατακρινοῦσιν. Fut act ind 3rd pl κατακρίνω. Here, "sentence someone to death" (BDAG, 519), with the accusative identifying the person sentenced and the dative specifying the nature of the sentence.

αὐτὸν. Accusative direct object of κατακρινοῦσιν.

θανάτῳ. Dative of reference.

παραδώσουσιν. Fut act ind 3rd pl παραδίδωμι (see above).

αὐτὸν. Accusative direct object of παραδώσουσιν.

τοῖς ἔθνεσιν. Dative indirect object of παραδώσουσιν.

10:34 καὶ ἐμπαίξουσιν αὐτῷ καὶ ἐμπτύσουσιν αὐτῷ καὶ μαστιγώσ- ουσιν αὐτὸν καὶ ἀποκτενοῦσιν, καὶ μετὰ τρεῖς ἡμέρας ἀναστήσεται.

ἐμπαίξουσιν. Fut act ind 3rd pl ἐμπαίζω. The subject shifts here from the actions of the religious leaders (v. 33) to the Roman authorities to whom Jesus has been "handed over" (παραδώσουσιν αὐτὸν τοῖς ἔθνεσιν, v. 33).

αὐτῷ. Dative complement of ἐμπαίξουσιν.

ἐμπτύσουσιν. Fut act ind 3rd pl ἐμπτύω.

αὐτῷ. Dative complement of ἐμπτύσουσιν.

μαστιγώσουσιν. Fut act ind 3rd pl μαστιγόω. In recording the fulfillment of these events in 15:15, Mark uses the synonymous Latin term φραγελλόω, while John 19:1 has μαστιγόω.

αὐτὸν. Accusative direct object of μαστιγώσουσιν.

ἀποκτενοῦσιν. Fut act ind 3rd pl ἀποκτείνω. The direct object (αὐτόν) is understood.

μετὰ τρεῖς ἡμέρας. Temporal.

ἀναστήσεται. Fut mid ind 3rd sg ἀνίστημι. The -ησ- is not a second future passive form marker (shortened from θησ), but rather is the stem vowel *alpha* lengthened with the addition of the future form marker (-σ-).

Mark 10:35-40

³⁵James and John, the sons of Zebedee, came to him and said to him, "Teacher, we would like that you would do for us whatever we ask you." ³⁶So he said to them, "What do you want me to do for you?" ³⁷They said to him, "Grant to us that we may sit one on your right and one on your left in your glory. ³⁸But Jesus said to them, "You don't understand what you are asking. Are you able to drink the cup which I will drink? Or to be baptized with the baptism with

which I will be baptized?" ³⁹They replied, "We are able." But Jesus
said to them, "You will drink the cup that I drink and you will be
baptized with the baptism with which I will be baptized, ⁴⁰but to sit
on my right or my left is not mine to give, but it is (for those) for
whom it is prepared.

**10:35 Καὶ προσπορεύονται αὐτῷ Ἰάκωβος καὶ Ἰωάννης οἱ υἱοὶ
Ζεβεδαίου λέγοντες αὐτῷ, Διδάσκαλε, θέλομεν ἵνα ὃ ἐὰν αἰτήσωμέν σε ποιήσῃς ἡμῖν.**

προσπορεύονται. Pres mid ind 3rd pl προσπορεύομαι. The present tense introduces a new paragraph (see 1:21).

αὐτῷ. Dative of destination. More commonly in Koine texts this
would be expressed with a prepositional phrase, usually with εἰς.

Ἰάκωβος καὶ Ἰωάννης. Nominative subject of προσπορεύονται.

οἱ υἱοὶ. Nominative in apposition to Ἰάκωβος καὶ Ἰωάννης.

λέγοντες. Pres act ptc masc nom pl λέγω (attendant circumstance). This participle does not fit the usual criteria for a participle
of attendant circumstance (for which see Wallace 1996, 642), but the
use of the present tense and the word order is likely due to the previous use of the present to mark the beginning of the new paragraph
(the narrative present). See also 1:21 on εἰσπορεύονται.

αὐτῷ. Dative indirect object of λέγοντες.

Διδάσκαλε. Vocative (see also 4:38).

θέλομεν. Pres act ind 1st pl θέλω.

ἵνα. Introduces a clause that indicates the content of the two disciples' desire. BDAG notes that "in this case the ἵνα-constr. serves as
a substitute for an inf. that supplements a verb" (476.2; cf. Wallace
(1996, 476).

ὃ ἐὰν αἰτήσωμέν σε. Indefinite relative clause functioning as the
direct object of ποιήσῃς.

αἰτήσωμέν. Aor act subj 1st pl αἰτέω. Subjunctive with ἐὰν.

σε. Accusative direct object of αἰτήσωμεν.

ποιήσῃς. Aor act subj 2nd sg ποιέω. Subjunctive with ἵνα.

ἡμῖν. Dative of advantage.

10:36 ὁ δὲ εἶπεν αὐτοῖς· Τί θέλετέ [με] ποιήσω ὑμῖν;

ὁ. Nominative subject of εἶπεν. On the use of ὁ δέ to change subjects, see 1:45.

εἶπεν. Aor act ind 3rd sg λέγω.

αὐτοῖς. Dative indirect object of εἶπεν.

Τί θέλετέ [με] ποιήσω ὑμῖν. Clausal complement (direct discourse) of εἶπεν, taking the form of a deliberative question.

Τί. Accusative direct object of ποιήσω.

θέλετέ. Pres act ind 2nd pl θέλω.

[με]. The presence of this word results in a very awkward construction. There are several possible solutions to the problem. It might be a textual corruption, it might involve ellipsis, or it might be a transitional construction. A possible analysis of the text as it stands might suggest that με is the accusative direct object of θέλετε in an object-complement double accusative construction. If so, then the clause Τί . . . ποιήσω ὑμῖν would be the accusative complement. France (414) considers the presence of με (א¹ B Ψ) to constitute a "syntactically impossible reading," preferring to omit με (C Θ ƒ¹, ¹³) with ἵνα understood: Τί θέλετέ ἵνα ποιήσω ὑμῖν. The Byzantine text (א² A 𝔐) has smoothed the awkwardness: Τί θέλετέ ποιῆσαί με ὑμῖν. Alternatively, since θέλω often takes a complementary infinitive, the ellipsis may involve ποιῆσαι given the presence of the accusative με: Τί θέλετέ με ποιῆσαι; ποιήσω ὑμῖν ("What do you want me to do? I will do it for you.") In this case ποιήσω would be be future indicative rather than aorist subjunctive. See also the syntactical pattern in 15:9.

ποιήσω. Aor act subj 1st sg ποιέω. Subjunctive as part of a deliberative question.

ὑμῖν. Dative of advantage.

10:37 οἱ δὲ εἶπαν αὐτῷ, δὸς ἡμῖν ἵνα εἷς σου ἐκ δεξιῶν καὶ εἷς ἐξ ἀριστερῶν καθίσωμεν ἐν τῇ δόξῃ σου.

οἱ. Nominative subject of εἶπαν. On the use of οἱ δέ to change subjects, see 1:45.

εἶπαν. Aor act ind 3rd pl λέγω.

αὐτῷ. Dative indirect object of εἶπαν.

δὸς. Aor act impv 2nd sg δίδωμι. In this context δίδωμι followed by ἵνα means "to grant that" (BDAG, 243.17.b).

ἡμῖν. Dative indirect object of δός.

ἵνα. Introduces a clause that functions as the direct object of δός indicating what is to be granted.

εἷς . . . καὶ εἷς. Nominative subject of καθίσωμεν.

σου. The position of σου is a bit unusual since it identifies at whose side (ἐκ δεξιῶν καὶ . . . ἐξ ἀριστερῶν) the disciples request to sit. For other modifiers in advance of a prepositional phrase, juxtaposed with an unrelated nominative, see 5:30, τίς μου ἥψατο τῶν ἱματίων (cf. Matt 12:50; Luke 11:19; John 12:47; John 13:6; 1 Cor 11:24).

ἐκ δεξιῶν . . . ἐξ ἀριστερῶν. Idiomatic phrases indicating positions of honor: "on the right (side) . . . on the left (side)." See the similar expression in verse 37 and 14:62. The adjective ἀριστερός ("left") is used substantivally in this verse: "the left hand" or "the left side" (BDAG, 131).

καθίσωμεν. Aor act subj 1st pl καθίζω. Subjunctive with ἵνα.

ἐν τῇ δόξῃ. Locative.

10:38 ὁ δὲ Ἰησοῦς εἶπεν αὐτοῖς, Οὐκ οἴδατε τί αἰτεῖσθε. δύνασθε πιεῖν τὸ ποτήριον ὃ ἐγὼ πίνω ἢ τὸ βάπτισμα ὃ ἐγὼ βαπτίζομαι βαπτισθῆναι;

ὁ . . . Ἰησοῦς. Nominative subject of εἶπεν.

δὲ. The use of δέ contrasts the disciples' request with Jesus' reply.

εἶπεν. Aor act ind 3rd sg λέγω.

Οὐκ οἴδατε . . . βαπτισθῆναι. Clausal complement (direct discourse) of εἶπεν.

οἴδατε. Prf act ind 2nd pl οἶδα. Here the sense is probably "understand" (BDAG, 694.4).

τί. Accusative direct object of αἰτεῖσθε.

αἰτεῖσθε. Pres mid ind 2nd pl αἰτέω.

δύνασθε. Pres mid ind 2nd pl δύναμαι.

πιεῖν. Aor act inf πίνω (complementary).

τὸ ποτήριον. Accusative direct object of πιεῖν.

ὃ. Accusative direct object of πίνω.

ἐγὼ. Nominative subject of πίνω.

πίνω. Pres act ind 1st sg πίνω. The time reference is future.

ἤ. The disjunctive particle indicates an alternative: "are you able to do this or this?"

τὸ βάπτισμα. Accusative of retained object with βαπτισθῆναι (see Wallace, 1996, 197, who cites a similar statement in Luke 7:29, βαπτισθέντες τὸ βάπτισμα). BDF §153 refers to it as an accusative of content qualified by the following relative clause.

ὃ. Accusative direct object of βαπτίζομαι.

ἐγὼ. Nominative subject of βαπτίζομαι.

βαπτίζομαι. Pres pass ind 1st sg βαπτίζω. The time reference is future.

βαπτισθῆναι. Aor pass inf βαπτίζω (complementary to δύνασθε). The expression τὸ βάπτισμα ὃ ἐγὼ βαπτίζομαι βαπτισθῆναι is a figurative expression that refers to "the power of calamity to overwhelm.

Can you, he asks, be immersed in that which has overwhelmed me?" (Gould, 200). "The sufferer is regarded as plunged and half-drowned in his grief or loss" (Swete, 237).

10:39 οἱ δὲ εἶπαν αὐτῷ, Δυνάμεθα. ὁ δὲ Ἰησοῦς εἶπεν αὐτοῖς, Τὸ ποτήριον ὃ ἐγὼ πίνω πίεσθε καὶ τὸ βάπτισμα ὃ ἐγὼ βαπτίζομαι βαπτισθήσεσθε,

οἱ δὲ. Nominative subject of εἶπαν. On the use of οἱ δέ to change subjects, see 1:45.

εἶπαν. Aor act ind 3rd pl λέγω.

αὐτῷ. Dative indirect object of εἶπαν.

δυνάμεθα. Pres mid ind 1st pl δύναμαι. This one word serves as the clausal complement (direct discourse) of εἶπαν.

ὁ . . . Ἰησοῦς. Nominative subject of εἶπεν.

δὲ. The use of δέ contrasts the disciples' affirmation with Jesus' reply.

εἶπεν. Aor act ind 3rd sg λέγω.

αὐτοῖς. Dative indirect object of εἶπεν.

Τὸ ποτήριον . . . οἷς ἡτοίμασται (v. 40). Clausal complement (direct discourse) of εἶπεν.

Τὸ ποτήριον. Accusative direct object of πίεσθε.

ὃ. Accusative direct object of πίνω.

ἐγὼ. Nominative subject of πίνω.

πίνω. Pres act ind 1st sg πίνω. The time reference is future.

πίεσθε. Fut mid ind 2nd pl πίνω.

τὸ βάπτισμα. Accusative of retained object with βαπτισθήσεσθε (see v. 38).

ὃ. Accusative direct object of βαπτίζομαι.

ἐγὼ. Nominative subject of βαπτίζομαι.

βαπτίζομαι. Pres pass ind 1st sg βαπτίζω. The time reference is future.

βαπτισθήσεσθε. Fut pass ind 2nd pl βαπτίζω.

10:40 τὸ δὲ καθίσαι ἐκ δεξιῶν μου ἢ ἐξ εὐωνύμων οὐκ ἔστιν ἐμὸν δοῦναι, ἀλλ' οἷς ἡτοίμασται.

τὸ . . . καθίσαι. Aor act inf καθίζω. The article is a nominalizer, indicating that the infinitive is functioning as a noun. The infinitival clause, τὸ δὲ καθίσαι ἐκ δεξιῶν μου ἢ ἐξ εὐωνύμων, functions as the subject of ἔστιν.

δὲ. The use of δέ contrasts the drinking and baptizing with the sitting.

ἐκ δεξιῶν . . . ἢ ἐξ εὐωνύμων. Source, but in an idiomatic expression: "on the right or on the left" (see also v. 37; 14:62). The original request used ἀριστερός rather than the synonymous εὐώνυμος. Although εὐώνυμος may have had connotations of bad luck in older usage (LSJ, 740, s.v. εὐώνυμος, A.III), which Gundry (578) tries to import here (cf. Duckwitz, 177, who calls it a "disagreeable word"), it appears that by Koine times it simply meant "left hand/ side" and was used interchangeably with ἀριστερός (LN 82.7 lists both together; see also BDAG, LEH, and Muraoka). Collins (498) suggests that the variation here is simply stylistic.

ἔστιν. Pres act ind 3rd sg εἰμί. On the accent, see 12:32.

ἐμὸν. Accusative subject of δοῦναι.

δοῦναι. Aor act inf δίδωμι. The infinitival clause, ἐμὸν δοῦναι, functions as the predicate of εἰμί.

ἀλλ' οἷς ἡτοίμασται. This phrase "is a compressed expression in which the relative stands in for the main clause; we must assume a main verb such as 'it will be given,' contrasting with the preceding statement that it is not for Jesus to give it" (France, 417). The original text was written in uncials with no word division or diacritics: ΑΛΛΟΙΣ. It can thus be read as in the UBS⁴, or as ἄλλοις ἡτοίμασται ("it is prepared for others"). "The seats beside Jesus, then, are reserved either for certain ones who have already been designated (and these might well be the sons of Zebedee themselves), or for others (excluding the sons of Zebedee)" (Aland, 277). The text as given is probably correct, though it does appear with the alternate word division in one late Greek ms (225) and some early versions (e.g., it sa^ms sy^s). For another example of this relatively rare ambiguity, see Matt 9:18 (εἰς ἐλθών versus εἰσελθών).

ἀλλ'. The conjunction introduces the positive contrast to the preceding negative statement. The statement introduced is elliptical, assuming ἔστιν from the preceding clause.

οἷς. Dative of advantage.

ἡτοίμασται. Prf pass ind 3rd sg ἑτοιμάζω. The implied agent of the passive verb is probably to be understood as God.

Mark 10:41-45

[41]When they heard (about this), the Ten became indignant with James and John. [42]Having summoned them, Jesus said to them, "You know that those who are recognized as rulers of the Gentiles lord it over them and their great ones dominate them, [43]but it must not be like that among you; rather, whoever desires to be greatest

among you must be your servant, ⁴⁴and whoever desires to be first must be a slave of all. ⁴⁵For not even the Son of Man came to be served, but to serve and to give his life as a ransom for many.

10:41 Καὶ ἀκούσαντες οἱ δέκα ἤρξαντο ἀγανακτεῖν περὶ Ἰακώβου καὶ Ἰωάννου.

ἀκούσαντες. Aor act ptc masc nom pl ἀκούω (temporal).

οἱ δέκα. Nominative subject of ἤρξαντο. The reference is not to "the Ten" as a group (contrast οἱ δωδέκα, "the Twelve," in Luke 8:1; 9:12; Acts 6:2), but means "the *remaining* ten (disciples)." Here, "a single definite number is separated off from a larger amount and labeled with the article" (Wackernagel, 569; cf. BDF §265; see also Matt 18:12, 13; 20:24; 25:2 v.l.; Luke 15:4; 17:17; Rev 17:10).

ἤρξαντο. Aor mid ind 3rd pl ἄρχω. With the infinitive, this phrase would formally be expressed as "began to be indignant/angry" (ESV, NRSV), but here it seems more likely that the point is "they became indignant" (e.g., NIV, NET) or "they got angry."

ἀγανακτεῖν. Pres act inf ἀγανακτέω (complementary).

περὶ Ἰακώβου καὶ Ἰωάννου. Reference.

10:42 καὶ προσκαλεσάμενος αὐτοὺς ὁ Ἰησοῦς λέγει αὐτοῖς, Οἴδατε ὅτι οἱ δοκοῦντες ἄρχειν τῶν ἐθνῶν κατακυριεύουσιν αὐτῶν καὶ οἱ μεγάλοι αὐτῶν κατεξουσιάζουσιν αὐτῶν.

προσκαλεσάμενος. Aor mid ptc masc nom sg προσκαλέομαι (temporal).

αὐτοὺς. Accusative direct object of προσκαλεσάμενος.

ὁ Ἰησοῦς. Nominative subject of λέγει.

λέγει. Pres act ind 3rd sg λέγω.

αὐτοῖς. Dative indirect object of λέγω.

Οἴδατε ὅτι . . . λύτρον ἀντὶ πολλῶν (v. 45). Clausal complement (direct discourse) of λέγει.

Οἴδατε. Prf act ind 2nd pl οἶδα.

ὅτι. Introduces the clausal complement of οἴδατε.

οἱ δοκοῦντες ἄρχειν. Formally, "the ones considered to rule." Manson argues that "the meaning required by the context for οἱ δοκοῦντες ἄρχειν is something like 'Those who aspire to rule'" (313–15). He then translates the verse, "You know that those who aspire to rule over the Gentiles subjugate them and the greatest of them (sc. τῶν ἀρχοντων) rule despotically."

οἱ δοκοῦντες. Pres act ptc masc nom pl δοκέω (substantival).

Nominative subject of κατακυριεύουσιν. On the use of δοκέω, see 6:49.

ἄρχειν. Pres act inf ἄρχω (complementary).

τῶν ἐθνῶν. Genitive direct object of ἄρχειν, as is common with verbs of ruling (see two more later in this verse; see also Robertson, 510). This might be described as a genitive of subordination (see Wallace 1996, 103–4).

κατακυριεύουσιν. Pres act ind 3rd pl κατακυριεύω ("to dominate, control," *CL*, 191). "It is possible that κατακυριεύω is somewhat more emphatic in meaning than κυριεύω" (LN 37.48 n. 6). Cranfield points out that "in the LXX the verb is nearly always used of the rule of an alien. The κατα- gives it the sense of using lordship over people to their disadvantage and to one's own advantage" (341). Though the evidence is not as extensive as Cranfield suggests (if for no other reason than the frequency with which it refers to God's dominion), his sentiments are correct in this context as well as in 1 Pet 5:3, which he compares to Jesus' statement here.

αὐτῶν. Genitive direct object of κατακυριεύουσιν (see on ἐθνῶν above).

οἱ μεγάλοι. Nominative subject of κατεξουσιάζουσιν.

κατεξουσιάζουσιν. Pres act ind 3rd pl κατεξουσιάζω ("to exercise unquestioned authority over," *CL*, 195). This word is "scarcely to be found in other Gk" (BDAG, 531); though the related noun κατεξουσία occurs twice in inscriptional material, the verb form is not otherwise attested until after NT times. "It is possible that κατεξουσιάζω is somewhat more emphatic in meaning than ἐξουσιάζω" (LN 37.48 n. 5).

αὐτῶν. Genitive direct object of κατεξουσιάζουσιν (see on ἐθνῶν above).

10:43 οὐχ οὕτως δέ ἐστιν ἐν ὑμῖν, ἀλλ᾽ ὃς ἂν θέλῃ μέγας γενέσθαι ἐν ὑμῖν ἔσται ὑμῶν διάκονος,

οὕτως δέ. This comparative adverb with δέ contrasts the pattern of earthly, authority-based relationships in verse 42 with the type of relationships that are to characterize Jesus' followers: service rather than authority.

ἐστιν. Pres act ind 3rd sg εἰμί. Although this indicative might be read as a statement of fact ("it is not this way among you"; NASB, NET), the contextual force is that of a prohibition: "it must not be like that among you" (HCSB; cf. ESV, NIV).

ἐν ὑμῖν. Association; with a plural object ἐν is often best expressed in English as "among."

ἀλλ'. This contrasting conjunction, almost always used with a preceding negative clause, here introduces a contrast with the statement of verse 42, functioning as an explanation of the prohibition in verse 43a.

ὃς ἂν θέλῃ μέγας γενέσθαι ἐν ὑμῖν. The relative clause functions as the subject of ἔσται.

ὃς ἄν. Indefinite relative pronoun ("whoever") functioning as the nominative subject of θέλῃ.

θέλῃ. Pres act subj 3rd sg θέλω. Subjunctive with ὃς ἄν.

μέγας. Predicate adjective. The infinitive (γενέσθαι) normally takes an accusative predicate, but here μέγας is nominative. Since it is parallel with πρῶτος in the next phrase, μέγας probably has a superlative sense here: "greatest" (see Cranfield, 341).

γενέσθαι. Aor mid inf γίνομαι (complementary).

ἐν ὑμῖν. Association.

ἔσται. Fut mid ind 3rd sg εἰμί. The future tense functions imperatively: "must be" (contra Gundry, 580, who argues that "what Mark's Jesus offers then [and despite the usual, unscrutinous understanding], is prediction, not command.)" Gundry's thesis, however, requires extensive and deliberate reworking of 9:33-35, 43-45 to create the necessary foil for this passage (his comments relate to both instances of ἔσται in vv. 43 and 44).

10:44 καὶ ὃς ἂν θέλῃ ἐν ὑμῖν εἶναι πρῶτος ἔσται πάντων δοῦλος·

καὶ. The coordinating conjunction places verse 43b and verse 44 in parallel, restating the same idea in different terms ("first" rather than "great").

ὃς ἂν θέλῃ ἐν ὑμῖν εἶναι πρῶτος. The relative clause functions as the subject of ἔσται.

ὃς ἄν. Indefinite relative pronoun ("whoever") functioning as the nominative subject of θέλῃ.

θέλῃ. Pres act subj 3rd sg θέλω. Subjunctive with ὃς ἄν.

εἶναι. Pres act inf εἰμί (complementary).

πρῶτος. Predicate adjective. The infinitive (γενέσθαι) normally takes an accusative predicate, but here μέγας is nominative.

ἔσται. Fut mid ind 3rd sg εἰμί. The switch from γενέσθαι to εἶναι in the parallel clauses is simply for stylistic variety.

πάντων. Possessive genitive.

δοῦλος. Predicate nominative of ἔσται.

10:45 καὶ γὰρ ὁ υἱὸς τοῦ ἀνθρώπου οὐκ ἦλθεν διακονηθῆναι ἀλλὰ διακονῆσαι καὶ δοῦναι τὴν ψυχὴν αὐτοῦ λύτρον ἀντὶ πολλῶν.

For a helpful summary of the background of the concepts (linguistic and conceptual) expressed in this verse from Isaiah 53, see the summary in France (420–21, and the additional bibliography given there) and Bolt (71–73).

καί. Adverbial: "even." This stresses the magnitude of the example cited.

γάρ. Introduces a clause that explains the reason for the preceding instructions.

ὁ υἱὸς. Nominative subject of ἦλθεν. On ὁ υἱὸς τοῦ ἀνθρώπου see 2:10.

ἦλθεν. Aor act ind 3rd sg ἔρχομαι (see also 1:24).

διακονηθῆναι. Aor pass inf διακονέω (purpose).

διακονῆσαι. Aor act inf διακονέω (purpose).

καί. The conjunction ought not be viewed as strictly coordinate, as if the serving (διακονῆσαι) and the giving (δοῦναι) were distinct actions. Rather, Jesus served ultimately by giving his life as a ransom. Lane (378 n. 75) calls this instance of καί explanatory, while Gundry (588) calls it epexegetical.

δοῦναι. Aor act inf δίδωμι (purpose).

τὴν ψυχὴν. Accusative direct object of δοῦναι. The meaning of ψυχή here is "life," not "soul," a reflexive use (i.e., equivalent to "himself") with possible Semitic influence (so Gundry, 588).

λύτρον. Complement in an object-complement double accusative construction. The noun λύτρον refers to "ransom."

ἀντὶ πολλῶν. Substitution. The prepositional phrase is adjectival, modifying λύτρον (not δοῦναι). This is at least partly indicated by word order (so Stein 2008, 488) with the prepositional phrase separated from the main verb. For more on ἀντί in this context, see esp. Wallace (1996, 365–67). "Many" (πολύς), here, is not "a large number less than all," but is probably to be understood in a Semitic sense (see Maloney 1981, 139–42, 221 n. 326; Jeremias, 6:543–45) as the equivalent of πᾶς, i.e., used to express the extensiveness of the action (all of a small group is not as "big" a statement as "many"). Note that in 3:10 πολύς is replaced in the synoptic parallel in Matt 12:15 with πᾶς. See the same use in Isa 53:12 ("many," but || "all" in v. 6) and Rom 5:12 ("all," but || "many" in v. 15). Calvin's comment is that "'many' is used, not for a definite number, but for a large number, in that He sets Himself over against all others. And this is the meaning also in Rom. 5.15, where Paul is not talking of a part of mankind but of the whole human race" (Calvin 2:277).

Mark 10:46-52

⁴⁶Then they came to Jericho. As Jesus was leaving Jericho with his disciples and a large crowd, the son of Timaeus, Bartimaeus, a blind beggar, was sitting by the road. ⁴⁷When he heard that it was Jesus the Nazarene he began to shout and say, "Son of David, Jesus, have mercy on me!" ⁴⁸Many rebuked him (telling him) that he should be quiet, but he shouted even more loudly, "Son of David, have mercy on me!" ⁴⁹Jesus, having stopped, said, "Call him." So they called the blind man, saying to him, "Be encouraged! Get up! He is calling you." ⁵⁰Having tossed aside his cloak and leaped to his feet, he came to Jesus. ⁵¹Jesus said to him, "What do you want me to do for you?" The blind man said to him, "Rabbi, I want to see again. ⁵²Jesus said to him, "Go. Your faith has healed you." Immediately, he regained his sight and he followed him on the road.

10:46 Καὶ ἔρχονται εἰς Ἰεριχώ. καὶ ἐκπορευομένου αὐτοῦ ἀπὸ Ἰεριχὼ καὶ τῶν μαθητῶν αὐτοῦ καὶ ὄχλου ἱκανοῦ ὁ υἱὸς Τιμαίου Βαρτιμαῖος, τυφλὸς προσαίτης, ἐκάθητο παρὰ τὴν ὁδόν.

ἔρχονται. Pres mid ind 3rd pl ἔρχομαι. The narrative present tense introduces a new paragraph (see 1:21).

εἰς Ἰεριχώ. Spatial.

ἐκπορευομένου. Pres mid ptc masc gen sg ἐκπορεύομαι. Genitive absolute (see 1:32), temporal. The participle is singular to agree with the closest subject, αὐτοῦ; this may also mark the primary subject with the remaining two genitives as secondary (see Wallace 1996, 401, who discusses this construction with reference to finite verbs; it appears that the same is true of nonfinite forms as well).

αὐτοῦ ... καὶ τῶν μαθητῶν αὐτοῦ καὶ ὄχλου ἱκανοῦ. Genitive subject of ἐκπορευομένου. It is a bit unusual to have a triple subject in a genitive absolute construction.

ἀπὸ Ἰεριχώ. Separation.

ὄχλου ἱκανοῦ. This is the only time that Mark describes the extent of a crowd using ἱκανός. Luke does so more often (Luke 7:12; Acts 11:24, 26; 19:26). When he describes the size of the crowd, Mark normally uses πολύς (5:21, 24; 6:34; 8:1; 9:14; 12:37), though once each he employs πλεῖστος (4:1) and ἱκανός (here).

ὁ υἱὸς. Nominative subject of ἐκάθητο.

Τιμαίου. Genitive of relationship. Τίμαιος is familiar as a Greek name, and it is possible that in the mixed culture of first-century Palestine it was borne by this Jewish beggar's father (cf. Ἀνδρέας and Φίλιππος among Jesus' Jewish disciples), though it could represent a Semitic name such as *Ṭimʾay* (France, 423).

Βαρτιμαῖος. Nominative in apposition to ὁ υἱός. This name is formed from the Aramaic bar, "son," added to the patronym, Τιμαῖος, making this name equivalent to ὁ υἱὸς Τιμαίου.

προσαίτης. Nominative in apposition to ὁ υἱός ("beggar"). This rare word occurs only here and in John 9:8, and is not found elsewhere in literature related to the NT. The cognate verb, προσαιτέω, occurs in John 9:8, LXX Job 27:14, and in *T. Job* 22:3; 24:8.

ἐκάθητο. Impf mid ind 3rd sg κάθημαι.

παρὰ τὴν ὁδόν. Spatial.

10:47 καὶ ἀκούσας ὅτι Ἰησοῦς ὁ Ναζαρηνός ἐστιν ἤρξατο κράζειν καὶ λέγειν, Υἱὲ Δαυὶδ Ἰησοῦ, ἐλέησόν με.

ἀκούσας. Aor act ptc masc nom sg ἀκούω (temporal).

ὅτι. Introduces the clausal complement (indirect discourse) of ἀκούσας (see 1:15).

Ἰησοῦς. Predicate nominative.

ὁ Ναζαρηνός. Nominative in apposition to Ἰησοῦς. Jesus is identified as a Nazarene four times in Mark, each time with a slightly different grammatical form of the adjective Ναζαρηνός, but all equivalent in meaning: 1:24; 10:47; 14:67; 16:6. He is also identified as coming from Nazareth in 1:9.

ἐστιν. Pres act ind 3rd sg εἰμί. As is normal in Greek, the verb retains the same tense in indirect discourse as the original statement.

ἤρξατο. Aor mid ind 3rd sg ἄρχω.

κράζειν. Pres act inf κράζω (complementary).

λέγειν. Pres act inf λέγω (complementary).

Υἱὲ Δαυὶδ Ἰησοῦ, ἐλέησόν με. Clausal complement (direct discourse) of κράζειν καὶ λέγειν. This is the only incident in Mark in which Jesus is explicitly addressed as "Son of David." The phrase Υἱὲ Δαυίδ is "functionally equivalent to Χριστός, but the voicing of David's name increases the loading of royal and nationalistic ideology which it carries" (France, 423).

Υἱὲ . . . Ἰησοῦ. Vocative (the vocative Ἰησοῦ is identical with the genitive).

ἐλέησόν. Aor act impv 2nd sg ἐλεέω.

με. Accusative direct object of ἐλέησον.

10:48 καὶ ἐπετίμων αὐτῷ πολλοὶ ἵνα σιωπήσῃ· ὁ δὲ πολλῷ μᾶλλον ἔκραζεν, Υἱὲ Δαυίδ, ἐλέησόν με.

ἐπετίμων. Impf act ind 3rd pl ἐπιτιμάω.

αὐτῷ. Dative complement of ἐπετίμων.

πολλοὶ. Nominative subject of ἐπετίμων.

ἵνα. Introduces a clause (indirect discourse) giving the content of the command (ἐπετίμων). BDAG notes that "in this case the ἵνα-constr. serves as a substitute for an inf. that supplements a verb" (476.2; cf. Wallace, 1996, 476). NET takes the ἵνα as indicating purpose: "Many scolded him to get him to be quiet."

σιωπήσῃ. Aor act subj 3rd sg σιωπάω. Subjunctive with ἵνα.

ὁ. Nominative subject of ἔκραζεν. On the use of ὁ δέ to change subjects, see 1:45.

πολλῷ μᾶλλον. This is an adverbial expression, "much more, all the more," or perhaps in this context, "even more loudly" (BDAG, 613.1, s.v. μᾶλλον). BDAG describes πολλῷ as "the dat. of degree of difference" (849.2.a.β.ℷ, s.v. πολύς). μᾶλλον is the comparative form of the adverb μάλα.

ἔκραζεν. Impf act ind 3rd sg κράζω.

Υἱὲ Δαυίδ, ἐλέησόν με. See verse 47.

ἐλέησόν. Aor act impv 2nd sg ἐλεέω.

με. Accusative direct object of ἐλέησον.

10:49 καὶ στὰς ὁ Ἰησοῦς εἶπεν, Φωνήσατε αὐτόν. καὶ φωνοῦσιν τὸν τυφλὸν λέγοντες αὐτῷ, Θάρσει, ἔγειρε, φωνεῖ σε.

στὰς. Aor act ptc masc nom sg ἵστημι (temporal). Used intransitively, this verb can mean "to stop," i.e., "stand still." Although that seems the most likely sense in this context, since Jesus has most recently been described as traveling (ἐκπορευομένου, v. 46), it is conceivable that ἵστημι could indicate that Jesus stood up, having paused along the way to sit and teach (cf. Evans 2001, 133).

εἶπεν. Aor act ind 3rd sg λέγω.

Φωνήσατε αὐτόν. Clausal complement (direct discourse) of εἶπεν.

Φωνήσατε. Aor act impv 2nd pl φωνέω. The text is not specific as to whom this command is addressed. It could be either his disciples, unspecified people nearby, or the πολλοί of verse 48 (the preference of Stein 2008, 496). This is a less common word to use in the sense of "to invite, summon," for which καλέω (e.g., 1:20; 2:17; 3:31, etc.) or προσκαλέω (3:13, 23; 6:7, etc.) are more frequently employed (but see 9:35; 15:35).

αὐτόν. Accusative direct object of φωνήσατε.

φωνοῦσιν. Pres act ind 3rd pl φωνέω. Presumably the subject is the same group to whom the command was addressed, likely the crowd (ὄχλου) of verse 46.

τὸν τυφλὸν. Accusative direct object of φωνοῦσιν.

λέγοντες. Pres act ptc masc nom pl λέγω (means; redundant adverbial participle of speaking; see 3:33).

αὐτῷ. Dative indirect object of λέγοντες.

Θάρσει, ἔγειρε, φωνεῖ σε. Clausal complement (direct discourse) of λέγοντες.

Θάρσει. Pres act impv 2nd sg θαρσέω. This word of encouragement ("cheer up, take courage, be encouraged") is always used (7 times) as an imperative in the NT. The imperative also dominates in the LXX (22/24) and Pseudepigrapha (all 11), but not in other Koine literature. The only other use in Mark is by Jesus in 6:50.

ἔγειρε. Pres act impv 2nd sg ἐγείρω.

φωνεῖ. Pres act ind 3rd sg φωνέω. The subject is Jesus.

σε. Accusative direct object of φωνεῖ.

10:50 ὁ δὲ ἀποβαλὼν τὸ ἱμάτιον αὐτοῦ ἀναπηδήσας ἦλθεν πρὸς τὸν Ἰησοῦν.

ὁ. Nominative subject of ἦλθεν. On the use of ὁ δέ to change subjects, see 1:45.

ἀποβαλὼν. Aor act ptc masc nom sg ἀποβάλλω (temporal). Here, "to toss/throw aside," but the word has a much broader semantic range in Koine than one would suspect from its NT usage (see BDAG, 107).

τὸ ἱμάτιον. Accusative direct object of ἀποβαλών.

ἀναπηδήσας. Aor act ptc masc nom sg ἀναπηδάω (temporal; "to leap/jump up"). This NT *hapax legomenon* occurs a half dozen times in the LXX (e.g., 1 Sam 20:34; Tob 2:4). The use of the two adverbial participles may be included "to show the man's eagerness" (Gould, 204).

ἦλθεν. Aor act ind 3rd sg ἔρχομαι.

10:51 καὶ ἀποκριθεὶς αὐτῷ ὁ Ἰησοῦς εἶπεν, Τί σοι θέλεις ποιήσω; ὁ δὲ τυφλὸς εἶπεν αὐτῷ, Ραββουνι, ἵνα ἀναβλέψω.

ἀποκριθεὶς. Aor mid ptc masc nom sg ἀποκρίνομαι (means; redundant adverbial participle of speaking). On this intransitive, "θη middle" form, see 3:33.

αὐτῷ. Dative indirect object of εἶπεν.

ὁ Ἰησοῦς. Nominative subject of εἶπεν.

εἶπεν. Aor act ind 3rd sg λέγω.

Τί σοι θέλεις ποιήσω. Clausal complement (direct discourse) of εἶπεν: "What do you want that I should do for you?"

Τί σοι . . . ποιήσω. Clausal complement of θέλεις.

Τί. Accusative direct object of ποιήσω.

σοι. Dative of advantage.

θέλεις. Pres act ind 2nd sg θέλω.

ποιήσω. Aor act subj 1st sg ποιέω. On the lack of a ἵνα, see 15:9.

ὁ . . . τυφλὸς. Nominative subject of εἶπεν.

δὲ. The use of δέ instead of καί is due to the change of speakers.

εἶπεν. Aor act ind 3rd sg λέγω.

Ραββουνι, ἵνα ἀναβλέψω. Clausal complement (direct discourse) of εἶπεν.

Ραββουνι. The indeclinable Aramaic loanword with a first person suffix ("my Rabbi, my lord, my master") functions as a vocative. The only other NT use (John 20:16) explicitly translates ῥαββουνί as διδάσκαλε. The more common form in the NT is ῥαββί.

ἵνα. Introduces the clausal complement of an elided θέλω. Although this has been explained as an imperatival ἵνα elsewhere (BDAG, 477.2.g; Wallace 1996, 477; Stein 2008, 498), the first person form of ἀναβλέψω makes this unlikely; imperatival uses of ἵνα normally occur with second or occasionally third person verbs.

ἀναβλέψω. Aor act subj 1st sg ἀναβλέπω. Subjunctive with ἵνα. Although ἀναβλέπω can mean "to look up" (e.g., 6:41), the ἀνά prefix can also mean "again," thus "to see again" (cf. 10:52), as here. In some cases the force of ἀνά appears to be diminished to the point where ἀναβλέπω means simply "to gain sight," rather than to regain what had been lost (e.g., of the man born blind, John 9:11). If ἀνά does have its full force here, then this beggar may have once been able to see and asks for the restoration of his sight.

10:52 καὶ ὁ Ἰησοῦς εἶπεν αὐτῷ, Ὕπαγε, ἡ πίστις σου σέσωκέν σε. καὶ εὐθὺς ἀνέβλεψεν καὶ ἠκολούθει αὐτῷ ἐν τῇ ὁδῷ.

ὁ Ἰησοῦς. Nominative subject of εἶπεν.

εἶπεν. Aor act ind 3rd sg λέγω.

αὐτῷ. Dative indirect object of εἶπεν.

Ὕπαγε, ἡ πίστις σου σέσωκέν σε. Clausal complement (direct discourse) of εἶπεν.

Ὕπαγε. Pres act impv 2nd sg ὑπάγω.

ἡ πίστις. Nominative subject of σέσωκεν.

σέσωκέν. Prf act ind 3rd sg σῴζω. Although this is an active voice verb and the subject is ἡ πίστις, this should not be taken to mean that the man's faith by itself was the agent of his healing. The whole point of the context is that it is Jesus who performed the healing. The statement is likely another way of saying "because you believed, I healed you."

σε. Accusative direct object of σέσωκεν.

καὶ εὐθὺς. The context suggests that this is one of the few instances in Mark in which καὶ εὐθύς means "immediately" (see 1:10). This is confirmed by the other Synoptics where it is represented with εὐθέως (Matt 20:34) and παραχρῆμα (Luke 18:43).

ἀνέβλεψεν. Aor act ind 3rd sg ἀναβλέπω.

ἠκολούθει. Impf act ind 3rd sg ἀκολουθέω. On the possibility that this is an inceptive imperfect as in HCSB and ISV, see 1:21.

αὐτῷ. Dative complement of ἠκολούθει.

ἐν τῇ ὁδῷ. Locative.

Mark 11:1-11

[1]When they approached Jerusalem, in the vicinity of Bethpage and Bethany, near the Mount of Olives, he sent two of his disciples [2]and he said to them, "Go into the village ahead of you and just as you are entering it you will find a tethered colt upon which no one has ever ridden; untie it and bring (it to me). [3]If anyone should say to you, 'Why are you doing this?' then say (to him), 'The Lord has need of (the colt) and he will send it back here soon.' [4]So they went and found the colt whom was tethered near a door, outside in the street, and they untied it. [5]Now some of those who were standing there said to them, "What are you doing, untying the colt?" [6]So they answered them as Jesus had instructed (them), and they allowed them (to take the colt). [7]They led the colt to Jesus and put their cloaks on it, and he sat on it. [8]Many people spread their cloaks on the road, and others (spread) leafy branches, having cut (them) from the fields. [9]Those who walked ahead and those who followed were shouting, "Hosanna! Blessed is the one who comes in the name of the Lord! [10]Blessed is the coming kingdom of our father David! Hosanna in the highest!" [11]He entered Jerusalem, into the temple and having looked around at everything, because it was already late, he retired to Bethany with the Twelve.

11:1 Καὶ ὅτε ἐγγίζουσιν εἰς Ἱεροσόλυμα εἰς Βηθφαγὴ καὶ Βηθανίαν πρὸς τὸ Ὄρος τῶν Ἐλαιῶν, ἀποστέλλει δύο τῶν μαθητῶν αὐτοῦ

ἐγγίζουσιν. Pres act ind 3rd pl ἐγγίζω. The two narrative present tenses mark both the beginning of a new paragraph and a change of location for the participants (see 1:21). The assumed subject is Jesus and his disciples, continued from 10:46 (contra France, 430, who includes the ὄχλου ἱκανοῦ mentioned in 10:46). Although the intervening verses have made reference to a crowd and a blind man, that Mark intends the reader to still think of Jesus and the disciples as the subject is verified by the reference to them in the last clause of this verse. That a crowd was present (πολλοί, v. 8) does not require that this verb refer to them. On the use of the plural verb here, see 5:38.

εἰς Ἱεροσόλυμα. Spatial ("to" rather than "into"; see Zerwick §97). Although Ἱεροσόλυμα is indeclinable (see 3:8), that it is accusative is confirmed by the parallel prepositional phrase following, which has an explicit accusative object (Βηθανίαν).

εἰς Βηθφαγὴ καὶ Βηθανίαν. Spatial ("in the vicinity of," BDAG, 288–89.1.a.α). Βηθφαγή is indeclinable, but here it is accusative as shown by the explicit accusative Βηθανίαν. This second εἰς phrase restricts the first; Mark first gives the general, "metro" location (Jerusalem), then the more specific, "suburban" location (Bethphage and Bethany). For a similar repetition of εἰς, see verse 11; 5:1; Matt 8:28; 21:1; 28:16; Luke 1:39; 2:4, 39; John 11:54 (Hort, 144).

πρὸς τὸ Ὄρος τῶν Ἐλαιῶν. Spatial ("near, at," BDAG, 875.3.g). For πρός used with ἐγγίζω of movement toward a geographical location, see also Luke 19:37; LXX 2 Sam 11:20.

ἀποστέλλει. Pres act ind 3rd sg ἀποστέλλω.

δύο. Accusative direct object of ἀποστέλλει.

τῶν μαθητῶν. Partitive genitive (see 8:8).

11:2 καὶ λέγει αὐτοῖς, Ὑπάγετε εἰς τὴν κώμην τὴν κατέναντι ὑμῶν, καὶ εὐθὺς εἰσπορευόμενοι εἰς αὐτὴν εὑρήσετε πῶλον δεδεμένον ἐφ᾽ ὃν οὐδεὶς οὔπω ἀνθρώπων ἐκάθισεν· λύσατε αὐτὸν καὶ φέρετε.

λέγει. Pres act ind 3rd sg λέγω.

αὐτοῖς. Dative indirect object of λέγει.

Ὑπάγετε εἰς ... πάλιν ὧδε (v. 3). Clausal complement (direct discourse) of λέγει.

Ὑπάγετε. Pres act impv 2nd pl ὑπάγω.

εἰς τὴν κώμην τὴν κατέναντι ὑμῶν. Spatial. The second τήν functions as an adjectivizer, changing the prepositional phrase κατέναντι ὑμῶν into an adjectival modifier of τὴν κώμην. Although κατέναντι is usually an adverb, here it functions as a preposition with the genitive (BDAG, 530.2.b; "straight ahead of," *CL*, 195.a).

καὶ εὐθὺς. In this instance of καὶ εὐθύς Mark appears to mean that the disciples will find the donkey tied near the edge of the village, "just as" they enter (the imperfective aspect and the lexis of εἰσπορευόμενοι contribute to this nuance); it says as much about distance as it does time (if it is near the edge of the village, they will find it as soon as they enter), so there is a dual spatial/temporal reference in this context (see also 1:10).

εἰσπορευόμενοι. Pres mid ptc masc nom pl εἰσπορεύομαι (temporal).

εὑρήσετε. Fut act ind 2nd pl εὑρίσκω.

πῶλον. Accusative direct object of εὑρήσετε. From Mark's account alone it would not be clear if πῶλος referred to the colt of a horse or a donkey, but Matthew's account identifies the πῶλος as that of an ὄνος, "donkey" (Matt 21:2-5; see also John 12:14-15). Bauer (220–29) has challenged the validity of appealing to the other gospel accounts, arguing that πῶλος without further description always means "horse" (see also BDAG, 900; Gundry, 626; Evans 2001, 142). For a helpful response to Bauer, see France, 431; cf. Collins, 517–18. The likelihood of finding a horse tied in a small Jewish village is rather remote.

δεδεμένον. Prf pass ptc masc acc sg δέω (attributive). On the significance of the perfect participle, see Porter (1997, 118).

ἐφ᾽ ὅν. Spatial.

οὐδεὶς. Nominative subject of ἐκάθισεν.

ἀνθρώπων. Partitive genitive (see 8:8), modifying οὐδείς ("no one of the human group").

ἐκάθισεν. Aor act ind 3rd sg καθίζω.

λύσατε. Aor act impv 2nd pl λύω.

αὐτὸν. Accusative direct object of λύσατε.

φέρετε. Pres act impv 2nd pl φέρω. This statement is elliptical.

11:3 καὶ ἐάν τις ὑμῖν εἴπῃ, Τί ποιεῖτε τοῦτο; εἴπατε, Ὁ κύριος αὐτοῦ χρείαν ἔχει, καὶ εὐθὺς αὐτὸν ἀποστέλλει πάλιν ὧδε.

This verse contains a number of ambiguities and there are several ways to understand the meaning of the statements, especially in the second half of the verse. These have also introduced a variety of textual variants at some points. The basic grammatical/syntactical options are identified below.

ἐάν τις ὑμῖν εἴπῃ . . . εἴπατε. . . . Third-class conditional statement reflecting a future potential situation.

τις. Nominative subject of εἴπῃ.

ὑμῖν. Dative indirect object of εἴπῃ.

εἴπῃ. Aor act subj 3rd sg λέγω.

Τί ποιεῖτε τοῦτο. Clausal complement (direct discourse) of εἴπῃ.

Τί. Interrogative adverb: "why?" The corresponding question asked in verse 5 is "what?" but the presence of τοῦτο here makes "why?" the most natural way to understand the statement.

ποιεῖτε. Pres act ind 2nd pl ποιέω.

τοῦτο. Accusative direct object of ποιεῖτε.

εἴπατε. Aor act impv 2nd pl λέγω.

Ὁ κύριος. Nominative subject of ἔχει. Danker suggests that this passage contains an "apparent wordplay" on the meaning of κύριος (CL, 211.2.e), i.e., the statement refers directly to the colt's owner, but since Jesus is κύριος in a greater sense, it is also true of him. Johansson offers an appealing alternative, though acknowledging that "the question of the referent is in the final analysis insoluble" (107–8). He suggests that in verse 3 the reference is to God, but that the referent shifts to Jesus in verse 7, who is the one who actually uses the animal, thus associating God and Jesus. Mark is more reticent than the other Gospel writers to refer to Jesus as κύριος, possibly doing so directly as ὁ κύριος only twice (here and 5:19; 13:20 is only remotely possible). This title does appear in OT quotations applied to Jesus (1:3; and by implication in 11:9; 12:36, 37), as a vocative with reference to Jesus (7:28, though this is probably only the honorific "sir"), and as a descriptive term (2:28). Elsewhere in Mark, κύριος refers to God (12:29, 30; 13:20) or is the simple descriptive "master/owner" (12:9; 13:35), though both of these latter references occur in parables that have their focus on Jesus. Cranfield thinks that "it seems unlikely that [Jesus] would refer to himself as 'the Lord'" (349; see also Lane, 391 n. 3; contra Gundry, 624; Stein 2008, 504). If, however, this is an example of "impressment" of an animal for one who had such a right (and both government officials as well as rabbis did have such rights), then we may be trying to read too much into the title κύριος in this particular setting (see Derrett, 2.167–77).

αὐτοῦ. This pronoun could be taken as a possessive genitive, modifying Ὁ κύριος ("his master/owner"), but it is more likely the genitive complement of χρείαν ἔχει ("has need of him"; see also ἔχει below).

χρείαν. Accusative direct object of ἔχει.

ἔχει. Pres act ind 3rd sg ἔχω. With ἔχω the accusative can specify what is "had" and the genitive what it is that one needs: "χρείαν ἔχειν τινός (have) need (of) someone or someth." (BDAG, 1088.1, s.v. χρεία).

καὶ εὐθὺς. In this context, καὶ εὐθύς (see 1:10) may mean "without delay" (if the subject of ἀποστέλλει is τις) or "soon" (if the subject is ὁ κύριος). See further on ἀποστέλλει below.

αὐτὸν. Accusative direct object of ἀποστέλλει.

ἀποστέλλει. Pres act ind 3rd sg ἀποστέλλω. The time reference is future. The singular may refer back to τις in the preceding clause (i.e., the person who asks what the disciples are doing; cf. ISV), but more likely refers to ὁ κύριος (so most translations), given the presence of πάλιν ὧδε.

11:4 καὶ ἀπῆλθον καὶ εὗρον πῶλον δεδεμένον πρὸς θύραν ἔξω ἐπὶ τοῦ ἀμφόδου καὶ λύουσιν αὐτόν.

ἀπῆλθον. Aor act ind 3rd pl ἀπέρχομαι.

εὗρον. Aor act ind 3rd pl εὑρίσκω.

πῶλον. Accusative direct object of εὗρον.

δεδεμένον. Prf pass ptc masc acc sg δέω (attributive).

πρὸς θύραν. Spatial. The colt was tied "at/near the door," not "to the door" (see also 1:33; 2:2).

ἐπὶ τοῦ ἀμφόδου. Spatial. The noun ἄμφοδον ("street") occurs only here in the NT.

λύουσιν. Pres act ind 3rd pl λύω.

αὐτόν. Accusative direct object of λύουσιν.

11:5 καί τινες τῶν ἐκεῖ ἑστηκότων ἔλεγον αὐτοῖς, Τί ποιεῖτε λύοντες τὸν πῶλον;

τινες. Nominative subject of ἔλεγον.

τῶν . . . ἑστηκότων. Prf act ptc masc gen pl ἵστημι (substantival). Partitive genitive (see 8:8).

ἔλεγον. Impf act ind 3rd pl λέγω. The imperfect functions, as it often does, to introduce direct discourse.

αὐτοῖς. Dative indirect object of ἔλεγον.

Τί ποιεῖτε λύοντες τὸν πῶλον. Clausal complement (direct discourse) of ἔλεγον.

Τί. Accusative direct object of ποιεῖτε.

ποιεῖτε. Pres act ind 2nd pl ποιέω.

λύοντες. Pres act ptc masc nom pl λύω (means).

τὸν πῶλον. Accusative direct object of λύοντες.

11:6 οἱ δὲ εἶπαν αὐτοῖς καθὼς εἶπεν ὁ Ἰησοῦς, καὶ ἀφῆκαν αὐτούς.

οἱ. Nominative subject of εἶπαν. On the use of οἱ δέ to change subjects, see 1:45.

εἶπαν. Aor act ind 3rd pl λέγω.

αὐτοῖς. Dative indirect object of εἶπαν.

καθὼς. After a verb of speaking the comparative adverb καθώς may introduce indirect discourse (BDAG, 494.5), but here the statement is only referenced obliquely, perhaps because the content of the statement has just been given two sentences earlier.

εἶπεν. Aor act ind 3rd sg λέγω.

ὁ Ἰησοῦς. Nominative subject of εἶπεν.

ἀφῆκαν. Aor act ind 3rd pl ἀφίημι. This verb should be understood in the sense of "give permission" (cf. BDAG, 157.5.a). The common translation, "let them go" (NIV, ESV, NET, HCSB, ISV) implies in English that the disciples were being detained, but the context says nothing about that, only a question of authorization has been asked. It is better, therefore, to translate "they allowed them (to take the colt)" (cf. NRSV) with the nature of the permission supplied from the context for clarity.

αὐτούς. Accusative direct object of ἀφῆκαν.

11:7 καὶ φέρουσιν τὸν πῶλον πρὸς τὸν Ἰησοῦν καὶ ἐπιβάλλουσιν αὐτῷ τὰ ἱμάτια αὐτῶν, καὶ ἐκάθισεν ἐπ᾽ αὐτόν.

φέρουσιν. Pres act ind 3rd pl φέρω.

τὸν πῶλον. Accusative direct object of φέρουσιν.

πρὸς τὸν Ἰησοῦν. Spatial.

ἐπιβάλλουσιν. Pres act ind 3rd pl ἐπιβάλλω.

αὐτῷ. Dative of location.

τὰ ἱμάτια. Accusative direct object of ἐπιβάλλουσιν. Although ἱμάτιον can refer to any garment, it presumably refers to their cloaks in this context.

ἐκάθισεν. Aor act ind 3rd sg καθίζω.

ἐπ᾽ αὐτόν. Spatial.

11:8 καὶ πολλοὶ τὰ ἱμάτια αὐτῶν ἔστρωσαν εἰς τὴν ὁδόν, ἄλλοι δὲ στιβάδας κόψαντες ἐκ τῶν ἀγρῶν.

πολλοὶ. Nominative subject of ἔστρωσαν.

τὰ ἱμάτια. Accusative direct object of ἔστρωσαν.

ἔστρωσαν. Aor act ind 3rd pl στρώννυμι ("to spread," BDAG, 949.1).

εἰς τὴν ὁδόν. Spatial.

ἄλλοι. Nominative subject of an implied ἔστρωσαν. The lack of an expressed verb may have prompted the textual variant found in A D Θ *f*[1, 13] 𝔐: ἄλλοι δὲ στοιβάδας ἔκοπτον ἐκ τῶν δένδρων, καὶ ἐστρώννυον εἰς τὴν ὁδόν ("others cut branches from the trees and spread [them] on the road"). It is possible that this is due to the Matthean parallel (ἄλλοι δὲ ἔκοπτον κλάδους ἀπὸ τῶν δένδρων καὶ ἐστρώννυον ἐν τῇ ὁδῷ, 21:8), as NA[27] suggests, but the wording of the first half is sufficiently different to suggest that these may be independent attempts to make the statement more clear.

δέ. The conjunction δέ distinguishes two groups: one spreads their garments, the other used leafy branches.

στιβάδας. Accusative direct object of an implied ἔστρωσαν. The noun στιβάς (only here in the NT) refers to "leafy branches" (BDAG, 945). Gundry argues that στιβάς ordinarily means "straw, grass, reeds, and suchlike" (629), rather than branches from a tree (e.g., palm branches), and that the association with ἀγρός ("fields") here makes that the most likely meaning. That is possible, though trees (or bushes) often grow along fields and ἀγρός can mean "countryside" as well as "fields" (BDAG, 15).

κόψαντες. Aor act ptc masc nom pl κόπτω (temporal).

ἐκ τῶν ἀγρῶν. Source.

11:9 καὶ οἱ προάγοντες καὶ οἱ ἀκολουθοῦντες ἔκραζον, Ὡσαννά· Εὐλογημένος ὁ ἐρχόμενος ἐν ὀνόματι κυρίου·

οἱ προάγοντες καὶ οἱ ἀκολουθοῦντες. Pres act ptc masc nom pl προάγω, ἀκολουθέω. Nominative subject of ἔκραζον. This need not be understood as two crowds, one from Jerusalem and one from Bethany (contra Swete, 250), but rather simply as Jesus being in the midst of a crowd with some ahead (οἱ προάγοντες) and some behind (οἱ ἀκολουθοῦντες).

ἔκραζον. Impf act ind 3rd pl κράζω.

Ὡσαννά· Εὐλογημένος ... [10]ἐν τοῖς ὑψίστοις. Clausal complement (direct discourse) of ἔκραζον. This cry contains two portions from the Hebrew text of Ps 118:25-26. Ὡσαννά is a transliteration of the Hebrew *hôšî῾â nā᾿* (LXX: σῶσον δή). εὐλογημένος ὁ ἐρχόμενος ἐν ὀνόματι κυρίου is identical to the LXX. The other half of the statement (v. 10) is not quoted from the OT, though it reflects common OT idioms.

Ὡσαννά. Although originally a part of the liturgy as part of the Hallel, "by the first century ... its use in Ps 118 was no longer understood literally as a cry by those shouting for God . . . to now save the people of Israel from their enemies ['save, I pray!']. Being repeated by pilgrims each year at the various major festivals, it had become more idiomatic in nature and was by then an expression of joy and jubilation, much as in the use of the word today" (Stein 2008, 505). For the possibility that a wordplay on Jesus' name is involved here, see Gundry, 630.

Εὐλογημένος. Prf pass ptc masc nom sg εὐλογέω. Predicate participle in a verbless clause.

ὁ ἐρχόμενος. Pres mid ptc masc nom sg ἔρχομαι (substantival). Nominative subject in a verbless clause. "It is a question of feeling, whether ἐστί or ἔστε is to be supplied here; whether it invokes a blessing on the coming king and his kingdom, or pronounces him blessed. Either is grammatically allowable" (Gould, 209). The phrase ὁ ἐρχόμενος ἐν ὀνόματι κυρίου is probably not, on its own, a Messianic title, but "the context seems to cast a messianic light on the phrase" (Gundry, 630).

ἐν ὀνόματι κυρίου. "With authority to act on behalf of the Lord" (Gundry, 631).

11:10 Εὐλογημένη ἡ ἐρχομένη βασιλεία τοῦ πατρὸς ἡμῶν Δαυίδ· Ὡσαννὰ ἐν τοῖς ὑψίστοις.

Εὐλογημένη. Prf pass ptc fem nom sg εὐλογέω. Predicate participle in a verbless clause.

ἡ . . . βασιλεία. Nominative subject in a verbless clause.

ἐρχομένη. Pres mid ptc fem nom sg ἔρχομαι (attributive).

Ὡσαννὰ. See verse 9.

ἐν τοῖς ὑψίστοις. Spatial. The expression refers to heaven: "in the highest (place)."

11:11 Καὶ εἰσῆλθεν εἰς Ἱεροσόλυμα εἰς τὸ ἱερὸν καὶ περιβλεψά-μενος πάντα, ὀψίας ἤδη οὔσης τῆς ὥρας, ἐξῆλθεν εἰς Βηθανίαν μετὰ τῶν δώδεκα.

εἰσῆλθεν. Aor act ind 3rd sg εἰσέρχομαι.

εἰς Ἱεροσόλυμα. Spatial. On the form of Ἱεροσόλυμα, see 3:8.

εἰς τὸ ἱερὸν. Spatial. The second phrase narrows the reference further. For a similar repetition of εἰς, see verse 1. The use of ἱερόν generally refers to the entire temple complex (cf. ναός, which is commonly the sanctuary proper).

περιβλεψάμενος. Aor mid ptc masc nom sg περιβλέπω (temporal).

πάντα. Accusative direct object of περιβλεψάμενος.

ὀψίας ἤδη οὔσης τῆς ὥρας. A temporal expression indicating that it was already late in the evening ("the hour being already late").

ὀψίας. Predicate genitive adjective.

οὔσης. Pres act ptc fem gen sg εἰμί. Genitive absolute (see 1:32), causal.

τῆς ὥρας. Genitive subject of οὔσης.

ἐξῆλθεν. Aor act ind 3rd sg ἐξέρχομαι.

εἰς Βηθανίαν. Spatial.

μετὰ τῶν δώδεκα. Association.

Mark 11:12-19

[12]On the next day as they were leaving Bethany he was hungry. [13]Seeing a fig tree from a distance that had leaves, he went (to see) if perhaps he would find something on it. And coming to it he found nothing except leaves, for it was not the season for figs. [14]So he said to it, "May no one ever eat fruit from you again!" And his disciples heard (him).

[15]Then they went into Jerusalem and entering the temple he began to throw out those who were selling and buying in the temple, and he overturned the tables of the money changers and the seats of those who were selling doves. [16]He did not permit anyone to carry merchandise through the temple. [17]Then he taught and said to them, "Is it not written, 'My house will be called a house of prayer for all people'? But you have made it a den of thieves." [18]Now the chief priests and the scribes heard (this) and they were seeking how they might destroy him, for they feared him, for all the crowd was amazed because of his teaching. [19]When evening came, they went out of the city.

This pericope is another example of Mark's "sandwich stories" in which two events are described, with one sandwiched in the middle of the other. Here the cleansing of the temple (vv. 15-19) is enclosed in the account of the barren fig tree (vv. 12-14, 20-25). This sandwich uses the outer story to focus attention on and to explain the significance of the inner story: the barren fig tree is a picture of the temple, Jesus' cursing of the tree functions as his pronouncement of judgment on the temple. "Barrenness occurs in the OT as an expression of Israel's failure to produce appropriate fruit for God (e.g., Jer 8:13; Mic 1:7), as well as an expression of God's judgment (e.g., Jer 7:20; Hos 9:16)" (Evans 2001, 155).

11:12 Καὶ τῇ ἐπαύριον ἐξελθόντων αὐτῶν ἀπὸ Βηθανίας ἐπείνασεν.

τῇ ἐπαύριον. Dative of time. ἐπαύριον is an adverb used as part of an elliptical phrase (τῇ ἐπαύριον ἡμέρᾳ). This is the only occurrence of ἐπαύριον in Mark (it is most common in Acts); in the NT it occurs only in this elliptical expression and only with the dative (see also *TDM*, 64–65, 67; cf. BDAG, LSJ).

ἐξελθόντων. Aor act ptc masc gen pl ἐξέρχομαι. Genitive absolute (see 1:32), temporal. On the use of the plural verb here, see 5:38.

αὐτῶν. Genitive subject of ἐξελθόντων. For further discussion and examples of the genitive absolute, see 1:32; and regarding the subject in such a construction, see 5:2.

ἀπὸ Βηθανίας. Separation. Mark normally uses ἐκ with ἐξέρχομαι, which would be typical of Greek syntax in repeating the prefixed preposition, but ἀπό is beginning to replace ἐκ in Koine (MHT 3:259; see also Zerwick §§87–88). This is the only instance in Mark of ἀπό with ἐξέρχομαι, and there does not appear to be any difference in meaning.

ἐπείνασεν. Aor act ind 3rd sg πεινάω.

11:13 καὶ ἰδὼν συκῆν ἀπὸ μακρόθεν ἔχουσαν φύλλα ἦλθεν, εἰ ἄρα τι εὑρήσει ἐν αὐτῇ, καὶ ἐλθὼν ἐπ᾽ αὐτὴν οὐδὲν εὗρεν εἰ μὴ φύλλα· ὁ γὰρ καιρὸς οὐκ ἦν σύκων.

ἰδών. Aor act ptc masc nom sg ὁράω (temporal).
συκῆν. Accusative direct object of ἰδών.
ἀπὸ μακρόθεν. Locative ("from a distance," see 5:6).
ἔχουσαν. Pres act ptc fem acc sg ἔχω (attributive, modifying συκῆν).
φύλλα. Accusative direct object of ἔχουσαν.
ἦλθεν. Aor act ind 3rd sg ἔρχομαι.
εἰ ἄρα. Introduces a tentative, indirect question (BDAG, 127.3, s.v. ἄρα): "in these circumstances" (V. Taylor, 459). The particle εἰ is used "in virtual questions expressing an uncertain expectation associated with an effort to attain something" (Zerwick §403.c.β).
τι. Accusative direct object of εὑρήσει.
εὑρήσει. Fut act ind 3rd sg εὑρίσκω. A subjunctive would be more common in this sort of statement. "The vivid fut. εὑρήσει represents εὑρήσω [i.e., the first singular] in the implied direct question" (V. Taylor, 459).
ἐν αὐτῇ. Locative.

ἐλθών. Aor act ptc masc nom sg ἔρχομαι (temporal).

ἐπ᾽ αὐτήν. Spatial, modifying ἐλθών.

οὐδέν. Accusative direct object of εὗρεν.

εὗρεν. Aor act ind 3rd sg εὑρίσκω.

εἰ μή. Idiom: "except" (see 2:7).

φύλλα. Accusative direct object of an implied εὗρεν.

γάρ. Introduces an explanatory phrase that clarifies that it is not figs for which Jesus was looking since it was not yet the season (καιρός) for them. It could be explained as giving the reason for ἦλθεν, εἰ ἄρα τι εὑρήσει ἐν αὐτῇ: "How then does the unseasonability of *figs* explain why Jesus did not find *buds*? It does not, and the nonsense of thinking that it does shows that the γάρ-clause, 'for the season was not of figs,' takes two steps backward to explain why Jesus went to find 'something' instead of 'figs' or 'fruit'" (Gundry, 636). Edwards paraphrases, "It was, of course, not the season for figs, but it was for *paggim*" (2002, 340). France thinks this is too awkward and places too much weight on τι, preferring instead to conclude that "for Mark, Jesus' frustration *was* horticulturally unreasonable" (441 n. 43; cf. Stein 2008, 513). It would seem, however, that it is γάρ that would be unreasonable and awkward given France's analysis.

ὁ . . . καιρός. Predicate nominative.

ἦν. Impf act ind 3rd sg εἰμί.

σύκων. Genitive of time: "season *for figs*."

11:14 καὶ ἀποκριθεὶς εἶπεν αὐτῇ, Μηκέτι εἰς τὸν αἰῶνα ἐκ σοῦ μηδεὶς καρπὸν φάγοι. καὶ ἤκουον οἱ μαθηταὶ αὐτοῦ.

ἀποκριθείς. Aor mid ptc masc nom sg ἀποκρίνομαι (means; redundant participle of speaking). On this intransitive, "θη middle" form, see 3:33. The use of this verb is typical, not "striking" as Gundry suggests (638). It simply means "to respond" (here, to the situation).

εἶπεν. Aor act ind 3rd sg λέγω.

αὐτῇ. Dative indirect object of εἶπεν.

Μηκέτι . . . μηδεὶς καρπὸν φάγοι. Clausal complement (direct discourse) of εἶπεν. This is a rather emphatic statement with two μή–negatives, the temporal phrase εἰς τὸν αἰῶνα, and the rare optative form (esp. without ἄν).

εἰς τὸν αἰῶνα. Temporal idiomatic expression that here means "never again" (BDAG, 32.1.b, s.v. αἰών).

ἐκ σοῦ. Source.

μηδείς. Nominative subject of φάγοι.

καρπὸν. Accusative direct object of φάγοι.

φάγοι. Aor act opt 3rd sg ἐσθίω. This is the only optative mood verb in Mark. The optative is usually described as the mood of "wish" (Latin, *opto*), though it has a broader range of use. It was dying out in the Koine; there are only sixty-eight instances in the NT, with twenty-eight occurring in Luke–Acts, none in Matthew, and only one in John. Lee lists this as an instance of "elevated tone" in Mark's record of Jesus' words, "in keeping with the status of the speaker" (13–15; see also 14:7). The LXX has far more optatives (590), though in relative frequency the difference is not that great. In the present passage the optative has been described as expressing an "adverse wish" (BDF §384), though perhaps imprecation is the better term, since this statement is described in verse 21 as a curse (καταράομαι; cf. Acts 8:20). In Matthew's account the statement is worded slightly differently and the optative is replaced by a subjunctive: μηκέτι ἐκ σοῦ καρπὸς γένηται εἰς τὸν αἰῶνα (21:19).

ἤκουον. Impf act ind 3rd pl ἀκούω. The imperfect is used here to provide background information that will be important later in the narrative (cf. Bruce, 417).

οἱ μαθηταὶ. Nominative subject of ἤκουον.

11:15 Καὶ ἔρχονται εἰς Ἱεροσόλυμα. καὶ εἰσελθὼν εἰς τὸ ἱερὸν ἤρξατο ἐκβάλλειν τοὺς πωλοῦντας καὶ τοὺς ἀγοράζοντας ἐν τῷ ἱερῷ, καὶ τὰς τραπέζας τῶν κολλυβιστῶν καὶ τὰς καθέδρας τῶν πωλούντων τὰς περιστερὰς κατέστρεψεν,

Verses 15-19 function as the center of a typical Markan "sandwich story." The outer story consists of verses 12-14 and 20-21 (see also 3:22).

ἔρχονται. Pres mid ind 3rd pl ἔρχομαι. The present tense introduces a new paragraph (see 1:21). On the use of the plural verb here, see 5:38.

εἰς Ἱεροσόλυμα. Spatial. On the form of Ἱεροσόλυμα, see 3:8.

εἰσελθὼν. Aor act ptc masc nom sg εἰσέρχομαι (temporal).

εἰς τὸ ἱερὸν. Spatial. The reference is to the temple complex generally, not the sanctuary proper (which is more commonly referred to by ναός). In the context it becomes apparent that the Court of the Gentiles is intended since that is where the temple market was located.

ἤρξατο. Aor mid ind 3rd sg ἄρχω.

ἐκβάλλειν. Pres act inf ἐκβάλλω (complementary).

τοὺς πωλοῦντας καὶ τοὺς ἀγοράζοντας. Pres act ptc masc acc pl πωλέω, ἀγοράζω (substantival). Accusative direct object of ἤρξατο ἐκβάλλειν.

ἐν τῷ ἱερῷ. Locative.

τὰς τραπέζας … καὶ τὰς καθέδρας. Accusative direct object of κατέστρεψεν. The noun καθέδρα means "chair, seat" (BDAG, 490).

τῶν κολλυβιστῶν. Possessive genitive modifying τραπέζας. A κολλυβιστής is a "money changer" (BDAG, 556).

τῶν πωλούντων. Pres act ptc masc gen pl πωλέω (substantival). Possessive genitive modifying τὰς καθέδρας.

τὰς περιστερὰς. Accusative direct object of πωλούντων.

κατέστρεψεν. Aor act ind 3rd sg καταστρέφω ("upset, overturn," BDAG, 528.1).

11:16 καὶ οὐκ ἤφιεν ἵνα τις διενέγκῃ σκεῦος διὰ τοῦ ἱεροῦ.

ἤφιεν. Impf act ind 3rd sg ἀφίημι. On the form, see 1:34 (the only other imperfect of ἀφίημι in the NT).

ἵνα. When ἀφίημι has a verbal complement following, it is normally an infinitive (e.g., 1:34; 5:37; 7:12, 27; 10:14; 15:36). This is the only instance in the NT of its use with ἵνα). Grammatically parallel is the use of a ἵνα clause as a substitute for an infinitive (see BDAG, 476.2.a, s.v. ἵνα), which occurs frequently in the NT and in Mark.

τις. Nominative subject of διενέγκῃ.

διενέγκῃ. Aor act subj 3rd sg διαφέρω. Subjunctive with ἵνα.

σκεῦος. Accusative direct object of διενέγκῃ. This is a very broad word, not limited to "vessels," but it should not be expanded to include "anything" (e.g., RSV, NRSV, ESV). "The manner in which σκεῦος is translated depends in many instances upon the specific context. It may, of course, be rendered by a highly generic expression such as English 'thing,' but wherever the context refers to some particular type of object, it is preferable to employ a specific referent" (LN 6.1). In this context "merchandise" appears to be justifiable in light of the buying and selling referenced in the preceding verse (NIV, NET; cf. NASB; see also the NET note).

διὰ τοῦ ἱεροῦ. Spatial.

11:17 καὶ ἐδίδασκεν καὶ ἔλεγεν αὐτοῖς, Οὐ γέγραπται ὅτι Ὁ οἶκός μου οἶκος προσευχῆς κληθήσεται πᾶσιν τοῖς ἔθνεσιν; ὑμεῖς δὲ πεποιήκατε αὐτὸν σπήλαιον λῃστῶν.

ἐδίδασκεν. Impf act ind 3rd sg διδάσκω. On the possibility that this is an inceptive imperfect as in several modern translations, see 1:21.

ἔλεγεν. Impf act ind 3rd sg λέγω. This is the only combination in the NT of these two verbs in the imperfect (though they occur together with one or the other as a participle in 12:35; cf. Matt 5:2); "it may indicate continuous teaching, in which more was said than is recorded" (V. Taylor, 463). Gundry, however, overstates the significance of three imperfect verbs in close proximity (ἤφιεν, ἐδίδασκεν, ἔλεγεν), insisting that the prohibition and teaching/speaking were taking place "simultaneously with his beginning to throw out the sellers and buyers and with his overturning the tables of the dove-sellers" (640). This not only mixes two sentences (note the punctuation in both the Greek text and the English versions, vv. 15-16, 17), but also assumes *Aktionsart* values for the tenses. The imperfects are not part of the main storyline, which is presented with aorist verbs (ἤρξατο ἐκβάλλειν, κατέστρεψεν, v. 15), but rather introduce background information (ἤφιεν, v. 16) and explanation (ἐδίδασκεν, ἔλεγεν, v. 17). Although there are not explicit temporal deictic indicators in the context (other than the narrative sequence of events), the events described seem best suited to a teaching time following the temple cleansing. The function of Jesus' teaching is to explain (after "the dust has settled") the reasons for his actions. It does not seem reasonable to think that Jesus shouting out verse 17 while turning over tables would be described as ἐδίδασκεν καὶ ἔλεγεν αὐτοῖς, despite Gundry's claim that "the awkwardness of saying that 'he was teaching' while throwing out traffickers and overturning tables shows the extent to which Mark goes to stress Jesus' exercise of didactic authority" (640).

αὐτοῖς. Dative indirect object of ἔλεγεν.

Οὐ γέγραπται . . . σπήλαιον λῃστῶν. Clausal complement (direct discourse) of ἔλεγεν.

γέγραπται. Prf pass ind 3rd sg γράφω. Used with the negative οὐ in a rhetorical question, a positive answer is implied.

ὅτι. On the recitative use of ὅτι, here used with γέγραπται to introduce an exact OT quotation from LXX Isa 56:7, see 1:15.

Ὁ οἶκός. Nominative subject of κληθήσεται.

μου. The genitive pronoun μου refers to God in the Isaianic context. It could be taken as a claim of temple ownership by Jesus in the Markan context (with μου referring to Jesus; so Gundry, 640), but if so it is only by implication and is not grammatically explicit.

οἶκος. Complement in a subject-complement double nominative construction with a passive verb (on the construction, see Culy 2009, 86). (With an active verb this would have been an

object-complement double accusative construction.) That it is anarthrous probably points to its qualitative force: "the Jerusalem temple
should have the function or nature of being a house of prayer for all
the nations" (Harner, 78).

προσευχῆς. This genitive describes the purpose for which God
intended the temple, "a house intended for prayer."

κληθήσεται. Fut pass ind 3rd sg καλέω.

πᾶσιν τοῖς ἔθνεσιν. Dative of advantage.

ὑμεῖς. Nominative subject of πεποιήκατε. This explicit nominative pronoun contrasts with μου in the previous clause.

δὲ. The conjunction contrasts the content of the OT quotation
(God's purpose for the temple) with current conditions in the
temple by citing two words from Jer 7:11 (σπήλαιον λῃστῶν). The
phrase is sufficiently distinctive to identify the passage to which
Jesus alludes; it occurs nowhere else in the LXX.

πεποιήκατε. Prf act ind 2nd pl ποιέω. The stative aspect describes
the contemporary conditions at the temple. Matthew uses a present
tense (ποιεῖτε, 21:13) and Luke an aorist (ἐποιήσατε, 19:46).

αὐτὸν. Accusative direct object of πεποιήκατε.

σπήλαιον. Complement in an object-complement double accusative construction.

λῃστῶν. "A den *characterized by thieves.*"

**11:18 καὶ ἤκουσαν οἱ ἀρχιερεῖς καὶ οἱ γραμματεῖς καὶ ἐζήτουν
πῶς αὐτὸν ἀπολέσωσιν· ἐφοβοῦντο γὰρ αὐτόν, πᾶς γὰρ ὁ ὄχλος
ἐξεπλήσσετο ἐπὶ τῇ διδαχῇ αὐτοῦ.**

καὶ ἤκουσαν ... καὶ ἐζήτουν. The parataxis here points to the
"definite connection ... between the cleansing of the Temple and
the plot of the chief priests and scribes against Jesus" (Cranfield,
359). As often when Mark connects an aorist with an imperfect, the
aorist describes the main, storyline event and the imperfect records
an oblique comment, sometimes indicating a consequence or explanation of the lead verb (e.g., 5:42; 7:35).

ἤκουσαν. Aor act ind 3rd pl ἀκούω.

οἱ ἀρχιερεῖς καὶ οἱ γραμματεῖς. Nominative subject of ἤκουσαν
... καὶ ἐζήτουν.

ἐζήτουν. Impf act ind 3rd pl ζητέω. On the possibility that this is
an inceptive imperfect as in ISV and NLT, see 1:21. There is no contextual evidence to suggest that this is an iterative statement (contra
Stein 2008, 518).

πῶς. "Used in an indirect sense, and the clause implies a

deliberative question: 'How are we to destroy him?" (V. Taylor, 464; cf. Lane, 403 n. 33).

αὐτὸν. Accusative direct object of ἀπολέσωσιν.

ἀπολέσωσιν. Aor act subj 3rd pl ἀπόλλυμι (deliberative subjunctive).

ἐφοβοῦντο. Impf mid ind 3rd pl φοβέομαι. The imperfect is used in an explanatory γάρ clause giving background information as to why they were trying to destroy Jesus.

αὐτὸν. Accusative direct object of ἐφοβοῦντο.

ὁ ὄχλος. Nominative subject of ἐξεπλήσσετο.

ἐξεπλήσσετο. Impf mid ind 3rd sg ἐκπλήσσω (see also 1:22). The imperfect is used in an additional explanatory γάρ clause giving background information as to why they feared Jesus; the second γάρ clause is subordinate to the first. Although two sequential γάρ clauses without an intervening conjunction or other clause are not common (there are about two dozen in the NT: Matt 6:32; Mark 9:6; Luke 6:44; 8:29; 20:36; John 3:34; 5:46; Acts 4:34; 26:26; 27:34; Rom 1:16; 2:1; 5:7; 6:14; 7:15; 13:4, 6; 1 Cor 9:16 [3×!]; 16:7; 2 Cor 10:14; 11:2; 12:6, 11; Gal 3:10; Heb 5:13), it is not a matter of "infelicity" (as Gundry, 641, claims).

ἐπὶ τῇ διδαχῇ. Cause. The teaching probably includes not only the oral teaching mentioned in verse 17, but also Jesus' actions (cf. 1:27).

11:19 Καὶ ὅταν ὀψὲ ἐγένετο, ἐξεπορεύοντο ἔξω τῆς πόλεως.

ὅταν. The use of ὅταν with an indicative, and especially an aorist, is unusual, though it is not uncommon in the vernacular Koine. The reference is probably to a specific event rather than a summary of a repeated pattern (Cranfield, 359; contra Swete, 258, who sees a reference to "the Lord's practice on each of the first three days of Holy Week"), given the perfective aspect of ἐγένετο (see 3:11).

ὀψὲ. Predicate adverb ("late") used almost as a substantive here: "evening" (BDAG, 746.2).

ἐγένετο. Aor mid ind 3rd sg γίνομαι.

ἐξεπορεύοντο. Impf mid ind 3rd pl ἐκπορεύομαι. To see the imperfect as implying an inceptive (Stein 2008, 519) or iterative (Gundry, 647) situation reads more into a tense than can be justified from the context. The flow of the narrative makes it obvious that the unexpressed subject is Jesus and his disciples.

ἔξω τῆς πόλεως. The adverb ἔξω here functions as a preposition with the genitive to indicate where they went.

Mark 11:20-26

[20]As they passed by early in the morning they saw the fig tree withered from the roots. [21]Peter, remembering, said to him, "Rabbi, Look! The fig tree which you cursed is withered. [22]Answering, Jesus said to them, "Have faith in God. [23]Truly I say to you that whoever says to this mountain, 'Arise and be cast into the sea,' and does not doubt in his heart, but believes that what he says will take place, it will happen for him. [24]Therefore, I say to you, whatever you pray and ask, believe that you will receive (it), and it will be yours. [25]And whenever you stand to pray, if you have anything against anyone, forgive, in order that your Father who is in heaven will also forgive you your offenses."

11:20 Καὶ παραπορευόμενοι πρωῒ εἶδον τὴν συκῆν ἐξηραμμένην ἐκ ῥιζῶν.

παραπορευόμενοι. Pres mid ptc masc nom pl παραπορεύομαι (temporal; "go/pass by/through").

πρωῒ. Temporal adverb ("early"), modifying παραπορευόμενοι, that is sometimes as specific as the fourth watch of the night (3–6 a.m.). To emphasize that πρωῒ refers to what the disciples could see "in the *clear morning light*" that they might not have noticed as they passed the tree in the dark the previous evening (so Bruce, 418) is to overread the text.

εἶδον. Aor act ind 3rd pl ὁράω. The unexpressed subject is Jesus and the disciples.

τὴν συκῆν. Accusative direct object of εἶδον.

ἐξηραμμένην ἐκ ῥιζῶν. Lane (408 n. 48) suggests that this wording is close enough to LXX Hos 9:16 (τὰς ῥίζας αὐτοῦ ἐξηράνθη) to justify an intentional allusion by Mark. Given the topic of Hosea (particularly ch. 9) and Jesus' purpose for cursing the fig tree, this may be a credible suggestion, despite there being only two words that match (and only in lexical form).

ἐξηραμμένην. Prf pass ptc fem acc sg ξηραίνω (attributive). The stative aspect describes the condition of the tree as observed by the disciples. That this was a permanent condition is consistent with Jesus' statement (μηκέτι εἰς τὸν αἰῶνα ἐκ σοῦ μηδεὶς καρπὸν φάγοι, v. 14), but cannot be based on the perfect tense (contra Gundry, 648).

ἐκ ῥιζῶν. Source, in contrast to wilted leaves.

11:21 καὶ ἀναμνησθεὶς ὁ Πέτρος λέγει αὐτῷ, Ῥαββί, ἴδε ἡ συκῆ ἣν κατηράσω ἐξήρανται.

ἀναμνησθεὶς. Aor mid ptc masc nom sg ἀναμιμνήσκομαι. This is a "θη middle" form, not passive (see 2:2). In the middle or passive this verb means "to remember."

ὁ Πέτρος. Nominative subject of λέγει.

λέγει. Pres act ind 3rd sg λέγω.

αὐτῷ. Dative indirect object of λέγει.

Ῥαββί, ἴδε . . . ἐξήρανται. Clausal complement (direct discourse) of λέγει.

Ῥαββί, ἴδε. The vocative followed by an interjection appears to indicate that Peter was startled. On ἴδε, see 3:34. BDAG (466.3) classes ἴδε as meaning "here" in this verse, but that makes for a very awkward statement since a form of εἰμί would then have to be supplied. It is better to take it as an interjection and allow ἐξήρανται to function as the main verb (so most translations). On ῥαββί, see 9:5.

ἡ συκῆ. Nominative subject of ἐξήρανται.

ἣν. Accusative direct object of κατηράσω.

κατηράσω. Aor mid ind 2nd sg καταράομαι ("to curse"). In earlier literature καταράομαι was normally followed by a dative (Gould, 215 n. 1), but in the NT the two instances with a complement are accusative (see also Jas 3:9).

ἐξήρανται. Prf pass ind 3rd sg ξηραίνω. The stative aspect describes the condition of the fig tree when Peter saw it.

11:22 καὶ ἀποκριθεὶς ὁ Ἰησοῦς λέγει αὐτοῖς, Ἔχετε πίστιν θεοῦ.

ἀποκριθεὶς. Aor mid ptc masc nom sg ἀποκρίνομαι (means; redundant participle of speaking). On this intransitive, "θη middle" form, see 3:33.

ὁ Ἰησοῦς. Nominative subject of λέγει.

λέγει. Pres act ind 3rd sg λέγω.

αὐτοῖς. Dative indirect object of λέγει.

Ἔχετε πίστιν θεοῦ . . . τὰ παραπτώματα ὑμῶν (v. 25). Clausal complement (direct discourse) of λέγει.

Ἔχετε. Pres act impv 2nd pl ἔχω.

πίστιν. Accusative direct object of ἔχετε.

θεοῦ. Objective genitive (so Wallace 1996, 116, and many commentators): "faith in God" (cf. "faith which rests on God," Swete, 259). It is "a more arresting expression for πιστεύετε θεῷ, but does not differ in meaning" (France, 448). "The suggestion that the genitive is subjective—'have the sort of faith God has'—is surely a monstrosity of exegesis" (Cranfield, 361; see also Gundry, 651 for additional discussion).

11:23 ἀμὴν λέγω ὑμῖν ὅτι ὃς ἂν εἴπῃ τῷ ὄρει τούτῳ, Ἄρθητι καὶ βλήθητι εἰς τὴν θάλασσαν, καὶ μὴ διακριθῇ ἐν τῇ καρδίᾳ αὐτοῦ ἀλλὰ πιστεύῃ ὅτι ὃ λαλεῖ γίνεται, ἔσται αὐτῷ.

ἀμὴν λέγω ὑμῖν. See 3:28.

λέγω. Pres act ind 1st sg λέγω.

ὅτι. Introduces the clausal complement (direct discourse) of λέγω.

ὃς ἂν. Indefinite relative pronoun ("whoever") functioning as the nominative subject of εἴπῃ.

εἴπῃ. Aor act subj 3rd sg λέγω. Subjunctive with ἄν.

τῷ ὄρει τούτῳ. Dative indirect object of εἴπῃ. Given the geographical location of this statement, the referent of "this mountain" is presumably the Mount of Olives. The demonstrative "points . . . to a particular rather than a general referent" (Evans 2001, 188, though he sees it as a reference to the Temple Mount). It is possible, however, that no particular referent is intended, especially if the following statement is taken as proverbial.

Ἄρθητι καὶ βλήθητι εἰς τὴν θάλασσαν. Clausal complement (direct discourse) of εἴπῃ.

Ἄρθητι. Aor pass impv 2nd sg αἴρω. Both this imperative and the following one are part of a "performative statement . . . couched in imperatival terms for rhetorical effect" (Wallace 1996, 492 n. 7). The agent of the passive voice is not identified, but the tenor and context of the statement (i.e., prayer, προσεύχεσθε, v. 24) suggest that God is understood as the one who would perform these actions.

βλήθητι. Aor pass impv 2nd sg βάλλω.

εἰς τὴν θάλασσαν. Spatial.

διακριθῇ. Aor mid subj 3rd sg διακρίνω. This is a "θη middle" form, not passive (see 2:2). Subjunctive with ἄν. The use of διακρίνω with the meaning "to doubt, waver," rather than the more common "to separate, distinguish, evaluate," is first found in the NT (BDAG, 231.6).

ἐν τῇ καρδίᾳ. Sphere.

ἀλλὰ. Introduces a contrasting statement following the negative μὴ διακριθῇ.

πιστεύῃ. Pres act subj 3rd sg πιστεύω. Subjunctive with ἄν.

ὅτι. Introduces a content clause specifying what is to be believed.

ὃ λαλεῖ. The relative clause functions as the nominative subject of γίνεται.

ὅ. Accusative direct object of λαλεῖ.

λαλεῖ. Pres act ind 3rd sg λαλέω.

γίνεται. Pres mid ind 3rd sg γίνομαι. The time reference is future. For γίνομαι meaning "to take place," see BDAG (197.4). Stein questionably wants to translate this verb as present time ("is coming about") suggesting that it "adds additional emphasis and encouragement to seek the kind of faith commanded" (2008, 520).

ἔσται. Fut mid ind 3rd sg εἰμί. For εἰμί with the dative meaning "happen to/for them," see BDAG (285.6).

αὐτῷ. Dative of advantage.

11:24 διὰ τοῦτο λέγω ὑμῖν, πάντα ὅσα προσεύχεσθε καὶ αἰτεῖσθε, πιστεύετε ὅτι ἐλάβετε, καὶ ἔσται ὑμῖν.

διὰ τοῦτο. Introduces an inference: "for this reason, therefore."

λέγω. Pres act ind 1st sg λέγω.

ὑμῖν. Dative indirect object of λέγω.

πάντα ὅσα. Accusative direct object of προσεύχεσθε καὶ αἰτεῖσθε ("whatever").

προσεύχεσθε καὶ αἰτεῖσθε. Translations vary as to whether or not this is an example of hendiadys: "whatever you *ask in prayer*" (e.g., RSV, ESV; cf. NIV, NRSV, ISV) or "whatever you *pray and ask* for" (e.g., NET; cf. NASB, HCSB). On hendiadys, see BDF (§442.16), Young (243), and Zerwick (§460).

προσεύχεσθε. Pres mid ind 2nd pl προσεύχομαι.

αἰτεῖσθε. Pres mid ind 2nd pl αἰτέω.

πιστεύετε. Pres act impv 2nd pl πιστεύω (see 1:15). The imperative expresses an implied condition, "if you believe" (Robertson, 1023.c.β; see also Burton §269.c).

ἐλάβετε. Aor act ind 2nd pl λαμβάνω. The lexis of πιστεύετε ὅτι ἐλάβετε and the mood of πιστεύετε imply a future situation. "An aorist after a future condition is, to a certain extent, futuristic" (BDF §333.2). This does not require that one believe "that you have received it already" as France (450) suggests, nor does it reflect a Semitic "prophetic perfect" as Evans (2001, 184 n. e) claims.

ἔσται. Fut mid ind 3rd sg εἰμί.

ὑμῖν. Dative of possession with an equative verb (see Wallace 1996, 149–51).

11:25 καὶ ὅταν στήκετε προσευχόμενοι, ἀφίετε εἴ τι ἔχετε κατά τινος, ἵνα καὶ ὁ πατὴρ ὑμῶν ὁ ἐν τοῖς οὐρανοῖς ἀφῇ ὑμῖν τὰ παραπτώματα ὑμῶν.

ὅταν. The use of ὅταν with a present indicative verb is not common in Mark. In this case the imperfective aspect of στήκετε is probably employed to reference action periodically repeated (so RSV and most English translations; contra NIV). See 3:11 and *TDM*, 87–88 for further discussion.

στήκετε. Pres act ind 2nd pl στήκω.

προσευχόμενοι. Pres mid ptc masc nom pl προσεύχομαι. The participle could be purpose ("when you stand to pray") or temporal ("when you stand while you are praying"), but the latter seems redundant following a temporal ὅταν clause. Attendant circumstance does not seem likely given the tenses and word order. Perhaps, in light of the rest of the sentence, we are to think of a particular occasion for prayer in the synagogue or temple in which it would be customary to stand; if so, purpose makes good sense.

ἀφίετε. Pres act impv 2nd pl ἀφίημι. This is a one-word apodosis of a first-class condition; the protasis follows in the next clause.

εἴ. Introduces the protasis of a first-class condition.

τι. Accusative direct object of ἔχετε.

ἔχετε. Pres act ind 2nd pl ἔχω.

κατά τινος. Opposition.

ἵνα. Introduces a purpose clause that provides a rationale for obeying the command in the apodosis of the preceding conditional statement.

ὁ πατὴρ. Nominative subject of ἀφῇ. John likewise uses πατὴρ ὑμῶν only once (20:17), Luke has it three times (6:36; 12:30, 32), but it is more common in Matthew (5:16, 45, 48; 6:1, 8, 14, 15, 26, 32; 7:11; 10:20, 29; 18:14; cf. 23:9). It appears nowhere else in the NT and the concept is rare in the LXX (cf. Mal 2:10).

ὁ ἐν τοῖς οὐρανοῖς. The article ὁ is an adjectivizer changing the prepositional phrase into an adjective modifying ὁ πατήρ.

ἀφῇ. Aor act subj 3rd sg ἀφίημι. Subjunctive with ἵνα.

ὑμῖν. Dative of advantage.

τὰ παραπτώματα. Accusative direct object of ἀφῇ. Although common in Paul (16 uses), this word is rare in the Gospels; other than this verse it occurs only in Matt 6:14, 15.

11:26

Verse 26 is a later scribal addition found in the Majority Text, probably picked up from the D or Θ texts (the earliest mss with this verse). It is not present in earlier manuscripts such as ℵ B L W Δ Ψ etc.

Mark 11:27-33

²⁷They came again to Jerusalem, and while he was walking in the temple the chief priests and the scribes and the elders came to him ²⁸and said to him, "By what authority do you do these things? Who gave you this authority that you do these things?" ²⁹But Jesus said to them, "I will ask you a question. Answer me and I will tell you by what authority I do these things. ³⁰The baptism that John performed—was it from heaven or from humans? Answer me!" ³¹They deliberated among themselves, "If we say, 'from heaven,' he will say, '[Then] why didn't you believe him?' ³²But if we say, 'from humans. . . .'" They feared the populace, for everyone truly thought John to be a prophet. ³³So they answered Jesus, "We don't know." Jesus said to them, "Neither will I tell you by what authority I do these things."

11:27 Καὶ ἔρχονται πάλιν εἰς Ἰεροσόλυμα. καὶ ἐν τῷ ἱερῷ περιπατοῦντος αὐτοῦ ἔρχονται πρὸς αὐτὸν οἱ ἀρχιερεῖς καὶ οἱ γραμματεῖς καὶ οἱ πρεσβύτεροι

ἔρχονται. Pres mid ind 3rd pl ἔρχομαι. The present tense with past time reference (narrative present) introduces a new paragraph (see 1:21 on εἰσπορεύονται). On the use of the plural verb here, see 5:38. The unexpressed subject is Jesus and the disciples.

πάλιν. This is now the third time that Jesus has entered the city; the first two are mentioned in 11:11, 15.

εἰς Ἰεροσόλυμα. Spatial. On the form of Ἰεροσόλυμα, see 3:8.

ἐν τῷ ἱερῷ. Locative.

περιπατοῦντος. Pres act ptc masc gen sg περιπατέω. Genitive absolute (see 1:32), temporal.

αὐτοῦ. Genitive subject of περιπατοῦντος. On the overlap of reference with αὐτόν in the main clause, see 5:2 and 14:3.

ἔρχονται. Pres mid ind 3rd pl ἔρχομαι. The present tense with past time reference (narrative present) introduces new participants into the discourse (see 1:21 on εἰσπορεύονται).

πρὸς αὐτὸν. Spatial.

οἱ ἀρχιερεῖς καὶ οἱ γραμματεῖς καὶ οἱ πρεσβύτεροι. Nominative subject of ἔρχονται. Swete (262) deduces from the repeated article that the persons mentioned are official representatives of their respective groups. Although that seems probable from the context, it is not likely justified by the articles alone.

11:28 καὶ ἔλεγον αὐτῷ, Ἐν ποίᾳ ἐξουσίᾳ ταῦτα ποιεῖς; ἢ τίς σοι ἔδωκεν τὴν ἐξουσίαν ταύτην ἵνα ταῦτα ποιῇς;

ἔλεγον. Impf act ind 3rd pl λέγω.

αὐτῷ. Dative indirect object of ἔλεγον.

Ἐν ποίᾳ ἐξουσίᾳ. Instrumental. The interrogative pronoun ποῖος modifies ἐξουσίᾳ. "In some cases [ποῖος] takes the place of the gen. of the interrog. τίς (in dir. as well as indir. questions. . . .)" (BDAG, 843.2.a.γ, s.v. ποῖος), thus "by whose authority?" Alternatively, it may "[center] attention on the nature of the authority" (Gundry, 657; this would be BDAG's category 1, "interrogative ref. to class or kind"), but that seems less likely in this context. "Nothing in the story or in the Jesus tradition as such would suggest that Jesus was, or that the authorities would think he was, simply taking matters into his own hands. The very question assumes an authorization" (Evans 2001, 201).

ταῦτα. Accusative direct object of ποιεῖς. The antecedent of ταῦτα must be the events of verses 15-17 since the speakers would have no way of knowing about the events described in the intervening verses (19-25). That the near demonstrative pronoun along with the present tense of ποιεῖς (see below) indicates "that Jesus continues to have stopped the commercial traffic in the temple" (so Gundry, 657) seems quite unlikely. The demonstrative need not indicate temporal proximity, only what is uppermost in the minds of the religious leaders, and that is certainly the events of the temple cleansing the previous day—something they have likely discussed at considerable length in the interval. Although it is grammatically possible that the plural ταῦτα refers to multiple events regarding which the Jewish leaders ask for Jesus' authority (so Stein 2008, 523), the cleansing of the temple could just as well be referred to with a plural, viewed as a sequence of events.

ποιεῖς. Pres act ind 2nd sg ποιέω. The present tense is more likely due to the use of imperfective aspect in dialogue than to any temporal point. The same is true of ποιῇς in the second question.

ἤ. The disjunctive particle introduces an alternative question. When used with an interrogative word it usually joins a string of questions (BDAG, 432.1.d; this text is cited at 1.d.δ, but the usage evidenced in all "d entries" is relevant). This connector is perhaps Mark's narrative addition to join two questions that were asked, rather than part of the original statement. If so (and perhaps even if not), the ἤ need not be translated in English. To do so with an "or" (e.g., ESV, NET) suggests, in English, two alternate questions of which Jesus could answer either. Jesus' interlocutors, however, were demanding answers to all their questions.

τίς. Nominative subject of ἔδωκεν.

σοι. Dative indirect object of ἔδωκεν.

ἔδωκεν. Aor act ind 3rd sg δίδωμι.

τὴν ἐξουσίαν ταύτην. Accusative direct object of ἔδωκεν.

ἵνα. Introduces a clause that is epexegetical to ἐξουσίαν. Alternatively, Gundry (666) argues for an ecbatic ἵνα (i.e., result).

ταῦτα. Accusative direct object of ποιῇς.

ποιῇς. Pres act subj 2nd sg ποιέω. Subjunctive with ἵνα. On the tense, see ποιεῖς above.

11:29 ὁ δὲ Ἰησοῦς εἶπεν αὐτοῖς, Ἐπερωτήσω ὑμᾶς ἕνα λόγον, καὶ ἀποκρίθητέ μοι καὶ ἐρῶ ὑμῖν ἐν ποίᾳ ἐξουσίᾳ ταῦτα ποιῶ·

ὁ ... Ἰησοῦς. Nominative subject of εἶπεν.

δὲ. The use of δέ rather than καί marks the change of speakers.

εἶπεν. Aor act ind 3rd sg λέγω.

αὐτοῖς. Dative indirect object of εἶπεν.

Ἐπερωτήσω ὑμᾶς ... ³⁰ἀποκρίθητέ μοι. Clausal complement (direct discourse) of εἶπεν.

Ἐπερωτήσω. Fut act ind 1st sg ἐπερωτάω. On ἐπερωτάω versus the simple form ἐρωτάω, see 4:10.

ὑμᾶς. Accusative direct object of ἐπερωτήσω.

ἕνα λόγον. Accusative complement in an object-complement double accusative construction. In this context λογός is best represented in English as "thing" or, better yet, "question" (BDAG, 599.1.a.β). Zerwick suggests that ἕνα/εἷς should be understood as equivalent to the indefinite τις here: "Let me ask you a question" (§155). Alternatively, some think that the singularity of εἷς should be stressed: "ἕνα λόγον ... puts all the weight of the discussion on one point" (Evans 2001, 204; cf. Swete, 263).

ἀποκρίθητέ. Aor mid impv 2nd pl ἀποκρίνομαι. On this intransitive, "θη middle" form, see 3:33. The second accent on ἀποκρίθητέ comes from the enclitic μοι. The imperative conveys an implicit condition with the following clause introduced by καί functioning like an apodosis: "if you answer me, then I will tell you" (see Cranfield, 363). This may be a more colloquial way to express a condition (so Bruce, 420). The ‖ Matt 21:24 phrases it as a formal, third-class condition, ἐὰν εἴπητέ μοι κἀγὼ ὑμῖν ἐρῶ. Alternatively, it might be viewed as a "demand, which borders on disrespect" (Evans 2001, 205), but that probably reads too much into the statement as such.

μοι. Dative complement of ἀποκρίθητε.

ἐρῶ. Fut act ind 1st sg λέγω.

ὑμῖν. Dative complement of ἐρῶ.

ἐν ποίᾳ ἐξουσίᾳ. Instrumental: "according to what authority." The interrogative pronoun ποῖος modifies ἐξουσίᾳ.

ταῦτα. Accusative direct object of ποιῶ.

ποιῶ. Pres act ind 1st sg ποιέω.

11:30 τὸ βάπτισμα τὸ Ἰωάννου ἐξ οὐρανοῦ ἦν ἢ ἐξ ἀνθρώπων; ἀποκρίθητέ μοι.

τὸ βάπτισμα τὸ Ἰωάννου. Nominative subject of ἦν. The second τό is an adjectivizer, changing the genitive substantive Ἰωάννου into an adjective modifying βάπτισμα: "the 'of John' baptism." Wallace (1996, 213–15) suggests that this construction, in comparison with τὸ βάπτισμα Ἰωάννου, is used "primarily for emphasis," but if so, it is slight. This is not a common construction in the NT, though it is similar to the use of an article with a prepositional phrase (e.g., οἱ γραμματεῖς οἱ ἀπὸ Ἱεροσολύμων, 3:22). The only other NT instances in which an article governs a noun of a different case in second attributive position is the parallel statement in Matt 21:25 and a dative example in Acts 15:1 (τῷ ἔθει τῷ Μωϋσέως). The only explicit genitive form in the LXX is Dan 8:26 (τὸ ὅραμα τὸ ἑσπέρας).

ἐξ οὐρανοῦ ... ἢ ἐξ ἀνθρώπων. Source. The use of οὐρανός as a periphrasis for God is a typical idiom for a first-century Jewish writer.

ἦν. Impf act ind 3rd sg εἰμί.

ἀποκρίθητέ. Aor mid impv 2nd pl ἀποκρίνομαι. On this intransitive, "θη middle" form, see 3:33.

μοι. Dative complement of ἀποκρίθητε.

11:31 καὶ διελογίζοντο πρὸς ἑαυτοὺς λέγοντες, Ἐὰν εἴπωμεν, Ἐξ οὐρανοῦ, ἐρεῖ, Διὰ τί [οὖν] οὐκ ἐπιστεύσατε αὐτῷ;

διελογίζοντο. Impf mid ind 3rd pl διαλογίζομαι. On the possibility that this is an inceptive imperfect as in HCSB, see 1:21. The seven instances of διαλογίζομαι in Mark (2:6, 8 [2×]; 8:16, 17; 9:33; 11:31) appears to be "always in contexts of people trying to evade the force of Jesus' words or claims on them" (Edwards 2002, 353), though this may be slightly overstated (e.g., 8:16-17 is a matter of comprehension, not evasion). Mark appears to use it often as a negative term (see 9:33) as does Matthew; Luke's usage is broader and is not as frequently negative. The translations are divided as to whether to use a neutral term such as "discuss" (e.g., NASB, NIV, NET, ESV) or a negative term such as "argue" (e.g., NJB, REB, NRSB, HCSB, CEB). Since there is no specific evidence in the context that there was a debate, the translation above uses "they deliberated," reflecting BDAG's definition: "to think or reason carefully, esp. about the implications of someth" (232.1).

πρὸς ἑαυτούς. Association. Here, ἑαυτούς has the sense of ἀλλήλους (Cranfield, 363).

λέγοντες. Pres act ptc masc nom pl λέγω (means; redundant participle of speaking; see 1:7).

Ἐὰν εἴπωμεν, ... ³²**Ἐξ ἀνθρώπων.** Clausal complement (direct discourse) of λέγοντες. The quotation, which consists of two third-class conditions, ends abruptly without supplying an apodosis for the second conditional statement, suggesting that the discussion was left unresolved in their deliberation, a conclusion confirmed by the answer they finally give in verse 33: οὐκ οἴδαμεν. NJB catches the tone of the context nicely (though perhaps not with sufficient grammatical justification) with "But dare we say human?"

Ἐὰν. Introduces the protasis of the first of two third-class conditional statements.

εἴπωμεν. Aor act subj 1st pl λέγω. Subjunctive with ἐάν.

Ἐξ οὐρανοῦ. Source. This is a verbless clause for which ἔστιν is assumed.

ἐρεῖ. Fut act ind 3rd sg λέγω. This verb introduces the apodosis of the conditional statement.

Διὰ τί [οὖν] οὐκ ἐπιστεύσατε αὐτῷ. This embedded discourse is a hypothetical statement quoting what they *think* Jesus would say based on the answer they propose in the protasis.

Διὰ τί [οὖν]. Idiomatic for "why then?"

ἐπιστεύσατε. Aor act ind 2nd pl πιστεύω.

αὐτῷ. Dative complement of ἐπιστεύσατε. The antecedent is almost certainly John, though it is grammatically possible—but unlikely as a complement of πιστεύω—to take the pronoun as neuter with John's baptism as the antecedent. It is more common in Mark for πιστεύω to be absolute than to be followed by a dative (see 1:15 for a discussion of the various complements of πιστεύω).

11:32 ἀλλὰ εἴπωμεν, Ἐξ ἀνθρώπων; — ἐφοβοῦντο τὸν ὄχλον· ἅπαντες γὰρ εἶχον τὸν Ἰωάννην ὄντως ὅτι προφήτης ἦν.

ἀλλά. Introduces an alternative possible answer that contrasts with the first suggestion.

εἴπωμεν. Aor act subj 1st pl λέγω. Subjunctive with ἐάν as part of a deliberative statement. It forms the beginning of a second protasis for the third-class condition introduced by ἐάν in the previous verse; this statement, however, is not completed. In place of an apodosis, Mark inserts an explanatory γάρ clause, leaving the apodosis to be implied, i.e., that the people would react negatively against the religious leaders. The broken construction (aposiopesis; cf. 2:10) is not found in the other Synoptics. Matthew 21:26 words it as an actual apodosis with a first plural verb: ἐὰν δὲ εἴπωμεν· ἐξ ἀνθρώπων, φοβούμεθα τὸν ὄχλον. Luke 20:6 is even more explicit: ἐὰν δὲ εἴπωμεν· ἐξ ἀνθρώπων, ὁ λαὸς ἅπας καταλιθάσει ἡμᾶς.

Ἐξ ἀνθρώπων. Source. This is a verbless clause for which ἔστιν is assumed. This statement proposes that John's baptism has only human authority. The plural might suggest "John and his followers/disciples," but more likely it is simply idiomatic for "human authority."

ἐφοβοῦντο τὸν ὄχλον ... προφήτης ἦν. The second half of the verse is an editorial comment in which Mark explains why it is that the religious leaders were reticent to answer that John's baptism was only of human authority, not divine.

ἐφοβοῦντο. Impf mid ind 3rd pl φοβέομαι. The imperfect is used to provide background information.

τὸν ὄχλον. Accusative direct object of ἐφοβοῦντο. This is not the usual use of ὄχλος to mean "a large group of people," but rather refers to "a large number of people of relatively low status *the (common) people, populace* ... in contrast to the rulers" (BDAG, 745.1.b.α), "often with the implication of disdain and low esteem" (LN 87.64).

ἅπαντες. Nominative subject of εἶχον. The referent here is not "everyone without exception" (the religious leaders were not of such a mind), but all of the just mentioned group, i.e., all the common people.

γάρ. The γάρ clause explains why the leadership feared (ἐφοβοῦντο) the crowd.

εἶχον. Impf act ind 3rd pl ἔχω. Here this common verb means "to have an opinion about someth., consider, look upon, view" (BDAG, 421.6). There are some minor textual variants here: both ᾔδεισαν (D W Θ 565 2542) and οἴδασι (700) are found in place of εἶχον, variants that Collins suggests may be "clarifications of the idiom" (538 n. *d*). Although BDAG notes that this use of ἔχω is normally "w. acc. as obj. and predicate acc." (421.6), here the predicate accusative slot (perhaps better, "clausal complement") is filled by a ὅτι clause. The imperfect tense is used as part of an explanatory, background statement, not because it "refers to a time previous to the perception" (contra Robertson, 887.θ).

τὸν Ἰωάννην. Accusative direct object of εἶχον. One might have expected that Ἰωάννην would have appeared in the ὅτι clause (ἅπαντες γὰρ εἶχον ὄντως ὅτι ὁ Ἰωάννης προφήτης ἦν), but it is not uncommon for verbs of perceiving/knowing to attract their object from the subordinate clause (Winer 1874, 626 §66.5.a; see also αὐτόν in 12:34). Alternatively, this may be explained as a case of prolepsis in which the subject of the subordinate clause is introduced in the main clause as an accusative object (see BDF §476.1.1).

ὄντως. The adverb most likely modifies εἶχον (so RV, ASV, ISV; Gould, 219; Swete, 264) rather than ἦν (contra V. Taylor, 471; Cranfield, 363; Bruce, 420; Lane, 412 n. 65; Gundry, 658; France, 455; NIV, NRSV, ESV, NET; cf. BDAG, 715.a): "they truly thought that," not "they thought he really was." Many defending the connection with ἦν admit that the order is "strange" (e.g., France, 455), concluding that Mark moved ὄντως ahead of ὅτι for emphasis. That is possible, but it seems more likely that Mark situated the adverb as part of the main clause.

ὅτι. Introduces a clause that explains what they thought (εἶχον) about John (see BDAG, 731.1.d, s.v., ὅτι; 421.6, s.v. ἔχω).

προφήτης. Predicate nominative. As an anarthrous preverbal noun προφήτης might be either indefinite or qualitative. "The predicate here may be regarded as indefinite in the sense that the people regarded John as a prophet. But it also has a qualitative force, since the context indicates that this view of John as 'prophet' made the Jewish leaders reluctant to speak disparagingly of the baptism that he administered. There is no basis for regarding the predicate as definite, for the passage does not deal with any particular figure who is to be identified as 'the prophet'" (Harner, 78).

ἦν. Impf act ind 3rd sg εἰμί.

11:33 καὶ ἀποκριθέντες τῷ Ἰησοῦ λέγουσιν, Οὐκ οἴδαμεν. καὶ ὁ Ἰησοῦς λέγει αὐτοῖς, Οὐδὲ ἐγὼ λέγω ὑμῖν ἐν ποίᾳ ἐξουσίᾳ ταῦτα ποιῶ.

ἀποκριθέντες. Aor mid ptc masc nom pl ἀποκρίνομαι (means; redundant participle of speaking; see 1:7). On this intransitive, "θη middle" form, see 3:33.

τῷ Ἰησοῦ. Dative indirect object of ἀποκριθέντες.

λέγουσιν. Pres act ind 3rd pl λέγω. The time reference is past, with the narrative present perhaps functioning to mark the change of speakers or to focus attention on their final answer in the debate (see also 1:21 on εἰσπορεύονται).

Οὐκ οἴδαμεν. Clausal complement (direct discourse) of λέγουσιν.

οἴδαμεν. Prf act ind 1st pl οἶδα.

ὁ Ἰησοῦς. Nominative subject of λέγει.

λέγει. Pres act ind 3rd sg λέγω. The time reference is past, with the narrative present perhaps functioning to mark the change of speakers or to highlight Jesus' forceful reply (see also 1:21 on εἰσπορεύονται).

αὐτοῖς. Dative indirect object of λέγει.

Οὐδὲ ἐγὼ λέγω … ταῦτα ποιῶ. Clausal complement (direct discourse) of λέγει.

ἐγώ. Nominative subject of λέγω.

λέγω. Pres act ind 1st sg λέγω.

ὑμῖν. Dative indirect object of λέγω.

ἐν ποίᾳ ἐξουσίᾳ. Instrumental: "according to what authority." The interrogative pronoun ποῖος modifies ἐξουσίᾳ.

ταῦτα. Accusative direct object of ποιῶ.

ποιῶ. Pres act ind 1st sg ποιέω.

Mark 12:1-12

¹Then he began to speak to them in parables: "A man planted a vineyard, surrounded it with a hedge, dug a wine trough, built a watchtower, leased it to tenant farmers, and then left on a journey. ²At harvest time he sent a slave to the tenant farmers in order to collect a share of the fruit from the vineyard. ³Having seized him, they beat him and sent him away empty-handed. ⁴Once again he sent another slave to them, and that one they struck on the head and treated shamefully. ⁵He sent another and that one they killed, and many others (they mistreated), beating some and killing others.

⁶"He still had one (to send), a beloved son. He finally sent him to them, saying, 'They will respect my son.' ⁷But those tenant farmers

said to one another, 'This is the heir! Come on, let's kill him and the inheritance will be ours!' [8]So having seized (him), they killed him and threw him outside the vineyard.

[9]"[Therefore,] what will the owner of the vineyard do? He will come and destroy the tenant farmers and give the vineyard to others. [10]Have you never read this Scripture? 'A stone which the builders rejected, this has become the cornerstone; [11]this is from the Lord and it is marvelous in our eyes'?"

[12]And so they sought to seize him for they realized that he spoke the parable against them, but they feared the populace. Leaving him they went away.

12:1 Καὶ ἤρξατο αὐτοῖς ἐν παραβολαῖς λαλεῖν, Ἀμπελῶνα ἄνθρωπος ἐφύτευσεν καὶ περιέθηκεν φραγμὸν καὶ ὤρυξεν ὑπολήνιον καὶ ᾠκοδόμησεν πύργον καὶ ἐξέδετο αὐτὸν γεωργοῖς καὶ ἀπεδήμησεν.

Jesus' parable, though not a direct quotation, is based on Isaiah 5:1-2. There are numerous vocabulary parallels including the following words and phrases found in the LXX: ἐφύτευσα ἄμπελον, φραγμὸν περιέθηκα, ὤρυξα, and ᾠκοδόμησα πύργον.

ἤρξατο. Aor mid ind 3rd sg ἄρχω.

αὐτοῖς. Dative indirect object of λαλεῖν. The antecedent of the pronoun is the group of religious leaders who had challenged his authority.

ἐν παραβολαῖς. Instrumental. V. Taylor (473) and Cranfield (364) prefer to describe it as manner ("parabolically"), pointing out that the plural need not imply multiple parables (which is true regardless of the classification; Bruce, 420, calls it a generic plural; see also France, 458). It is possible, however, that Jesus spoke multiple parables; Mark and || Luke 20:9-18 record only one, but || Matt 21:28–24:14 records four at this point in the narrative. In two earlier uses of ἐν παραβολαῖς in Mark (3:23; 4:1) multiple parables are recorded (see Gundry, 683).

λαλεῖν. Pres act inf λαλέω (complementary).

Ἀμπελῶνα ἄνθρωπος . . . [11]ἐν ὀφθαλμοῖς ἡμῶν. Clausal complement (direct discourse) of λαλεῖν.

Ἀμπελῶνα. Accusative direct object of ἐφύτευσεν.

ἄνθρωπος. Nominative subject of ἐφύτευσεν.

ἐφύτευσεν. Aor act ind 3rd sg φυτεύω.

περιέθηκεν. Aor act ind 3rd sg περιτίθημι. If φραγμός is translated as "fence" or "wall," then περιέθηκεν should be translated, "he

built . . . around." If φραγμός is translated "hedge," then the verb
should be translated, "he planted . . . around" or as above.

φραγμὸν. Accusative direct object of περιέθηκεν. A φραγμός
functions as a fence, but it may take the form of a hedge or a wall:
"someth. manufactured or grown that demarcates or functions as a
fence" (*CL*, 375; cf. BDAG, 1064; LN 7.59).

ὤρυξεν. Aor act ind 3rd sg ὀρύσσω ("to dig").

ὑπολήνιον. Accusative direct object of ὤρυξεν. An ὑπολήνιον
(only here in the NT) is the trough located below a wine press to
collect the juice from the grapes ("wine trough/vat," (BDAG, 1039).

ᾠκοδόμησεν. Aor act ind 3rd sg οἰκοδομέω.

πύργον. Accusative direct object of ᾠκοδόμησεν. A πύργος was
probably a watchtower; though "farm building" (perhaps, "shed" or
"barn") has also been suggested, it has not generally been accepted
by scholars (BDAG, 800; LN 7.23).

ἐξέδετο. Aor mid ind 3rd sg ἐκδίδωμι ("to hire out, lease," BDAG,
300). In verse 9, the same idea is expressed with δίδωμι.

αὐτὸν. Accusative direct object of ἐξέδετο.

γεωργοῖς. Dative indirect object of ἐξέδετο.

ἀπεδήμησεν. Aor act ind 3rd sg ἀποδημέω. This is the same word
used to describe the "prodigal" who traveled to a distant country in
Luke 15:13.

**12:2 καὶ ἀπέστειλεν πρὸς τοὺς γεωργοὺς τῷ καιρῷ δοῦλον ἵνα
παρὰ τῶν γεωργῶν λάβῃ ἀπὸ τῶν καρπῶν τοῦ ἀμπελῶνος·**

ἀπέστειλεν. Aor act ind 3rd sg ἀποστέλλω.

πρὸς τοὺς γεωργοὺς. Spatial.

τῷ καιρῷ. Dative of time. Here, given the context, this phrase ("at
the time/season") clearly refers to harvest time.

δοῦλον. Accusative direct object of ἀπέστειλεν.

ἵνα. Introduces a purpose clause.

παρὰ τῶν γεωργῶν. Source.

λάβῃ. Aor act subj 3rd sg λαμβάνω. Subjunctive with ἵνα.

ἀπὸ τῶν καρπῶν. On the preposition with the genitive in place
of an accusative direct object, see 7:28 on ἀπὸ τῶν ψιχίων. Evans
rightly notes that "we should not imagine that the owner expects
the servant to return with wagons loaded with grapes or barrels of
wine. Rather the servant is to return with money from the sale of the
grapes and wine" (2001, 233; contra Gundry, 685). However, Evans
seriously overstates the evidence when he claims that καρπός "is
often understood as money" (2001, 233; the references he cites from

MM and BAG do not substantiate such a claim). I am unaware of any specific texts that use καρπός as an exact equivalent of "money" or even of "profit" (the closest is Phil 4:17), though it is quite obvious that καρπός can refer metaphorically to the results or outcome of an action or situation (see examples in BDAG, 510.1.b).

12:3 καὶ λαβόντες αὐτὸν ἔδειραν καὶ ἀπέστειλαν κενόν.

λαβόντες. Aor act ptc masc nom pl λαμβάνω (temporal). Here, "lay hands on, seize w. acc. of the pers. who is seized by force" (BDAG, 584.3). Stein (2008, 540) classes this as a complementary participle (also v. 8; on the category, see Wallace 1996, 646), but there is no verb that makes a meaningful combination.

αὐτὸν. Accusative direct object of λαβόντες. This same object is assumed by both finite verbs that follow.

ἔδειραν. Aor act ind 3rd pl δέρω. Diachronically, δέρω meant "to skin, flay" (BDAG, 219; the cognate nouns are δέρρις, δέρος, and δέρμα, all meaning "skin, hide") and was typically used in reference to an animal (e.g., LXX 2 Chr 29:34), but it could also be used, even in classical Greek, in a metaphorical sense, "to beat, whip" (see LSJ, 380; cf. our English idiom, "I'll tan your hide!"). This is the normal usage in the Koine, particularly in colloquial speech, and exclusively so in the NT.

ἀπέστειλαν. Aor act ind 3rd pl ἀποστέλλω.

κενόν. Complement in an object-complement double accusative construction with the implied direct object being αὐτόν. The expression ἀποστέλλειν τινά means to "send someone away empty-handed" (BDAG, 539.1, s.v. κενός).

12:4 καὶ πάλιν ἀπέστειλεν πρὸς αὐτοὺς ἄλλον δοῦλον· κἀκεῖνον ἐκεφαλίωσαν καὶ ἠτίμασαν.

ἀπέστειλεν. Aor act ind 3rd sg ἀποστέλλω.

πρὸς αὐτοὺς. Spatial.

ἄλλον δοῦλον. Accusative direct object of ἀπέστειλεν.

κἀκεῖνον. Accusative direct object of ἐκεφαλίωσαν καὶ ἠτίμασαν. On the crasis form, see verse 4.

ἐκεφαλίωσαν. Aor act ind 3rd pl κεφαλιόω. This verb (only here in the NT) "is usually taken to mean 'to strike on the head, treat brutally (with reference to the head),' but as such is entirely unattested" (BDF §108.1.1; see also Hort, 153). The verb may mean "to decapitate" (see BDF §108.1.1), but the context does not suggest such a harsh sense; the parallel ἀτιμάζω portrays these events as shame, not necessarily death.

ἠτίμασαν. Aor act ind 3rd pl ἀτιμάζω. Perhaps the καί connecting ἐκεφαλίωσαν and ἠτίμασαν should be taken in an explicative sense rather than conjoining two distinct events (see BDAG, 495.1.c, s.v. καί) or as indicating a hendiadys: "shameful beating" (see BDAG, 494.1.a.δ, s.v. καί).

12:5 καὶ ἄλλον ἀπέστειλεν· κἀκεῖνον ἀπέκτειναν, καὶ πολλοὺς ἄλλους, οὓς μὲν δέροντες, οὓς δὲ ἀποκτέννοντες.

ἄλλον. Accusative direct object of ἀπέστειλεν.

ἀπέστειλεν. Aor act ind 3rd sg ἀποστέλλω.

κἀκεῖνον. Accusative direct object of ἀπέκτειναν. This is a crasis form of καί + ἐκεῖνος ("and that one," BDAG, 500.2.b). The smooth breathing mark over the alpha is retained from ἐκεῖνος.

ἀπέκτειναν. Aor act ind 3rd pl ἀποκτείνω.

πολλοὺς ἄλλους. Accusative direct object of an assumed verb. From the sense of the context and especially the two adverbial participles that follow, we should probably understand a verb to the effect of "they mistreated" (see Conrad 2004).

οὓς μὲν δέροντες, οὓς δὲ. The μέν . . . δέ construction marks a series; the relative pronouns are the accusative direct objects of the two participles. On the use of μέν as a "prestige feature," see 4:4.

δέροντες. Pres act ptc masc nom pl δέρω (means).

ἀποκτέννοντες. Pres act ptc masc nom pl ἀποκτέννω (means). The spelling ἀποκτέννω, a new form in the Koine, is rare in the NT (elsewhere only Matt 10:28; 2 Cor 3:6; Rev 6:11) and the LXX (8 times), the usual form being ἀποκτείνω. There is no difference in meaning.

12:6 ἔτι ἕνα εἶχεν υἱὸν ἀγαπητόν· ἀπέστειλεν αὐτὸν ἔσχατον πρὸς αὐτοὺς λέγων ὅτι Ἐντραπήσονται τὸν υἱόν μου.

ἕνα. Accusative direct object of εἶχεν.

εἶχεν. Impf act ind 3rd sg ἔχω.

υἱὸν ἀγαπητόν. Accusative in apposition to ἕνα. The only other occurrences of this phrase in Mark are 1:11 and 9:7, both in reference to Jesus.

ἀπέστειλεν. Aor act ind 3rd sg ἀποστέλλω.

αὐτόν. Accusative direct object of ἀπέστειλεν.

ἔσχατον. This word could be an adjective (used where English would use an adverb; Smyth §1042); the form would then be a masculine accusative singular to agree with αὐτόν, either as the complement in an object-complement double accusative construction, or substantivally in apposition to αὐτόν ("sent him, the last one"). Perhaps better is to view it as a neuter functioning as an adverbial accusative (the form is identical; see BDAG, 398.2.b) modifying ἀπέστειλεν, "last of all he sent him." "When one action is opposed to another in order of sequence, the adverbs . . ., not the adjectives . . ., must be used" (Smyth §1042.b.N).

πρὸς αὐτούς. Spatial.

λέγων. Pres act ptc masc nom sg λέγω (temporal).

ὅτι. Introduces the clausal complement (direct discourse) of λέγων (see 1:15).

ἐντραπήσονται. Fut mid ind 3rd pl ἐντρέπω. This is a "θη middle" form (see 2:2), but it follows the second future middle/passive pattern, so the θ does not appear. This verb appears with seemingly opposite senses here and in 1 Cor 4:14. The basic meaning is "to turn, turn about." Used in a metaphorical sense, one may turn away in shame (BDAG, 341.1) or turn toward someone to show deference or respect (BDAG, 341.2); the context must determine which is intended.

τὸν υἱόν. Accusative direct object of ἐντραπήσονται.

12:7 ἐκεῖνοι δὲ οἱ γεωργοὶ πρὸς ἑαυτοὺς εἶπαν ὅτι Οὗτός ἐστιν ὁ κληρονόμος· δεῦτε ἀποκτείνωμεν αὐτόν, καὶ ἡμῶν ἔσται ἡ κληρονομία.

ἐκεῖνοι δὲ . . . ἀποκτείνωμεν αὐτόν. Compare the account of Joseph's brothers' words in Gen 37:20, εἶπαν δὲ ἕκαστος πρὸς τὸν ἀδελφὸν αὐτοῦ. . . . νῦν οὖν δεῦτε ἀποκτείνωμεν αὐτὸν. Whether the verbal parallel is intentional or merely an interesting coincidence is uncertain.

ἐκεῖνοι . . . οἱ γεωργοί. Nominative subject of εἶπαν.

δὲ. The use of δέ contrasts the father's expectations (v. 6c) with the actual results.

πρὸς ἑαυτούς. A πρός prepositional phrase may function in place of a dative indirect object. This is the only instance in the NT in which πρὸς ἑαυτούς precedes the verb that it modifies.

εἶπαν. Aor act ind 3rd pl λέγω.

ὅτι. Introduces the clausal complement (direct discourse) of εἶπαν (see 1:15).

Οὗτός. Nominative subject of ἐστιν.

ἐστιν. Pres act ind 3rd sg εἰμί.

ὁ κληρονόμος. Predicate nominative.

δεῦτε. An adverb functioning as a hortatory particle (an interjection): "come on!" With a singular verb, δεῦρο is used; with a plural verb, the form is δεῦτε.

ἀποκτείνωμεν. Aor act subj 1st pl ἀποκτείνω (hortatory).

αὐτόν. Accusative direct object of ἀποκτείνωμεν.

ἡμῶν. Possessive genitive with an equative verb, though Robertson (497.3) prefers to describe it as a predicate genitive, citing the parallel in Luke 20:14 (ἡμῶν γένηται ἡ κληρονομία).

ἔσται. Fut mid ind 3rd sg εἰμί.

ἡ κληρονομία. Nominative subject of ἔσται.

12:8 καὶ λαβόντες ἀπέκτειναν αὐτὸν καὶ ἐξέβαλον αὐτὸν ἔξω τοῦ ἀμπελῶνος.

λαβόντες. Aor act ptc masc nom pl λαμβάνω (temporal).

ἀπέκτειναν. Aor act ind 3rd pl ἀποκτείνω.

αὐτὸν. Accusative direct object of ἀπέκτειναν.

ἐξέβαλον. Aor act ind 3rd pl ἐκβάλλω.

αὐτὸν. Accusative direct object of ἐξέβαλον.

ἔξω τοῦ ἀμπελῶνος. The adverb ἔξω is used as a preposition with the genitive to indicate where the corpse was thrown (BDAG, 354.1.b).

12:9 τί [οὖν] ποιήσει ὁ κύριος τοῦ ἀμπελῶνος; ἐλεύσεται καὶ ἀπολέσει τοὺς γεωργοὺς καὶ δώσει τὸν ἀμπελῶνα ἄλλοις.

τί. Accusative direct object ποιήσει.

[οὖν]. Introduces a rhetorical question to apply the significance of the parable. The answer is obvious, but Jesus goes on to state it explicitly.

ποιήσει. Fut act ind 3rd sg ποιέω.

ὁ κύριος. Nominative subject of ποιήσει. Here, κύριος is best taken as "owner" (RSV, NASB, NIV, NRSV, ESV, HCSB), rather than "Lord" (contra ASV, NASB mg.; Stein 2008, 537). The parable is best understood as running through verse 9, with Jesus' application not coming until verse 10.

ἐλεύσεται. Fut mid ind 3rd sg ἔρχομαι. It is possible that the answer beginning here is offered by the crowd rather than Jesus (if so, Jesus' words resume in v. 10), but it seems more likely that Jesus both asks (v. 9a) and answers (v. 9b) the question.

ἀπολέσει. Fut act ind 3rd sg ἀπόλλυμι. This is a more general word than ἀποκτείνω. Whether the change is deliberate or simply for stylistic variety is debatable.

τοὺς γεωργοὺς. Accusative direct object of ἀπολέσει.

δώσει. Fut act ind 3rd sg δίδωμι. This idea is paralleled with ἐκδίδωμι in verse 1. Matthew uses ἐκδίδωμι in both statements (21:33, 41), while Luke's verbs (20:9, 16) are the same as Mark's.

τὸν ἀμπελῶνα. Accusative direct object of δώσει.

ἄλλοις. Dative indirect object of δώσει.

12:10 οὐδὲ τὴν γραφὴν ταύτην ἀνέγνωτε, Λίθον ὃν ἀπεδοκίμασαν οἱ οἰκοδομοῦντες, οὗτος ἐγενήθη εἰς κεφαλὴν γωνίας·

οὐδὲ. The use of a form of οὐ in an indicative mood rhetorical question implies a positive answer: "You have read, haven't you?" Though framed as a question, it has the force of a rebuke, implying that they should have understood the significance of the OT text that is cited.

τὴν γραφὴν ταύτην. Accusative direct object of ἀνέγνωτε. The demonstrative pronoun refers forward to the verbatim quotation from LXX Ps 117:22-23 (Ps 118 in Heb. and Eng.). Grammatically, the quotation is in apposition to ταύτην. This is the only use of the singular ἡ γραφή in Mark as a reference to the OT; the plural occurs twice (12:24; 14:49). By appending ταύτην the reference is limited to a specific portion of Scripture.

ἀνέγνωτε. Aor act ind 2nd pl ἀναγινώσκω.

Λίθον. This word introduces the subject of the verb ἐγενήθη in the main clause, but its case is attracted to the relative pronoun in the intervening clause ("inverse attraction"; normally the relative is attracted to the case of its antecedent, see BDF §295; Wallace 1996, 339). To adjust for this case discrepancy, the main clause has the subject repeated with a demonstrative pronoun in nominative case (οὗτος).

ὃν. Accusative direct object of ἀπεδοκίμασαν.

ἀπεδοκίμασαν. Aor act ind 3rd pl ἀποδοκιμάζω.

οἱ οἰκοδομοῦντες. Pres act ptc masc nom pl οἰκοδομέω (substantival). Nominative subject of ἀπεδοκίμασαν.

οὗτος. Nominative subject of ἐγενήθη (see also above on λίθον).

ἐγενήθη. Aor mid ind 3rd sg γίνομαι. This is a "θη middle" form, not passive (see 2:2).

εἰς κεφαλὴν γωνίας. A predicate nominative may be replaced by εἰς + accusative (see Wallace 1996, 47). The collocation κεφαλὴν γωνίας might refer to a "cap/keystone" (e.g., Jeremias, 4:274–75;

France, 463), but the reference here is more likely to a "cornerstone" (the same figure is used in Eph 2:20-22, though there the term is ἀκρογωνιαίου, apparently a synonym). The LXX represents the Hebrew *rō'š pinnāh* quite formally. On the meaning of the expression, France notes that "our ignorance of Hebrew architectural terminology at this point does not, however, affect the sense of the quotation: the one rejected has become the most important of all" (463).

12:11 παρὰ κυρίου ἐγένετο αὕτη καὶ ἔστιν θαυμαστὴ ἐν ὀφθαλμοῖς ἡμῶν;

παρὰ κυρίου. Source (or possibly agency).

ἐγένετο. Aor mid ind 3rd sg γίνομαι.

αὕτη. Nominative subject of ἐγένετο. The grammatical antecedent of the feminine pronoun could be κεφαλήν in the preceding verse, thus, "this (corner stone) has come from the Lord" (so Gould, 222; Duckwitz, 193). Alternatively, αὕτη could be taken as a reference to the event so described (i.e., οὗτος ἐγενήθη εἰς κεφαλὴν γωνίας), but in that case the gender would be puzzling. The most probable explanation is that the feminine gender is due to a very formal translation in the LXX (the Hebrew text has a feminine demonstrative pronoun here) that is carried over unchanged in the quotation here (BDF §138.2; Robertson, 254.4.b; Conybeare and Stock §47).

ἔστιν. Pres act ind 3rd sg εἰμί. On the accent, see 12:32.

θαυμαστὴ. Predicate adjective. See also 1:22 on ἐκπλήσσω.

ἐν ὀφθαλμοῖς. Locative, though metaphorical. The question mark at the end of verse 11 closes the question started in verse 10, rather than being part of the quotation.

12:12 Καὶ ἐζήτουν αὐτὸν κρατῆσαι, καὶ ἐφοβήθησαν τὸν ὄχλον, ἔγνωσαν γὰρ ὅτι πρὸς αὐτοὺς τὴν παραβολὴν εἶπεν. καὶ ἀφέντες αὐτὸν ἀπῆλθον.

Καὶ. Introducing "a result that comes fr. what precedes" (BDAG, 495.1.b.ζ): "and so."

ἐζήτουν. Impf act ind 3rd pl ζητέω. The third plural subject implicitly shifts from the tenant farmers to the religious leaders to whom Jesus addressed the preceding parable. Edwards (2002, 361) suggests that "conniving" is the appropriate nuance for ζητέω here.

αὐτὸν. Accusative direct object of κρατῆσαι.

κρατῆσαι. Aor act inf κρατέω. The infinitive clause, αὐτὸν κρατῆσαι, functions as the direct object of ἐζήτουν.

καὶ. We might have expected ἀλλά here or perhaps δέ, but καί serves the same function since the context makes it clear that though they wanted to seize him (v. 12a), they went away without doing so (v. 12d). BDAG (495.1.f, see also 1.b.η) notes that καί can introduce contrasts (cf. Maloney 1981, 69; Cranfield, 369; Zerwick §455.b.β; contra Winer 1874, 437 §53.3.b, who cites this text in claiming that καί is never adversative).

ἐφοβήθησαν. Aor mid ind 3rd pl φοβέομαι. This is a "θη middle" form (see 2:2).

τὸν ὄχλον. Accusative direct object of ἐφοβήθησαν. On the meaning of ὄχλος, see 11:32.

ἔγνωσαν. Aor act ind 3rd pl γινώσκω. The subject is οἱ ἀρχιερεῖς καὶ οἱ γραμματεῖς καὶ οἱ πρεσβύτεροι, last explicitly mentioned in 11:27, but referenced by pronouns and verbal subjects in 11:28, 31, 32, 33; 12:1, and in this verse by ἐζήτουν and ἐφοβήθησαν. Though the subject could be understood grammatically to shift from the religious leaders to the crowd (i.e., the leaders feared the crowd because *the crowd* understood that Jesus had spoken the parable against the leaders; so Gundry, 664), the flow of the context makes that very unlikely. The same referent to the leaders continues with ἀπῆλθον in the last clause of this verse and on into the following paragraph (ἀποστέλλουσιν, v. 13).

γὰρ. Introduces an explanation as to why they wanted to seize Jesus.

ὅτι. Introduces the clausal complement of ἔγνωσαν.

πρὸς αὐτοὺς. Opposition.

τὴν παραβολὴν. Accusative direct object of εἶπεν.

εἶπεν. Aor act ind 3rd sg λέγω.

ἀφέντες. Aor act ptc masc nom pl ἀφίημι (temporal). The participial form of ἀφίημι or ἀνίστημι is often used with a verb of motion in the Koine, especially in the Gospels and the LXX (Doudna, 55–57, 117–22). ἔρχομαι is used in a similar manner in 7:25; 12:42; 14:45; and 16:1. Zerwick explains these as Semitic idioms in which "one who does something in another place does it ἀπελθών (Mk 14,12); one who goes away, does so, ἀναστάς or ἐγερθείς or πορευθείς (Hebrew *wayyaqom wayyabo'*)" (126–27 §§363–65). He also points out that "they render a Semitic mannerism of speech by expressing what in ordinary Greek would not be expressed at all." For more on this verb, see 15:37 on ἀφείς.

αὐτόν. Accusative direct object of ἀφέντες.

ἀπῆλθον. Aor act ind 3rd pl ἀπέρχομαι.

Mark 12:13-17

[13]Then they sent some of the Pharisees and the Herodians to him in order to catch him in an unguarded statement. [14]Upon arriving they said to him, "Teacher, we know you are a man of integrity and you don't care what anybody thinks or says about you, for you are not afraid of what they think, but you teach God's way on the basis of truth; is it permitted to pay a head tax to Caesar or not? Should we pay or not pay?" [15]But knowing their hypocrisy, he said to them, "Why are you testing me? Bring me a denarius so that I can look at it." [16]So they brought (one to him). He asked them, "Whose image is this and whose inscription?" They said to him, "Caesar's." [17]Then Jesus said to them, "Give the things that belong to Caesar to Caesar and the things that belong to God give to God." And they were amazed at him.

12:13 Καὶ ἀποστέλλουσιν πρὸς αὐτόν τινας τῶν Φαρισαίων καὶ τῶν Ἡρῳδιανῶν ἵνα αὐτὸν ἀγρεύσωσιν λόγῳ.

ἀποστέλλουσιν. Pres act ind 3rd pl ἀποστέλλω. The present tense introduces a new paragraph (see 1:21). The subject is οἱ ἀρχιερεῖς καὶ οἱ γραμματεῖς καὶ οἱ πρεσβύτεροι (11:27), the reference to whom has been continued with verbs (ἔλεγον, 11:28; διελογίζοντο, 11:31; λέγουσιν, 11:33; ἐζήτουν, ἐφοβήθησαν, ἔγνωσαν, ἀπῆλθον, 12:12) and pronouns (αὐτοῖς, 11:29, 33; 12:1; αὐτούς, 12:12) to this point (contra V. Taylor, 478; and Cranfield, 369, who take this as an indefinite plural, a classification that should only be used when there is no sensible antecedent and the referent must shift to a different party to make sense).

πρὸς αὐτόν. Spatial.

τινας. Accusative direct object of ἀποστέλλουσιν.

τῶν Φαρισαίων καὶ τῶν Ἡρῳδιανῶν. Partitive genitive (see 8:8). They are sent by the chief priests and the scribes and the elders (11:27, 33; 12:1, 12), but it is dubious that we are to picture the Jerusalem authorities selecting Galilean representatives for this task (contra Gundry, 696). Rather, the partitive genitive simply identifies a subset of the larger group(s).

ἵνα. Introduces a purpose clause.

αὐτὸν. Accusative direct object of ἀγρεύσωσιν.

ἀγρεύσωσιν. Aor act subj 3rd pl ἀγρεύω ("to catch unawares"; only here in the NT). Subjunctive with ἵνα. In the LXX (Prov 5:22; 6:25, 26; Job 10:16; Hos 5:2) this word can mean not only "to catch," but also "to hunt" (LEH, 5); it is often used metaphorically in the LXX, as here. When ἀγρεύω is used with λόγῳ the idea is best expressed as "to catch in an unguarded statement" (BDAG, 15).

λόγῳ. Dative of means ("by their word," i.e., the question they were going to ask; so GNB) or dative of respect ("to catch him in his word/talk," i.e., in Jesus' answer to their question; so RSV, NASB, NIV, NRSV, NET, ESV, HCSB, NCV, ISV).

12:14 καὶ ἐλθόντες λέγουσιν αὐτῷ, Διδάσκαλε, οἴδαμεν ὅτι ἀληθὴς εἶ καὶ οὐ μέλει σοι περὶ οὐδενός· οὐ γὰρ βλέπεις εἰς πρόσωπον ἀνθρώπων, ἀλλ' ἐπ' ἀληθείας τὴν ὁδὸν τοῦ θεοῦ διδάσκεις· ἔξεστιν δοῦναι κῆνσον Καίσαρι ἢ οὔ; δῶμεν ἢ μὴ δῶμεν;

ἐλθόντες. Aor act ptc masc nom pl ἔρχομαι (temporal).

λέγουσιν. Pres act ind 3rd pl λέγω.

αὐτῷ. Dative indirect object of λέγουσιν.

Διδάσκαλε, οἴδαμεν . . . ἢ μὴ δῶμεν. Clausal complement (direct discourse) of λέγουσιν.

Διδάσκαλε. Vocative (see also 4:38).

οἴδαμεν. Prf act ind 1st pl οἶδα.

ὅτι. Introduces a noun clause that functions as the clausal complement of οἴδαμεν.

ἀληθὴς. Predicate adjective: "truthful, righteous, honest." The translation follows the NIV.

εἶ. Pres act ind 2nd sg εἰμί.

οὐ μέλει σοι περὶ οὐδενός. This is an awkward phrase to translate due to the double negative and the idiomatic nature of the statement (formally, "it is not a concern to you concerning no one") BDAG (626.1.b, s.v. μέλει) suggests, *"you court no one's favor or you don't care what anybody thinks or says about you."*

μέλει. Pres act ind 3rd sg μέλει (μέλω). Although μέλω is an impersonal verb, the third singular form can be used either personally or impersonally, thus meriting a separate lexical listing in BDAG (626).

σοι. Dative complement of μέλει.

περὶ οὐδενός. Reference.

οὐ . . . βλέπεις εἰς πρόσωπον ἀνθρώπων. Another idiomatic expression (formally, "for you don't look on the face of people") for which BDAG (179.4, s.v. βλέπω) suggests, *"you don't regard someone's opinion* in the sense of being afraid of what someone might think" (for similar idioms, see France, 467–68).

βλέπεις. Pres act ind 2nd sg βλέπω.

εἰς πρόσωπον. Respect, or perhaps locative.

ἐπ᾽ ἀληθείας. Cause: "on the basis of truth."

τὴν ὁδὸν. Accusative direct object of διδάσκεις.

διδάσκεις. Pres act ind 2nd sg διδάσκω.

ἔξεστιν. Pres act ind 3rd sg ἔξεστιν. This verb implies a Jewish legal question: Is it permitted under Jewish law to pay taxes to a Gentile power?

δοῦναι. Aor act inf δίδωμι (subject of ἔξεστιν). When used in a monetary context, δίδωμι means "to pay" (BDAG, 242.6.a).

κῆνσον. Accusative direct object of δοῦναι. This Latin loanword (κῆνσος, from census; see 4:21 on ὑπὸ τὸν μόδιον . . . ἢ ὑπὸ τὴν κλίνην) refers to a per capita "head tax" (BDAG, 542) in contrast to τέλος, which refers to a revenue tax, toll, or custom duty (BDAG, 999.5). The later textual variant (e.g., D Θ) ἐπικεφάλαιον ("poll-tax") reflects this understanding.

δῶμεν. Aor act subj 1st pl δίδωμι (deliberative subjunctive).

12:15 ὁ δὲ εἰδὼς αὐτῶν τὴν ὑπόκρισιν εἶπεν αὐτοῖς, Τί με πειράζετε; φέρετέ μοι δηνάριον ἵνα ἴδω.

ὁ. Nominative subject of εἶπεν. On the use of ὁ δέ to change subjects, see 1:45. The use of δέ also reflects the contrast, evident in the context, between the pious-sounding query of verse 14 and Jesus' perception of the motive.

εἰδὼς. Prf act ptc masc nom sg οἶδα (causal).

τὴν ὑπόκρισιν. Accusative direct object of εἰδώς.

εἶπεν. Aor act ind 3rd sg λέγω.

αὐτοῖς. Dative indirect object of εἶπεν.

Τί με πειράζετε . . . ἵνα ἴδω. Clausal complement (direct discourse) of εἶπεν.

Τί. The interrogative pronoun introduces a rhetorical question that functions as a statement to the effect: "I know what you're up to."

με. Accusative direct object of πειράζετε.

πειράζετε. Pres act ind 2nd pl πειράζω.

φέρετέ. Pres act impv 2nd pl φέρω.

μοι. Dative indirect object of φέρετε.

δηνάριον. Accusative direct object of φέρετε. A Latin loanword (see 4:21 on ὑπὸ τὸν μόδιον . . . ἢ ὑπὸ τὴν κλίνην).

ἵνα. Introduces a purpose clause.

ἴδω. Aor act subj 1st sg ὁράω. Subjunctive with ἵνα.

12:16 οἱ δὲ ἤνεγκαν. καὶ λέγει αὐτοῖς, Τίνος ἡ εἰκὼν αὕτη καὶ ἡ ἐπιγραφή; οἱ δὲ εἶπαν αὐτῷ, Καίσαρος.

οἱ. Nominative subject of ἤνεγκαν. On the use of οἱ δέ to change subjects, see 1:45.

ἤνεγκαν. Aor act ind 3rd pl φέρω.

λέγει. Pres act ind 3rd sg λέγω.

αὐτοῖς. Dative indirect object of λέγει.

Τίνος ἡ εἰκὼν αὕτη καὶ ἡ ἐπιγραφή. Clausal complement (direct discourse) of λέγει. A verbless clause with a form of εἰμί omitted as is common in questions (BDF §127.3).

Τίνος. Possessive genitive modifying εἰκών.

ἡ εἰκὼν ... καὶ ἡ ἐπιγραφή. Nominative subject of a verbless clause.

αὕτη. Predicate nominative of a verbless clause.

ἡ ἐπιγραφή. This word ordinarily refers to "a document incised on stone, but also of identifying notices on any kind of material" (BDAG, 369; see also 15:26).

οἱ. Nominative subject of εἶπαν. On the use of οἱ δέ to change speakers, see 1:45.

εἶπαν. Aor act ind 3rd pl λέγω.

αὐτῷ. Dative indirect object of εἶπαν.

Καίσαρος. Clausal complement (direct discourse) of εἶπαν. Possessive genitive.

12:17 ὁ δὲ Ἰησοῦς εἶπεν αὐτοῖς, Τὰ Καίσαρος ἀπόδοτε Καίσαρι καὶ τὰ τοῦ θεοῦ τῷ θεῷ. καὶ ἐξεθαύμαζον ἐπ᾽ αὐτῷ.

ὁ ... Ἰησοῦς. Nominative subject of εἶπεν.

δὲ. The use of δέ reflects the change of speakers at this point.

εἶπεν. Aor act ind 3rd sg λέγω.

αὐτοῖς. Dative indirect object of εἶπεν.

Τὰ Καίσαρος ... τῷ θεῷ. Clausal complement (direct discourse) of εἶπεν.

Τὰ Καίσαρος. The article τά is a nominalizer, changing the (possessive) genitive noun Καίσαρος into the accusative direct object of ἀπόδοτε ("the things of Caesar," i.e., "the things that belong to Caesar").

ἀπόδοτε. Aor act impv 2nd pl ἀποδίδωμι. In the question (v. 14), δίδωμι was used. The shift to ἀποδίδωμι might imply that the payment is a debt (so Swete, 276), i.e., a financial obligation to the government, but it is only used for payment of taxes here in the NT (and || Matt 22:21; Luke 20:25), so the point should not be pressed, especially since the simpler form, δίδωμι, is regularly used for financial obligations (e.g., Matt 27:10).

Καίσαρι. Dative indirect object of ἀπόδοτε.

τὰ τοῦ θεοῦ. The article τά is a nominalizer, changing the (possessive) genitive noun τοῦ θεοῦ into the accusative direct object of an implied ἀπόδοτε ("the things of God," i.e., "the things that belong to God"). The same expression occurs in 8:33 where it is contrasted with τὰ τῶν ἀνθρώπων.

τῷ θεῷ. Dative indirect object of an implied ἀπόδοτε.

ἐξεθαύμαζον. Impf act ind 3rd pl ἐκθαυμάζω. The prefixed preposition ἐκ– may be perfective/emphatic (Robertson, 597; France, 469), but other uses do not seem to have that force, meaning simply "to admire" in some contexts. The synoptic parallels use the simple form θαυμάζω (Matt 22:22; Luke 20:26). Bruce cautions against reading too much into the prefixed form due to "the tendency in late Greek to use compounds" (422). This is not a common word; it occurs only here in the NT, twice in the LXX (Sir 27:23; 43:18) and in the Pseudepigrapha (*Let. Aris.* 312; 4 Macc 17:17), three times in Josephus (*Ant.* 5:279; 18:291, 309), and once in Philo (*Dreams* 2.70). The subject of this verb is τινας τῶν Φαρισαίων καὶ τῶν Ἡρῳδιανῶν (v. 13); the reference to them has been consistent in the intervening verses, suggesting that this is not a comment regarding the reaction of the onlookers, but of those attempting to entrap Jesus in his words. To suggest that they have become "his admirers" (Collins, 557) may give them too much credit (ἐκθαυμάζω need not be such a positive statement), but "there is gentle irony in Mark's closing comment that his adversaries marveled greatly at Jesus" (Lane, 425). See also 1:22 on ἐκπλήσσω.

ἐπ᾽ αὐτῷ. Causal.

Mark 12:18-27

[18]Then some Sadducees, who say there is no resurrection, came to him and asked him (a question), saying, [19]"Teacher, Moses wrote for us that if a brother of someone should die and leave a wife and not leave children, then his brother must take his wife and beget children for his brother. [20]There were seven brothers. The first one took a wife and when he died he did not leave children. [21]So the second took her and he died, not leaving children; and the third (did)

likewise. ²²Indeed, the seven did not leave children. Last of all the woman died. ²³In the resurrection [when they rise], whose wife will she be? For the seven had her as a wife."

²⁴Jesus said to them, "Isn't this the reason why you are deceived: because you understand neither the Scriptures nor the power of God? ²⁵For when they rise from the dead they will neither marry nor be given in marriage, but they will be similar to angels in heaven. ²⁶But concerning the dead, that they will rise, you have read, haven't you, in the Book of Moses, (in the passage) about the bush, how God spoke to (Moses), saying, 'I am the God of Abraham and the God of Isaac, and the God of Jacob'? ²⁷He is not the God of the dead but of the living; you are greatly mistaken."

12:18 Καὶ ἔρχονται Σαδδουκαῖοι πρὸς αὐτόν, οἵτινες λέγουσιν ἀνάστασιν μὴ εἶναι, καὶ ἐπηρώτων αὐτὸν λέγοντες,

ἔρχονται. Pres mid ind 3rd pl ἔρχομαι. The present tense introduces a new paragraph (see 1:21).

Σαδδουκαῖοι. Nominative subject of ἔρχονται. This is the only explicit mention of the Sadducees in Mark.

πρὸς αὐτόν. Spatial.

οἵτινες. The nominative indefinite relative pronoun functions as the subject of λέγουσιν and introduces an explanatory phrase telling the reader who the Sadducees are and how they differ from the previous delegation comprised of Pharisees and Herodians.

λέγουσιν. Pres act ind 3rd pl λέγω. The present tense does not indicate that this is a characterization of the Sadducees' general position (contra France, 473). While it is true that this is a general statement rather than something true only of the group in view, this cannot be proved by the tense.

ἀνάστασιν μὴ εἶναι. Clausal complement (indirect discourse) of λέγουσιν. It is possible that μή is used with the infinitive in indirect discourse "when the statement quoted is not a fact, but an opinion" (Hort, 157).

ἀνάστασιν. Accusative subject of εἶναι. This and verse 23 are the only occurrences of ἀνάστασις in Mark, though the cognate verb form, ἀνίστημι, occurs in 8:31; 9:9, 10, 31; 10:34; 12:23, 25.

εἶναι. Pres act inf εἰμί (indirect discourse).

ἐπηρώτων. Impf act ind 3rd pl ἐπερωτάω. On ἐπερωτάω versus the simple form ἐρωτάω, see 4:10. The use of the imperfect here to introduce discourse is due to the group nature of the question; this is typical of Mark's use of the imperfect (see, e.g., 2:24; 3:21, 22, 30; 4:41; 5:31; 6:14, 35; see also Decker 2013a, 354–56).

αὐτὸν. Accusative direct object of ἐπηρώτων.

λέγοντες. Pres act ptc masc nom pl λέγω (means; redundant participle of speaking; see 1:7; 3:33). The statement that is introduced extends from verse 19 through verse 23 and functions as the clausal complement (direct discourse) of λέγοντες.

12:19 Διδάσκαλε, Μωϋσῆς ἔγραψεν ἡμῖν ὅτι ἐάν τινος ἀδελφὸς ἀποθάνῃ καὶ καταλίπῃ γυναῖκα καὶ μὴ ἀφῇ τέκνον, ἵνα λάβῃ ὁ ἀδελφὸς αὐτοῦ τὴν γυναῖκα καὶ ἐξαναστήσῃ σπέρμα τῷ ἀδελφῷ αὐτοῦ.

Διδάσκαλε. Vocative (see also 4:38).

Μωϋσῆς. Nominative subject of ἔγραψεν.

ἔγραψεν. Aor act ind 3rd sg γράφω.

ἡμῖν. Dative indirect object of ἔγραψεν.

ὅτι. On the recitative use of ὅτι to introduce direct discourse, here used with γράφω to introduce an OT reference, see 1:15. The OT text is not quoted directly; rather, the Sadducees summarize the gist of Deut 25:5 in their own words.

ἐάν. Introduces a third-class condition. The protasis is compound, τινος ἀδελφὸς ἀποθάνῃ καὶ καταλίπῃ γυναῖκα καὶ μὴ ἀφῇ τέκνον, followed by an imperatival ἵνα (Zerwick, 415) in the apodosis.

τινος. Genitive of relationship modifying ἀδελφὸς.

ἀδελφὸς. Nominative subject of ἀποθάνῃ.

ἀποθάνῃ. Aor act subj 3rd sg ἀποθνῄσκω. Subjunctive with ἐάν.

καταλίπῃ. Aor act subj 3rd sg καταλείπω. Subjunctive with ἐάν.

γυναῖκα. Accusative direct object of καταλίπῃ.

καὶ. Coordinating conjunction, but here used in an adversative context, "but, and yet, and in spite of that, nevertheless" (Maloney 1981, 69–70; see also BDAG, 1.b.η).

ἀφῇ. Aor act subj 3rd sg ἀφίημι. Subjunctive with ἐάν.

τέκνον. Accusative direct object of ἀφῇ.

ἵνα. An imperatival ἵνα (e.g., "the man must take," ESV) indicating the content of Moses' command. Alternatively, Μωϋσῆς ἔγραψεν might be assumed in the apodosis with ἵνα introducing indirect discourse: "(Moses also wrote) that his brother should . . ." (see BDAG, 476.2.a.δ). Gundry suggests that the ἵνα simply shifts the statement from direct to indirect discourse (701).

λάβῃ. Aor act subj 3rd sg λαμβάνω.

ὁ ἀδελφὸς. Nominative subject of λάβῃ.

αὐτοῦ. Modifies ἀδελφός, following the typical pattern of genitives modifying the noun in front of them, and given the context and the parallel phrase at the end of the verse (τῷ ἀδελφῷ αὐτοῦ).

τὴν γυναῖκα. Accusative direct object of λάβῃ.

ἐξαναστήσῃ. Aor act subj 3rd sg ἐξανίστημι ("to rise up," but here metaphorically "to beget progeny," BDAG, 345.2).

σπέρμα. Accusative direct object of ἐξαναστήσῃ.

τῷ ἀδελφῷ. Dative of advantage.

12:20 ἑπτὰ ἀδελφοὶ ἦσαν· καὶ ὁ πρῶτος ἔλαβεν γυναῖκα καὶ ἀποθνῄσκων οὐκ ἀφῆκεν σπέρμα·

ἑπτὰ ἀδελφοὶ. Predicate nominative.

ἦσαν. Impf act ind 3rd pl εἰμί.

ὁ πρῶτος. Nominative subject of ἔλαβεν.

ἔλαβεν. Aor act ind 3rd sg λαμβάνω.

γυναῖκα. Accusative direct object of ἔλαβεν.

ἀποθνῄσκων. Pres act ptc masc nom sg ἀποθνῄσκω (temporal).

ἀφῆκεν. Aor act ind 3rd sg ἀφίημι.

σπέρμα. Accusative direct object of ἀφῆκεν.

12:21 καὶ ὁ δεύτερος ἔλαβεν αὐτὴν καὶ ἀπέθανεν μὴ καταλιπὼν σπέρμα· καὶ ὁ τρίτος ὡσαύτως·

ὁ δεύτερος. Nominative subject of ἔλαβεν.

ἔλαβεν. Aor act ind 3rd sg λαμβάνω.

αὐτὴν. Accusative direct object of ἔλαβεν.

ἀπέθανεν. Aor act ind 3rd sg ἀποθνῄσκω.

καταλιπὼν. Aor act ptc masc nom sg καταλείπω (attendant circumstance). The participle is negated by μή, not because it gives something "the tone of 'so the story goes'" (Gould, 228 n. 2), but because μή is the normal negative for a nonfinite form.

ὁ τρίτος. Nominative subject of an implied ἔλαβεν.

12:22 καὶ οἱ ἑπτὰ οὐκ ἀφῆκαν σπέρμα. ἔσχατον πάντων καὶ ἡ γυνὴ ἀπέθανεν.

οἱ ἑπτὰ. Nominative subject of ἀφῆκαν.

ἀφῆκαν. Aor act ind 3rd pl ἀφίημι.

σπέρμα. Accusative direct object of ἀφῆκαν.

ἔσχατον. The neuter adjective functions as an adverb (BDAG, 398.2.b) modifying ἀπέθανεν. The accompanying πάντων functions somewhat like a partitive genitive (though there is no head noun) referring to the entire series of events described in verses 20-22a.

ἡ γυνὴ. Nominative subject of ἀπέθανεν.

ἀπέθανεν. Aor act ind 3rd sg ἀποθνῄσκω.

12:23 ἐν τῇ ἀναστάσει [ὅταν ἀναστῶσιν] τίνος αὐτῶν ἔσται γυνή; οἱ γὰρ ἑπτὰ ἔσχον αὐτὴν γυναῖκα.

ἐν τῇ ἀναστάσει. Temporal.

ἀναστῶσιν. Aor act subj 3rd pl ἀνίστημι. Subjunctive with ὅταν. The phrase ὅταν ἀναστῶσιν is certainly redundant with ἐν τῇ ἀναστάσει, but this very redundancy leads many text critics to conclude that it must be original (there does not appear to be any way it could be an unintentional error), despite the substantive external evidence for its omission (ℵ B C* D L W Ψ). Mark is often redundant, so such a statement would not be surprising (see Metzger 1994, 93).

τίνος αὐτῶν ἔσται γυνή. Lit. "She will be wife of which of them?"

τίνος. Genitive interrogative pronoun modifying γυνή.

αὐτῶν. Partitive genitive (see 8:8).

ἔσται. Fut mid ind 3rd sg εἰμί.

ἡ γυνὴ. Predicate nominative.

οἱ ... ἑπτὰ. Nominative subject of ἔσχον.

ἔσχον. Aor act ind 3rd pl ἔχω.

αὐτὴν. Accusative direct object of ἔσχον.

γυναῖκα. Complement in an object-complement double accusative construction.

12:24 ἔφη αὐτοῖς ὁ Ἰησοῦς, Οὐ διὰ τοῦτο πλανᾶσθε μὴ εἰδότες τὰς γραφὰς μηδὲ τὴν δύναμιν τοῦ θεοῦ;

ἔφη. Aor act ind 3rd sg φημί.

αὐτοῖς. Dative indirect object of ἔφη.

ὁ Ἰησοῦς. Nominative subject of ἔφη.

Οὐ διὰ τοῦτο πλανᾶσθε ... ²⁷πολὺ πλανᾶσθε. Clausal complement (direct discourse) of ἔφη.

διὰ τοῦτο. Causal. This expression "usually refers to something going before, and it may do so here, pointing to their question as involving ignorant presuppositions regarding the future state. ... But it is more natural to connect it with the following clause" (Bruce, 423; see also V. Taylor, 483). If so, Jesus' meaning is "Isn't this the reason why you are deceived: [it is] because you understand neither the Scriptures nor the power of God?" Alternatively, Gundry

(705–6) argues for a retrospective reference to the Sadducees' story since a prospective use is typically followed by an explanatory clause in apposition (BDAG, 740.1.a.δ), but he does not consider the possibility that the causal participle clause fills this role.

πλανᾶσθε. Pres mid ind 2nd pl πλανάω. The main verb in the question is negated with οὐ, implying a positive answer. Jesus' question serves the rhetorical purpose of declaring the error of the Sadducees. On the use of πλανάω here and in verse 27, see BDAG (822.2.c.γ).

μὴ ... μηδὲ. Marks a negative sequence: "neither ... nor." The participle εἰδότες is negated by μή, not because "the statement is made by Jesus as a conjecture, of which he asks their opinion" (Gould, 229 n. 1), but because μή is the normal negative for a nonfinite form.

εἰδότες. Prf act ptc masc nom pl οἶδα (causal). The participial clause (μὴ εἰδότες ... τοῦ θεοῦ) is in apposition to τοῦτο.

τὰς γραφὰς μηδὲ τὴν δύναμιν. Accusative direct object of εἰδότες.

12:25 ὅταν γὰρ ἐκ νεκρῶν ἀναστῶσιν οὔτε γαμοῦσιν οὔτε γαμίζονται, ἀλλ᾽ εἰσὶν ὡς ἄγγελοι ἐν τοῖς οὐρανοῖς.

ὅταν. The temporal particle is typically used in Mark with an aorist subjunctive to reference a singular event (i.e., "when," not "whenever") that precedes the action of the main verb (see *TDM*, 87–88).

ἐκ νεκρῶν. Source. On the lack of an article, see on 6:14.

ἀναστῶσιν. Aor act subj 3rd pl ἀνίστημι. Subjunctive with ὅταν. The third plural subject refers to the seven brothers and the oft-married woman. This introductory reference to the resurrection and the ὅταν + subjunctive construction give the following three present indicative forms future time reference.

οὔτε γαμοῦσιν οὔτε γαμίζονται. On the collocation γαμέω/γαμίζω as a reference to the social institution of marriage (rather than the beginning of a marriage relationship), see the expanded parallel in Luke 20:34–36 (so Makujina, 57–74; cf. the same idiom in Luke 17:26–28 and Matt 24:38).

γαμοῦσιν. Pres act ind 3rd pl γαμέω. The active voice of γαμοῦσιν is contrasted with the passive γαμίζονται, initially reflecting the situation of the seven brothers and the woman respectively, though the use of the plural in both forms suggests that Jesus is now speaking more broadly of men and women generally (see above). The use of ὅταν + subjunctive sets the temporal reference to a potential future situation (i.e., a narrative future from the perspective of the fictive event described; see v. 18). Alternatively, the present tenses here might be viewed as gnomic; the difference is insignificant.

γαμίζονται. Pres pass ind 3rd pl γαμίζω.

εἰσὶν. Pres act ind 3rd pl εἰμί.

ὡς ἄγγελοι. Predicate nominative to εἰσίν, in which ὡς is used as an adjective (BDAG, 1104.2.c.β, s.v. ὡς, citing ‖ Matt 22:30): "they are similar to angels." Alternatively, ἄγγελοι could also be described as the nominative subject of an implied εἰσίν in a comparative clause: "they are as the angels are."

ἐν τοῖς οὐρανοῖς. Locative. The word order would suggest that the prepositional phrase is probably best taken as adjectival (despite the lack of an article) describing the angels (Swete, 281). Were it taken adverbially, it would instead describe the situation of people in general when they were in heaven. Note that the comparison is to marital status (γαμέω), not sexual identification.

12:26 περὶ δὲ τῶν νεκρῶν ὅτι ἐγείρονται οὐκ ἀνέγνωτε ἐν τῇ βίβλῳ Μωϋσέως ἐπὶ τοῦ βάτου πῶς εἶπεν αὐτῷ ὁ θεὸς λέγων, Ἐγὼ ὁ θεὸς Ἀβραὰμ καὶ [ὁ] θεὸς Ἰσαὰκ καὶ [ὁ] θεὸς Ἰακώβ;

περὶ δὲ τῶν νεκρῶν. Reference. The use of περὶ δέ at the beginning of a paragraph typically indicates a transition in the discussion (see also 13:32), whether to a new topic altogether or to a new aspect of the topic already under discussion.

ὅτι. Epexegetical, introducing the specifics regarding the dead concerning which Jesus will comment. The formal equivalent given in the translation above would more naturally be expressed in English as, "Now as for the dead being raised" (NET).

ἐγείρονται. Pres pass ind 3rd pl ἐγείρω. The temporal reference is unrestricted as part of a gnomic statement (or it could be viewed as future).

ἀνέγνωτε. Aor act ind 2nd pl ἀναγινώσκω. This verb is negated with οὐκ, which in a rhetorical question of this nature implies a positive answer; Jesus assumes that they have read the passage in question.

ἐν τῇ βίβλῳ Μωϋσέως. Locative. The reference is to the Pentateuch as a whole (note the singular τῇ βίβλῳ). This is the only NT reference to "the book of Moses"; it appears in the LXX as τῇ Μωυσέως βίβλῳ (1 Esd 5:48; 7:6, 9). The term βιβλίον is used instead of βίβλος in 2 Chr 35:12; Ezra 6:18; 1 Esd 1:12 (see also τῷ βιβλίῳ τοῦ νόμου Μωυσῆ in Josh 23:6; cf. Neh 8:1; 13:1).

ἐπὶ τοῦ βάτου. Spatial. "ἐ. τοῦ ... βάτου *at the thornbush* = *in the passage about the thornbush* (i.e. Ex 3:1ff) Mk 12:26; Lk 20:37" (BDAG, 363.2.a, s.v. ἐπί). The word βάτος appears as either masculine or feminine, though both use second declension endings. The masculine, as here, is more common in Koine, with the feminine more commonly found in Attic texts (cf. ἐπὶ τῆς βάτου in ‖ Luke 20:37).

πῶς. The interrogative particle introduces the content of the passage about the bush to which Jesus refers.

εἶπεν. Aor act ind 3rd sg λέγω.

αὐτῷ. Dative indirect object of εἶπεν.

ὁ θεὸς. Nominative subject of εἶπεν.

λέγων. Pres act ptc masc nom sg λέγω (means; redundant participle of speaking; see 3:33).

Ἐγὼ ὁ θεὸς Ἀβραὰμ ... Ἰακώβ. Clausal complement (direct discourse) of λέγων. The question mark following this embedded quote goes with the larger statement, not the quotation from LXX Exod 3:6. Mark does not include the εἰμι that is found in the LXX, making it a verbless clause as in the MT. (‖ Matt 22:32 matches the LXX and includes the verb; Luke 20:37 paraphrases the statement.)

Ἐγὼ. Nominative subject in a verbless clause.

ὁ θεὸς Ἀβραὰμ καὶ [ὁ] θεὸς Ἰσαὰκ καὶ [ὁ] θεὸς Ἰακώβ. Predicate nominative in a verbless clause. The three proper names are all indeclinable, but are to be understood as genitives. The presence (as in most mss) or absence (as in B D W) of the second and third article makes no difference in meaning.

12:27 οὐκ ἔστιν θεὸς νεκρῶν ἀλλὰ ζώντων· πολὺ πλανᾶσθε.

ἔστιν. Pres act ind 3rd sg εἰμί. On the accent, see 12:32.

θεὸς. Predicate nominative.

νεκρῶν ἀλλὰ ζώντων. Both the adjective and the participle are substantival, with the conjunction contrasting the two groups.

ζώντων. Pres act ptc masc gen pl ζάω (substantival).

πολὺ. Adverbial use of πολύς. This is the only adverbial use in Mark of the singular (see 1:45).

πλανᾶσθε. Pres mid ind 2nd pl πλανάω.

Mark 12:28-34

[28]Now one of the scribes, having come and heard them debating, having observed that (Jesus) answered them well, asked him, "What is the most important commandment of all?" [29]Jesus answered,

"Most important is 'Hear Israel, the Lord our God, the Lord is one. [30]Love the Lord your God with all your heart and with all your soul and with all your mind and with all your strength.' [31]A second is this, 'Love your neighbor as yourself.' There is no commandment greater than these." [32]The scribe said to him, "Well (said), Teacher. You have spoken truly that he is one and there is no other but him; [33]and to love him with all your heart, and with all your understanding, and with all your strength, and to love your neighbor as yourself is more important than all the burnt offerings and sacrifices." [34]Jesus, seeing him answer wisely, said to him, "You are not far from the kingdom of God." So no one any longer dared to question him.

12:28 Καὶ προσελθὼν εἷς τῶν γραμματέων ἀκούσας αὐτῶν συζητούντων, ἰδὼν ὅτι καλῶς ἀπεκρίθη αὐτοῖς ἐπηρώτησεν αὐτόν, Ποία ἐστὶν ἐντολὴ πρώτη πάντων;

προσελθών. Aor act ptc masc nom sg προσέρχομαι (temporal). All three participles are taken here in parallel (see the translation), but it is possible that "the second and third . . . may be viewed as the ground of the first = one of the scribes, having heard [ἀκούσας] them disputing, and being conscious [ἰδών] that He (Jesus) answered them well, approached [προσελθών] and asked Him, etc." (Bruce, 424).

εἷς. Nominative subject of ἐπηρώτησεν. On the use of εἷς with the partitive genitive, not as an equivalent to τις in this context, see 10:17 and 14:10.

τῶν γραμματέων. Partitive genitive (see 8:8).

ἀκούσας. Aor act ptc masc nom sg ἀκούω (temporal).

αὐτῶν. Genitive direct object of ἀκούσας. The referent is Jesus and the Sadducees.

συζητούντων. Pres act ptc masc gen pl συζητέω (complement in an object-complement double genitive construction).

ἰδών. Aor act ptc masc nom sg ὁράω (temporal).

ὅτι. Introduces the clausal complement of ἰδών.

ἀπεκρίθη. Aor mid ind 3rd sg ἀποκρίνομαι. On this intransitive, "θη middle" form, see 3:33.

αὐτοῖς. Dative complement of ἀπεκρίθη.

ἐπηρώτησεν. Aor act ind 3rd sg ἐπερωτάω. On ἐπερωτάω versus the simple form ἐρωτάω, see 4:10.

αὐτόν. Accusative direct object of ἐπηρώτησεν.

Ποία ἐστὶν ἐντολὴ πρώτη πάντων. Clausal complement (direct discourse) of ἐπηρώτησεν.

Ποία. The interrogative pronoun modifies ἐντολή. The meaning is no different here than τίς (Cranfield, 376; contra Gould, 231). As Gundry rightly notes, "'what kind of' asks for a description. Yet Jesus answers by identifying a commandment, not by describing one" (714).

ἐστὶν. Pres act ind 3rd sg εἰμί.

ἐντολὴ. Nominative subject of ἐστίν.

πρώτη. Predicate adjective. The meaning is not "first" (in a numerical or chronological sense), but "most important" (BDAG, 893.2.a.α). Hort describes it as "a strong superlative, = 'absolutely first'" (159).

πάντων. Partitive genitive (see 8:8) referring to the entire corpus of commandments. The gender is neuter in place of the expected feminine (to agree with ἐντολή); this is probably an idiomatic, "frozen masc.-neut. form" (BDF §164.1.1; cf. Zerwick §12). "Since πάντων, 'of all' (v 28), does not agree in gender with ἐντολή, 'commandment,' the interpretation has arisen that 'first of all' does not mean 'foremost of all the commandments,' but 'the commandment that is more important than everything else, whether other commandments or not.' But Jesus' stating that there is no other *commandment* greater than the two he has quoted (v 31) shows that πάντων occurs ad sensum, perhaps stereotypically, to intensify the superlative 'first'" (Gundry, 714; see Edwards 2002, 370, as an example of the argument which Gundry rejects).

12:29 ἀπεκρίθη ὁ Ἰησοῦς ὅτι Πρώτη ἐστίν, Ἄκουε, Ἰσραήλ, κύριος ὁ θεὸς ἡμῶν κύριος εἷς ἐστιν,

ἀπεκρίθη. Aor mid ind 3rd sg ἀποκρίνομαι. This is one of the few uses in Mark of ἀποκρίνομαι without an associated participle of speaking to introduce direct discourse (see also 9:17 and 12:29). On this intransitive, "θη middle" form, see 3:33.

ὁ Ἰησοῦς. Nominative subject of ἀπεκρίθη.

ὅτι. Introduces the clausal complement (direct discourse) of ἀπεκρίθη (see 1:15).

Πρώτη. Adjective modifying an understood ἐντολή (from the previous phrase): "the first commandment." *First* is here used in the sense of "most important" (see v. 31).

ἐστίν. Pres act ind 3rd sg εἰμί.

Ἄκουε, Ἰσραήλ . . . ³⁰τῆς ἰσχύος σου. This quotation from Deut 6:4-5, the first part of the *Šĕmaʿ*, functions as the subject of ἐστίν. With two unmarked constituents, the known entity is typically the subject (Wallace 1996, 42). In this situation the subject is not marked grammatically, but the OT quotation is known, and the point of the question is which is first. The last two phrases of the quotation vary from the LXX, inserting a phrase not found in the MT or LXX (καὶ ἐξ ὅλης τῆς διανοίας σου) and substituting a synonym (ἰσχύος for δυνάμεώς).

Ἄκουε. Pres act impv 2nd sg ἀκούω.

Ἰσραήλ. Vocative.

κύριος. Nominative subject of ἐστιν.

ὁ θεὸς. Nominative in apposition to κύριος. The LXX reproduces the Hebrew syntax exactly, including the repetition of YHWH/ κύριος, even though it produces an abrupt, somewhat redundant expression in Greek.

κύριος. Nominative subject of ἐστιν.

εἷς. Predicate nominative of ἐστιν.

ἐστιν. Pres act ind 3rd sg εἰμί.

12:30 καὶ ἀγαπήσεις κύριον τὸν θεόν σου ἐξ ὅλης τῆς καρδίας σου καὶ ἐξ ὅλης τῆς ψυχῆς σου καὶ ἐξ ὅλης τῆς διανοίας σου καὶ ἐξ ὅλης τῆς ἰσχύος σου.

ἀγαπήσεις. Fut act ind 2nd sg ἀγαπάω. The future has an imperatival sense, reflecting the force of the OT quote.

κύριον. Accusative direct object of ἀγαπήσεις.

τὸν θεόν. Accusative in apposition to κύριον.

ἐξ … καὶ ἐξ … καὶ ἐξ … καὶ ἐξ. Source. For a helpful discussion of the meaning of the four objects in these phrases (καρδίας, ψυχῆς, διανοίας, ἰσχύος), see Stein (2008, 561).

12:31 δευτέρα αὕτη, Ἀγαπήσεις τὸν πλησίον σου ὡς σεαυτόν. μείζων τούτων ἄλλη ἐντολὴ οὐκ ἔστιν.

Jesus' use of πρώτη (v. 29) and Δευτέρα indicate "priority and order," but "there is a sense in which these two separate commands are brought together by Jesus and form a single command. This is seen in 12:31, where Jesus says that no other commandment (singular) [ἄλλη ἐντολὴ οὐκ ἔστιν] is greater than these … and in 12:33, where the scribe repeats Jesus' two commandments and says that this 'is' (ἐστίν …) greater than all whole burnt offerings and sacrifices. All the other commandments can be understood as an explication of this one, two-part command" (Stein 2008, 562).

δευτέρα. Predicate nominative of an implied ἔστιν.

αὕτη. Nominative subject of an implied ἔστιν.

Ἀγαπήσεις τὸν πλησίον σου ὡς σεαυτόν. This clause, quoted exactly from LXX Lev 19:18, serves as the "postcedent" of the pronoun αὕτη.

Ἀγαπήσεις. Fut act ind 2nd sg ἀγαπάω.

τὸν πλησίον. Accusative direct object of ἀγαπήσεις. πλησίον is the adverbial accusative form of the adjective πλησίος ("nearby"), but in the NT it is used with the article as a substantive ("neighbor, friend").

ὡς σεαυτόν. Comparative clause in which σεαυτόν functions as the accusative direct object of an implied verb (ὡς ἀγαπᾷς σεαυτόν).

μείζων. Predicate adjective.

τούτων. Genitive of comparison.

ἄλλη ἐντολὴ. Nominative subject of ἔστιν.

ἔστιν. Pres act ind 3rd sg εἰμί.

12:32 καὶ εἶπεν αὐτῷ ὁ γραμματεύς, Καλῶς, διδάσκαλε, ἐπ' ἀληθείας εἶπες ὅτι εἷς ἐστιν καὶ οὐκ ἔστιν ἄλλος πλὴν αὐτοῦ·

εἶπεν. Aor act ind 3rd sg λέγω.

αὐτῷ. Dative indirect object of εἶπεν.

ὁ γραμματεύς. Nominative subject of εἶπεν.

Καλῶς. Predicate adverb of an elliptical statement with an understood verb, perhaps εἶπες (i.e., "you speak well"). The one-word statement can stand alone in both Greek and English: "Good!" (or, "well said," Swete, 286; see also V. Taylor, 488; BDAG, 506.4.c). For a similar use of καλῶς as a one-word response, see Rom 11:20 and perhaps 1 Kgs (3 Kgdms) 2:18. In response to the initial question posed by the scribe (v. 28), this one-word exclamation in essence says, "You have answered well/correctly."

διδάσκαλε. Vocative (see also 4:38).

ἐπ' ἀληθείας. Cause: "on the basis of truth."

εἶπες. Aor act ind 2nd sg λέγω.

ὅτι. Introduces the clausal complement (indirect discourse) of εἶπες (see 1:15).

εἷς. Predicate nominative.

ἐστιν. Pres act ind 3rd sg εἰμί. The verb form ἐστίν is an enclitic, so here loses its accent since the preceding one-syllable word has a circumflex. It is most commonly enclitic, occurring without an accent fifty-two times in Mark. The same form three words later is not enclitic and has an acute on the first syllable (ἔστιν) both because the preceding word is οὐκ and because there it signifies existence (see Carson, 50 §EPR.8.2–3; Smyth §187). Accenting the first syllable (here the penult) is a less common form in Mark, occurring only nine times (6:4; 7:2; 9:40; 10:40; 12:11, 27, 31, 32; 16:6), almost always when following a form of οὐκ (once it follows τοῦτ᾽). The other nonenclitic form, ἐστίν, occurs twelve times in Mark (2:1; 3:35; 6:15, 55; 9:43, 45; 12:29; 13:28), the accent usually being retained because the word comes at the end of a clause (also four with grave, ἐστὶν, not clause final: 4:26; 9:21; 10:14; 12:28).

ἔστιν. Pres act ind 3rd sg εἰμί. Impersonal subject from the verb, "there is."

ἄλλος. Predicate nominative.

πλὴν αὐτοῦ. Although technically an adverb, πλήν is usually used as a conjunction, but here it functions as a preposition with the genitive indicating an exception (BDAG, 826.2). The only other NT uses of πλήν as a preposition are Acts 8:1; 15:28; 27:22 (it is more common in the LXX where there are 84 instances; Josephus has 42 instances).

12:33 καὶ τὸ ἀγαπᾶν αὐτὸν ἐξ ὅλης τῆς καρδίας καὶ ἐξ ὅλης τῆς συνέσεως καὶ ἐξ ὅλης τῆς ἰσχύος καὶ τὸ ἀγαπᾶν τὸν πλησίον ὡς ἑαυτὸν περισσότερόν ἐστιν πάντων τῶν ὁλοκαυτωμάτων καὶ θυσιῶν.

τὸ ἀγαπᾶν αὐτὸν . . . καὶ τὸ ἀγαπᾶν τὸν πλησίον. The infinitive clause functions as the nominative subject of ἐστιν. Each of the infinitives represent, in indirect discourse, the finite imperative form, ἀγαπήσεις, in the original statement.

ἀγαπᾶν. Pres act inf ἀγαπάω (see above).

αὐτὸν. Accusative direct object of ἀγαπᾶν.

ἐξ . . . καὶ ἐξ . . . καὶ ἐξ. . . . Source (see also v. 30).

ἀγαπᾶν. Pres act inf ἀγαπάω (see above).

τὸν πλησίον. Accusative direct object of ἀγαπᾶν.

ὡς ἑαυτὸν. See verse 31.

περισσότερόν. Comparative adjective form of περισσός, functioning as a predicate adjective. The double accent is due to the enclitic form following (ἐστιν).

ἐστιν. Pres act ind 3rd sg εἰμί.

πάντων τῶν ὁλοκαυτωμάτων καὶ θυσιῶν. Genitive of comparison with περισσότερον. The noun ὁλοκαύτωμα refers to a "whole burnt offering."

12:34 καὶ ὁ Ἰησοῦς ἰδὼν [αὐτὸν] ὅτι νουνεχῶς ἀπεκρίθη εἶπεν αὐτῷ, Οὐ μακρὰν εἶ ἀπὸ τῆς βασιλείας τοῦ θεοῦ. καὶ οὐδεὶς οὐκέτι ἐτόλμα αὐτὸν ἐπερωτῆσαι.

ὁ Ἰησοῦς. Nominative subject of εἶπεν.

ἰδὼν. Aor act ptc masc nom sg ὁράω (causal/temporal).

[αὐτὸν]. Accusative direct object of ἰδών. On the position of αὐτόν, cf. τὸν Ἰωάννην in 11:32. This is an example of *prolepsis* in which the subject of the subordinate clause is introduced in the main clause as an accusative object (see BDF §476.1).

ὅτι. Epexegetical to αὐτόν.

νουνεχῶς. Adverb modifying ἀπεκρίθη ("with display of intelligence, *thoughtfully, wisely*," CL, 243; only here in the NT and nowhere else in Greek texts related to the Bible). The expression νοῦν ἔχειν, meaning "to have sense, be sensible" or "to have one's mind directed to something" (LSJ), is fairly common; and there is also an adjectival form, νουνεχή ("with understanding, sensible, discreet," LSJ).

ἀπεκρίθη. Aor pass ind 3rd sg ἀποκρίνομαι. On this intransitive, "θη middle" form, see 3:33.

εἶπεν. Aor act ind 3rd sg λέγω.

αὐτῷ. Dative indirect object of εἶπεν.

Οὐ μακρὰν εἶ ... τοῦ θεοῦ. Clausal complement (direct discourse) of εἶπεν. This may be an example of litotes. If so, "this means that Jesus' statement should be taken positively, not negatively. The understated emphasis is on the scribe's nearness to the kingdom of God, not the fact that he does not yet belong to the kingdom" (Collins, 577).

μακρὰν. Predicate adverb.

εἶ. Pres act ind 2nd sg εἰμί.

ἀπὸ τῆς βασιλείας. Separation.

τοῦ θεοῦ. Subjective genitive indicating the regent of the kingdom: the kingdom over which God reigns.

οὐδεὶς. Nominative subject of ἐτόλμα. The double negative, οὐδεὶς οὐκέτι, is emphatic.

οὐκέτι. Adverb, "no longer, any more."

ἐτόλμα. Impf act ind 3rd sg τολμάω.

αὐτὸν. Accusative direct object of ἐπερωτῆσαι.

ἐπερωτῆσαι. Aor act inf ἐπερωτάω (complementary). On ἐπερωτάω versus the simple form ἐρωτάω, see 4:10.

Mark 12:35-40

³⁵While teaching in the temple Jesus said, "How is it the scribes say that the Messiah is the son of David? ³⁶David himself spoke by the Holy Spirit, 'The Lord said to my Lord, "Sit at my right hand until I place your enemies under your feet."' ³⁷David himself calls him Lord; how then is he his son?" Now the large crowd enjoyed listening to him.

³⁸As he was teaching he said, "Beware of the scribes who like to walk around in long robes (and who like) greetings in the markets and places of honor in the synagogues ³⁹and the best seats at dinners, ⁴⁰who devour widows' houses and who say long prayers for appearance's sake; these are the ones who will receive very severe punishment."

12:35 Καὶ ἀποκριθεὶς ὁ Ἰησοῦς ἔλεγεν διδάσκων ἐν τῷ ἱερῷ, Πῶς λέγουσιν οἱ γραμματεῖς ὅτι ὁ Χριστὸς υἱὸς Δαυίδ ἐστιν;

ἀποκριθεὶς. Aor pass ptc masc nom sg ἀποκρίνομαι (means; redundant participle of speaking; see 1:7). On this intransitive, "θη middle" form, see 3:33. "Since Jesus has already answered the scribe in verse 34ab and since Mark's statement that 'nobody was daring to question him any more' has intervened in v 34c, Jesus' 'answering' does not mean that he answers the scribe, but that he responds to the lack of further questions by asking his own questions about the scribes" (Gundry, 717). Mark does not specify to whom the question was addressed. The question functions as a rhetorical device to introduce the subject of Jesus' teaching. The ‖ Luke 20:41 has the question addressed to "them" (εἶπεν δὲ πρὸς αὐτούς), but without specification as to the referent. In Matt 22:41, a similar question is addressed to the Pharisees. Given the location of the statement of Mark 12:34 ‖ Matt 22:46—following the question in Matthew, but preceding it in Mark—it is possible that Jesus addressed a question first to the Pharisees, then, having silenced them, used their response (Matt 22:42, λέγουσιν αὐτῷ· τοῦ Δαυίδ) as a rhetorical question addressed to the crowd (Mark 12:35).

ὁ Ἰησοῦς. Nominative subject of ἔλεγεν.

ἔλεγεν. Impf act ind 3rd sg λέγω. On the possibility that this is an inceptive imperfect as in the NASB, see 1:21.

διδάσκων. Pres act ptc masc nom sg διδάσκω (temporal; cf. ἐν τῇ διδαχῇ αὐτοῦ in v. 38).

ἐν τῷ ἱερῷ. Locative.

Πῶς λέγουσιν ... ἐστιν υἱός. Clausal complement (direct

discourse) of ἔλεγεν. Compare the introductory wording (πῶς λέγουσιν οἱ γραμματεῖς ὅτι) with the question asked by the disciples in 9:11, λέγουσιν οἱ γραμματεῖς ὅτι.

Πῶς. Interrogative particle ("How?") used in this context with "the special mng. *with what right? with what evidence? in what sense?*" (BDAG, 900.1.a.α).

λέγουσιν. Pres act ind 3rd pl λέγω.

οἱ γραμματεῖς. Nominative subject of λέγουσιν.

ὅτι. Introduces the clausal complement of λέγουσιν (see 1:15). This could be taken as either direct or indirect discourse, but most likely it represents just a summary of a commonly known position, rather than citing a particular statement by the scribes.

ὁ Χριστὸς. Nominative subject of ἐστιν. The sense of ὁ Χριστός here is "the Messiah."

υἱὸς Δαυίδ. Predicate nominative of ἐστιν with an indeclinable genitive modifier (Δαυίδ). Although this expression could be understood as either definite or indefinite, it is likely qualitative as an anarthrous preverbal noun. "The predicate would be definite if it signified 'the son of David' as some well-known figure of Jewish expectation. It would be indefinite if it simply meant someone descended from David. It would be qualitative if it emphasized Davidic descent as an aspect or condition of messiahship. The first or the second possibility, of course, does not preclude the third. The primary emphasis of the passage as a whole (12:35-37) seems to lie in the question of Davidic descent. The passage gives no further clues, on the other hand, whether Mark was thinking of 'the' son or 'a' son of David. Again the qualitative force of the predicate noun seems to be more prominent than its definiteness or indefiniteness" (Harner, 79).

ἐστιν. Pres act ind 3rd sg εἰμί.

12:36 αὐτὸς Δαυὶδ εἶπεν ἐν τῷ πνεύματι τῷ ἁγίῳ, Εἶπεν κύριος τῷ κυρίῳ μου, Κάθου ἐκ δεξιῶν μου, ἕως ἂν θῶ τοὺς ἐχθρούς σου ὑποκάτω τῶν ποδῶν σου.

αὐτὸς. The intensive adjective emphasizes David as the author of Ps 110.

Δαυίδ. Nominative subject of εἶπεν.

εἶπεν. Aor act ind 3rd sg λέγω.

ἐν τῷ πνεύματι τῷ ἁγίῳ. Locative, used metaphorically to describe David's relationship to the Spirit as he spoke (cf. Acts 1:16; 2:29-31; 28:25).

Εἶπεν κύριος . . . τῶν ποδῶν σου. Clausal complement (direct discourse) of εἶπεν. The statement is quoted from Ps 110:1 (LXX: 109:1), with only a few minor variations, none of which affect the meaning. The most significant is the substitution of ὑποκάτω for ὑποπόδιον (B D W 28 2542 *pc*; the remaining witnesses read ὑποπόδιον). The || Matt 22:44 also has ὑποκάτω supported by a broader range of witnesses; Luke 20:43 is uniformly ὑποπόδιον (other than D). The LXX is a close formal equivalent of the Hebrew text.

Εἶπεν. Aor act ind 3rd sg λέγω.

κύριος. Nominative subject of εἶπεν.

τῷ κυρίῳ. Dative indirect object of εἶπεν.

μου. The addition of μου helps to distinguish David (subject of the first εἶπεν), from both the subject of this clause (κύριος) and the addressee of the second εἶπεν (τῷ κυρίῳ μου), i.e., three parties are in view. The third party is described as David's lord/κύριος, distinct from the first κύριος who speaks the words of the following clause (Κάθου . . .) in which the second μου now refers to the first κύριος, as does the first singular subject of θῶ, and both instances of σου refer to the second κύριος who is also described as David's lord/κύριος.

κάθου. Pres mid impv 2nd sg κάθημαι.

ἐκ δεξιῶν μου. On this idiomatic phrase, see 10:37.

ἕως ἄν. Introduces a temporal clause (*TDM*, 88–89); the same expression is used in 6:19 and 9:1.

θῶ. Aor act subj 1st sg τίθημι. Subjunctive with ἕως ἄν.

τοὺς ἐχθρούς. Accusative direct object of θῶ.

ὑποκάτω τῶν ποδῶν. Although ὑποκάτω is technically an adverb ("under, below"), in the NT it functions only as a preposition with the genitive (BDAG, 1038), most commonly with τῶν ποδῶν as the object (5 of 11 instances). In this context, the figure is that of "the one who is vanquished lies beneath the victor's feet" (BDAG, 858.1.b, s.v. πούς).

12:37 αὐτὸς Δαυὶδ λέγει αὐτὸν κύριον, καὶ πόθεν αὐτοῦ ἐστιν υἱός; Καὶ [ὁ] πολὺς ὄχλος ἤκουεν αὐτοῦ ἡδέως.

αὐτὸς. Adjectival intensive use.

Δαυὶδ. Nominative subject of λέγει.

λέγει. Pres act ind 3rd sg λέγω.

αὐτὸν. Accusative direct object of λέγει.

κύριον. Complement in an object-complement double accusative construction.

καὶ πόθεν. "How then?" Here πόθεν is an interrogative that asks for a reason (BDAG, 838.3): "How is it?" (contra Gundry, 718–19, 721–23, who insists that πόθεν retains its usual sense, "from where?").

αὐτοῦ. The genitive modifies υἱός despite being separated by the verb (an unusual word order).

ἐστιν. Pres act ind 3rd sg εἰμί.

υἱός. Predicate nominative.

Καὶ [ὁ] πολὺς ὄχλος ἤκουεν αὐτοῦ ἡδέως. A similar statement occurs in 6:20. Cranfield (383) suggests that this clause introduces the next pericope (vv. 38-40), rather than commenting on their response to the preceding event. In NA^{27}/UBS^4 verse 37b stands as a separate paragraph, perhaps suggesting somewhat of a transitional statement. Most English versions punctuate verse 37b as part of the preceding pericope, though it is a new paragraph in the TEV and NIV.

[ὁ] πολὺς ὄχλος. Nominative subject of ἤκουεν. This phrase has been taken to refer to the populace generally, i.e., "the common people" (KJV, ASV; so also Cranfield, 383), but is more commonly understood simply as a reference to the size of the crowd (BDAG, 745.1.a, s.v. ὄχλος; most English versions).

ἤκουεν. Impf act ind 3rd sg ἀκούω.

αὐτοῦ. Genitive direct object of ἤκουεν.

ἡδέως. This is the adverb form of the adjective ἡδύς (BDAG, 434), "gladly." On the collocation of ἡδέως with ἀκούω, see Josephus, *Ant.* 3.191, where God is said to hear gladly/readily the prayers of the high priest.

12:38 Καὶ ἐν τῇ διδαχῇ αὐτοῦ ἔλεγεν, Βλέπετε ἀπὸ τῶν γραμματέων τῶν θελόντων ἐν στολαῖς περιπατεῖν καὶ ἀσπασμοὺς ἐν ταῖς ἀγοραῖς

ἐν τῇ διδαχῇ. Temporal (formally, "in the teaching"; see BDAG, 329.10.c, "in the course of his teaching"). The implication is that Mark records but a part of a larger didactic situation. Matthew 23 records much more of the content of Jesus' teaching at this point.

ἔλεγεν. Impf act ind 3rd sg λέγω.

Βλέπετε ἀπὸ τῶν γραμματέων ... ⁴⁰περισσότερον κρίμα. Clausal complement (direct discourse) of ἔλεγεν.

Βλέπετε. Pres act impv 2nd pl βλέπω. On the meaning of βλέπω in this context, see 8:15.

ἀπὸ τῶν γραμματέων. Causal. On the use of ἀπό with the genitive following an imperatival βλέπετε, see 8:15.

θελόντων. Pres act ptc masc gen pl θέλω (attributive). This verb is completed by a mixed construction (an infinitive followed by three accusative objects, with the four complements linked by καί). The use of the infinitive may be due to the fact that "there is no convenient noun for 'walking about'" (France, 490). The || Luke 20:46 does not have the mixed construction, but uses a second participle instead.

ἐν στολαῖς. The use of ἐν to describe being clothed is fairly common (see BDAG, 327.2.a), though this is the only such instance in Mark whose usual construction in this situation is a participle with an accusative (see 1:6; 14:51; 16:5). The closest parallel in Mark is the use of the dative case in 15:46 (ἐνείλησεν τῇ σινδόνι). Edwards proposes that στολή refers to the "full-length prayer shawls with tassels attached to the four corners. . . . These blanket-like mantles known as *tallits*, distinguished rabbis and scholars as men of wealth and eminence" (2002, 378). France, however, counters that "this is not required by the context and is not a known use of στολή" (490 n. 102). He argues that it is a festive or celebratory robe that "suggests 'dressing up'" as a mark of social prominence (490). The translation above follows Louw and Nida (6.174).

περιπατεῖν. Pres act inf περιπατέω. The infinitive phrase, ἐν στολαῖς περιπατεῖν, functions as the first part of the direct object of θελόντων.

ἀσπασμοὺς. Accusative (second part of the) direct object of θελόντων.

ἐν ταῖς ἀγοραῖς. Locative.

12:39 καὶ πρωτοκαθεδρίας ἐν ταῖς συναγωγαῖς καὶ πρωτοκλισίας ἐν τοῖς δείπνοις,

πρωτοκαθεδρίας. Accusative (third part of the) direct object of θελόντων (v. 38). A πρωτοκαθεδρία was "a place of honor at a special event of gathering, *best seat*" (*CL*, 309; BDAG, 892).

ἐν ταῖς συναγωγαῖς. Locative.

πρωτοκλισίας. Accusative (fourth part of the) direct object of θελόντων (v. 38). A πρωτοκλισία was a "prominent reclining position at a dinner, *place of honor*" (*CL*, 309; BDAG, 892).

ἐν τοῖς δείπνοις. Locative.

12:40 οἱ κατεσθίοντες τὰς οἰκίας τῶν χηρῶν καὶ προφάσει μακρὰ προσευχόμενοι· οὗτοι λήμψονται περισσότερον κρίμα.

οἱ κατεσθίοντες . . . καὶ . . . προσευχόμενοι. Nominative absolutes or "hanging nominatives" (Wallace 1996, 654), which further describe τῶν γραμματέων of verse 38 (this is not a new group or a subgroup of the scribes; France, 491) and specify the logical subject of the following clause. A change of subjects at this point would have suggested the use of δέ, but there is no conjunction at the beginning of verse 40.

κατεσθίοντες. Pres act ptc masc nom pl κατεσθίω (substantival, see above). Stein (2008, 574–75) discusses a half dozen ways in which the actions described by this word might be understood.

τὰς οἰκίας. Accusative direct object of κατεσθίοντες. BDAG (695.1.a) suggests that the reference is somewhat larger than the physical structure: "rob widows of their houses (and household goods)." The nearly synonymous οἶκος can refer to "a house and what is in it, *property, possessions, estate*" (BDAG, 699.4); in classical Greek οἰκία referred to the structure and οἶκος to "the whole of a deceased person's possessions, what he leaves behind" (Michel, 5:131), i.e., an estate, but this distinction is no longer true in Koine. The context would seem to justify the broader reference for οἰκία in this passage.

τῶν χηρῶν. Genitive of possession.

προφάσει μακρὰ προσευχόμενοι. Formally, "with pretense long-praying ones" (see the translation).

προφάσει. Dative of manner. A πρόφασις is a "falsely alleged motive, *pretext, ostensible reason*" (BDAG, 889), but here the idea seems to be "for show" (Gundry, 728).

μακρὰ. Adverbial accusative form of μακρός.

προσευχόμενοι. Pres mid ptc masc nom pl προσεύχομαι (substantival, see above).

οὗτοι. Nominative subject of λήμψονται. The near demonstrative pronoun resumes the subject previously introduced (the two nominative absolutes) "with special emphasis" (BDAG, 741.1.a.ε). Thus, "these are the ones who."

λήμψονται. Fut mid ind 3rd pl λαμβάνω.

περισσότερον. Comparative adjective form of περισσός. Since there is no other value in the context with which to compare, it is possible that this is to be understood as an elative rather than a comparative (cf. the NIV's "will be punished most severely"). Alternatively, France proposes that it be understood to refer to "the more obvious guilt of these people than of other less blatant sinners" (492; cf. Collins, 586).

κρίμα. Accusative direct object of λήμψονται.

Mark 12:41-44

⁴¹Having sat down opposite the offering box, Jesus observed how the crowd was throwing money into the offering box. Many wealthy people threw in much. ⁴²Coming, a poor widow threw in two *lepta*, which is (equivalent to) a *quadrans*. ⁴³So summoning his disciples he said to them, "Truly I say to you that this poor widow has thrown in more than all those who threw (money) into the offering box; ⁴⁴for everyone else threw in out of their abundance, but she, out of her poverty, threw in everything she had—all her livelihood.

12:41 Καὶ καθίσας κατέναντι τοῦ γαζοφυλακίου ἐθεώρει πῶς ὁ ὄχλος βάλλει χαλκὸν εἰς τὸ γαζοφυλάκιον. καὶ πολλοὶ πλούσιοι ἔβαλλον πολλά·

καθίσας. Aor act ptc masc nom sg καθίζω (temporal).

κατέναντι τοῦ γαζοφυλακίου. By form, κατέναντι is an adverb, but it can be used (as it is here) as a preposition with the genitive expressing location. Normally, γαζοφυλάκιον would refer to a treasury or treasure room (e.g., Matt 27:6; LXX 2 Kgs 23:11; Neh 10:37), but in this passage, as in || Luke 21:1, the referent appears to be narrower, since money is thrown into it; thus, "offering box" (LN 6.141; but BDAG, 186.2). According to the Mishnah there were thirteen such offering boxes in the temple, each with a trumpet-shaped opening (*m. Šeqal.* 6:5).

ἐθεώρει. Impf act ind 3rd sg θεωρέω. The imperfect is used to set the scene, telling the reader what Jesus was doing when the events of this pericope take place.

πῶς. The interrogative adverb is used in an indirect question focused on the *manner* in which something was done.

ὁ ὄχλος. Nominative subject of βάλλει.

βάλλει. Pres act ind 3rd sg βάλλω. This pericope provides a good illustration of verbal aspect, both in the use of the various aspects and their distinction from *Aktionsart*. In 12:41 imperfective aspect is used to describe the actions of the crowd in terms of a process: ἐθεώρει πῶς ὁ ὄχλος βάλλει χαλκὸν εἰς τὸ γαζοφυλάκιον ("he was observing how the crowd *was throwing* money into the offering box"). Then in verse 44, referring to the same event, perfective aspect is used, which views the action as a whole: πάντες ἐκ τοῦ περισσεύοντος αὐτοῖς ἔβαλον ("all out of their abundance *threw*"). We would be foolish to insist that two different kinds of actions are being described just because one verse uses βάλλει and the other ἔβαλον. Given the presumed nature of the offering box (see above on γαζοφυλάκιον), "throw" is understandable, without any necessary nuance of an ostentatious action; the widow's meager offering is described with the same verb. If γαζοφυλάκιον refers to the treasury, then this verb may be translated "put" (see BDAG, 163.3.b).

χαλκὸν. Accusative direct object of βάλλει. χαλκός is a term for anything made of metal, particularly copper or bronze (e.g., statues, gongs, kettles, vases, etc.), but it was often used as a term for money in general, typically with reference to copper coins (BDAG, 1076). The woman's gift was of copper (λεπτά, v. 42), but presumably the wealthy who threw in large sums (ἔβαλλον πολλά) would be giving silver and gold coins; thus the general sense "money" is in view here. The only other NT uses with this meaning are 6:8 and Matt 10:9.

εἰς τὸ γαζοφυλάκιον. Spatial.

πολλοὶ πλούσιοι. Nominative subject of ἔβαλλον.

ἔβαλλον. Impf act ind 3rd pl βάλλω. Following the proximate imperfective verb βάλλει, the first storyline verb, this remote imperfective form adds supplementary detail. The actions of the wealthy are the not the primary focus; they are simply the contrasting backdrop for the poor widow's actions.

πολλά. Accusative direct object of ἔβαλλον. The adjective is substantival: "much money" or "large sums/amounts" (cf. RSV, NIV); πολλά does not describe or represent χαλκόν per se since they do not agree in gender, but is a general term for whatever might be given. Gundry's (728) suggestion that this is an adverbial accusative does not seem appropriate since that would "qualify the action of the verb rather than indicating quantity or extent" (Wallace 1996, 200).

12:42 καὶ ἐλθοῦσα μία χήρα πτωχὴ ἔβαλεν λεπτὰ δύο, ὅ ἐστιν κοδράντης.

ἐλθοῦσα. Aor act ptc fem nom sg ἔρχομαι (attendant circumstance). The participle is somewhat superfluous (so V. Taylor, 497), but this usage is not uncommon in the Koine (see 12:12 on ἀφέντες).

μία χήρα πτωχὴ. Nominative subject of ἔβαλεν. The number μία (εἷς) is equivalent to τις here and functions like indefinite article (see 5:22; 10:17). Swete (293) suggests that πτωχός here refers to pauper in contrast to peasant status.

ἔβαλεν. Aor act ind 3rd sg βάλλω. On the aspect, see verse 41 on βάλλει.

λεπτὰ δύο. Accusative direct object of ἔβαλεν. A λεπτός, a designation for a Jewish coin (*perûṭâ*), was the smallest denomination (copper) coin in circulation at the time, worth only 1/128 of a *denarius* (BDAG, 592). According to Evans (2001, 282–83) λεπτὰ δύο was the value of a handful of flour.

ὅ ἐστιν. On this formulaic phrase, see 3:17.

ἐστιν. Pres act ind 3rd sg εἰμί.

κοδράντης. Predicate nominative. A *quadrans*, a Latin loanword (see 4:21 on ὑπὸ τὸν μόδιον … ἢ ὑπὸ τὴν κλίνην), was a bronze Roman coin worth two *lepta* or 1/64 of a *denarius* (BDAG, 550), the smallest denomination Roman coin at the time (Collins, 589). The fact that Mark explicitly converts the amount to the western, Roman equivalent (ὅ ἐστιν κοδράντης) "supports the view that he was writing in the west, as the *quadrans* was not in circulation in the east" (Cranfield, 386; cf. Lane 443 n. 85).

12:43 καὶ προσκαλεσάμενος τοὺς μαθητὰς αὐτοῦ εἶπεν αὐτοῖς, Ἀμὴν λέγω ὑμῖν ὅτι ἡ χήρα αὕτη ἡ πτωχὴ πλεῖον πάντων ἔβαλεν τῶν βαλλόντων εἰς τὸ γαζοφυλάκιον·

προσκαλεσάμενος. Aor mid ptc masc nom sg προσκαλέομαι (temporal).

τοὺς μαθητὰς. Accusative direct object of προσκαλεσάμενος.

εἶπεν. Aor act ind 3rd sg λέγω.

αὐτοῖς. Dative indirect object of εἶπεν.

ἀμὴν λέγω … ⁴⁴ὅλον τὸν βίον αὐτῆς. Clausal complement (direct discourse) of εἶπεν.

Ἀμὴν λέγω ὑμῖν. See 3:28.

λέγω. Pres act ind 1st sg λέγω.

ὑμῖν. Dative indirect object of λέγω.

ὅτι. Introduces the clausal complement (direct discourse) of λέγω.

ἡ χήρα αὕτη ἡ πτωχὴ. Nominative subject of ἔβαλεν.

πλεῖον. Comparative adverb form of πολύς used substantivally as the accusative direct object of ἔβαλεν.

πάντων … τῶν βαλλόντων. Genitive of comparison.

ἔβαλεν. Aor act ind 3rd sg βάλλω. On the aspect, see verse 41 on βάλλει.

τῶν βαλλόντων. Pres act ptc masc gen pl βάλλω (substantival).

εἰς τὸ γαζοφυλάκιον. Spatial. On γαζοφυλάκιον, see verse 41.

12:44 πάντες γὰρ ἐκ τοῦ περισσεύοντος αὐτοῖς ἔβαλον, αὕτη δὲ ἐκ τῆς ὑστερήσεως αὐτῆς πάντα ὅσα εἶχεν ἔβαλεν ὅλον τὸν βίον αὐτῆς.

πάντες. Nominative subject of ἔβαλον.

γὰρ. Introduces an explanation as to how it is that the poor widow's two *lepta* can be considered to be more (πλεῖον) than the "much" (πολλά) of the wealthy.

ἐκ τοῦ περισσεύοντος. Source.

περισσεύοντος. Pres act ptc neut gen sg περισσεύω (substantival). Contrasts between περισσεύω and expressions of scarcity or poverty are common: ὑστέρησις (here), ὑστέρημα (Luke 21:4; cf. 2 Cor 9:12), πτωχεία (2 Cor 8:2), τοῦ μὴ ἔχοντος (Matt 25:29; cf. 13:12), and ταπεινόω and ὑστερέω (Phil 4:12; *Diogn.* 5:13; cf. Philo, *Heir* 191).

αὐτοῖς. Dative of advantage: "what abounded to them."

ἔβαλον. Aor act ind 3rd pl βάλλω. On the aspect, see verse 41 on βάλλει.

αὕτη. Nominative subject of ἔβαλεν.

δὲ. The use of δέ reflects the contrast between abundance (περισσεύοντος) and poverty (ὑστερήσεως).

ἐκ τῆς ὑστερήσεως. Source. ὑστέρησις ("poverty") is an uncommon word that is the equivalent of the more common ὑστέρημα.

πάντα. Accusative direct object of ἔβαλεν.

ὅσα. Accusative direct object of εἶχεν.

εἶχεν. Impf act ind 3rd sg ἔχω.

ἔβαλεν. Aor act ind 3rd sg βάλλω. On the aspect, see verse 41 on βάλλει.

ὅλον τὸν βίον. Accusative in apposition to πάντα. The reference of βίος here is not to life per se, but to "the resources which one has as a means of living" (LN 57.18).

Mark 13:1-4

[1]As Jesus was leaving the temple one of his disciples said to him, "Teacher. Look! What (massive) stones and what (impressive) buildings!" [2]Jesus said to him, "Do you see these great buildings? A stone will not remain here on a stone which will not be thrown down." [3]While he was sitting on the Mount of Olives opposite the temple, Peter, James, John, and Andrew asked him privately, [4]"Tell us, when will these things happen and what will be the sign when all these things are to be accomplished?"

13:1 Καὶ ἐκπορευομένου αὐτοῦ ἐκ τοῦ ἱεροῦ λέγει αὐτῷ εἷς τῶν μαθητῶν αὐτοῦ, Διδάσκαλε, ἴδε ποταποὶ λίθοι καὶ ποταπαὶ οἰκοδομαί.

ἐκπορευομένου. Pres mid ptc masc gen sg ἐκπορεύομαι. Genitive absolute (see 1:32), temporal.

αὐτοῦ. Genitive subject of ἐκπορευομένου. On the overlap of reference with αὐτῷ in the main clause, see 5:2 and 14:3.

ἐκ τοῦ ἱεροῦ. Separation. The term ἱερόν normally refers to the entire temple complex (in contrast to ναός, the sanctuary proper, which Mark uses only in 14:58; 15:29, 38).

λέγει. Pres act ind 3rd sg λέγω.

αὐτῷ. Dative indirect object of λέγει.

εἷς. Nominative subject of λέγει. On the use of εἷς with the partitive genitive, see 10:17 and 14:10.

τῶν μαθητῶν. Partitive genitive (8:8).

Διδάσκαλε, ἴδε ποταποὶ λίθοι καὶ ποταπαὶ οἰκοδομαί. Clausal complement (direct discourse) of λέγει.

Διδάσκαλε. Vocative (see also 4:38).

ἴδε. See 3:34. This instance of ἴδε appears to retain its verbal qualities.

ποταποὶ λίθοι καὶ ποταπαὶ οἰκοδομαί. With the particle ἴδε the nominative specifies "that which is to be observed" (BDAG, 466, s.v. ἴδε). Wallace (1996, 60 n. 88) classes this as an example of a nominative of exclamation.

ποταποὶ ... ποταπαὶ. Although ποταπός is an interrogative adjective ("of what sort?"), "somet[imes] the context calls for the sense *how great, how wonderful* Mk 13:1ab" (BDAG, 856). This is an "exclamatory sense" (Hort, 163).

13:2 καὶ ὁ Ἰησοῦς εἶπεν αὐτῷ, Βλέπεις ταύτας τὰς μεγάλας οἰκοδομάς; οὐ μὴ ἀφεθῇ ὧδε λίθος ἐπὶ λίθον ὃς οὐ μὴ καταλυθῇ.

ὁ Ἰησοῦς. Nominative subject of εἶπεν.

εἶπεν. Aor act ind 3rd sg λέγω.

αὐτῷ. Dative indirect object of εἶπεν.

Βλέπεις ταύτας ... οὐ μὴ καταλυθῇ. Clausal complement (direct discourse) of εἶπεν. The first statement is usually understood as a question because it is a response to an exclamation, but it could be taken as a second exclamation: "Look at these great buildings!"

Βλέπεις. Pres act ind 2nd sg βλέπω.

ταύτας τὰς μεγάλας οἰκοδομάς. Accusative direct object of βλέπω.

ἀφεθῇ. Aor pass subj 3rd sg ἀφίημι. Subjunctive with οὐ μή, which may be emphatic here (see 9:1). Some commentators see the repetition of οὐ μή with the aorist subjunctive as giving the passage a "decisive tone" (V. Taylor, 501) or as suggesting "the total nature of the destruction" (Lane, 452). On double negatives in general, see 1:44.

ὧδε. This adverb of place may add vividness, "almost suggesting a gesture" (V. Taylor, 501).

λίθος. Nominative subject of ἀφεθῇ.

ἐπὶ λίθον. Spatial.

ὅς. Nominative subject of καταλυθῇ.

οὐ μὴ. On the use of οὐ μή, see above .

καταλυθῇ. Aor pass subj 3rd sg καταλύω. Subjunctive with οὐ μή.

13:3 Καὶ καθημένου αὐτοῦ εἰς τὸ Ὄρος τῶν Ἐλαιῶν κατέναντι τοῦ ἱεροῦ ἐπηρώτα αὐτὸν κατ᾽ ἰδίαν Πέτρος καὶ Ἰάκωβος καὶ Ἰωάννης καὶ Ἀνδρέας,

καθημένου. Pres mid ptc masc gen sg κάθημαι. Genitive absolute (see 1:32), temporal.

αὐτοῦ. Genitive subject of καθημένου. On the overlap of reference with αὐτόν in the main clause, see 5:2 and 14:3.

εἰς τὸ Ὄρος. Locative.

κατέναντι τοῦ ἱεροῦ. Spatial. The adverb κατέναντι here functions as a preposition with the genitive.

ἐπηρώτα. Impf act ind 3rd sg ἐπερωτάω. On ἐπερωτάω versus the simple form ἐρωτάω, see 4:10. The singular verb, which is followed by four nominatives, likely focuses on Peter as the speaker, who is accompanied by three other disciples. Matthew's account (24:3) makes it a more general statement with a plural verb, while Luke 21:7 is more general yet with no subject specified.

αὐτὸν. Accusative direct object of ἐπηρώτα.

κατ᾽ ἰδίαν. "Privately" (see 4:34).

Πέτρος καὶ . . . καὶ Ἀνδρέας. Nominative subject of ἐπηρώτα.

13:4 Εἰπὸν ἡμῖν, πότε ταῦτα ἔσται καὶ τί τὸ σημεῖον ὅταν μέλλῃ ταῦτα συντελεῖσθαι πάντα;

εἰπὸν. Aor act impv 2nd sg λέγω.

ἡμῖν. Dative indirect object of εἰπόν.

ταῦτα. Nominative subject of ἔσται. Because ταῦτα is plural (twice in this verse) it is probable that the disciples are asking about multiple events (cf. NET note; Bock 2005, 517).

ἔσται. Fut mid ind 3rd sg εἰμί.

καί. Coordinating conjunction joining two questions.

τί. Predicate nominative of an implied ἔσται.

τὸ σημεῖον. Nominative subject of an implied ἔσται.

ὅταν μέλλῃ ταῦτα συντελεῖσθαι πάντα. The wording here might echo Dan 12:7, συντελεσθήσεται πάντα ταῦτα (so Lane, 454–55).

μέλλῃ. Pres act subj 3rd sg μέλλω. Subjunctive with ὅταν.

ταῦτα ... πάντα. Nominative subject (a collective reference, "all this") of μέλλῃ.

συντελεῖσθαι. Pres mid inf συντελέω (complementary; cf. Acts 21:27). BDAG translates the clause, "when all this is to come to an end" (975.4; cf. *CL*, 1.b), but notes that it might mean, "when all this is to be accomplished" (975.2). Gundry's (737) argument that with the prefixed preposition (σύν-) the meaning is "to be brought to completion *together*" is not justified by the usage of the word, nor is it supported by any of the standard lexica. The singular verb is used with a neuter plural subject (see 4:4).

Mark 13:5-13

[5]Then Jesus began to say to them, "Watch out that no one deceives you. [6]Many will come in my name claiming, 'I am he,' and they will deceive many. [7]But when you hear wars and news about wars, do not be afraid. This must be, but the end is not yet. [8]For nation will rise against nation and kingdom against kingdom. There will be earthquakes in various places. There will be famines. These (events) are the beginning of great sorrows. [9]But be on your guard: people will hand you over to the local councils and you will be beaten in synagogues and you will stand before governors and kings for my sake as a testimony to them. [10]The gospel must first be preached to all the nations. [11]Now when they arrest you and hand you over (for trial), do not worry ahead of time about what you should say. Instead, say whatever is given to you at that time; for you are not the ones who are speaking, but the Holy Spirit. [12]Brother will hand over brother to death, a father (will hand over) a child, and children will rebel against parents and hand them over to be killed. [13]You will be hated by all because of my name, but the one who endures to the end will be delivered.

13:5 ὁ δὲ Ἰησοῦς ἤρξατο λέγειν αὐτοῖς, Βλέπετε μή τις ὑμᾶς πλανήσῃ·

ὁ ... Ἰησοῦς. Nominative subject of ἤρξατο λέγειν. The use of δέ marks the shift of speaker from the disciples in verse 4 to Jesus in verse 5.

ἤρξατο. Aor mid ind 3rd sg ἄρχω.

λέγειν. Pres act inf λέγω (complementary).

αὐτοῖς. Dative indirect object of λέγειν.

Βλέπετε... ³⁸γρηγορεῖτε. Clausal complement (direct discourse) of λέγειν.

Βλέπετε. Pres act impv 2nd pl βλέπω. When the context suggests the meaning "be ready to learn about someth. that is needed or is hazardous, *watch, look to, beware of*" (BDAG, 179.5), the imperative is usually followed by a form of μή and the aorist subjunctive. On negated imperatives generally, see 10:14 on κωλύετε. Half of Mark's instances of the imperative βλέπετε ("look out, beware") occur in this chapter (vv. 5, 9, 23, 33). The conjunction γάρ, in relative terms, is also more frequent than elsewhere in the book (vv. 8, 11, 19, 22, 33, 35). Both of these features reflect a chapter that consists of parenesis, the specific elements of which are explained by the frequent γάρ clauses (see Lane, 445–46).

μή. Though the negative routinely functions adverbially, it can, as here, function as a negative conjunction, "that ... (not), lest" (BDAG, 646.2.a), most commonly in this case followed by an aorist subjunctive (πλανήσῃ).

τις. Nominative subject of πλανήσῃ.

ὑμᾶς. Accusative direct object of πλανήσῃ.

πλανήσῃ. Aor act subj 3rd sg πλανάω.

13:6 πολλοὶ ἐλεύσονται ἐπὶ τῷ ὀνόματί μου λέγοντες ὅτι Ἐγώ εἰμι, καὶ πολλοὺς πλανήσουσιν.

πολλοί. Nominative subject of ἐλεύσονται.

ἐλεύσονται. Fut mid ind 3rd pl ἔρχομαι.

ἐπὶ τῷ ὀνόματί μου. This idiom "focuses on the authorizing function of the one named in the gen." (BDAG, 366.17, s.v. ἐπί; see also 9:37, 39). This phrase would ordinarily mean "claiming to be sent by me," but the collocation with λέγοντες ὅτι Ἐγώ εἰμι suggests that the claim here is to Jesus' title and authority (Lane, 457), i.e., they claim to be Messiah himself. This is made explicit in Matt 24:5.

λέγοντες. Pres act ptc masc nom pl λέγω (attributive).

ὅτι. Introduces the clausal complement (direct discourse) of λέγοντες (see 1:15).

εἰμι. Pres act ind 1st sg εἰμί. Here, Ἐγώ εἰμι ("I am [he]") implies, "I am the Messiah." This is explicit in Matt 24:5, ἐγώ εἰμι ὁ χριστός.

πολλοὺς. Accusative direct object of πλανήσουσιν.

πλανήσουσιν. Fut act ind 3rd pl πλανάω.

13:7 ὅταν δὲ ἀκούσητε πολέμους καὶ ἀκοὰς πολέμων, μὴ θρο-εῖσθε· δεῖ γενέσθαι, ἀλλ᾽ οὔπω τὸ τέλος.

ὅταν. Temporal particle introducing an informal conditional statement.

δὲ. The use of δέ rather than καί reflects the shift from prophetic statement in verse 6 to the exhortation in verse 7. This sort of topic shift occurs multiple times in the discourse, sometimes in conjunction with a temporal shift as here (ὅταν δέ), other times not (see vv. 9, 13, 14, 15, 17, 18, 23, 28, 31, 32, 37).

ἀκούσητε. Aor act subj 2nd pl ἀκούω. Subjunctive with ὅταν.

πολέμους καὶ ἀκοὰς. Accusative direct object of ἀκούσητε. "After ἀκούσητε πολέμους the additional ἀκοὰς πολέμων is formally redundant, but the rounded and memorable prophetic phrase which results is typical of Mark's style" (France, 511).

θροεῖσθε. Pres pass impv 2nd pl θροέω. In the passive this verb means "to be disturbed or frightened" (BDAG, 460). Though there is no explicit agent marker here, the middle voice seems less likely in the context; the form is more likely passive with the agent implied by the ὅταν clause (what they hear is the potential cause of fear). On the negated imperative, see 10:14.

δεῖ. Pres act ind 3rd sg δεῖ.

γενέσθαι. Aor mid inf γίνομαι (complementary).

οὔπω. Predicate adverb in a verbless clause.

τὸ τέλος. Nominative subject in a verbless clause.

13:8 ἐγερθήσεται γὰρ ἔθνος ἐπ᾽ ἔθνος καὶ βασιλεία ἐπὶ βασιλείαν, ἔσονται σεισμοὶ κατὰ τόπους, ἔσονται λιμοί· ἀρχὴ ὠδίνων ταῦτα.

ἐγερθήσεται. Fut mid ind 3rd sg ἐγείρω. Here, "rise up . . . of nations rising in arms" (BDAG, 272.11). This is an intransitive, "θη middle" form (see 2:2).

γὰρ. Introduces a statement that explains why it is that οὔπω τὸ τέλος (v. 7).

ἔθνος. Nominative subject of ἐγερθήσεται.

ἐπ᾽ ἔθνος. Opposition (BDAG, 366.12.b), with reference to military aggression.

βασιλεία. Nominative subject of an implied ἐγερθήσεται.

ἐπὶ βασιλείαν. Spatial (see above on ἐπ᾽ ἔθνος).

ἔσονται. Fut mid ind 3rd pl εἰμί.

σεισμοὶ. Nominative subject of ἔσονται.

κατὰ τόπους. Spatial ("in place after place" or "in various regions," BDAG, 511.B.1.a, s.v. κατά; 1011.1.d, s.v. τόπος).

ἔσονται. Fut mid ind 3rd pl εἰμί.

λιμοί. Nominative subject of ἔσονται.

ἀρχὴ. Predicate nominative in a verbless clause.

ὠδίνων. The noun ὠδίν refers to the "experience of pains associated with childbirth" (BDAG, 1102) or simply "great suffering" (LN 24.87; cf. 1 Thess 5:3). Cranfield suggests that this expression parallels "the Rabbinic expression 'the birth-pangs of the Messiah' . . . [which] was probably already current in the time of Jesus" (397).

ταῦτα. Nominative subject in a verbless clause. The neuter is used as a collective term to include the events described by both masculine and feminine terms in the preceding context.

13:9 βλέπετε δὲ ὑμεῖς ἑαυτούς· παραδώσουσιν ὑμᾶς εἰς συνέδρια καὶ εἰς συναγωγὰς δαρήσεσθε καὶ ἐπὶ ἡγεμόνων καὶ βασιλέων σταθήσεσθε ἕνεκεν ἐμοῦ εἰς μαρτύριον αὐτοῖς.

βλέπετε . . . ὑμεῖς ἑαυτούς. Formally, "Beware! You (beware of) yourselves."

βλέπετε. Pres act impv 2nd pl βλέπω. This is the second of four uses of βλέπετε as an imperative in this chapter (see v. 5).

δὲ. The use of δέ rather than καί reflects another shift from prophetic statement in verse 8 to exhortation in verse 9 (see also v. 7 on δέ).

ὑμεῖς. Nominative subject of βλέπετε. It is not common to have a nominative subject expressed with an imperative in Greek, though it does occur about forty-five times in the NT (out of more than 1,400 second person imperatives), usually with ὑμεῖς (e.g., 6:37; 13:23), but occasionally with συ (e.g., Luke 9:60; John 17:5).

ἑαυτούς. Accusative direct object of βλέπετε. An accusative that indicates the object of which one is to beware occurs seldom in the NT (see 2 John 8; Phil 3:2).

παραδώσουσιν. Fut act ind 3rd pl παραδίδωμι. Indefinite plural (see 1:22). On the meaning and use of παραδίδωμι in Mark, see 3:19.

ὑμᾶς. Accusative direct object of παραδώσουσιν.

εἰς συνέδρια. Locative. The use of the plural form of συνέδριον makes it clear that local councils rather than the Sanhedrin in Jerusalem are in view. Although the usual assumption is that these are Jewish councils, the word can also be used in a Gentile context (see Evans 2001, 309).

εἰς συναγωγὰς. Locative (equivalent to ἐν as it often is in Koine).

δαρήσεσθε. Fut pass ind 2nd pl δέρω.

ἐπὶ ἡγεμόνων καὶ βασιλέων. The preposition ἐπί can be used as a "marker of involvement in an official proceeding, *before*, w. gen., of pers., esp. in the language of lawsuits" (BDAG, 363.3). Although ἡγεμών can refer in a general sense to "rulers," here it may refer to the "head imperial provincial administrator, *governor* in the provinces" (BDAG, 433.2) as may be seen in the experiences of the early Christians: Paul, e.g., appeared before both Roman proconsuls (ὁ ἀνθύπατος; see Acts 13:7, 12; 18:12; 19:38) and governors (ὁ ἡγεμών; see Acts 23:24; 24:27).

σταθήσεσθε. Fut mid ind 2nd pl ἵστημι. With regard to judicial proceedings, this verb means "to appear" (*CL*, 178.2.d) as in "appear in court." This is an intransitive, "θη middle" form (see 2:2).

ἕνεκεν ἐμοῦ. See 10:29.

εἰς μαρτύριον. Purpose.

αὐτοῖς. Dative of reference, or perhaps interest. In the latter case, whether advantage or disadvantage is in view is not clear since the result could be positive or negative in any given situation (Wallace 1996, 144, lists this passage as a possible dative of disadvantage; cf. Strathmann, 4:502–3).

13:10 καὶ εἰς πάντα τὰ ἔθνη πρῶτον δεῖ κηρυχθῆναι τὸ εὐαγγέλιον.

εἰς πάντα τὰ ἔθνη. Locative, though extent ("unto, as far as") is also possible (see Cranfield, 399).

δεῖ. Pres act ind 3rd sg δεῖ.

κηρυχθῆναι. Aor pass inf κηρύσσω. The infinitival clause, κηρυχθῆναι τὸ εὐαγγέλιον, is the subject of δεῖ, "for the gospel to be preached is necessary."

τὸ εὐαγγέλιον. Accusative subject of κηρυχθῆναι.

13:11 καὶ ὅταν ἄγωσιν ὑμᾶς παραδιδόντες, μὴ προμεριμνᾶτε τί λαλήσητε, ἀλλ᾽ ὃ ἐὰν δοθῇ ὑμῖν ἐν ἐκείνῃ τῇ ὥρᾳ τοῦτο λαλεῖτε· οὐ γάρ ἐστε ὑμεῖς οἱ λαλοῦντες ἀλλὰ τὸ πνεῦμα τὸ ἅγιον.

ἄγωσιν. Pres act subj 3rd pl ἄγω. Here, "to take into custody, *lead away, arrest*, legal [technical term] w. acc." (BDAG, 16.2).

παραδιδόντες. Pres act ptc masc nom pl παραδίδωμι (attendant circumstance). Here, a technical term "of police and courts 'hand over into [the] custody [of]'" (BDAG, 762.1.b). The purpose is not explicit; it may refer to handing over for trial or for punishment.

In light of the following clause, the first seems most likely. On the meaning and use of παραδίδωμι in Mark, see 1:14 and 3:19.

προμεριμνᾶτε. Pres act impv 2nd pl προμεριμνάω. The verb means "to worry beforehand, *concern oneself or be anxious before-hand* w. indir. quest. foll." (BDAG, 872). This word "may be a Markan coinage" (V. Taylor, 508), since it is not found in any other Greek literature prior to or contemporary with the NT. On the negated imperative, see 10:14. That they are not to worry ahead of time does not mean there should be no thought given as to what should be said. Even by "application" this text does not authorize lack of preparation by Jesus' followers—something I once heard justified publicly from this text, followed by a demonstration that indeed there had been no forethought! As France puts it, "the prom-ise . . . is for hard-pressed disciples on trial, not for lazy preachers!" (517).

τί. Accusative direct object of λαλήσητε in an indirect question.

λαλήσητε. Aor act subj 2nd pl λαλέω (deliberative subjunctive in an indirect question).

ἀλλ'. Introduces the contrasting positive statement following μὴ προμεριμνᾶτε.

ὃ ἐὰν δοθῇ ὑμῖν ἐν ἐκείνῃ τῇ ὥρᾳ. The relative clause serves as the antecedent of the following τοῦτο.

ὃ ἐὰν. Indefinite relative pronoun ("whoever") functioning as the nominative subject of δοθῇ.

δοθῇ. Aor pass subj 3rd sg δίδωμι. Subjunctive with ἐάν.

ὑμῖν. Dative indirect object of δοθῇ.

ἐν ἐκείνῃ τῇ ὥρᾳ. Temporal.

τοῦτο. Accusative direct object of λαλεῖτε. The antecedent of τοῦτο is the preceding relative clause.

λαλεῖτε. Pres act impv 2nd pl λαλέω.

γάρ. Introduces an explanation as to why they should not worry, but speak what is given.

ἐστε. Pres act ind 2nd pl εἰμί.

ὑμεῖς. Nominative subject of ἐστε.

οἱ λαλοῦντες. Pres act ptc masc nom pl λαλέω (substantival). Predicate nominative.

ἀλλὰ. Introduces the positive counter to οὐ . . . ἐστε ὑμεῖς οἱ λαλοῦντες.

τὸ πνεῦμα τὸ ἅγιον. Nominative subject of an implied ἔστιν (τὸ λαλοῦν). This is partially fleshed out in ‖ Matt 10:20.

13:12 καὶ παραδώσει ἀδελφὸς ἀδελφὸν εἰς θάνατον καὶ πατὴρ τέκνον, καὶ ἐπαναστήσονται τέκνα ἐπὶ γονεῖς καὶ θανατώσουσιν αὐτούς·

παραδώσει. Fut act ind 3rd sg παραδίδωμι. On the meaning and use of παραδίδωμι in Mark, see 1:14 and 3:19.

ἀδελφὸς. Nominative subject of παραδώσει.

ἀδελφὸν. Accusative direct object of παραδώσει.

εἰς θάνατον. Result.

πατὴρ. Nominative subject of an implied παραδώσει.

τέκνον. Accusative direct object of an implied παραδώσει.

ἐπαναστήσονται. Fut mid ind 3rd pl ἐπανίστημι ("to rise up in open defiance of authority, with the presumed intention to overthrow it or to act in complete opposition to its demands," LN 39.34).

τέκνα. Nominative subject of ἐπαναστήσονται.

ἐπὶ γονεῖς. Opposition.

θανατώσουσιν. Fut act ind 3rd pl θανατόω. This could refer to children murdering their parents ("put them to death," HCSB), but in the context of various legal proceedings and betrayals (vv. 9-12a), this most likely refers to an indirect action ("have them put to death"; NIV, NRSV; see also Cranfield, 401).

αὐτούς. Accusative direct object of θανατώσουσιν.

13:13 καὶ ἔσεσθε μισούμενοι ὑπὸ πάντων διὰ τὸ ὄνομά μου. ὁ δὲ ὑπομείνας εἰς τέλος οὗτος σωθήσεται.

ἔσεσθε. Fut mid ind 2nd pl εἰμί.

μισούμενοι. Pres pass ptc masc nom pl μισέω (future imperfective periphrastic). This construction enables the expression of imperfective aspect in future time (see also v. 25, ἔσονται . . . πίπτοντες).

ὑπὸ πάντων. Introduces the agent of the passive μισούμενοι. The use of πάς should be taken as a general statement or perhaps qualitatively: "every element of society: rulers, religious leaders, citizens, slaves, criminals, philosophers, one's own family, and so on" (Stein 2008, 601).

διὰ τὸ ὄνομά μου. Causal.

ὁ . . . ὑπομείνας. Aor act ptc masc nom sg ὑπομένω (substantival). Hanging (or pendent) nominative, resumed by οὗτος in the main clause, also known as *casus pendens* (see 6:16).

δὲ. The use of δέ rather than καί reflects the shift from prophetic statement in verse 12 to encouragement in verse 13 (see v. 7 on δέ).

εἰς τέλος. Temporal, modifying ὑπομείνας (or perhaps σωθήσεται): "at last, in the end" (Swete, 304).

οὗτος. Nominative subject of σωθήσεται.

σωθήσεται. Fut pass ind 3rd sg σῴζω.

Mark 13:14-23

[14]"So when you see the Abomination of Desolation standing
where it ought not" — The reader must understand! — "then those
who are in Judea must flee to the mountains. [15]The one who is on
the housetop must neither come down nor go inside to take anything out of his house, [16]and the one in the field must not return to
retrieve his cloak. [17]But woe for those women who are pregnant and
those who are breastfeeding in those days. [18]So pray that it may not
happen in winter, [19]for those days will be a time of tribulation such
as has not been from the beginning of creation which God created
until the present and never will be (after that). [20]If the Lord does not
cut short the days, then no one will survive; but for the sake of the
elect whom he elected, he will cut short the days. [21]Then if anyone
says to you, 'Look! Here is the Messiah! Look! There (he is)!' do not
believe (it). [22]For false messiahs and false prophets will appear and
will produce signs and wonders in order to deceive, if it were possible, the elect. [23]So be on your guard! I have told you all these things
ahead of time.

13:14 Ὅταν δὲ ἴδητε τὸ βδέλυγμα τῆς ἐρημώσεως ἑστηκότα ὅπου
οὐ δεῖ, ὁ ἀναγινώσκων νοείτω, τότε οἱ ἐν τῇ Ἰουδαίᾳ φευγέτωσαν
εἰς τὰ ὄρη,

Ὅταν. This correlative conjunction introduces a temporal clause
that functions much like an informal conditional statement.

δὲ. The use of δέ rather than καί reflects the shift from encouragement in verse 13 to prophetic statement in verse 14 (see v. 7 on δέ).

ἴδητε. Aor act subj 2nd pl ὁράω. Subjunctive with ὅταν.

τὸ βδέλυγμα. Accusative direct object of ἴδητε. Although
βδέλυγμα can refer to something that is "disgusting that arouses
wrath, *loathsome thing*" (BDAG, 172.1), in the phrase τὸ βδέλυγμα
τῆς ἐρημώσεως it "appears to refer to someth[ing] that is abhorred
because it defiles a sacred place and causes it to be left desolate"
(BDAG, 172.2).

τῆς ἐρημώσεως. The noun ἐρήμωσις refers to "devastation,
destruction, depopulation" (BDAG, 392) and is related to ἔρημος
and ἐρημόω.

ἑστηκότα. Prf act ptc masc acc sg ἵστημι (attributive). The participle should agree with the neuter βδέλυγμα, but this is a *constructio ad sensum* (BDF §134.3.3), suggesting that the abomination is either a person or perhaps the image of a person (cf. Swete, 305; Hort, 167).

δεῖ. Pres act ind 3rd sg δεῖ (impersonal; contra ESV: "standing where *he* ought not to be").

ὁ ἀναγινώσκων νοείτω. This is a parenthetical, editorial comment by Mark to underline the significance of Jesus' statement. Jesus would not have referred to his "readers," but rather to his "hearers." Though it is possible that Jesus could refer to those who were reading Daniel (who uses the same phrase τὸ βδέλυγμα τῆς ἐρημώσεως in 12:11), given that there has been no explicit reference to any scriptural text in Jesus' discourse, the literacy rate in the ancient world, and especially the scarcity of written copies of the Scriptures, that is highly unlikely. Gundry makes the interesting suggestion that "'the reader' would not mean a private reader, but a public reader to whom an audience is listening (cf. Rev 1:3), the command to understand may imply that the public reader should understand the masculine participle so as not to shift to the grammatically regular but predictively inferior neuter gender" (742–43). In any event, this statement is one of the evidences for some literary relationship between Mark and Matthew (see 24:15-16) in that it is very improbable that two writers would insert the identical editorial comment at the exact same place in their respective texts. Parenthetical comments such as this are common in Mark's Gospel, e.g., 3:30; 7:3-4, 11, 19; 13:14.

ὁ ἀναγινώσκων. Pres act ptc masc nom sg ἀναγινώσκω (substantival).

νοείτω. Pres act impv 3rd sg νοέω.

τότε. BDF (§459.2) notes that this use of τότε as a connective particle is "unclassical."

οἱ ἐν τῇ Ἰουδαίᾳ. The article functions as a nominalizer, changing the locative prepositional phrase into a nominative substantive that functions as the subject of φευγέτωσαν.

φευγέτωσαν. Pres act impv 3rd pl φεύγω.

εἰς τὰ ὄρη. Spatial.

13:15 ὁ [δὲ] ἐπὶ τοῦ δώματος μὴ καταβάτω μηδὲ εἰσελθάτω ἆραί τι ἐκ τῆς οἰκίας αὐτοῦ,

ὁ ... ἐπὶ τοῦ δώματος. The article functions as a nominalizer, changing the spatial prepositional phrase into the nominative subject of καταβάτω. The use of δέ reflects the shift from a general statement in verse 14 to the two specific instances cited in verses 15-16 (both linked with καί; see also v. 7 on δὲ).

μὴ καταβάτω μηδὲ εἰσελθάτω. This double imperative is "probably best understood as a combined command 'do not go down and enter' or 'do not go down to enter' (cf. 13:16)" (Stein 2008, 605 n. 16).

μὴ . . . μηδὲ. "Neither . . . nor."

καταβάτω. Aor act impv 3rd sg καταβαίνω. Wallace notes "only 8 instances of the aorist imperative in prohibitions, all with Jesus as the speaker" (1996, 487 n. 99). The customary form of a prohibition uses the present imperative.

εἰσελθάτω. Aor act impv 3rd sg εἰσέρχομαι.

ἆραί. Aor act inf αἴρω (purpose).

τι. Accusative object of ἆραι.

ἐκ τῆς οἰκίας. Partitive, unusual with both an indefinite pronoun (τι) and a preposition; see 9:17.

13:16 καὶ ὁ εἰς τὸν ἀγρὸν μὴ ἐπιστρεψάτω εἰς τὰ ὀπίσω ἆραι τὸ ἱμάτιον αὐτοῦ.

ὁ εἰς τὸν ἀγρὸν. The article functions as a nominalizer, changing the spatial prepositional phrase into the nominative subject of ἐπιστρεψάτω ("the one who is in the field," i.e., a farm worker).

ἐπιστρεψάτω. Aor act impv 3rd sg ἐπιστρέφω.

εἰς τὰ ὀπίσω. Spatial. Formally, "to the things behind," but most translations combine this phrase with ἐπιστρεψάτω and render it "turn back" (see BDAG, 716.1.a.α).

ἆραι. Aor act inf αἴρω (purpose).

τὸ ἱμάτιον. Accusative object of the infinitive ἆραι.

13:17 οὐαὶ δὲ ταῖς ἐν γαστρὶ ἐχούσαις καὶ ταῖς θηλαζούσαις ἐν ἐκείναις ταῖς ἡμέραις.

οὐαὶ. "Interjection denoting pain or displeasure, *woe, alas* . . . w. dat. of pers. or thing concerning whom . . . pain is expressed" (BDAG, 734.1.a; see also 14:21).

δὲ. The use of δέ shifts the topic from where a person might be (on the housetop or in the field) to a specific kind of person: a pregnant woman (see also v. 7 on δὲ).

ταῖς ἐν γαστρὶ ἐχούσαις. Dative of interest/disadvantage. The idiomatic expression "ἐν γαστρὶ ἔχειν *be pregnant*" (BDAG, 190.2, s.v. γαστήρ) dates to classical times.

ταῖς … ἐχούσαις. Pres act ptc fem dat pl ἔχω (substantival).

ταῖς θηλαζούσαις. Pres act ptc fem dat pl θηλάζω (substantival; "to breast-feed an infant, *nurse*," BDAG, 455.1).

ἐν ἐκείναις ταῖς ἡμέραις. Temporal.

13:18 προσεύχεσθε δὲ ἵνα μὴ γένηται χειμῶνος·

προσεύχεσθε. Pres mid impv 2nd pl προσεύχομαι.

δὲ. The conjunction δέ shifts the narrative from warning to exhortation (see v. 7 on δέ).

γένηται. Aor mid subj 3rd sg γίνομαι. Subjunctive with ἵνα following a verb of entreaty gives the content of the request (see Burton §200; Wallace 1996, 475).

χειμῶνος. Genitive of time.

13:19 ἔσονται γὰρ αἱ ἡμέραι ἐκεῖναι θλῖψις οἵα οὐ γέγονεν τοιαύτη ἀπ' ἀρχῆς κτίσεως ἣν ἔκτισεν ὁ θεὸς ἕως τοῦ νῦν καὶ οὐ μὴ γένηται.

The wording of this verse is similar to LXX Dan 12:1b, which Lane describes as "virtually a citation" (471): ἐκείνη ἡ ἡμέρα θλίψεως, οἵα οὐκ ἐγενήθη ἀφ' οὗ ἐγενήθησαν ἕως τῆς ἡμέρας ἐκείνης.

ἔσονται. Fut mid ind 3rd pl εἰμί.

γὰρ. Introduces a clause that explains why woe is pronounced on pregnant and nursing mothers.

αἱ ἡμέραι ἐκεῖναι. Nominative subject of ἔσονται.

θλῖψις. Predicate nominative of ἔσονται. Although θλῖψις means simply "trouble, tribulation, suffering," in this context as an explanation of αἱ ἡμέραι ἐκεῖναι, it should probably be understood as a temporal expression: "time of tribulation."

οἵα. The qualitative (or correlative) relative pronoun is the nominative subject of γέγονεν.

γέγονεν. Prf act ind 3rd sg γίνομαι.

τοιαύτη. The repetition of a second pronoun referring to θλῖψις (fem nom sg) is redundant, but not uncommon (Robertson, 722.10; on possible Semitic influence, see 1:7; cf. 7:25). Grammatically it could be viewed as nominative in apposition to οἵα.

ἀπ' ἀρχῆς κτίσεως ἣν ἔκτισεν ὁ θεὸς. Or, "since God created the world" (NJB). For the cognate repetition (κτίσεως ἣν ἔκτισεν), see verse 20. The redundancy may be Semitic (Evans 2001, 322), "a good example of Mark's expansive phraseology (less politely, 'redundancy')" (France, 527), or "an instance of Markan expansion to clarify a biblical statement for his Gentile readers, who would not necessarily assume that the creation of the world was an act of God" (Lane, 465 n. 71).

ἀπ᾽ ἀρχῆς κτίσεως. Temporal.

ἣν. Accusative direct object of ἔκτισεν.

ἔκτισεν. Aor act ind 3rd sg κτίζω.

ὁ θεὸς. Nominative subject of ἔκτισεν.

ἕως τοῦ νῦν. Temporal: "up to the present time." The article functions as a nominalizer, changing the adverb νῦν into the genitive object of the (improper) preposition.

γένηται. Aor mid subj 3rd sg γίνομαι. The subjunctive is used with οὐ μή to express a very forceful negation (see also 9:41).

13:20 καὶ εἰ μὴ ἐκολόβωσεν κύριος τὰς ἡμέρας, οὐκ ἂν ἐσώθη πᾶσα σάρξ· ἀλλὰ διὰ τοὺς ἐκλεκτοὺς οὓς ἐξελέξατο ἐκολόβωσεν τὰς ἡμέρας.

εἰ μὴ ἐκολόβωσεν . . . οὐκ ἂν ἐσώθη. The second-class condition assumes the unreality of the protasis. Since both parts are negated, the result is a positive statement that the Lord will shorten the days and therefore some "flesh" would survive—which is stated positively in the next clause (ἀλλὰ . . . ἐκολόβωσεν τὰς ἡμέρας).

εἰ μὴ. Idiomatic, "except"; see 2:7.

ἐκολόβωσεν. Aor act ind 3rd sg κολοβόω ("to shorten, cut short, curtail"). The time reference is ambiguous since the statement can be read as a past action by God to shorten the days or a future action; an aorist can refer to past, present, or future events.

κύριος. Nominative subject of ἐκολόβωσεν. It is remotely possible that κύριος refers to Jesus, though the link is indirect (see Johansson, 108–9).

τὰς ἡμέρας. Accusative direct object of ἐκολόβωσεν.

ἐσώθη. Aor pass ind 3rd sg σῴζω. Although the sense of σῴζω is ambiguous, the contextual references to the physical challenges in the preceding verses would favor the use of σῴζω as the preservation of physical life.

πᾶσα σάρξ. Nominative subject of ἐσώθη. In this context σάρξ probably refers to human life, with πᾶσα σάρξ meaning "every person, everyone" (BDAG, 915.3.a, s.v. σάρξ). The phrase occurs ten times in the NT, almost invariably as a reference to "all people" (Luke 3:6 might be understood more broadly; 1 Cor 15:39 does not use the phrase in its usual idiomatic sense); it occurs nearly sixty times in the LXX in reference to human life (e.g., LXX Ps 145:21), animal life (e.g., Sir 17:4), or all animate life (e.g., Gen 9:15-17; Sir 40:8).

διὰ τοὺς ἐκλεκτούς. Causal.

οὓς. Accusative direct object of ἐξελέξατο.

ἐξελέξατο. Aor mid ind 3rd sg ἐκλέγομαι. The cognate repetition (ἐκλεκτοὺς οὓς ἐξελέξατο) is typical of a Semitically influenced style (cf. κτίσεως ἣν ἔκτισεν in verse 19, and τὸ βάπτισμα ὃ ἐγὼ βαπτίζομαι in 10:38, 39).

ἐκολόβωσεν. Aor act ind 3rd sg κολοβόω.

τὰς ἡμέρας. Accusative direct object of ἐκολόβωσεν.

13:21 καὶ τότε ἐάν τις ὑμῖν εἴπῃ, Ἴδε ὧδε ὁ Χριστός, Ἴδε ἐκεῖ, μὴ πιστεύετε·

ἐάν. Introduces a third-class condition.

τις. Nominative subject of εἴπῃ.

ὑμῖν. Dative indirect object of εἴπῃ.

εἴπῃ. Aor act subj 3rd sg λέγω. Subjunctive with ἐάν.

Ἴδε ὧδε ὁ Χριστός, Ἴδε ἐκεῖ. Clausal complement (direct discourse) of εἴπῃ. Both statements are nominal clauses in which a form of εἰμί must be supplied as is common in exclamations (BDF §127.4).

Ἴδε. See 3:34.

ὧδε. Predicate adverb in a verbless clause.

ὁ Χριστός. Nominative subject in a verbless clause.

πιστεύετε. Pres act impv 2nd pl πιστεύω. On πιστεύω, see 1:15. On the negated imperative, see 10:14. "The command μὴ πιστεύετε is left unqualified and can be completed in one of two ways: 'Do not believe it' or 'Do not believe him' (where the reference is to 'anyone' at the beginning of the sentence" (Lane, 465 n. 72).

13:22 ἐγερθήσονται γὰρ ψευδόχριστοι καὶ ψευδοπροφῆται καὶ δώσουσιν σημεῖα καὶ τέρατα πρὸς τὸ ἀποπλανᾶν, εἰ δυνατόν, τοὺς ἐκλεκτούς.

ἐγερθήσονται. Fut mid ind 3rd pl ἐγείρω. This is an intransitive, "θη middle" form (see 2:2). This verb is often used of the appearance of a prophet on the scene (see Matt 11:11; Luke 7:16; John 7:52).

ψευδόχριστοι καὶ ψευδοπροφῆται. Nominative subject of ἐγερθήσονται.

δώσουσιν. Fut act ind 3rd pl δίδωμι. This is a less common use of δίδωμι that means "to cause to happen, esp. in ref. to physical

phenomena, *produce, make, cause, give*" (BDAG, 242.4; see also
v. 24; Acts 2:19; LXX Joel 3:3).

σημεῖα καὶ τέρατα. Accusative direct object of δώσουσιν. On
σημεῖον and τέρας as words for "miracle," see 6:2.

πρὸς τὸ ἀποπλανᾶν. Purpose. This is the only use of πρὸς τό +
infinitive to indicate purpose in Mark (V. Taylor, 516).

ἀποπλανᾶν. Pres act inf ἀποπλανάω ("to mislead, deceive").
Used with πρὸς τό to introduce a purpose clause (only here in Mark;
V. Taylor, 516).

εἰ δυνατόν. Elliptical (verbless) protasis of a first-class condition.

τοὺς ἐκλεκτούς. Accusative direct object of ἀποπλανᾶν.

13:23 ὑμεῖς δὲ βλέπετε· προείρηκα ὑμῖν πάντα.

ὑμεῖς. Nominative subject (emphatic) of βλέπετε.

δὲ. The use of δέ shifts the narrative from prophetic statement to
exhortation (see v. 7).

βλέπετε. Pres act impv 2nd pl βλέπω. Here, the meaning is "be
aware, be on guard." This is the third of four uses of βλέπετε as an
imperative in this chapter (see v. 5).

προείρηκα. Prf act ind 1st sg προλέγω/προεῖπον. This (and ‖ Matt
24:25) is the only instance of προλέγω with Jesus as the speaker.

ὑμῖν. Dative indirect object of προείρηκα.

πάντα. Accusative direct object of προείρηκα.

Mark 13:24-31

[24]"But in those days, after that tribulation, the sun will be darkened and the moon will not give its light, [25]the stars will fall from
heaven and the heavenly powers will be shaken. [26]And then they will
see the Son of Man coming in the clouds with great power and glory.
[27]And then he will send his angels and they will gather his elect from
the four winds, from the ends of the earth to the ends of heaven.

[28]"Now learn the lesson from the fig tree. When its branch
becomes tender and it is sprouting leaves, you know that summer
is near. [29]So also you: when you see these things take place, then
you will know that he is near, at your very door. [30]Truly I say to you
that this generation will not pass away until all these things happen.
[31]Heaven and earth will pass away, but my words will never pass
away."

13:24 Ἀλλὰ ἐν ἐκείναις ταῖς ἡμέραις μετὰ τὴν θλῖψιν ἐκείνην ὁ ἥλιος σκοτισθήσεται, καὶ ἡ σελήνη οὐ δώσει τὸ φέγγος αὐτῆς,

The OT quotation in verses 24-25 draws language from LXX Isa 13:10.

Ἀλλὰ ἐν ἐκείναις ταῖς ἡμέραις μετὰ τὴν θλῖψιν ἐκείνην. This double temporal phrase is introduced with the contrasting conjunction ἀλλά, which contrasts the events of αἱ ἡμέραι ἐκεῖναι (v. 19) which are described in verses 14-23 and which begin with the "abomination of desolation" (v. 14), with events μετά ("after") τὴν θλῖψιν ἐκείνην. This new set of events, described in verses 24-27 as consisting of solar and stellar signs and the coming of the Son of Man (τὸν υἱὸν τοῦ ἀνθρώπου ἐρχόμενον), are still part of "those days" (ἐν ἐκείναις ταῖς ἡμέραις), but constitute subsequent events. Given the deictic reference of ἐν ἐκείναις ταῖς ἡμέραις and the almost invariable temporal meaning of μετά when it is used with the accusative (BDAG, 637.B.2), this must be a temporal statement. Jesus' prophetic discourse appears to describe three distinct series: the preaching of the gospel and the reaction to it (vv. 5-13), the θλῖψις marked by the abomination of desolation (vv. 14-23), and the events associated with the coming of the Son of Man (vv. 24-27).

ἐκείναις. On the adjectival use of demonstratives in Mark, see 4:11.

ὁ ἥλιος. Nominative subject of σκοτισθήσεται.

σκοτισθήσεται. Fut pass ind 3rd sg σκοτίζω ("to be/become dark/darkened," BDAG, 932.1). As a part of the supernatural signs announcing the coming of the Son of Man, God is the implied agent.

ἡ σελήνη. Nominative subject of δώσει.

δώσει. Fut act ind 3rd sg δίδωμι.

τὸ φέγγος. Accusative direct object of δώσει ("light").

13:25 καὶ οἱ ἀστέρες ἔσονται ἐκ τοῦ οὐρανοῦ πίπτοντες, καὶ αἱ δυνάμεις αἱ ἐν τοῖς οὐρανοῖς σαλευθήσονται.

οἱ ἀστέρες. Nominative subject of ἔσονται . . . πίπτοντες.

ἔσονται . . . πίπτοντες. This periphrastic construction enables the expression of imperfective aspect in future time (see also v. 13). Since neither εἰμί nor future tense-forms appear to be aspectual, the use of an imperfective periphrastic with a future form of εἰμί is the only way to grammaticalize "future imperfectivity." The functionally equivalent form, πίπτονται (which does not occur in the NT or related texts), would carry the same value in this context. The Matthean ‖ 24:29 has a future middle, πεσοῦνται (as do several Greek mss of Mark: W 565 700). The imperfective value of this periphrastic comes from the participle; the future expectation comes from the future tense-form of εἰμί, the future being more closely related to mood than to tense. On periphrastics, see the Introduction and 1:6 on ἐνδεδυμένος.

ἔσονται. Fut mid ind 3rd pl εἰμί.

ἐκ τοῦ οὐρανοῦ. Source.

πίπτοντες. Pres act ptc masc nom pl πίπτω (future imperfective periphrastic, see above).

αἱ δυνάμεις αἱ ἐν τοῖς οὐρανοῖς. Nominative subject of σαλευθήσονται. The second article functions as an adjectivizer, changing the prepositional phrase ἐν τοῖς οὐρανοῖς into an adjective modifying δυνάμεις. The identity of these "powers" is debated. BDAG (263.4) identifies them as "heavenly bodies [i.e., the stars] thought of as armies" and translates "the armies of heaven," presumably due to the parallel with οἱ ἀστέρες. Most commentators agree, typically appealing to similar terminology in the OT prophets (Isa 34:4 is often cited). On the other hand, they might be viewed as supernatural beings in a sense common in Paul (e.g., Eph 1:21; V. Taylor, 518, mentions this possibility, but does not adopt it).

σαλευθήσονται. Fut pass ind 3rd pl σαλεύω.

13:26 καὶ τότε ὄψονται τὸν υἱὸν τοῦ ἀνθρώπου ἐρχόμενον ἐν νεφέλαις μετὰ δυνάμεως πολλῆς καὶ δόξης.

καὶ τότε. This phrase places the following event in sequence following the heavenly signs narrated in verse 24-25.

ὄψονται. Fut mid ind 3rd pl ὁράω. Indefinite plural (see 1:22). To take this as an equivalent of a passive ("will be seen"), as does Collins (614 n. 168), shifts the focus unduly.

τὸν υἱὸν τοῦ ἀνθρώπου. Accusative direct object of ὄψονται. See 2:10.

ἐρχόμενον. Pres mid ptc masc acc sg ἔρχομαι (complement in an object-complement double accusative construction).

ἐν νεφέλαις. Locative.

μετὰ δυνάμεως πολλῆς καὶ δόξης. Manner: "in a very powerful, glorious manner."

13:27 καὶ τότε ἀποστελεῖ τοὺς ἀγγέλους καὶ ἐπισυνάξει τοὺς
ἐκλεκτοὺς [αὐτοῦ] ἐκ τῶν τεσσάρων ἀνέμων ἀπ᾽ ἄκρου γῆς ἕως
ἄκρου οὐρανοῦ.

καὶ τότε. This phrase places the following event in sequence following the sighting of the Son of Man coming (v. 26).

ἀποστελεῖ. Fut act ind 3rd sg ἀποστέλλω. The subject is not
expressed in this clause, but the third person reference is to the Son
of Man (v. 26).

τοὺς ἀγγέλους. Accusative direct object of ἀποστελεῖ. In this
eschatological context ἄγγελος must refer to angels, not simply
messengers; the nature of their task would imply the same conclusion. The article is possessive ("his angels"); Matthew's parallel
statement is more explicit: ἀποστελεῖ τοὺς ἀγγέλους αὐτοῦ (24:31);
scribes sometimes added αὐτοῦ in the manuscripts (ℵ A C Θ Ψ $f^{1,13}$
𝔐).

ἐπισυνάξει. Fut act ind 3rd sg ἐπισυνάγω.

τοὺς ἐκλεκτοὺς. Accusative direct object of ἐπισυνάξει.

[αὐτοῦ]. The brackets suggesting some uncertainty regarding the
originality of this word do not appear to be necessary. If external evidence is given significant weight, the decision seems fairly clear cut;
the pronoun is omitted only by D L W Ψ f^1 and a few minuscules,
but included by ℵ A B C Θ 083 f^{13} 𝔐.

ἐκ τῶν τεσσάρων ἀνέμων. Source ("from the four winds," i.e.,
from all directions).

ἀπ᾽ ἄκρου γῆς. Source. In both this phrase and the next ἄκρον
refers to the end or extremity of something. Alternatively, Swete
suggests that it be understood as "from any one to any other opposite meeting-point of earth and sky" (313).

ἕως ἄκρου οὐρανοῦ. Although technically a conjunction, ἕως
often functions as it does here as a preposition governing the genitive. The combination ἐκ τῶν τεσσάρων ἀνέμων ἀπ᾽ ἄκρου γῆς ἕως
ἄκρου οὐρανοῦ is a way of saying "everywhere, wherever they are"
(cf. Evans 2001, 330).

13:28 Ἀπὸ δὲ τῆς συκῆς μάθετε τὴν παραβολήν· ὅταν ἤδη ὁ
κλάδος αὐτῆς ἁπαλὸς γένηται καὶ ἐκφύῃ τὰ φύλλα, γινώσκετε ὅτι
ἐγγὺς τὸ θέρος ἐστίν·

Ἀπὸ ... τῆς συκῆς. Source. The use of the conjunction δέ shifts
the narrative from prophetic statement to parable (see v. 7).

μάθετε. Aor act impv 2nd pl μανθάνω.

τὴν παραβολήν. Accusative direct object of μάθετε. Formally, "learn the parable," i.e., learn the lesson from the parable. This text illustrates the fact that the word παραβολή need not refer to a story, but may also refer to an extended simile, as here.

ὅταν ἤδη. The temporal subordinating conjunction ὅταν, together with the temporal adverb ἤδη, which implies completion, means "as soon as" or simply "when." ὅταν is normally used with the subjunctive (though it begins to appear with the indicative in the Koine) and can be used with either imperfective (here, ἐκφύῃ) or perfective aspect (here, γένηται) verbs. The key deictic marker in this instance is ἤδη. The perfective aorist is appropriate in the description of the sap beginning to flow, but the imperfective present is used to describe the leafing out process, which continues for some time (see *TDM*, 87–88). The use of ὅταν + subjunctive forms an informal condition.

ὁ κλάδος. Nominative subject of γένηται καὶ ἐκφύῃ.

ἁπαλὸς. Predicate adjective. ἁπαλός ("tender") can refer to a branch producing a sprout (as the sap begins to flow and it becomes "tender," swelling into a bud), or to young animals who are not yet grown and strong, or people who are sensitive, vulnerable, or inexperienced. In the LXX it occurs nine times, all with reference to people or animals.

γένηται. Aor mid subj 3rd sg γίνομαι. Subjunctive with ὅταν.

ἐκφύῃ. Pres act subj 3rd sg ἐκφύω ("to put forth," BDAG, 312). If this word were accented as ἐκφυῇ (so BDF §76.2.2), it would be a second aorist middle subjunctive (θη middle) and would be "used intr., and make τὰ φύλλα the subj.: *the leaves sprout*" (BDAG, 312).

τὰ φύλλα. Accusative direct object of ἐκφύῃ.

γινώσκετε. Pres act ind 2nd pl γινώσκω.

ὅτι. Introduces the clausal complement of γινώσκετε.

ἐγγὺς. Predicate adverb.

τὸ θέρος. Nominative subject of ἐστίν ("summer").

ἐστίν. Pres act ind 3rd sg εἰμί.

13:29 οὕτως καὶ ὑμεῖς, ὅταν ἴδητε ταῦτα γινόμενα, γινώσκετε ὅτι ἐγγύς ἐστιν ἐπὶ θύραις.

οὕτως καὶ ὑμεῖς. An elliptical statement: "even so you also *should know*." The use of οὕτως indicates a comparison between the informal conditions in verses 28 and 29.

ἴδητε. Aor act subj 2nd pl ὁράω. Subjunctive with ὅταν (see v. 28). The informal condition formed by ὅταν + subjunctive (protasis) has an apodosis consisting of γινώσκετε + ὅτι clause: "when you see . . . then you will know that. . . ."

ταῦτα. Accusative direct object of ἴδητε.

γινόμενα. Pres mid ptc neut acc pl γίνομαι (complement in an object-complement double accusative construction).

γινώσκετε. Pres act impv 2nd pl γινώσκω.

ὅτι. Introduces the clausal complement of γινώσκετε.

ἐγγύς. Predicate adverb.

ἐστιν. Pres act ind 3rd sg εἰμί. Whether the subject is "he," i.e., the Son of Man (cf. NASB, NET, NRSV, ESV, HCSB) or "it" (cf. NIV) is debatable, but the specific reference to the Son of Man in verse 26 makes the former most likely. Although there is a reference to an event in verse 28 (the coming of summer), verse 29 shifts the reference back to the person by using the comparative οὕτως. France (538) insists strongly that it must be "it," though this is because he limits the statement (and the entire discourse) to the destruction of the temple in AD 70.

ἐπὶ θύραις. This prepositional phrase, which stands in apposition to the predicate adverb, is an idiomatic expression of nearness (BDAG, 462.1.b.α, s.v. θύρα; cf. Acts 5:9; Jas 5:9; Philo, *Agriculture*, 148, ὅταν ὁ πόλεμος ἐγγὺς καὶ ἐπὶ θύραις. The use of the plural "θύραι of one door is rare in the NT. . . . The appearance of equivalents using the singular . . . makes it likely the old set phrase was obsolescent and formal-sounding" (Lee, 23). For the singular πρὸς τὴν θύραν in Mark, see 1:33; 2:2; 11:4.

13:30 ἀμὴν λέγω ὑμῖν ὅτι οὐ μὴ παρέλθῃ ἡ γενεὰ αὕτη μέχρις οὗ ταῦτα πάντα γένηται.

Ἀμὴν λέγω ὑμῖν. See 3:28.

λέγω. Pres act ind 1st sg λέγω.

ὑμῖν. Dative indirect object of λέγω.

ὅτι. Introduces the clausal complement (direct discourse) of λέγω.

παρέλθῃ. Aor act subj 3rd sg παρέρχομαι. Subjunctive with οὐ μή (see 9:1; on double negatives in general, see 1:44).

ἡ γενεὰ αὕτη. Nominative subject of παρέλθῃ. The expression γενεά οὗτος occurs four times in Mark: 8:12 (2×), 38; 13:30. The referent of "this generation" in the present verse is not easily identified and several alternatives have been proposed. The decision cannot be made on grammatical grounds. Bock (2005, 523–24) and France (539) provide helpful summaries of issues.

μέχρις οὗ. The improper preposition μέχρι, which governs the genitive case, functions as a temporal conjunction indicating "continuance in time up to a point" (BDAG, 644.2.b). It is often spelled μέχρις before a vowel as it is here.

ταῦτα πάντα. Nominative subject of γένηται. The reference could be to all the events described in verses 5-29 or only those of verses 24-29.

γένηται. Aor mid subj 3rd sg γίνομαι. Subjunctive with μέχρις οὗ.

13:31 ὁ οὐρανὸς καὶ ἡ γῆ παρελεύσονται, οἱ δὲ λόγοι μου οὐ μὴ παρελεύσονται.

ὁ οὐρανὸς καὶ ἡ γῆ. Nominative subject of παρελεύσονται.
παρελεύσονται. Fut mid ind 3rd pl παρέρχομαι.
οἱ . . . λόγοι. Nominative subject of παρελεύσονται. The use of δέ introduces a contrast between the contingent nature of the created order and the certainty of the fulfillment of Jesus' words (echoing v. 30).

οὐ μή. Emphatic negation (on οὐ μή, see 9:1; on double negatives in general, see 1:44). The usual idiom is οὐ μή with an aorist subjunctive, but a dozen times in the NT it occurs as here with a future indicative (see also 14:31; Matt 15:6; 16:22; 26:35; Luke 21:33; John 4:14; 6:35; 10:5; Heb 10:17; Rev 3:5; 9:6; 18:14).

παρελεύσονται. Fut mid ind 3rd pl παρέρχομαι. The force of this statement does not relate to the perpetual existence of Jesus' spoken words (or a written record of them, and especially not in any one particular form, whether in Aramaic, Greek, or a translation), but to the assurance of the fulfillment of the events predicted in his words. This is evident in the parallel expression, ἕως ἂν πάντα ταῦτα γένηται (v. 30; cf. the similar statement in Matt 5:18, which is linked with an explanatory γάρ to the "fulfillment" language [πληρῶσαι] of v. 17).

Mark 13:32-37

[32]"Now no one knows about that day or hour, not even the angels in heaven nor the Son, but only the Father. [33]Watch out! Be alert! For you do not know when the time will come. [34](It is) like a man away on a journey who having left his house and given his slaves responsibility, to each his own task, commanded the doorkeeper that he should stay awake and alert. [35]Therefore, stay awake and alert—for you do not know when the master of the house is coming, whether at evening, or midnight, or cockcrow, or in the morning—[36]so that

he does not find you sleeping if he comes unexpectedly. [37]Now what I say to you, I say to all: Stay awake and alert!"

13:32 Περὶ δὲ τῆς ἡμέρας ἐκείνης ἢ τῆς ὥρας οὐδεὶς οἶδεν, οὐδὲ οἱ ἄγγελοι ἐν οὐρανῷ οὐδὲ ὁ υἱός, εἰ μὴ ὁ πατήρ.

Περὶ δὲ τῆς ἡμέρας ἐκείνης ἢ τῆς ὥρας. Reference. The use of περὶ δέ at the beginning of a paragraph typically indicates a transition in the discussion (as it did at 12:26), whether to a new topic altogether or to a new aspect of the topic already under discussion. There is no explicit antecedent to "that day or hour" in the preceding context. The word ἡμέρα has occurred several times, but ὥρα has not. The phrase here is used to summarize the time when the events predicted are fulfilled with the addition of ὥρα suggesting that Jesus refers to the specific time of the climax of all these events (cf. Hartman, 520): the coming of the Son of Man (v. 26).

οὐδεὶς. Nominative subject of οἶδεν.

οἶδεν. Prf act ind 3rd sg οἶδα.

οὐδὲ οἱ ἄγγελοι . . . οὐδὲ ὁ υἱός. Nominative subject of an implied form of οἶδα. This phrase explains the extent of the οὐδείς in the preceding clause. This is the only instance of the "unadorned" ὁ υἱός as a title for Jesus in Mark (cf. Matt 11:27 ‖ Luke 10:22).

εἰ μὴ. Idiom: "except" (see 2:7).

ὁ πατήρ. Nominative subject of an elliptical statement: ὁ πατήρ οἶδεν περὶ τῆς ἡμέρας ἐκείνης ἢ τῆς ὥρας.

13:33 βλέπετε, ἀγρυπνεῖτε· οὐκ οἴδατε γὰρ πότε ὁ καιρός ἐστιν.

βλέπετε. Pres act impv 2nd pl βλέπω. This is the last of four uses of βλέπετε as an imperative in this chapter (see v. 5). In this final paragraph of the chapter "five times and in three different words Jesus warns the disciples to watch, to be alert" (βλέπετε, v. 33; ἀγρυπνεῖτε, v. 33; and γρηγορεῖτε, vv. 34, 35, 37; Edwards 2002, 408).

ἀγρυπνεῖτε. Pres act impv 2nd pl ἀγρυπνέω ("to be alert [i.e., to danger]," BDAG, 16; see also Luke 21:36; Eph 6:18; Heb 13:17). Danker (*CL*, 5) explains the formation as ὕπνος with an alpha privative, but that leaves the -γρ- unexplained. More likely is V. Taylor's explanation (523) that the verb is formed from ἄγρα ("the catching of prey") + ὕπνος, in which case the transparent etymology is well explained by Danker's definition: "to be on the hunt for sleep, to be sleepless, lie awake" (*CL*, 5), though here it is used metaphorically of "to be alert." The two imperatives are parallel and essentially synonymous for emphasis.

οἴδατε. Prf act ind 2nd pl οἶδα.

γὰρ. "The disciples' ignorance of the date of the Parousia is not an excuse for being unprepared, but a reason (γάρ) for unceasing vigilance" (Cranfield, 411).

πότε ὁ καιρός ἐστιν. Indirect question: "when the time will come." Clausal complement of οἴδατε.

ὁ καιρός. Nominative subject of ἐστιν.

ἐστιν. Pres act ind 3rd sg εἰμί. The collocation with καιρός justifies the translation "come."

13:34 ὡς ἄνθρωπος ἀπόδημος ἀφεὶς τὴν οἰκίαν αὐτοῦ καὶ δοὺς τοῖς δούλοις αὐτοῦ τὴν ἐξουσίαν ἑκάστῳ τὸ ἔργον αὐτοῦ καὶ τῷ θυρωρῷ ἐνετείλατο ἵνα γρηγορῇ.

The syntax of verse 34 has been described as awkward and inelegant (France, 545) due to the parallel of two participles with a finite verb. If, however, the participles are adjectival, then the parallel is only apparent. The second καί in this sentence (represented in the translation only by a comma) does seems awkward; it may have seemed necessary to indicate the resumption of the main statement since the subject has been separated from the main verb by two long participial clauses.

ὡς. The comparative serves to introduce a parable as part of a verbless clause: "(It is) like a man."

ἄνθρωπος ἀπόδημος. Nominative subject of ἐνετείλατο. The adjective (only here in the NT) means, "away on a journey" (BDAG, 109).

ἀφεὶς. Aor act ptc masc nom sg ἀφίημι (attributive).

τὴν οἰκίαν. Accusative direct object of ἀφείς.

δοὺς. Aor act ptc masc nom sg δίδωμι (attributive). The participle has two direct objects (τὴν ἐξουσίαν and τὸ ἔργον), each with an associated indirect object (τοῖς δούλοις and ἑκάστῳ respectively).

τοῖς δούλοις. Dative indirect object of δούς.

τὴν ἐξουσίαν. Accusative direct object of δούς. BDAG (353.3) suggests that ἐξουσίαν διδόναι τινί may be represented in English as "put someone in charge."

ἑκάστῳ. Dative indirect object of δούς. The phrase ἑκάστῳ τὸ ἔργον αὐτοῦ further explains the previous statement.

τὸ ἔργον. Accusative direct object of an implied δούς. The reference is to the slave's specific work assignment.

τῷ θυρωρῷ. Dative indirect object of ἐνετείλατο. The noun θυρωρός ("doorkeeper, gatekeeper") is always masculine in the NT, but it can also be feminine (BDAG, 462).

ἐνετείλατο. Aor mid ind 3rd sg ἐντέλλω.

ἵνα. Introduces the clausal complement of ἐνετείλατο.

γρηγορῇ. Pres act subj 3rd sg γρηγορέω. Subjunctive with ἵνα. This word is a "new formation in H[ellenistic] Gk. fr. ἐγρήγορα, the pf. of ἐγείρω" (BDAG, 208). There is no simple English equivalent, since it implies both staying awake and being alert. One can be awake without being alert, and though alertness would normally assume being awake, it does not specify wakefulness.

13:35 γρηγορεῖτε οὖν· οὐκ οἴδατε γὰρ πότε ὁ κύριος τῆς οἰκίας ἔρχεται, ἢ ὀψὲ ἢ μεσονύκτιον ἢ ἀλεκτοροφωνίας ἢ πρωΐ,

γρηγορεῖτε. Pres act impv 2nd pl γρηγορέω. On the meaning, see verse 34. "The porter's verb, γρηγορέω, is then turned into a direct exhortation to the readers, γρηγορεῖτε οὖν. . . . This explanatory clause is expressed still in terms of the situation of the parable, as if the readers were themselves in the position of the porter. It is a striking and effective way of drawing us directly into the application of the parable" (France, 545).

οὖν. The coordinating conjunction introduces Jesus' application of the parable; the imperative is addressed to his hearers.

οἴδατε. Prf act ind 2nd pl οἶδα.

γὰρ. The explanatory γάρ introduces why they should watch.

πότε ὁ κύριος . . . ἢ πρωΐ. An indirect question. The Roman designations used four numbered watches, but the terminology reflected here adapts common names for the Jewish watches, pushing them back one step to make room for the fourth Roman watch (see Martin, 685–701).

ὁ κύριος. Nominative subject of ἔρχεται.

ἔρχεται. Pres mid ind 3rd sg ἔρχομαι.

μεσονύκτιον. Accusative of time. Here, the adjective μεσονύκτιος is used in the neuter as an adverbial accusative ("at midnight"; BDAG, 634).

ἀλεκτοροφωνίας. Normally a genitive would refer to the period of time, but perhaps the parallel with the accusative suggests a specific time (cf. BDAG's suggestion: "at dawn"). It is true that with reference to time, "the accusative is widening its scope again" (Robertson, 471). The noun ἀλεκτοροφωνία refers to the "crowing of a cock/rooster" or the "name of the third watch of the night [12–3 AM]," BDAG, 41).

13:36 μὴ ἐλθὼν ἐξαίφνης εὕρῃ ὑμᾶς καθεύδοντας.

μὴ. The negative modifies εὕρῃ (not the participle ἐλθών), taking the place of a negative purpose clause: "so that he does not find."

ἐλθὼν . . . εὕρῃ . . . καθεύδοντας. See the verbal parallel in 14:40.

ἐλθών. Aor act ptc masc nom sg ἔρχομαι (conditional).

ἐξαίφνης. This is the only non-Lukan use of the adverb ("suddenly, unexpectedly") in the NT.

εὕρῃ. Aor act subj 3rd sg εὑρίσκω. Subjunctive with μή in a negative purpose clause.

ὑμᾶς. Accusative direct object of εὕρῃ.

καθεύδοντας. Pres act ptc masc acc pl καθεύδω (complement in an object-complement double accusative construction).

13:37 ὃ δὲ ὑμῖν λέγω πᾶσιν λέγω, γρηγορεῖτε.

ὃ. Accusative direct object of λέγω.

δὲ. The use of δέ extends the application of the prophetic parable (vv. 34-36) from the disciples to everyone.

ὑμῖν. Dative indirect object of λέγω.

λέγω. Pres act ind 1st sg λέγω.

πᾶσιν. Dative indirect object of (the second) λέγω.

λέγω. Pres act ind 1st sg λέγω.

γρηγορεῖτε. Pres act impv 2nd pl γρηγορέω. This one word clause functions as the clausal complement of (the second) λέγω. On the meaning, see verse 34.

Mark 14:1-11

[1]Now the Passover and the Feast of Unleavened Bread was after two days. The chief priests and the scribes were seeking how, if they could seize (him) by stealth, they might kill him, [2]for they said, "Not during the feast, lest there be an uproar from the people." [3]While Jesus was in Bethany having dinner at the home of Simon the Leper, a woman who had an alabaster vase of perfume made of very expensive, pure oil of nard, came (and) having broken the alabaster vase, poured (the perfume) over his head. [4]But some expressed their displeasure to each other, "Why this waste of perfume? [5]For it was possible to sell this perfume for more than 300 denarii and for it to be given to the poor!" So they scolded her indignantly. [6]But Jesus

said, "Leave her alone. Why do you cause trouble for her? She has done a good thing for me. [7]For you will always have the poor among you and you can do good for them whenever you want, but you will not always have me. [8]She did what she could; she anointed my body for burial ahead of time. [9]Truly I say to you, wherever the good news is proclaimed in all the world, what she has done will also be told in memory of her." [10]Then Judas Iscariot, one of the Twelve, went to the chief priests in order to hand Jesus over to them. [11]Now they, having heard (this), were glad and promised to give him money. So he sought how he might hand him over at an opportune time.

14:1 Ἦν δὲ τὸ πάσχα καὶ τὰ ἄζυμα μετὰ δύο ἡμέρας. καὶ ἐζήτουν οἱ ἀρχιερεῖς καὶ οἱ γραμματεῖς πῶς αὐτὸν ἐν δόλῳ κρατήσαντες ἀποκτείνωσιν·

Ἦν. Impf act ind 3rd sg εἰμί. It may be that the singular verb with the compound subject focuses attention on the first nominative (see Wallace 1996, 401–2).

δὲ. The use of δέ shifts from the prophetic discourse of verses 7-37 to historical narrative.

τὸ πάσχα καὶ τὰ ἄζυμα. Nominative subject of ἦν. Although τὸ πάσχα can refer either to the Passover lamb, the Passover meal, or the feast as a whole, "in the present passage [the Passover meal] seems to be intended, since τὸ π. is distinguished from τὰ ἄζυμα, the opening meal from the period of abstinence from leaven" (Swete, 319). On the plural of τὰ ἄζυμα, see 1:21.

μετὰ δύο ἡμέρας. Temporal. Evans translates, "It was now two days before the Passover" (2001, 353).

ἐζήτουν. Impf act ind 3rd pl ζητέω.

οἱ ἀρχιερεῖς καὶ οἱ γραμματεῖς. Nominative subject of ἐζήτουν.

πῶς. Introduces an indirect question that serves as the clausal complement of ἐζήτουν.

αὐτὸν. Accusative direct object of ἀποκτείνωσιν.

ἐν δόλῳ. Manner.

κρατήσαντες. Aor act ptc masc nom pl κρατέω. The participle could be temporal (they must first seize Jesus before they can kill him) or conditional (they could only kill him if they could seize him). Most English translations treat the participle as attendant circumstance (e.g., ESV), the construction here does not fit well with the usual criteria for an attendant circumstance participle (see Wallace 1996, 640–45).

ἀποκτείνωσιν. Pres (*or* aor) act subj 3rd pl ἀποκτείνω (deliberative subjunctive in an indirect question with πῶς; BDAG, 901.1.b.β, s.v. πῶς; see also v. 11). Both the tense and mood of the original verb (ἀποκτείνωμεν) are retained in the indirect statement, though the person changes from first to third. The forms of the present and aorist subjunctive of a liquid verb are identical.

14:2 ἔλεγον γάρ, Μὴ ἐν τῇ ἑορτῇ, μήποτε ἔσται θόρυβος τοῦ λαοῦ.

ἔλεγον. Impf act ind 3rd pl λέγω. The imperfect is used as part of an explanatory statement giving the background of the situation, not due to an *Aktionsart* value such as continuous (contra, e.g., NET note) or tendential (such factors may be true, but they cannot be based on the tense).

γάρ. The explanatory conjunction introduces a clause that explains the desire to seize Jesus ἐν δόλῳ.

Μὴ ἐν τῇ ἑορτῇ. A verbless clause that assumes a subjunctive form of κρατέω from the preceding verse.

ἐν τῇ ἑορτῇ. Temporal. Locative is also possible: "in the presence of the festival crowd" (Cranfield, 414, appealing to LSJ, 601.4, s.v. ἑορτή, "assembled multitude at a festival"). Evidence for the locative view is very limited, though LXX Ps 73:4 and John 7:11 provide additional possible examples (cited by Gundry, 808).

μήποτε. Introduces a negative purpose statement ("lest"). The two dozen NT instances of μήποτε almost always govern subjunctive verbs (17 aorist, 1 present, 1 perfect periphrastic), but there is a smattering of other forms that also occur: three future indicatives (here; Matt 7:6; Heb 3:12), one aorist indicative, one present indicative, and one optative (see also 3:11).

ἔσται. Fut mid ind 3rd sg εἰμί. Impersonal use of εἰμί.

θόρυβος. Predicate nominative.

τοῦ λαοῦ. Source.

14:3 Καὶ ὄντος αὐτοῦ ἐν Βηθανίᾳ ἐν τῇ οἰκίᾳ Σίμωνος τοῦ λεπροῦ, κατακειμένου αὐτοῦ ἦλθεν γυνὴ ἔχουσα ἀλάβαστρον μύρου νάρδου πιστικῆς πολυτελοῦς, συντρίψασα τὴν ἀλάβαστρον κατέχεεν αὐτοῦ τῆς κεφαλῆς.

Verses 3-9 function as the center of a typical Markan "sandwich story" (see also 3:22). The outer story consists of verses 1-2 and 10-11.

ὄντος. Pres act ptc masc gen sg εἰμί. Genitive absolute (see 1:32), temporal.

αὐτοῦ. Genitive subject of ὄντος. Generally the genitive subject of a genitive absolute does not recur in the sentence (there are more exceptions than many textbooks imply), but the referent of both genitive subjects in this double construction is the same as the third αὐτοῦ in the verse. It is better to define a genitive absolute as having a different subject from the main verb (though there are still exceptions), in which case this sentence fits the usual pattern since the first two instances of αὐτοῦ refer to Jesus, but the subject of both main verbs is the woman. See further at 5:2.

ἐν Βηθανίᾳ. Locative, "in Bethany."

ἐν τῇ οἰκίᾳ Σίμωνος. Locative. For οἰκίᾳ as "home," see 1:29.

κατακειμένου αὐτοῦ. This genitive absolute construction stands in apposition to the first one: "while he was in Bethany in the house of Simon the Leper, *while he was reclining to eat.*" McKnight (2001, 85) suggests that the occurrence of two genitive absolutes together at the beginning of a sentence is unusual and reflects a "grammatical irregularity" that is avoided by Matthew. Swete (320) describes it as a "disjointed style," while V. Taylor (539) calls it "strange" and Collins (641) views it as "very awkward." D. Black (90–91), however, challenges this prescriptive judgment. There is another double genitive absolute in verse 18, though there a single genitive pronoun functions as the subject of two genitive participles. Depending on textual choices, there could also be a double genitive absolute in 6:22. Though not common, such constructions are found in the other Synoptics (see Matt 13:19; Luke 3:21; 12:36; 14:29; 20:1; 22:55; 24:5, though without a genitive substantive in 12:36 and 22:55). Given the half dozen such examples in Luke, who is generally considered a more polished writer, it is probably not legitimate to view the use of two genitive absolutes together as irregular.

κατακειμένου. Pres mid ptc masc gen sg κατάκειμαι. Genitive absolute (see 1:32), temporal. On the meaning of κατάκειμαι, see 2:15.

αὐτοῦ. Genitive subject of κατακειμένου.

ἦλθεν. Aor act ind 3rd sg ἔρχομαι.

γυνὴ. Nominative subject of ἦλθεν.

ἔχουσα. Pres act ptc fem nom sg ἔχω (attributive).

ἀλάβαστρον. Accusative direct object of ἔχουσα. The noun ἀλάβαστρος occurs in all genders and refers to "a vessel w. a rather long neck which was broken off when the contents were used" (BDAG, 40).

μύρου νάρδου πιστικῆς πολυτελοῦς. The four genitives each describe a preceding word: the ἀλάβαστρον (alabaster jar) contained μύρου (perfume), which was made of νάρδου (nard), whose quality was πιστικῆς (pure) and which was valued as πολυτελοῦς (very expensive). Even if Edwards is correct that "Mark stumbles over himself in Greek to convey the value of the nard" (2002, 413), the statement is clear enough. France suggests that these four genitives "form a deliberately weighty phrase" to emphasize the nature of the perfume (551). Four contiguous genitives, each modifying the preceding, is not common (only || John 12:3 in the NT), but neither is it clumsy nor unnatural (cf. LXX Lev 5:15; Num 22:5; Josh 4:7). More commonly long genitive strings involve apposition, a list of parallel items, or spelled-out numbers (e.g., Mark 1:1; Rom 1:29; Rev 21:17).

νάρδου πιστικῆς. νάρδος is an aromatic oil extracted from the root of a perennial herb that is also known as nard or spikenard (BDAG, 666). πιστικός means "pure."

πολυτελοῦς. The adjective πολυτελής means "very expensive."

συντρίψασα. Aor act ptc fem nom sg συντρίβω (temporal).

τὴν ἀλάβαστρον. Accusative direct object of συντρίψασα.

κατέχεεν. Aor act ind 3rd sg καταχέω ("pour out," BDAG, 529–30). This verb is not coordinated with the previous finite verb in the sentence (as punctuated in the NA²⁷/UBS⁴), which is unusual for Mark. France (552) suggests that a new sentence should begin with συντρίψασα, but we would still be left with asyndeton, which is not typical in Mark.

τῆς κεφαλῆς. The genitive indicates over what the liquid is poured (BDAG, 529–30).

14:4 ἦσαν δέ τινες ἀγανακτοῦντες πρὸς ἑαυτούς, Εἰς τί ἡ ἀπώλεια αὕτη τοῦ μύρου γέγονεν;

ἦσαν. Impf act ind 3rd pl εἰμί.

δὲ. The use of δέ reflects the shift in subjects: the woman in verse 5, the onlookers in verse 6.

τινες. Nominative subject of ἦσαν . . . ἀγανακτοῦντες. Matthew's account specifies the subject as the disciples (26:8).

ἀγανακτοῦντες. Pres act ptc masc nom pl ἀγανακτέω (imperfective periphrastic; "to be indignant against what is assumed to be wrong"). The word ἀγανακτέω can function as a verb of speaking, though the speech act is only implied. Mark uses it here to introduce direct discourse (vv. 4b-5). Matthew's parallel uses a participle to make the speaking explicit (26:8). Though many translations take the participle as adjectival rather than periphrastic ("some were there who were indignant," cf. NIV, ESV, NRSV, NET, NJB, REB), if ἀγανακτέω is taken as a verb of speaking the periphrastic analysis is more likely.

πρὸς ἑαυτούς. Association. Cranfield suggests that this phrase is "perhaps to be explained as suggesting looks or remarks exchanged between them" (416), though V. Taylor thinks that "in the absence of a verb of saying, this idea is at best obscurely expressed" (531). BDAG (5, s.v. ἀγανακτέω) translates ἦσαν δέ τινες ἀγανακτοῦντες πρὸς ἑαυτούς as "some expressed their displeasure to each other," but acknowledges that elsewhere "πρός introduces the one against whom the displeasure is directed." In the NT, the object of the displeasure is elsewhere noted with περί (Matt 20:24; Mark 10:41). πρός, on the other hand, is commonly used with verbs of speaking to introduce the one being addressed (e.g., 8:16; 12:7; 16:3).

εἰς τί ἡ ἀπώλεια . . . τοῖς πτωχοῖς (v. 5). Clausal complement (direct discourse) of ἀγανακτοῦντες.

Εἰς τί. "Why?" (BDAG, 290.4.f, s.v., εἰς; see also 15:34).

ἡ ἀπώλεια αὕτη. Nominative subject of γέγονεν. Although ἀπώλεια usually has a stronger sense ("annihilation," BDAG, 127.2), here it means "waste" (BDAG, 127.1; see also V. Taylor, 531).

τοῦ μύρου. Objective genitive.

γέγονεν. Prf act ind 3rd sg γίνομαι. The perfect tense refers to the state that existed: the perfume is now spilled (the result of κατέχεεν, v. 3); formally, "Why has this waste of perfume come to be?"

14:5 ἠδύνατο γὰρ τοῦτο τὸ μύρον πραθῆναι ἐπάνω δηναρίων τριακοσίων καὶ δοθῆναι τοῖς πτωχοῖς· καὶ ἐνεβριμῶντο αὐτῇ.

ἠδύνατο. Impf mid ind 3rd sg δύναμαι. The augment appearing as *eta* is not the usual pattern, especially for a word beginning with a *delta*. In the NT, the aorist of δύναμαι always augments this way, but the imperfect uses the *eta* seven times and the more typical *epsilon* twelve times. In the LXX, the imperfect has eighteen *epsilon* forms and thirty-three *eta* forms; the aorist shows three forms augmented with *epsilon* and twenty-five with *eta* (see MHT 2:188 for possible explanations). One might translate, "it would have been possible."

τοῦτο τὸ μύρον. Nominative subject of ἠδύνατο.

πραθῆναι. Aor pass inf πιπράσκω (complementary). On the form, see MHT (2:254, 2:185.IV).

ἐπάνω δηναρίων τριακοσίων. The adverb ἐπάνω ("more than") is used with a number/quantity in the genitive case. This is a colloquial expression in Koine; classical Greek would have used πλείων instead of ἐπάνω (BDF §185.4; BDAG, 359.2). The amount suggested would be more than a year's wages for an average worker. The adjective τριακόσιοι means "three hundred."

δοθῆναι. Aor pass inf δίδωμι (complementary to ἠδύνατο). The subject of δοθῆναι is, grammatically speaking, τοῦτο τὸ μύρον, though as France points out, it "should be the money raised by the sale rather than the perfume itself" that is given, "but, compressed as it is, Mark's sentence is idiomatically clear and effective" (553).

τοῖς πτωχοῖς. Dative indirect object of δοθῆναι.

ἐνεβριμῶντο. Impf mid ind 3rd pl ἐμβριμάομαι ("to scold indignantly/harshly," BDAG, 322; see also 1:43). "Strong disapproval expressed in gesture and sound seem implied" (V. Taylor, 532). On the possibility that this is an inceptive imperfect as in HCSB, see 1:21.

αὐτῇ. Dative complement of ἐνεβριμῶντο. France notes that "the dative following ἐμβριμάομαι indicates (as in 1:43) that their hostility was openly directed against the woman" (553).

14:6 ὁ δὲ Ἰησοῦς εἶπεν, Ἄφετε αὐτήν· τί αὐτῇ κόπους παρέχετε; καλὸν ἔργον ἠργάσατο ἐν ἐμοί.

ὁ . . . Ἰησοῦς. Nominative subject of εἶπεν. The use of δέ reflects the shift of speakers from the onlookers in verses 4-5 to Jesus in verse 6.

εἶπεν. Aor act ind 3rd sg λέγω.

ἄφετε αὐτήν· . . . ⁹εἰς μνημόσυνον αὐτῆς. Clausal complement (direct discourse) of εἶπεν.

ἄφετε. Aor act impv 2nd pl ἀφίημι.

αὐτήν. Accusative direct object of ἄφετε.

τί. Interrogative: "why?"

αὐτῇ. Dative of disadvantage.

κόπους. Accusative direct object of παρέχετε.

παρέχετε. Pres act ind 2nd pl παρέχω.

καλὸν ἔργον. Accusative direct object of ἠργάσατο. The choice of καλός as the modifier of ἔργον rather than ἀγαθός appears to be idiolectal. Matthew, Mark, and John use only καλός (5 times total), as do Hebrews, James and 1 Peter (once each). Luke's only occurrence uses ἀγαθός. Pauline usage divides with six uses of ἀγαθός and eight of καλός (all of which are in the Pastorals). Evans (2001, 361) points out (following Daube) that καλὸν ἔργον was a technical expression for an act of charity.

ἠργάσατο. Aor mid ind 3rd sg ἐργάζομαι. Note the cognate forms of verb and object.

ἐν ἐμοί. Reference.

14:7 πάντοτε γὰρ τοὺς πτωχοὺς ἔχετε μεθ᾽ ἑαυτῶν καὶ ὅταν θέλητε δύνασθε αὐτοῖς εὖ ποιῆσαι, ἐμὲ δὲ οὐ πάντοτε ἔχετε.

γὰρ. The explanatory conjunction functions to introduce an explanation of why the protest of "waste" was misguided and responds specifically to the (self-righteous?) excuse that it would have been better used for charity.

τοὺς πτωχοὺς. Accusative direct object of ἔχετε.

ἔχετε. Pres act ind 2nd pl ἔχω. The time reference is future, or it could be considered timeless as part of a gnomic statement.

μεθ᾽ ἑαυτῶν. Spatial (or perhaps association: "with you").

ὅταν. In this instance, the sense is "whenever" (in Koine ὅταν with the subjunctive usually means simply "when"). The statement might also be treated as an informal condition, "if you want . . ." (cf. Duckwitz, 218).

θέλητε. Pres act subj 2nd pl θέλω. Subjunctive with ὅταν.

δύνασθε. Pres mid ind 2nd pl δύναμαι.

αὐτοῖς. Dative of advantage. The later reading αὐτούς (A Θ 𝔐) likely reflects more common usage of ποιέω with the accusative (BDAG, 841.4.a–d, s.v. ποιέω; for use with dative and an adverb as here, see 4.e), especially in classical Greek (LSJ, 1428.B.2, s.v. ποιέω).

εὖ. The collocation εὖ ποιέω means "do good, show kindness" (BDAG, 401.1, s.v. εὖ). The phrase occurs only here in the NT, but is common in the LXX (more than 50 times), usually with an accusative (εὖ σε ποιήσει or εὖ ἐποίησεν ὑμᾶς are frequent), but occasionally with the dative as here (e.g., Sir 12:5, εὖ ποίησον ταπεινῷ). "It is generally accepted that in later Greek εὖ was gradually superseded by καλῶς, a near synonym from early in classical Greek. Some such development was to be expected, given the shortness and irregularity of εὖ. It is in keeping with the tendencies of the Koine that the replacement is both 'fuller-sounding' and a regular formation related to a familiar word" (Lee, 11–12). The use of εὖ here gives Jesus' statement a more formal sound (contrast the more common καλῶς ποιέω in 7:37).

ποιῆσαι. Aor act inf ποιέω (complementary).

ἐμὲ. Accusative direct object of ἔχετε.

δὲ. The conjunction δέ contrasts the presence of the poor with the presence of Jesus.

ἔχετε. Pres act ind 2nd pl ἔχω. The time reference is future.

14:8 ὃ ἔσχεν ἐποίησεν· προέλαβεν μυρίσαι τὸ σῶμά μου εἰς τὸν ἐνταφιασμόν.

ὃ ἔσχεν ἐποίησεν. Formally, "what she had, she did" (see the similar wording at 12:44). Hort suggests that ποιῆσαι is to be supplied: "what she was able *to do*, she did" (172). The relative clause ὃ ἔσχεν functions as the direct object of ἐποίησεν.

ὅ. Accusative direct object of ἔσχεν.

ἔσχεν. Aor act ind 3rd sg ἔχω. The word ἔχω has a fairly wide semantic range. In this context it means "be in a position to do someth., can, be able" (BDAG, 421.5). This sense is typically followed by a complementary infinitive (e.g., Luke 14:14).

ἐποίησεν. Aor act ind 3rd sg ποιέω.

προέλαβεν. Aor act ind 3rd sg προλαμβάνω ("do someth. before the usual time, anticipate someth.," BDAG, 872.1.a). What is done in advance is indicated by the following infinitive (cf. *2 Clem.* 8:2; BDF §392.2.2). Robertson (551, see also 1120) suggests that this is a rare instance in which the infinitive expresses the main idea and the finite form functions almost like an adverb.

μυρίσαι. Aor act inf μυρίζω ("to anoint," BDAG, 661). Grammatically, μυρίσαι functions as the object of προέλαβεν (but see above on προέλαβεν). This NT *hapax legomenon* does not occur in the LXX, but does appear once each in Josephus (*Ant.* 19:358) and the Pseudepigrapha (*Apoc. Sedr.* 14:6).

τὸ σῶμά. Accusative direct object of μυρίσαι.

εἰς τὸν ἐνταφιασμόν. Reference. "The phrase indicates not here conscious intention, but the purpose which her action will actually serve" (Cranfield, 417), or as V. Taylor puts it, it was "not the woman's purpose, but the interpretation Jesus puts on her action" (533).

ἐνταφιασμόν. "The performance of what is customary for burial" (BDAG, 339). Both the noun (ἐνταφιαστής, "embalmer") and verb (ἐνταφιάζω, "to embalm, prepare for burial") form of this word occur several times in LXX Gen 50:2.

14:9 ἀμὴν δὲ λέγω ὑμῖν, ὅπου ἐὰν κηρυχθῇ τὸ εὐαγγέλιον εἰς ὅλον τὸν κόσμον, καὶ ὃ ἐποίησεν αὕτη λαληθήσεται εἰς μνημόσυνον αὐτῆς.

ἀμὴν . . . λέγω ὑμῖν. See 3:28.

δὲ. The use of δέ is probably due to the shift in grammatical subjects: the woman in verse 8, Jesus in verse 9.

λέγω. Pres act ind 1st sg λέγω.

ὑμῖν. Dative indirect object of λέγω.

ὅπου ἐὰν κηρυχθῇ ... εἰς μνημόσυνον αὐτῆς. Clausal complement (embedded direct discourse) of λέγω.

ὅπου ἐὰν. Particle of place with the indefinite particle ἐάν.
Although this might be taken as a temporal expression in some contexts ("whenever"), the following εἰς ὅλον τὸν κόσμον clarifies that
the expression in this instance is locative.

κηρυχθῇ. Aor pass subj 3rd sg κηρύσσω. Subjunctive with ὅπου
ἐάν. On ὅπου ἐάν/ἄν with the subjunctive, see 6:10.

τὸ εὐαγγέλιον. Nominative subject of κηρυχθῇ.

εἰς ὅλον τὸν κόσμον. Locative.

ὃ ἐποίησεν αὕτη. The relative clause functions as the subject of
λαληθήσεται.

ὃ. Accusative direct object of ἐποίησεν.

ἐποίησεν. Aor act ind 3rd sg ποιέω.

αὕτη. Nominative subject of ἐποίησεν.

λαληθήσεται. Fut pass ind 3rd sg λαλέω.

εἰς μνημόσυνον. Reference. μνημόσυνον refers to "memory"
(BDAG, 655) or "an instrument or means designed to cause to
remember—'memorial'" (LN 29.12). In Acts 10:4 it refers to a
memorial offering, a frequent LXX use.

αὐτῆς. Objective genitive (BDAG, 655.2, s.v. μνημόσυνον).

**14:10 Καὶ Ἰούδας Ἰσκαριὼθ ὁ εἷς τῶν δώδεκα ἀπῆλθεν πρὸς τοὺς
ἀρχιερεῖς ἵνα αὐτὸν παραδοῖ αὐτοῖς.**

Ἰούδας Ἰσκαριὼθ. Nominative subject of ἀπῆλθεν.

ὁ εἷς τῶν δώδεκα. The article ὁ functions as a nominalizer, changing the adjective εἷς (which is modified by a partitive genitive) into
a nominative in apposition to Ἰούδας Ἰσκαριὼθ. Wallace (1996,
239) cites this as an example of a "third attributive position," but
explaining it as a nominalizer seems to make better sense, since
the following phrase is not a modifier, but a restatement of the
head noun. Collins thinks the article makes it a titular form, "the
[notorious] one of the Twelve" (644; brackets in original). Gundry
(819) suggests that the article is to be understood as antecedent reference to 3:19 (the only place in Mark where the full name, Ἰούδας
Ἰσκαριὼθ, is used), but that is a very long span for such a use of the
article alone. BDF (§247.2.2) and Robertson (675.i) claim that ὁ εἷς
is the equivalent of τις, but that does not seem to yield good sense

in this text unless "*a certain* one of the Twelve" is meant. On the use of εἷς with the partitive genitive, see 10:17. On the use and referent of δώδεκα, see 4:10.

ἀπῆλθεν. Aor act ind 3rd sg ἀπέρχομαι.

πρὸς τοὺς ἀρχιερεῖς. Spatial.

ἵνα. Introduces a purpose clause.

αὐτὸν. Accusative direct object of παραδοῖ.

παραδοῖ. Aor act subj 3rd sg παραδίδωμι. Subjunctive with ἵνα. On the form, see 4:29. On the meaning and use of παραδίδωμι in Mark, see 1:14 and 3:19.

αὐτοῖς. Dative indirect object of παραδοῖ.

14:11 οἱ δὲ ἀκούσαντες ἐχάρησαν καὶ ἐπηγγείλαντο αὐτῷ ἀργύριον δοῦναι. καὶ ἐζήτει πῶς αὐτὸν εὐκαίρως παραδοῖ.

οἱ. Nominative subject of ἐχάρησαν. On the use of οἱ δέ to change subjects, see 1:45.

ἀκούσαντες. Aor act ptc masc nom pl ἀκούω (temporal, or less likely substantival: "the ones who heard," since the reference appears to still be specifically to the chief priests).

ἐχάρησαν. Aor pass ind 3rd pl χαίρω.

ἐπηγγείλαντο. Aor mid ind 3rd pl ἐπαγγέλλομαι. When the content of the promise is given, this verb most commonly includes an accusative direct object indicating what is given followed by a dative indirect object to specify to whom it is given (e.g., Jas 1:12; 2 Pet 2:19; 1 John 2:25). Occasionally, however, the accusative is replaced by an infinitive, as here (see also Acts 7:5). In some instances ἐπαγγέλλομαι takes an infinitive, a dative, and an accusative (see 3 Macc 1:4; *2 Clem.* 11:6; and Herm. *Vis.* 3.1).

αὐτῷ. Dative indirect object of δοῦναι

ἀργύριον. Accusative direct object of δοῦναι. Technically, ἀργύριον refers to the metal silver, but it is often used to refer to money.

δοῦναι. Aor act inf δίδωμι (indirect discourse).

ἐζήτει. Impf act ind 3rd sg ζητέω. (On the possibility that this is an inceptive imperfect as in a number of modern translations, see 1:21.)

εὐκαίρως. Adverb: "at an opportune time" (LN 67.6; see also 6:21.

παραδοῖ. Aor act subj 3rd sg παραδίδωμι (deliberative subjunctive in an indirect question with πῶς; see also v. 1). On the meaning and use of παραδίδωμι in Mark, see the discussions at 1:14 and 3:19.

Mark 14:12-21

[12]Now on the first day of the Feast of Unleavened Bread when people sacrificed their Passover lamb, Jesus' disciples asked him, "Where do you want us to go to prepare so that you may eat the Passover meal?" [13]So he sent two of his disciples and said to them, "Go into the city and a man who is carrying a water jar will meet you; follow him [14]and where he enters (a house), say to the owner of the house, 'the Teacher says, "Where is my guest room where I may eat the Passover meal with my disciples?"' [15]He will show you a large room upstairs, furnished and ready. Prepare for us there." [16]The disciples left, went into the city and found (it) just as Jesus told them, so they prepared the Passover meal. [17]When it came to be evening Jesus came with the Twelve. [18]While they were reclining at the table and eating Jesus said, "Truly I say to you that one of you will hand me over—one who is eating with me." [19]They began to grieve and to say to him one after the other, "It is not me, is it?" [20]But he said to them, "It is one of the Twelve—one who dips with me in the dish. [21]For on the one hand the Son of Man goes as it is written about him, but on the other hand, woe to that man by whom the Son of Man is handed over. It would be better for him if that man had not been born."

14:12 Καὶ τῇ πρώτῃ ἡμέρᾳ τῶν ἀζύμων, ὅτε τὸ πάσχα ἔθυον, λέγουσιν αὐτῷ οἱ μαθηταὶ αὐτοῦ, Ποῦ θέλεις ἀπελθόντες ἑτοιμάσωμεν ἵνα φάγῃς τὸ πάσχα;

τῇ πρώτῃ ἡμέρᾳ. Dative of time.

τῶν ἀζύμων. The adjective ἄζυμος means "unleavened," but is more commonly used as a substantive to refer to bread baked without leaven or, as here, the Feast of Unleavened Bread. On the plural, see 1:21.

τὸ πάσχα. Accusative direct object of ἔθυον. Most commonly πάσχα (an indeclinable, neuter noun) refers to the entire Passover festival including the Feast of Unleavened Bread, which immediately followed Passover (e.g., Matt 26:2; Mark 14:1; Luke 22:1; John 2:23; Acts 12:4), but it sometimes, as here, refers to the Passover lamb (see also Matt 26:17; Luke 22:7, 11, 15; John 18:28; 1 Cor 5:7) or to the meal that formed the centerpiece of the festival (e.g., Matt 26:18, 19; Mark 14:12b, 16; Luke 22:8, 13; Heb 11:28).

ἔθυον. Impf act ind 3rd pl θύω. Indefinite plural (see 1:22). The thrust of the context is to describe the usual events at this time during the feast so it would be legitimate to describe the *statement* as a "customary" one (though this ought not be attributed to the imperfect tense alone). Alternatively, Evans (2001, 373) proposes that the reference is not to the crowds, but to Jesus and his disciples, appealing to the subsequent question as the logical next step. Another, less likely, possibility is that the reference is to τοὺς ἀρχιερεῖς in verse 10 (so Maloney 2008, 142), but that is in a different pericope and the subject has changed with the new paragraph in verse 12.

λέγουσιν. Pres act ind 3rd pl λέγω. The narrative present is used to introduce a new paragraph (see 1:21 on εἰσπορεύονται).

αὐτῷ. Dative indirect object of λέγουσιν.

οἱ μαθηταὶ. Nominative subject of λέγουσιν.

Ποῦ θέλεις . . . τὸ πάσχα. Clausal complement (direct discourse) of λέγουσιν in the form of a deliberative question.

θέλεις. Pres act ind 2nd sg θέλω.

ἀπελθόντες ἑτοιμάσωμεν ἵνα φάγῃς τὸ πάσχα. Clausal complement of θέλεις.

ἀπελθόντες. Aor act ptc masc nom pl ἀπέρχομαι (temporal or perhaps attendant circumstance). The participle is redundant and somewhat clumsy; it is not included in the Synoptic parallels (Matt 26:17 and Luke 22:9).

ἑτοιμάσωμεν. Aor act subj 1st pl ἑτοιμάζω. On the lack of a ἵνα, see the discussion of the syntactical pattern in 15:9.

ἵνα. Introduces a purpose statement.

φάγῃς. Aor act subj 2nd sg ἐσθίω. Subjunctive with ἵνα. The singular reference to Jesus as the one to eat the feast is perhaps unexpected, but the crucial focus is on Jesus, not his disciples.

τὸ πάσχα. Accusative direct object of φάγῃς. Here πάσχα refers to the Passover meal as a whole (see above; see also Cranfield, 420–21).

14:13 καὶ ἀποστέλλει δύο τῶν μαθητῶν αὐτοῦ καὶ λέγει αὐτοῖς, Ὑπάγετε εἰς τὴν πόλιν, καὶ ἀπαντήσει ὑμῖν ἄνθρωπος κεράμιον ὕδατος βαστάζων· ἀκολουθήσατε αὐτῷ

ἀποστέλλει. Pres act ind 3rd sg ἀποστέλλω. The narrative present is used when new participants (here, δύο τῶν μαθητῶν αὐτοῦ rather than οἱ μαθηταὶ αὐτοῦ in general) are introduced, and in this instance there is also a geographical shift, both common features of narrative presents (see also 1:21 on εἰσπορεύονται).

δύο. Accusative direct object of ἀποστέλλει.

τῶν μαθητῶν. Partitive genitive (see 8:8).

λέγει. Pres act ind 3rd sg λέγω.

αὐτοῖς. Dative indirect object of λέγει.

Ὑπάγετε εἰς τὴν πόλιν . . .¹⁵ἐτοιμάσατε ἡμῖν. Clausal complement (direct discourse) of λέγει.

Ὑπάγετε. Pres act impv 2nd pl ὑπάγω.

εἰς τὴν πόλιν. Spatial.

ἀπαντήσει. Fut act ind 3rd sg ἀπαντάω "to meet (someone)"
(BDAG, 97; see also Luke 17:12). The more common synonym is
ὑπαντάω. Texts with one of these words usually have a variant reading with the other. As one evidence that Jesus has arranged for use
of the room in advance, France points to this third singular form,
suggesting "that the man is on the lookout for them, rather than a
chance encounter" (564).

ὑμῖν. Dative complement of ἀπαντήσει.

ἄνθρωπος. Nominative subject of ἀπαντήσει.

κεράμιον. Accusative direct object of βαστάζων ("an earthenware
vessel, jar," BDAG, 540). Α κεράμιον ὕδατος is a water jar, the genitive indicating the contents of the head noun.

βαστάζων. Pres act ptc masc nom sg βαστάζω (attributive modifying ἄνθρωπος).

ἀκολουθήσατε. Aor act impv 2nd pl ἀκολουθέω.

αὐτῷ. Dative complement of ἀκολουθήσατε.

**14:14 καὶ ὅπου ἐὰν εἰσέλθῃ εἴπατε τῷ οἰκοδεσπότῃ ὅτι Ὁ διδά-
σκαλος λέγει, Ποῦ ἐστιν τὸ κατάλυμά μου ὅπου τὸ πάσχα μετὰ
τῶν μαθητῶν μου φάγω;**

ὅπου ἐὰν. Introduces a locative clause.

εἰσέλθῃ. Aor act subj 3rd sg εἰσέρχομαι. Subjunctive with ὅπου
ἐάν. On ὅπου ἐάν/ἄν with the subjunctive, see 6:10.

εἴπατε. Aor act impv 2nd pl λέγω.

τῷ οἰκοδεσπότῃ. Dative indirect object of εἴπατε.

ὅτι. Introduces the clausal complement (direct discourse) of
εἴπατε (see 1:15).

Ὁ διδάσκαλος. Nominative subject of λέγει. The use of the article
may have a "titular" function (so Gundry, 822).

λέγει. Pres act ind 3rd sg λέγω.

Ποῦ ἐστιν τὸ κατάλυμά . . . φάγω. Clausal complement (embedded direct discourse) of λέγει.

ἐστιν. Pres act ind 3rd sg εἰμί.

τὸ κατάλυμά. Nominative subject of ἐστιν (a "lodging place,
guest room" or possibly even "dining room," BDAG, 521; also in
Luke 2:7 and ‖ 22:11. The fourteen uses in the LXX are similar in
most instances, though there is a much broader range of referents

including the Tabernacle (2 Sam 7:6) and a lion's lair (Jer 32:38; Eng. = 25:38).

μου. The inclusion of the personal pronoun seems to imply that the room had been prearranged. The genitive refers to "right of use rather than ownership" (Swete, 330).

ὅπου. Introduces a locative clause (see v. 14a).

τὸ πάσχα. On the meaning, see verse 12.

μετὰ τῶν μαθητῶν. Association.

φάγω. Aor act subj 1st sg ἐσθίω. Subjunctive with ὅπου.

14:15 καὶ αὐτὸς ὑμῖν δείξει ἀνάγαιον μέγα ἐστρωμένον ἕτοιμον· καὶ ἐκεῖ ἑτοιμάσατε ἡμῖν.

αὐτὸς. Nominative subject of δείξει. The pronoun is neither emphatic nor intensive (see 6:17).

ὑμῖν. Dative indirect object of δείξει.

δείξει. Fut act ind 3rd sg δείκνυμι.

ἀνάγαιον μέγα ἐστρωμένον ἕτοιμον. Accusative direct object of δείξει ("upstairs room," BDAG, 59) The more usual Koine word to describe an upper room was ὑπερῷον (e.g., Acts 1:13; 9:37, 39; 20:8; *1 Clem.* 12:3; and 21 times in the LXX). The noun is followed by three modifiers: μέγα, ἐστρωμένον, and ἕτοιμον, "large, furnished, ready."

ἐστρωμένον. Prf pass ptc neut acc sg στρωννύω/στρώννυμι (attributive). The word στρωννύω means "to spread," but the context determines what is spread. It could refer to "furnishing a room with couches" (Gould, 261; cf. BDAG, 949.2.a), "'a well laid out' banquet room" (Edwards 2002, 421), spreading a covering on the walls ("paneled"), or perhaps even to covering the floor with stone ("paved," see BDAG, 949.1).

ἑτοιμάσατε. Aor act impv 2nd pl ἑτοιμάζω.

ἡμῖν. Dative of advantage.

14:16 καὶ ἐξῆλθον οἱ μαθηταὶ καὶ ἦλθον εἰς τὴν πόλιν καὶ εὗρον καθὼς εἶπεν αὐτοῖς καὶ ἡτοίμασαν τὸ πάσχα.

ἐξῆλθον. Aor act ind 3rd pl ἐξέρχομαι.

οἱ μαθηταὶ. Nominative subject of ἐξῆλθον . . . καὶ ἦλθον . . . καὶ εὗρον . . . καὶ ἡτοίμασαν.

ἦλθον. Aor act ind 3rd pl ἔρχομαι.

εἰς τὴν πόλιν. Spatial.

εὗρον. Aor act ind 3rd pl εὑρίσκω.

καθώς. Introduces a comparative clause that compares the implied object of εὗρον with what Jesus has told them.

εἶπεν. Aor act ind 3rd sg λέγω.

αὐτοῖς. Dative indirect object of εἶπεν.

ἡτοίμασαν. Aor act ind 3rd pl ἑτοιμάζω.

τὸ πάσχα. Accusative direct object of ἡτοίμασαν. Here τὸ πάσχα refers to the Passover meal (see v. 12).

14:17 Καὶ ὀψίας γενομένης ἔρχεται μετὰ τῶν δώδεκα.

ὀψίας. Genitive subject of γενομένης.

γενομένης. Aor mid ptc fem gen sg γίνομαι. Genitive absolute (see 1:32), temporal.

ἔρχεται. Pres mid ind 3rd sg ἔρχομαι. The narrative present tense introduces a new paragraph and also marks a change in location (see 1:21 on εἰσπορεύονται).

μετὰ τῶν δώδεκα. Accompaniment. The term τῶν δώδεκα is a designation of the group of Jesus' disciples, even if not all twelve men were present (cf. John 20:24). In this instance two of them had gone on ahead, so Jesus' arrival with τῶν δώδεκα refers to the group of the remaining ten, unless the two had perhaps returned.

14:18 καὶ ἀνακειμένων αὐτῶν καὶ ἐσθιόντων ὁ Ἰησοῦς εἶπεν, Ἀμὴν λέγω ὑμῖν ὅτι εἷς ἐξ ὑμῶν παραδώσει με ὁ ἐσθίων μετ᾽ ἐμοῦ.

ἀνακειμένων. Pres mid ptc masc gen pl ἀνάκειμαι. Genitive absolute (see 1:32), temporal. On the use of the plural verb here, see 5:38. The word ἀνάκειμαι means "to recline" and can refer to someone who is "lying dead" (though only in a variant reading [𝔐] of Mark 5:40 in the NT), but it is almost always used as a synonym for "to dine" (BDAG, 65.2).

αὐτῶν. Genitive subject of ἀνακειμένων . . . καὶ ἐσθιόντων.

ἐσθιόντων. Pres act ptc masc gen pl ἐσθίω. Genitive absolute (see 1:32), temporal.

ὁ Ἰησοῦς. Nominative subject of εἶπεν.

εἶπεν. Aor act ind 3rd sg λέγω.

Ἀμὴν λέγω . . . μετ᾽ ἐμοῦ. Clausal complement (direct discourse) of εἶπεν.

Ἀμὴν λέγω ὑμῖν. See 3:28.

λέγω. Pres act ind 1st sg λέγω.

ὅτι. Introduces the clausal complement (direct discourse) of λέγω.

εἰς ἐξ ὑμῶν. On εἰς and ἐκ with a partitive genitive, see 9:17.

εἰς. Nominative subject of παραδώσει.

παραδώσει. Fut act ind 3rd sg παραδίδωμι. On the meaning and use of παραδίδωμι in Mark, see 1:14 and 3:19.

με. Accusative direct object of παραδώσει.

ὁ ἐσθίων. Pres act ptc masc nom sg ἐσθίω (substantival). Nominative in apposition to εἰς.

μετ᾽ ἐμοῦ. Association.

14:19 ἤρξαντο λυπεῖσθαι καὶ λέγειν αὐτῷ εἰς κατὰ εἰς, Μήτι ἐγώ;

ἤρξαντο. Aor mid ind 3rd pl ἄρχω.

λυπεῖσθαι. Pres mid inf λυπέω (complementary).

λέγειν. Pres act inf λέγω (complementary).

αὐτῷ. Dative indirect object of λέγειν.

εἰς κατὰ εἰς. A colloquial distributive expression equivalent to ἕκαστος (|| Matt 26:22, εἰς ἕκαστος): "one by one" or "one after the other" (BDAG, 293.5.e, s.v. εἰς). For parallels in Koine, see Doudna (39). On distributives generally, see 6:7. One would expect the second εἰς to be in the accusative (ἕνα) as the object of κατά, but in this idiomatic expression εἰς is apparently used as an indeclinable form, something which is more common in "later Greek," i.e., Koine (Robertson, 283; see also BDF §305; Rom 12:5; Rev 21:21; 3 Macc 5:34). For the more commonly expected form with a preposition, see 1 Cor 14:31 (καθ᾽ ἕνα). Moulton suggests that κατά should be viewed as functioning as an adverb in such instances (hence case agreement is not necessary), pointing to the (much) later development of the adverbs καθείς and καθένας as evidence (MHT 1:105; cf. Robertson, 606.i.2; Bruce, 436).

Μήτι ἐγώ. A nominal statement with εἰμί omitted as is common in questions (BDF §127.3). The use of μή implies that a negative answer is expected.

14:20 ὁ δὲ εἶπεν αὐτοῖς, Εἷς τῶν δώδεκα, ὁ ἐμβαπτόμενος μετ᾽ ἐμοῦ εἰς τὸ τρύβλιον.

ὁ. Nominative subject of εἶπεν. On the use of ὁ δέ to change subjects, see 1:45.

εἶπεν. Aor act ind 3rd sg λέγω.

αὐτοῖς. Dative indirect object of εἶπεν.

Εἷς τῶν δώδεκα ... ²¹ὁ ἄνθρωπος ἐκεῖνος. Clausal complement (direct discourse) of εἶπεν.

Εἷς τῶν δώδεκα. On εἷς and ἐκ with a partitive genitive, see 9:17. On the use of εἷς with the partitive genitive, see 10:17 and 14:10.

Εἷς. Predicate nominative of the assumed verb ἐστίν.

ὁ ἐμβαπτόμενος. Pres mid ptc masc nom sg ἐμβάπτω (substantival in apposition to Εἷς; "to dip [into]," BDAG, 321). To find in Mark's use of the middle voice (in contrast to the active in ‖ Matt 26:23) a "perfidious" nuance (so Gundry, 828) is to read too much significance into the voice. The action described would be judged duplicitous regardless of the voice used. In a similar statement in the same context John uses the simple form βάπτω twice (13:26). In both cases some mss read ἐμβάπτω.

μετ᾽ ἐμοῦ. Association.

εἰς τὸ τρύβλιον. Spatial. A τρύβλιον is a "bowl" or "dish." To "dip one's hand into the bowl together with someone" means to "share one's meal w. someone" (BDAG, 1018).

14:21 ὅτι ὁ μὲν υἱὸς τοῦ ἀνθρώπου ὑπάγει καθὼς γέγραπται περὶ αὐτοῦ, οὐαὶ δὲ τῷ ἀνθρώπῳ ἐκείνῳ δι᾽ οὗ ὁ υἱὸς τοῦ ἀνθρώπου παραδίδοται· καλὸν αὐτῷ εἰ οὐκ ἐγεννήθη ὁ ἄνθρωπος ἐκεῖνος.

ὅτι. Introduces a causal clause explaining the significance of the traitor's actions.

μὲν . . . δὲ. The paired conjunctions mark a contrast. Mark rarely uses the μέν . . . δέ construction (14:38; cf. 12:5; it is much more common in Matthew and Luke-Acts). On the use of μέν as a "prestige feature," see 4:4.

ὁ . . . υἱὸς. Nominative subject of ὑπάγει. On ὁ . . . υἱὸς τοῦ ἀνθρώπου, see 2:10.

ὑπάγει. Pres act ind 3rd sg ὑπάγω. The verb ὑπάγω is not used elsewhere in the Synoptics with reference to the cross (other than ‖ Matt 26:24), though it is a common Johannine theme (see John 8:21; 13:3, 33, 36; 14:4, 28; 16:5, 10). The present tense has future time reference, unless one were to claim that the events were already set in motion.

καθὼς. Introduces a comparative clause that clarifies that Jesus' "going" is in fulfillment of Scripture. The phrase καθὼς γέγραπται only occurs three times in Mark. Here, it is similar to the general reference in 9:13 rather than 1:2 which cites specific Scripture.

γέγραπται. Prf pass ind 3rd sg γράφω.

περὶ αὐτοῦ. Reference.

οὐαὶ. An interjection typically used without a verb (but see 1 Cor 9:16), though it implies something like ἔσται οὐαί. It is almost always followed by a dative identifying the party upon whom the woe is to come (cf. 13:17; Luke 6:25b is an exception; syntactic usage in Revelation differs from the rest of the NT). This word has "OT associations and a solemn biblical flavour" (Lee, 23).

τῷ ἀνθρώπῳ ἐκείνῳ. Dative of disadvantage. On the adjectival use of demonstratives in Mark, see 4:11. "That man" (used twice) carries a negative tone.

δι' οὗ. Intermediate agency. The use of διά rather than ὑπό "suggests the truth that the delivering up of Jesus is not simply an act of Judas, but part of a bigger purpose" (Cranfield, 424).

ὁ υἱὸς. Nominative subject of παραδίδοται.

παραδίδοται. Pres pass ind 3rd sg παραδίδωμι. On the meaning and use of παραδίδωμι in Mark, see 1:14 and 3:19. The present tense probably has future time reference if it refers to Judas' actions, which will follow shortly. If Mark intends to refer to the entire sequence that began in 14:10-11, then the description spans past and present and culminates in the (near) future.

καλὸν αὐτῷ εἰ οὐκ ἐγεννήθη ὁ ἄνθρωπος ἐκεῖνος. A similar statement (though only in Ethiopic, rather than Greek) occurs in 1 Enoch 38:2 regarding those who had denied the Lord: "when the Righteous One shall appear . . . it would have been better for them not to have been born" (Charlesworth, 1:30).

καλὸν αὐτῷ. A verbless clause with ἦν omitted as is common in exclamations (BDF §127.4; 128.3.3). Some mss insert ἦν after καλόν (א A C D Θ Ψ 𝔐), perhaps due to its presence in ‖ Matt 26:24. This clause functions as the apodosis of a second-class condition in which ἄν has been omitted and οὐ used in place of μή, perhaps to "enhance the poignancy of this unfulfilled conditional sentence by removing its contingent form" (Cranfield, 424). Moulton (MHT 1:199–201) says that this is the only NT example of this type of condition. Here, the positive adjective is used as a comparative ("better"), a common Koine escalation of comparative adjective forms.

αὐτῷ. Dative of advantage.

εἰ. Introduces the protasis of a second-class condition. On the view that this is to be understood as a second-class condition with the expected ἄν omitted, see Robertson (1169) and Swete (334).

ἐγεννήθη. Aor pass ind 3rd sg γεννάω.

ὁ ἄνθρωπος ἐκεῖνος. Nominative subject of ἐγεννήθη.

Mark 14:22-26

22Now while they were eating, having taken a loaf of bread and having blessed it, he broke it and gave it to them and said, "Take (it); this represents my body." ²³Then having taken a cup and given thanks, he gave (it) to them and they all drank from it. ²⁴He said to them, "This represents my blood of the covenant, which is poured out for many. ²⁵Truly I say to you that I will no longer drink from the fruit of the vine until that day when I drink this new wine in the kingdom of God." ²⁶So having sung (a hymn), they went out to the Mount of Olives.

14:22 Καὶ ἐσθιόντων αὐτῶν λαβὼν ἄρτον εὐλογήσας ἔκλασεν καὶ ἔδωκεν αὐτοῖς καὶ εἶπεν, Λάβετε, τοῦτό ἐστιν τὸ σῶμά μου.

ἐσθιόντων. Pres act ptc masc gen pl ἐσθίω. Genitive absolute (temporal).

αὐτῶν. Genitive subject of ἐσθιόντων, referring, as the following statement makes clear, to the disciples (the reference is continued with αὐτοῖς), not to Jesus and the disciples (though this does not mean that Jesus was not also eating with them). The subject of the genitive absolute is, as usual, not the same as the subject of the main statement, though the referent does recur in the indirect object of one of the main verbs (ἔδωκεν αὐτοῖς) and as the subject of the imperative (λάβετε) in the embedded discourse.

λαβὼν. Aor act ptc masc nom sg λαμβάνω (temporal). Both λαβών and εὐλογήσας, though often translated as finite verbs for English purposes (e.g., "He took bread, blessed and broke it," HCSB), express ideas subordinate to the main statement expressed by the finite verbs: ἔκλασεν καὶ ἔδωκεν αὐτοῖς καὶ εἶπεν.

ἄρτον. Accusative direct object of λαβών; also functions as the implied object of the following participle and two finite verbs (εὐλογήσας ἔκλασεν καὶ ἔδωκεν). The referent is a loaf of bread, in this instance one of the loaves being used for the Passover meal.

εὐλογήσας. Aor act ptc masc nom sg εὐλογέω (temporal).

ἔκλασεν. Aor act ind 3rd sg κλάω, "to break in pieces."

ἔδωκεν. Aor act ind 3rd sg δίδωμι.

αὐτοῖς. Dative indirect object of ἔδωκεν.

εἶπεν. Aor act ind 3rd sg λέγω.

Λάβετε, τοῦτό ἐστιν τὸ σῶμά μου. Clausal complement (direct discourse) of εἶπεν.

Λάβετε. Aor act impv 2nd pl λαμβάνω.

τοῦτό ἐστιν τὸ σῶμά μου. Bolt translates, "this represents me" (104 n. 46).

τοῦτό. Nominative subject of ἐστιν. The antecedent is ἄρτον which Jesus has taken, blessed, broken, and given, even though the gender is neuter (ἄρτον is masculine), the gender apparently being attracted to σῶμα following ("A pronoun subject may be made to agree with the predicate noun"; BDF §132).

ἐστιν. Pres act ind 3rd sg εἰμί. The meaning of this common verb in this statement has been debated for centuries. Is it identity or representation? BDAG, 284.2.c.α, lists this statement as "to show how someth. is to be understood *is a representation of, is the equivalent of*" (cf. LN 58.68, "to correspond to something else in certain significant features—'to correspond to, to stand for, to be a figure of, to represent x'"). See the commentaries (and the theologies!) for discussion.

τὸ σῶμά. Predicate nominative of εἰμί.

14:23 καὶ λαβὼν ποτήριον εὐχαριστήσας ἔδωκεν αὐτοῖς, καὶ ἔπιον ἐξ αὐτοῦ πάντες.

λαβών. Aor act ptc masc nom sg λαμβάνω (temporal).

ποτήριον. Accusative direct object of λαβών; also functions as the implied object of the following participle. The referent is to one of the traditional cups that formed part of the Passover celebration.

εὐχαριστήσας. Aor act ptc masc nom sg εὐχαριστέω (temporal). The bread was "blessed" (εὐλογέω, v. 22), but for the cup Jesus "gives thanks"; "such variation is typical of Jewish prayers in the first century" (Collins, 656).

ἔδωκεν. Aor act ind 3rd sg δίδωμι.

αὐτοῖς. Dative indirect object of ἔδωκεν.

ἔπιον ἐξ αὐτοῦ. For a genitive object (or, as here, a preposition with a genitive object) with verbs of eating or drinking, see the comments on ἐσθίουσιν ἀπὸ τῶν ψιχίων at 7:28. The singular αὐτοῦ with the plural subject πάντες implies that a common cup was used for the Passover at this time; later practice used individual cups (Cranfield, 426).

ἔπιον. Aor act ind 3rd pl πίνω. This is not an imperfect (as Evans' 2001, 385, translation, "all were drinking," appears to imply) but a second aorist form; the imperfect form would be ἔπινον.

πάντες. Nominative subject of ἔπιον. France (566) infers from this word that Judas was still present for the words of institution, but πάντες need only refer to all those who were present, not that all of the Twelve are present. (John 13:30 may suggest that Judas left prior to this, though John does not recount the actual institution of the Lord's Supper as do the Synoptics.)

14:24 καὶ εἶπεν αὐτοῖς, Τοῦτό ἐστιν τὸ αἷμά μου τῆς διαθήκης τὸ ἐκχυννόμενον ὑπὲρ πολλῶν.

εἶπεν. Aor act ind 3rd sg λέγω.

αὐτοῖς. Dative indirect object of εἶπεν.

τοῦτό ἐστιν τὸ αἷμά . . . ²⁵ἐν τῇ βασιλείᾳ τοῦ θεοῦ. Clausal complement (direct discourse) of εἶπεν.

τὸ αἷμά μου τῆς διαθήκης. The genitive τῆς διαθήκης identifies the purpose of the blood, i.e., the reason for Jesus' death was to provide the basis of the covenant (see below). As the old covenant was ratified by blood, so is the new. It is "the sign of [the covenant's] existence and the means by which it is effected" (V. Taylor, 546). The genitive μου identifies the blood as Jesus' blood (possession).

τῆς διαθήκης. The reference is to the new covenant (a textual variant makes this identification explicit as does ‖ Luke 22:20). The phraseology presents this covenant in explicit contrast to the old covenant: Exod 24:8, τὸ αἷμα τῆς διαθήκης. In classical Greek διαθήκη almost always referred to a "last will and testament"; the usual term for a covenant was συνθήκη. The LXX and NT, however, use διαθήκη exclusively for *covenant*, never for *will* (not even in Heb 9:16-17, though that is debated!), probably because συνθήκη implied an agreement between equal parties. "It is the declaration of one person's initiative, not the result of an agreement betw. two parties, like a compact or a contract. This is beyond doubt one of the main reasons why the LXX rendered בְּרִית by [διαθήκη]. In the 'covenants' of God, it was God alone who set the conditions; hence *covenant* can be used to trans. δ. only when this is kept in mind. So δ. acquires a mng. in the LXX which cannot be paralleled w. certainty in extrabiblical sources, namely 'decree,' 'declaration of purpose,' 'set of regulations,' etc. Our lit., which is very strongly influenced by the LXX in this area, seems as a rule to have understood the word in these senses" (BDAG, 228.2).

Τοῦτό. Nominative subject of ἐστιν.

ἐστιν. Pres act ind 3rd sg εἰμί. On the meaning of εἰμί in this context, see verse 22.

τὸ αἷμά. Predicate nominative of ἐστιν.

τὸ ἐκχυννόμενον. Pres pass ptc neut nom sg ἐκχύννω (adjectival attributive, modifying αἷμά). The time is future referring to the events of the Passion the next day. The usual form of this verb is ἐκχέω, but in Koine it often appears as ἐκχύννω (the formation χύννω perhaps developed to prevent confusion with the future χεῶ, so MHT 2:195 n. 4). This expression is related to the idiom αἷμα

ἐκχέω/ἐκχύννω, "to cause the death of someone by violent means—
'to murder, to kill'" (LN 20.84).

ὑπὲρ πολλῶν. Substitution. The use of πολύς instead of πάς is not
intended to limit the scope, but to stress the quantity. Calvin says
that "the word *many* does not mean a part of the world only, but
the whole human race: he contrasts *many* with *one*, as if to say that
he would not be the Redeemer of one man, but would taste death
to deliver man of their cursed guilt" (3:139). Gundry observes that
πολλῶν "describes 'all' as 'many' rather than delimiting 'many' as
fewer than 'all.'" (842). See the discussion of the equivalent expression, ἀντὶ πολλῶν, in 10:45.

**14:25 ἀμὴν λέγω ὑμῖν ὅτι οὐκέτι οὐ μὴ πίω ἐκ τοῦ γενήματος τῆς
ἀμπέλου ἕως τῆς ἡμέρας ἐκείνης ὅταν αὐτὸ πίνω καινὸν ἐν τῇ
βασιλείᾳ τοῦ θεοῦ.**

ἀμὴν λέγω ὑμῖν. See 3:28.

λέγω. Pres act ind 1st sg λέγω.

ὑμῖν. Dative indirect object of λέγω.

ὅτι. Introduces the clausal complement (direct discourse) of
λέγω.

οὐκέτι οὐ μὴ. An unusual and emphatic triple negative. On οὐ μή,
see 9:1. The use of οὐκέτι gives a temporal sense: "the extension of
time up to a point but not beyond, *no more, no longer, no further*"
(BDAG, 736.1, s.v. οὐκέτι), the corresponding limit of the negation
is expressed with ἕως τῆς ἡμέρας ἐκείνης ὅταν. That is, after "that
day" Jesus *will* once again drink "the fruit of the vine" with his followers in the kingdom. This is not a vow, but a "bittersweet prediction" of Jesus' coming absence (Gundry, 843). The statement of
abstinence relates only to the Passover meal, and that only because
he will not be present. "If he were to be present, he would certainly
eat and drink the Passover with his disciples, as he will do when
he comes back to transform the Passover meal into the messianic
banquet" (843).

πίω ἐκ τοῦ γενήματος. For a genitive object (or a preposition with
a genitive object) with verbs of eating or drinking, see the comments
on ἐσθίουσιν ἀπὸ τῶν ψιχίων at 7:28.

πίω. Aor act subj 1st sg πίνω.

ἐκ τοῦ γενήματος τῆς ἀμπέλου. Source. This description may
reflect an OT expression; cf. Hab 3:17, οὐκ ἔσται γενήματα ἐν ταῖς
ἀμπέλοις (likewise Pr Man 4:17) and Isa 32:12, ἀμπέλου γενήματος,
though I am not aware of a collocation of γένημα and ἀμπέλος

elsewhere in the NT or other related texts. The phrase serves as a synonym for οἶνος. The traditional Jewish thanksgiving for the wine was "Blessed are you God who creates the fruit of the vine" (*m. Ber.* 6:1; see Hartman, 565; France, 571). The use of similar phraseology by Jesus may verify that the later Mishnaic record reflects first-century practice.

τοῦ γενήματος. "That which comes into being through production, *product, fruit, yield*" whether vegetable or fruit (BDAG, 193). It is also used in ‖ Matt 26:29 and Luke 22:18, as well as metaphorically in 2 Cor 9:10. Note that this is a form of γένημα, a new word in Koine derived from γίνομαι (one *nu*, not two), rather than γέννημα ("product of the activity expressed by γεννάω 'that which is produced or born' . . . , *child, offspring*" (BDAG, 193). The usual distinction in Koine is that γένημα refers to the produce of plants, but that γέννημα is the offspring of animals or people (MM, 123; Deissmann 1901, 184; *New Docs* 2.79 §34). This word is an example of the contribution of the papyri to understanding Koine vocabulary. The two were formerly treated as spelling variants of the same word, the form with a single nu being viewed as incorrect (MM, 123).

ἕως τῆς ἡμέρας ἐκείνης. Although ἕως is formally a temporal conjunction, it may be used (as it is here), as a preposition with the genitive (BDAG, 1.b.α). The phraseology here makes it clear that the kingdom of God (τῇ βασιλείᾳ τοῦ θεοῦ) is envisioned as a future reality. See also the discussion on οὐκέτι above.

ὅταν. Temporal subordinating conjunction normally used with a subjunctive (see *TDM*, 87–88); here it introduces a clause epexegetical to τῆς ἡμέρας ἐκείνης.

αὐτὸ. Accusative direct object of πίνω. The antecedent is τοῦ γενήματος τῆς ἀμπέλου earlier in the verse (both are neuter singular).

πίνω. Pres act subj 1st sg πίνω. The two instances of the verb πίνω differ in tense. The first use, οὐκέτι οὐ μὴ πίω, is an aorist subjunctive, viewing the interval during which Jesus will not drink as a whole. The second, ὅταν αὐτὸ πίνω καινόν, is a present subjunctive. The present tense with ὅταν in a context referring to the future kingdom views the future action as a process; given the nature of the ceremonial drink (it is not based on the tense), it could be said that the statement refers to a repeated event.

καινὸν. An adjective seems out of place here since there is no adjacent substantive to modify. It has been said that it reflects an inaccurate translation of the original Aramaic (see Evans 2001, 395, for a survey of such proposals), but this is highly speculative. More likely options include taking καινόν adverbially (neuter accusative adjectives are often used adverbially) modifying πίνω, thus "drink it in a new way" (HCSB, CEB). Gundry (834) suggests that the word order may be intended to clarify that καινόν is intended adverbially rather than modifying αὐτό with which it agrees in gender, number, and case. A variation on this explanation holds that it refers to *Jesus* who is renewed (Evans 2001, 395), with the renewal apparently referring to the resurrection. Or καινόν could be viewed as substantival and equivalent to οἶνον καινόν ("I will drink this—the new wine," though elsewhere in the NT the expression is usually οἶνον νέον, e.g., 2:22). Or, if taken adjectivally, it could modify αὐτό; supplying the antecedent (which would be necessary to express it this way in English), "I will drink new wine" as suggested by HCSB mg. ("Or *drink new wine*"; see also GNB, CEV, NJB, GW). Separating the adjective from the word it modifies by the verb (not impossible: 13:4; 16:6; cf. Jas 2:8) seems to result in a somewhat clumsy statement here.

ἐν τῇ βασιλείᾳ τοῦ θεοῦ. Temporal with reference to a future situation (as the earlier part of the verse makes clear). The temporal use of ἐν in this phrase is similar to its use in 12:23.

τοῦ θεοῦ. Subjective genitive indicating the regent of the kingdom: the kingdom over which God reigns.

14:26 Καὶ ὑμνήσαντες ἐξῆλθον εἰς τὸ Ὄρος τῶν Ἐλαιῶν.

ὑμνήσαντες. Aor act ptc masc nom pl ὑμνέω (temporal; "to sing a song in a cultic setting, esp. of praise and celebration," BDAG, 1027).

ἐξῆλθον. Aor act ind 3rd pl ἐξέρχομαι. C. H. Turner (36–37, 42) plausibly speculates that this plural may reflect Mark's record of Peter's first person account ("we went out").

εἰς τὸ Ὄρος τῶν Ἐλαιῶν. Spatial, perhaps in the sense of "toward."

Mark 14:27-31

[27]Jesus said to them, "All of you will fall away, for it is written, 'I will strike the shepherd and the sheep will be scattered,' [28]but after I have risen I will go ahead of you into Galilee." [29]Peter said to him, "Even if all fall away, I will not." [30]Jesus said to him, "Truly I say to you that this very night before the rooster crows twice you will deny me three times." [31]But he replied emphatically, "If it is necessary

for me to die with you, I will never deny you." And all (the other disciples) were also saying similar things.

14:27 Καὶ λέγει αὐτοῖς ὁ Ἰησοῦς ὅτι Πάντες σκανδαλισθήσεσθε, ὅτι γέγραπται, Πατάξω τὸν ποιμένα, καὶ τὰ πρόβατα διασκορπισθήσονται.

λέγει. Pres act ind 3rd sg λέγω. Although editions of the Greek NT and translations differ as to where to place a paragraph break (before or after v. 26), it seems best to view verse 26 as the conclusion of the preceding paragraph with the narrative present λέγει marking a new paragraph, a common discourse function of the present tense (see also 1:21 on εἰσπορεύονται).

αὐτοῖς. Dative indirect object of λέγει.

ὁ Ἰησοῦς. Nominative subject of λέγει.

ὅτι. Introduces the clausal complement (direct discourse) of λέγει (see 1:15).

Πάντες. Nominative subject of σκανδαλισθήσεσθε.

σκανδαλισθήσεσθε. Fut pass ind 2nd pl σκανδαλίζω. On the meaning of this word, see 4:17. In this context it "refer[s] to a serious but temporary loss of faith" (R. Brown, 1:127 n. 24).

ὅτι. Causal, indicating that the disciples' desertion is the fulfillment of Scripture.

γέγραπται. Prf pass ind 3rd sg γράφω. A standard NT citation formula.

Πατάξω τὸν ποιμένα . . . διασκορπισθήσονται. The quotation from Zech 13:7 most closely matches the Hebrew text, rather than the LXX, giving a fairly formal equivalent at all points.

Πατάξω. Fut act ind 1st sg πατάσσω.

τὸν ποιμένα. Accusative direct object of πατάξω.

τὰ πρόβατα. Nominative subject of διασκορπισθήσονται.

διασκορπισθήσονται. Fut pass ind 3rd pl διασκορπίζω. The use of the compound form with διά– rather than the simple σκορπίζω ("to scatter") may indicate the nuance, "to cause a group or gathering to disperse or scatter, with possible emphasis on the distributive nature of the scattering (that is to say, each going in a different direction)" (LN 15.136), particularly given the sheep metaphor.

14:28 ἀλλὰ μετὰ τὸ ἐγερθῆναί με προάξω ὑμᾶς εἰς τὴν Γαλιλαίαν.

ἐγερθῆναί. Aor mid inf ἐγείρω. This is a "θη middle" intransitive form, not passive (see 2:2). Used with μετὰ τό to indicate subsequent time (see 1:14).

με. Accusative subject of ἐγερθῆναί.

προάξω. Fut act ind 1st sg προάγω. Cranfield summarizes three possible senses for this verb, concluding (correctly, I think) in favor of the third: "The verb can denote a literal walking in front of someone (as in x. 32). . . . It can also be used metaphorically . . . in the sense that it will be in obedience to his instructions that they will go to Galilee. But it is best to take the meaning here to be 'go somewhere earlier than someone' (as in vi. 45)" (429; see also V. Taylor, 549).

ὑμᾶς. Accusative direct object of προάξω.

εἰς τὴν Γαλιλαίαν. Spatial.

14:29 ὁ δὲ Πέτρος ἔφη αὐτῷ, Εἰ καὶ πάντες σκανδαλισθήσονται, ἀλλ᾽ οὐκ ἐγώ.

ὁ . . . Πέτρος. Nominative subject of ἔφη. The use of δέ reflects the shift in speakers from Jesus in verse 28 to Peter in verse 29.

ἔφη. Aor act ind 3rd sg φημί.

αὐτῷ. Dative indirect object of φημί.

Εἰ. Introduces the protasis of a first-class condition.

καὶ. Ascensive: "even." The use of εἰ καί together has the idea "even admitting that it is true" (Swete, 339), i.e., εἰ καί, as opposed to καί εἰ or κἄν, is concessive (Moule 1959, 167).

πάντες. Nominative subject of σκανδαλισθήσονται.

σκανδαλισθήσονται. Fut pass ind 3rd pl σκανδαλίζω. There are several textual variants at this point, most of which appear to supplement Mark's account with various elements of Matthew's fuller description; hence the longer text reflected in the KJV.

ἀλλ᾽ οὐκ ἐγώ. Apodosis of the first-class condition. Introducing this clause with ἀλλά creates a contrast between the protasis and apodosis.

ἐγώ. Nominative subject of the implied σκανδαλισθήσομαι.

14:30 καὶ λέγει αὐτῷ ὁ Ἰησοῦς, Ἀμὴν λέγω σοι ὅτι σὺ σήμερον ταύτῃ τῇ νυκτὶ πρὶν ἢ δὶς ἀλέκτορα φωνῆσαι τρίς με ἀπαρνήσῃ.

λέγει. Pres act ind 3rd sg λέγω.

αὐτῷ. Dative indirect object of λέγει.

ὁ Ἰησοῦς. Nominative subject of λέγει.

Ἀμὴν λέγω σοι. See 3:28. This is the only instance of this expression using the singular σοι.

λέγω. Pres act ind 1st sg λέγω.

ὅτι. Introduces the clausal complement (direct discourse) of λέγω.

σύ. Nominative subject of ἀπαρνήσῃ. The use of the explicit pronoun as subject is emphatic.

σήμερον ταύτῃ τῇ νυκτί. An idiom (formally, "today on this night") meaning, "this very night" (BDAG, 921, s.v. σήμερον). Jesus speaks in the evening, and since the Jewish day was calculated from sundown, that evening, the coming night, and the next day are all "today."

πρὶν ἢ δὶς ἀλέκτορα φωνῆσαι τρίς. This could refer to a rooster crowing in the predawn hours or perhaps "the reference is to the beginning of the fourth watch when the signal known as *gallicinium* ('cock-crowing') was given by bugle call" (V. Taylor, 550). If the variant reading ἐκ δευτέρου in verse 72 is valid (as most believe), then the reference is probably to a rooster rather than a bugle call, since that call would not be repeated at a later time (see Metzger 1994, 96, and especially the discussion of the related variant in verse 68; see also Edwards 2002, 430 n. 39; R. Brown, 1:606).

πρὶν ἤ. An idiom, "before," an "Ionism, very rare in Attic wr[iters], but common in the Koine" (BDAG, 433.2.d.α, s.v. ἤ). In the NT see Matt 1:18; Luke 2:26; Acts 7:2; 25:16.

δίς. Adverb: "twice."

ἀλέκτορα. Accusative subject of φωνῆσαι. See also verse 68.

φωνῆσαι. Aor act inf φωνέω. Used with πρὶν ἤ the infinitive introduces an event that is subsequent to the action of the main verb. "This is a very general word for sounds of all kinds. But the instances are rare in profane writers of its use for animal cries" (Gould, 267).

τρίς. Adverb: "three times."

με. Accusative direct object of ἀπαρνήσῃ.

ἀπαρνήσῃ. Fut mid ind 2nd sg ἀπαρνέομαι. There is probably no difference in meaning between ἀπαρνέομαι (used only in the Synoptics) and the simple form ἀρνέομαι, which is used throughout the NT (cf. the use of ἀρνέομαι in 12:7).

14:31 ὁ δὲ ἐκπερισσῶς ἐλάλει, Ἐὰν δέῃ με συναποθανεῖν σοι, οὐ μή σε ἀπαρνήσομαι. ὡσαύτως δὲ καὶ πάντες ἔλεγον.

ὁ. Nominative subject of ἐλάλει. On the use of ὁ δέ to change subjects, see 1:45.

ἐκπερισσῶς. Adverb: "emphatically, extraordinarily." BDAG (307) translates the expression ἐκπερισσῶς λαλεῖν as "*say with great emphasis,*" while R. Brown (1:117, 138) renders it "he was saying vehemently." This word does not occur in other Koine literature related to the Bible or in classical Greek, though the simple form περισσῶς is found in the NT (Matt 27:23; Mark 10:26; 15:14; Acts 26:11) and the LXX (Ps 30:24; 2 Macc 8:27). Cranfield (429–30) suggests that it is possibly a Markan coinage. That it was an unfamiliar word is suggested by the textual variants, which substitute more common words: Legg lists περισσῶς (L W Θ f^{13}), ἐκ περισσοῦ (A f^{1}), and ἐκπερίσας (Δ); the NA²⁷/UBS⁴ text is supported by ℵ B C D Ψ.

ἐλάλει. Impf act ind 3rd sg λαλέω.

Ἐὰν δέῃ με . . . σε ἀπαρνήσομαι. Clausal complement (direct discourse) of ἐλάλει.

Ἐάν. Introduces the protasis of a third-class condition.

δέῃ. Pres act subj 3rd sg δεῖ. Subjunctive with ἐάν.

με. Accusative subject of συναποθανεῖν.

συναποθανεῖν. Aor act inf συναποθνῄσκω (to "die with τινί someone," BDAG, 965; see also 2 Cor 7:3; 2 Tim 2:11. The infinitival clause, με συναποθανεῖν σοι, functions as the subject of δέῃ.

σοι. Dative of association.

οὐ μή. Emphatic negation (see 9:1; on οὐ μή with the future indicative, see 13:31; on double negatives in general, see 1:44). This is the only instance of οὐ μή in Mark that is not found in the words of Jesus, though it is in a strong statement of asseveration.

ἀπαρνήσομαι. Fut mid ind 1st sg ἀπαρνέομαι.

δὲ. The use of δέ reflects the shift of subject from Peter to all the disciples.

ὡσαύτως . . . ἔλεγον. Formally, "they were saying similarly."

καί. Adverbial: "also."

πάντες. Nominative subject of ἔλεγον.

ἔλεγον. Impf act ind 3rd pl λέγω.

Mark 14:32-42

³²Then they came to a place called Gethsemane and Jesus said to his disciples, "Sit here until I have prayed." ³³He took Peter and James and John with him and he began to be distressed and troubled. ³⁴He said to them, "My soul is grieved to the point of death; remain here and keep watch." ³⁵Having gone a little further he fell on the ground and prayed that if it were possible the hour would pass from him. ³⁶He said, "Abba, Father, all things are possible for you. Remove this cup from me; but not what I desire, but what you (desire)." ³⁷Then he came and found them sleeping and he said to Peter, "Simon, are you sleeping? Were you not able to watch for one

hour? ³⁸Watch and pray so that you do not come into temptation; for the spirit is willing, but the flesh is weak." ³⁹Again having gone away he prayed saying the same thing. ⁴⁰Again, having returned, he found them sleeping, for their eyes were heavy, and they did not know what to say to him. ⁴¹He came a third time and said to them, "Are you still asleep and resting? Enough! The hour has come. Look! The Son of Man is handed over into the hands of sinners. ⁴²Get up, let's go. Look! The one who hands me over is near."

14:32 Καὶ ἔρχονται εἰς χωρίον οὗ τὸ ὄνομα Γεθσημανὶ καὶ λέγει τοῖς μαθηταῖς αὐτοῦ, Καθίσατε ὧδε ἕως προσεύξωμαι.

ἔρχονται. Pres mid ind 3rd pl ἔρχομαι. The present tense introduces a new paragraph (see 1:21). On the use of the plural verb here, see 5:38. Gundry (853) suggests that there is an "unusually high concentration" of historical (i.e., narrative) presents in verses 32-45, listing eleven present tense verbs in fourteen verses that narrate past historical events (5 of these are λέγω). There are more present indicatives in chapter 14 than in any other chapter in Mark, but then it is the longest chapter in the Gospel. Although there are other passages in Mark with a higher concentration of present tense forms (e.g., 19 presents in 8:16-24), most of them are not narrative presents. Whether this translates to a display of excitement "over Jesus' entrance into the Passion" (Gundry, 853) is another question. Gundry appears to assume that the use of the present in this way is for vividness, but that is a controversial (if common) explanation (see also 1:21 on εἰσπορεύονται, and the summary in *TDM*, 101–4; cf. C. Campbell, 68–71, who points instead to 15:17-27 as a more significant concentration of such forms). The eighty-two instances of narrative presents in Mark that do not involve λέγω are found in 1:12, 21, 40; 2:3, 4, 15, 18a; 3:13a, b, 20a, b, 31; 4:1, 36, 37, 38a; 5:15a, b, 22a, b, 23, 35, 38a, b, 40a, b; 6:1a, b, 7, 30, 45, 48; 7:1, 5, 32a, b; 8:6, 22a, b, c; 9:2a, b; 10:1a, b; 35, 46, 49; 11:1a, b, 2, 4, 7a, b, 15, 21, 22, 27a, b; 12:13, 18; 14:13a, 17, 32a, 33, 37a, b, 41, 43, 51, 53, 66; 15:16, 17a, b, 20, 21, 22, 24a, b, 27; 16:2, 4. The use of λέγω as narrative present, seventy times in Mark, has not yet been satisfactorily described.

εἰς χωρίον. Spatial. The word χωρίον is the diminutive form of χώρα and refers to "a piece of land other than a populated area, *place, piece of land, field*" (BDAG, 1095).

οὗ τὸ ὄνομα Γεθσημανὶ. Formally, "of which the name (was) Gethsemane." "Ἦν . . . is always omitted in the phrases ᾧ (ᾗ) ὄνομα, οὗ τὸ ὄνομα Mk 14:32" (BDF §128.3). Γεθσημανὶ (indeclinable) is transliterated from Hebrew.

λέγει. Pres act ind 3rd sg λέγω.

τοῖς μαθηταῖς. Dative indirect object of λέγει.

Καθίσατε ὧδε ἕως προσεύξωμαι. Clausal complement (direct discourse) of λέγει.

Καθίσατε. Aor act impv 2nd pl καθίζω.

ἕως. The usual pattern is to find ἕως ἄν with an aorist subjunctive, but occasionally ἕως occurs alone, as here. The meaning is almost always "until" when used with a perfective verb, and usually so when the verb is imperfective (though it sometimes means "while" with the imperfective; see, e.g., 6:45; John 9:4). Almost all translations prefer "while" (NIV, NAB, NJB, CEV, NRSV, NCV, ESV, NET, HCSB), but NASB translates "until." BDAG (423) lists this reference under both options (1.a.β and 2.b). Despite being the minority decision of translators, it seems that "until I have prayed" is the intended meaning (see further *TDM*, 81–82; Fanning, 403–4).

προσεύξωμαι. Aor mid subj 1st sg προσεύχομαι. Subjunctive with ἕως.

14:33 καὶ παραλαμβάνει τὸν Πέτρον καὶ [τὸν] Ἰάκωβον καὶ [τὸν] Ἰωάννην μετ᾽ αὐτοῦ καὶ ἤρξατο ἐκθαμβεῖσθαι καὶ ἀδημονεῖν

παραλαμβάνει. Pres act ind 3rd sg παραλαμβάνω. Although this verb need not imply physical movement, it almost certainly does here (as it clearly does in 4:36; 5:40; 9:2; see the response of R. Brown, 1:151, to some who think otherwise).

τὸν Πέτρον ... καὶ [τὸν] Ἰωάννην. Accusative direct object of παραλαμβάνει.

μετ᾽ αὐτοῦ. Accompaniment.

ἤρξατο. Aor mid ind 3rd sg ἄρχω.

ἐκθαμβεῖσθαι. Pres mid inf ἐκθαμβέω (complementary). Here the sense is "to be distressed," given the parallel with ἀδημονεῖν (BDAG, 303). R. Brown comments, "'to be greatly distraught' ... a profound disarray, expressed physically before a terrifying event: a shuddering horror" (1:153). For more on the meaning and usage of ἐκθαμβέω in Mark, see 9:15. Reflecting on the multiple rare words used in this context (ἐκθαμβέω, ἀδημονέω, περίλυπος), Edwards comments that "the range and number of expressions describing [Jesus'] sorrow rival the lamentable description of the demoniac in 5:2-5" (2002, 432).

ἀδημονεῖν. Pres act inf ἀδημονέω (complementary; "to be

troubled," BDAG, 19). That the words ἐκθαμβέω, ἀδημονέω and λυπέω are very closely related in meaning can be seen in that Matthew's account at this point reads ἤρξατο λυπεῖσθαι καὶ ἀδημονεῖν. Lane (516) translates the phrase, "appalled and profoundly troubled."

14:34 καὶ λέγει αὐτοῖς, Περίλυπός ἐστιν ἡ ψυχή μου ἕως θανάτου· μείνατε ὧδε καὶ γρηγορεῖτε.

λέγει. Pres act ind 3rd sg λέγω.

αὐτοῖς. Dative indirect object of λέγει.

Περίλυπός ἐστιν . . . καὶ γρηγορεῖτε. Clausal complement (direct discourse) of λέγει.

Περίλυπός. Predicate adjective ("very sad, deeply grieved," BDAG, 802. The compound formation (περί + λύπη, *CL*, 280) is probably emphatic, made even more so by the addition of ἕως θανάτου.

ἐστιν. Pres act ind 3rd sg εἰμί.

ἡ ψυχή. Nominative subject of ἐστιν. A similar expression of the soul being grieved occurs in LXX Ps 41:6, 12 (Eng. = 42:5, 11), though there it is in the form of a question. This should not be treated as an OT quotation (despite it being so listed in NA[27]), though the phraseology may unconsciously echo OT language.

ἕως θανάτου. Although usually used as a conjunction, here ἕως functions as a preposition with the genitive meaning "to the point of" (‖ Matt 26:38). V. Taylor describes it as "a sorrow that threatens life itself" (553). The same expression ἕως θανάτου occurs in Jonah 4:9, also in the context of grief: Σφόδρα λελύπημαι ἐγὼ ἕως θανάτου (see also Isa 38:1; Sir 34:12; 37:2; 51:6; 4 Macc 1:9; 14:19). Alternatively, France argues that it "refers explicitly to the cause of that emotion (distress 'at the approach of death'), as the death which Jesus has long been predicting now fills the horizon" (583). Despite many similar explanations among the commentators (see R. Brown, 1:155 for a survey), many of whom appear to be attempting to take the wording of the text at full value, this expression is most likely a figurative expression of hyperbole, "I am very sad," with no reference to Jesus' impending death. He is "simply using a common linguistic form to express the depth of his sorrow" (Culy 2006, 107) much as an English speaker might say, "I'm starving/bored/scared to death."

μείνατε. Aor act impv 2nd pl μένω.

γρηγορεῖτε. Pres act impv 2nd pl γρηγορέω. The shift from perfective to imperfect imperative is appropriate: the simple command to stay followed by a command that involves a process (keeping watch). Being watchful and alert requires staying awake (though translating γρηγορέω as "stay awake," as, e.g., NRSV, ESV, NJB, REB, HCSB, misses the point; for one can be awake but not alert and watchful). The same verb is used three times in the parable of the absent householder (13:34-37).

14:35 καὶ προελθὼν μικρὸν ἔπιπτεν ἐπὶ τῆς γῆς καὶ προσηύχετο ἵνα εἰ δυνατόν ἐστιν παρέλθῃ ἀπ' αὐτοῦ ἡ ὥρα,

προελθὼν. Aor act ptc masc nom sg προέρχομαι (temporal).

μικρὸν. The adjective μικρός is often used adverbially, as here, usually of time (e.g., 14:70; frequently in John), but in this instance of space (as προελθὼν makes clear): "a short distance, a little way" (BDAG, 651.1.c). Although BDAG cites a classical parallel (Xenophon, 4th–5th cent. BC) and a later Koine writer (Dionysius Byzantius, ca. AD 200), the only other adverbial use in regard to distance in the NT is ‖ Matt 26:39 (cf. LXX 2 Sam 17:20). The parallel account in Luke 22:41 specifies the distance as ὡσεὶ λίθου βολήν ("about a stone's throw").

ἔπιπτεν. Impf act ind 3rd sg πίπτω. To read into this imperfect form (and the following one) an iterative idea (so Gundry, 854), or to conclude that he fell on the ground and prayed for a prolonged period, or fell and prayed repeatedly, is to attempt to wring too much significance out of a tense form. In this instance the remote (imperfect) form describes the setting of the event: background information.

ἐπὶ τῆς γῆς. Spatial.

προσηύχετο. Impf mid ind 3rd sg προσεύχομαι. On the possibility that this is an inceptive imperfect as in NASB and HCSB, see 1:21. The imperfect functions to introduce discourse (see Decker 2013a, 354–56).

ἵνα. Introduces indirect discourse.

εἰ. Introduces the protasis of a first-class condition.

δυνατόν. Predicate adjective.

ἐστιν. Pres act ind 3rd sg εἰμί.

παρέλθῃ. Aor act subj 3rd sg παρέρχομαι. Subjunctive with ἵνα.

ἀπ' αὐτοῦ. Separation.

ἡ ὥρα. Nominative subject of παρέλθῃ.

14:36 καὶ ἔλεγεν, Αββα ὁ πατήρ, πάντα δυνατά σοι· παρένεγκε τὸ ποτήριον τοῦτο ἀπ᾽ ἐμοῦ· ἀλλ᾽ οὐ τί ἐγὼ θέλω ἀλλὰ τί σύ.

ἔλεγεν. Impf act ind 3rd sg λέγω.

Αββα ὁ πατήρ ... ἀλλὰ τί σύ. Clausal complement (direct discourse) of ἔλεγεν.

Αββα ὁ πατήρ. Nominative of address (equivalent to the vocative πάτερ). Αββα is a transliteration of the Aramaic word 'abbā', an emphatic form that was used as a vocative. It was not the customary word used by a child of his father, i.e., it is not the equivalent of our "Daddy." In the Aramaic of Jesus' day (200 BC–AD 200), our "Daddy" would have been expressed as 'ăbî. Only after AD 200 does 'abbā' come to replace 'ăbî in a family setting and even then it is rarely used by Jewish speakers in address to God (never in the Mishnah and only once or twice in the Targums). We have no evidence in Judaism for any individual using 'abbā' as a personal address for God in or prior to the first century. Even the use of "father" (in Hebrew, Aramaic, or Greek) is rarely used by an individual in reference to God, though it is common as a corporate term. That 'abbā' and ὁ πατήρ/πάτερ do become part of Christian expression (e.g., Rom 8:15; Gal 4:6), both individually and corporately, is probably due to Jesus' unique use of this expression (only here in the Gospels). It does not, however, reflect a childish affection, but rather "the respectful intimacy of a son in a patriarchal family" (France, 584; the preceding summary is based largely on R. Brown, 1:172–75). For other transliterated Aramaic words in Mark, see 5:41; 7:11, 34.

πάντα. Nominative subject in a verbless clause.

δυνατά. Predicate adjective in a verbless clause.

σοι. Dative of advantage.

παρένεγκε. Aor act impv 2nd sg παραφέρω ("to take away, remove," especially when used with τὶ ἀπό τινος; BDAG, 772.2.c).

τὸ ποτήριον τοῦτο. Accusative direct object of παρένεγκε.

ἀπ᾽ ἐμοῦ. Separation.

ἀλλ᾽. . . ἀλλά. The double ἀλλά marks a pair of contrasting clauses. As he faced the certain agonies of the cross (ἡ ὥρα, v. 35; τὸ ποτήριον τοῦτο, v. 36), he would like, humanly speaking, to avoid such terrible suffering (παρένεγκε τὸ ποτήριον τοῦτο ἀπ᾽ ἐμοῦ). Although that is an honest expression of Jesus' emotions and desires (τί ἐγὼ θέλω), it is a desire that he has already set aside, having agreed with and submitted to the Father's will that he go to the cross as a sacrifice for sin (τί σὺ [θέλω]).

τί. Accusative direct object of θέλω. Here the indefinite pronoun may function as a relative—an uncommon use, but one adequately attested in the Koine. Robertson cites this text as the "plainest New Testament example of τίς as ὅς" (737). Swete, however, wonders if there might not be an interrogative sense here: "however, the question is not (οὐ, not μή) what is My will" (344). If so, then it is an indirect question.

ἐγώ. Nominative subject of θέλω.

θέλω. Pres act ind 1st sg θέλω.

τί. Accusative direct object of an implied θέλεις.

σύ. Nominative subject of an implied θέλεις.

14:37 καὶ ἔρχεται καὶ εὑρίσκει αὐτοὺς καθεύδοντας, καὶ λέγει τῷ Πέτρῳ, Σίμων, καθεύδεις; οὐκ ἴσχυσας μίαν ὥραν γρηγορῆσαι;

ἔρχεται. Pres mid ind 3rd sg ἔρχομαι.

εὑρίσκει. Pres act ind 3rd sg εὑρίσκω.

αὐτοὺς. Accusative direct object of εὑρίσκει.

καθεύδοντας. Pres act ptc masc acc pl καθεύδω (complement in an object-complement double accusative construction).

λέγει. Pres act ind 3rd sg λέγω.

τῷ Πέτρῳ. Dative indirect object of λέγει.

Σίμων, καθεύδεις ... ἡ δὲ σὰρξ ἀσθενής. Clausal complement (direct discourse) of λέγει.

Σίμων. Vocative. The vocative spelling is identical with the nominative. Although it is possible that the use of Peter's "old" name (3:16) is deliberate and perhaps even "ominous" (e.g., Bruce, 439), this is the only instance in Mark in which Jesus addresses Peter directly by name. Πέτρος occurs three times as often as Σίμων in Mark (19/6), but always in narrative descriptions by Mark. In the Gospels, when Jesus addresses him directly by name he uses Simon seven times (Matt 16:17; 17:25; Luke 22:31 [2×]; John 1:42; 21:15, 17) and Peter only twice (Matt 16:18; Luke 22:34). Such usage suggests that Jesus simply preferred to use Σίμων in direct address.

καθεύδεις. Pres act ind 2nd sg καθεύδω.

οὐκ. Questions with οὐκ normally imply a positive answer. Here that would seem to imply, "You are able, aren't you?" That is not consistent with what Mark has just told us: ἔρχεται καὶ εὑρίσκει αὐτοὺς καθεύδοντας (v. 37a) and what he will tell us twice again (vv. 40, 41), unless we conclude that they could have done so but chose not to stay awake. There are two alternatives at this point. First, we might conclude that the use of οὐ/μή with questions is a general pattern that does not fit the present context. Second, rather than questions, perhaps we should think of them as statements/ exclamations: "Simon, you are sleeping! You are not able to watch for one hour" (so Gundry, 855). Stein (2008, 663) follows Gundry on the first statement, but maintains the second as a question. He argues, however, that it is to be understood as a question of rebuke, taking this to blunt the significance of οὐ. Gundry's proposal makes the best sense in this context, though my translation follows the punctuation of the UBS⁴ text.

ἴσχυσας. Aor act ind 2nd sg ἰσχύω.

μίαν ὥραν. Accusative of time. The accusative case is often used with words having temporal semantics to express the extent or duration of a time period.

γρηγορῆσαι. Aor act inf γρηγορέω (complementary).

14:38 γρηγορεῖτε καὶ προσεύχεσθε, ἵνα μὴ ἔλθητε εἰς πειρασμόν· τὸ μὲν πνεῦμα πρόθυμον ἡ δὲ σὰρξ ἀσθενής.

γρηγορεῖτε. Pres act impv 2nd pl γρηγορέω. On the meaning of γρηγορέω, see 13:34.

προσεύχεσθε. Pres mid impv 2nd pl προσεύχομαι.

ἵνα. Introduces the clausal complement of προσεύχεσθε (so Moule 1959, 434; Gundry, 872; on ἵνα with object clauses, see Funk §659). As punctuated in the NA²⁷/UBS⁴, the ἵνα clause refers to both imperatives. This might be taken as a purpose statement explaining why they should watch and pray (e.g., NIV; cf. HCSB, NLT, CEB; Lane, 521 n. 90). R. Brown connects the ἵνα clause with both imperatives, but suggests that "the coordination of the two governing verbs 'watch' and 'pray' would then have a slightly distinguishing nuance: Not entering into trial would be the purpose of the watching and the object of the praying" (1:197). The other uses of προσεύχομαι followed by a ἵνα clause in the NT (other than this text and its parallels) appear to express the content of the prayer (Matt 24:20 || Mark 13:18; 1 Cor 14:13; Phil 1:9; Col 1:9; 4:3; 2 Thess 1:11; 2 Thess 3:1).

ἔλθητε. Aor act subj 2nd pl ἔρχομαι. Subjunctive with ἵνα.

εἰς πειρασμόν. Reference, or perhaps locative in a metaphorical sense.

τὸ μὲν πνεῦμα πρόθυμον ἡ δὲ σὰρξ ἀσθενής. This clause appears to explain why the sort of prayer just specified was appropriate (one might have expected γάρ rather than asyndeton, but the sense is obvious). In this familiar saying πνεῦμα probably refers to a person's volitional capacity and σάρξ to the human nature in its sinful inability to please God. This dominical saying (|| Matt 26:41) is the only instance in Koine texts related to the Bible in which πρόθυμος and ἀσθενής are collocated. It is also the only instance in the Gospels in which πνεῦμα and σάρξ are contrasted, though that is a common contrast elsewhere in the NT.

τὸ . . . πνεῦμα. Nominative subject in a verbless clause.

μὲν . . . δὲ. The correlative construction makes the parallel between τὸ πνεῦμα and ἡ σάρξ explicit. On the use of μέν as a "prestige feature," see 4:4.

πρόθυμον. Predicate adjective in a verbless clause ("ready, willing, eager").

ἡ . . . σάρξ. Nominative subject in a verbless clause.

ἀσθενής. Predicate adjective in a verbless clause.

14:39 καὶ πάλιν ἀπελθὼν προσηύξατο τὸν αὐτὸν λόγον εἰπών.

ἀπελθών. Aor act ptc masc nom sg ἀπέρχομαι (temporal).

προσηύξατο. Aor mid ind 3rd sg προσεύχομαι.

τὸν αὐτὸν λόγον. Accusative direct object of εἰπών. Adjectival identifying use of αὐτός: "the *same* thing." BDAG (600.1.a.β) suggests "prayer" and Lane (513 n. 73) proposes "request" for λόγος, but more natural English would prefer "thing" (Abbott-Smith, 271.1.6) in this context to avoid redundancy.

εἰπών. Aor act ptc masc nom sg λέγω (means; redundant participle of speaking; see also 1:7).

14:40 καὶ πάλιν ἐλθὼν εὖρεν αὐτοὺς καθεύδοντας, ἦσαν γὰρ αὐτῶν οἱ ὀφθαλμοὶ καταβαρυνόμενοι, καὶ οὐκ ᾔδεισαν τί ἀποκριθῶσιν αὐτῷ.

ἐλθὼν εὖρεν . . . καθεύδοντας. Lane (519–20 n. 86) points out a close verbal parallel with 13:36 (ἐλθών . . . εὕρῃ . . . καθεύδοντας).

ἐλθών. Aor act ptc masc nom sg ἔρχομαι (temporal).

εὖρεν. Aor act ind 3rd sg εὑρίσκω.

αὐτούς. Accusative direct object of εὖρεν.

καθεύδοντας. Pres act ptc masc acc pl καθεύδω (complement in an object-complement double accusative construction).

ἦσαν. Impf act ind 3rd pl εἰμί.

γὰρ. Explanatory.

οἱ ὀφθαλμοί. Nominative subject of ἦσαν . . . καταβαρυνόμενοι.

καταβαρυνόμενοι. Pres mid ptc masc nom pl καταβαρύνω (imperfective periphrastic; "to weigh down upon, to grow heavy upon").

οὐκ ᾔδεισαν τί ἀποκριθῶσιν αὐτῷ. Cf. the similar statement at the Transfiguration in 9:6, οὐ γὰρ ᾔδει τί ἀποκριθῇ.

ᾔδεισαν. Plprf act ind 3rd pl οἶδα.

τί ἀποκριθῶσιν αὐτῷ. An indirect question that functions as the clausal complement of ᾔδεισαν.

τί. Accusative direct object of ἀποκριθῶσιν.

ἀποκριθῶσιν. Aor mid subj 3rd pl ἀποκρίνομαι. On this intransitive, "θη middle" form, see 3:33. This verb may imply that when Jesus returned the second time he also posed a question to them, though the specific question is not recorded. It is also possible that ἀποκρίνομαι has the sense of "respond" without a specific question asked.

αὐτῷ. Dative indirect object of ἀποκριθῶσιν.

14:41 καὶ ἔρχεται τὸ τρίτον καὶ λέγει αὐτοῖς, Καθεύδετε τὸ λοιπὸν καὶ ἀναπαύεσθε· ἀπέχει· ἦλθεν ἡ ὥρα, ἰδοὺ παραδίδοται ὁ υἱὸς τοῦ ἀνθρώπου εἰς τὰς χεῖρας τῶν ἁμαρτωλῶν.

ἔρχεται. Pres mid ind 3rd sg ἔρχομαι.

τὸ τρίτον. The neuter articular form of the adjective τρίτος ("three") is used here as an adverb (i.e., an adverbial accusative), "the third time" (BDAG, 1016.1.b).

λέγει. Pres act ind 3rd sg λέγω.

αὐτοῖς. Dative indirect object of λέγει.

Καθεύδετε τὸ λοιπὸν . . . ⁴²με ἤγγικεν. Clausal complement (direct discourse) of λέγει. R. Brown (1:207) describes the first two clauses as "embarrassingly obscure" due to questions as to the type of statements (indicative, interrogative, or imperative), the meaning of τὸ λοιπόν, and the terse idiom ἀπέχει.

Καθεύδετε τὸ λοιπὸν καὶ ἀναπαύεσθε. Although punctuated in the NA²⁷/UBS⁴ as a statement, in English translations it is usually taken as a question (NIV, NASB, NRSV, NET, HCSB; see Cranfield, 435), but sometimes as a statement (KJV, ASV, ESV). It could also be taken imperatively (Gundry, 857) or as an exclamation (ISV: "you might as well keep on sleeping and resting"). Evans (2001, 416) argues that an imperative does not correspond well to the immediately following statement ἦλθεν ἡ ὥρα (see also BDAG's comments on λοιπόν below). The Lukan parallel (22:46) clearly makes the first a question, introducing it with an interrogative and omitting the second verb altogether.

Καθεύδετε. Pres act ind (or impv) 2nd pl καθεύδω.

τὸ λοιπὸν. The neuter accusative adjective λοιπός ("remaining") is used here as a temporal adverb ("still, meanwhile"). BDAG explains that "καθεύδετε τὸ λοιπόν, which is variously interpreted, conveys a mild rebuke: *you are still sleeping!* or: *do you intend to sleep on and on?*; the expression is prob. colloquial and is succinctly rendered by numerous versions: *Still asleep?* Mt 26:45; Mk 14:41. Also poss. for this pass.: *meanwhile, you are sleeping! you are sleeping in the meantime?* . . . w. the sense: 'A fine time you've chosen to sleep!'" (602.3.a.α). An alternative possibility is to class τὸ λοιπόν as a connecting particle equivalent to our English "so then" (R. Brown, 1:208). This is a valid use of τὸ λοιπόν in some passages, but Thrall (25–26) rejects it for this passage, especially if καθεύδετε is taken as an imperative (thus, "go on sleeping!"), though admitting that "the Marcan reference is in any case obscure" (26).

ἀναπαύεσθε. Pres mid ind (or impv) 2nd pl ἀναπαύω.

ἀπέχει. Pres act ind 3rd sg ἀπέχω. This impersonal expression might be understood as equivalent to the English expression "Enough!" (ISV: "Enough of that!"). This appears to be the preference of BDAG (102.2). The meaning would then be: "I have conquered in the struggle; I need your sympathy no longer; you may sleep now if you will" (Bruce, 440). Another possibility is that "the rather freq. expr. οὐδὲν ἀπέχει = 'nothing hinders' . . . would suggest for ἀπέχει in Mk 14:41 *that is a hindrance* (referring to the extreme drowsiness of the disciples at the decisive moment)" (BDAG, 102.3). Or it might be understood in light of its use as a commercial technical term meaning "provide a receipt for a sum paid in full," perhaps here in reference to Judas ("he has received the money," see BDAG, 102.1; so R. Brown, 1:209). Although the later two options could make sense, neither seems to fit the context. Evans (2001, 416–17; see also Gundry, 857), argues that this is a one-word question: "Is it [i.e., the end] far away?" He maintains that this is "the most common meaning" of ἀπέχει (at least in the LXX), and "it makes better sense in the context." Cranfield (435) lists a number of other proposals which are less likely.

ἦλθεν ἡ ὥρα. This is an expression characteristic of the Johannine corpus (John 4:21, 23; 5:25, 28; 7:30; 8:20; 12:23; 13:1; 16:2, 4, 21, 25, 32; 17:1; Rev 14:7, 15; 18:10). Mark is the only other writer to use it in the NT. The implication is that a time or event has been anticipated and is now imminent.

ἦλθεν. Aor act ind 3rd sg ἔρχομαι.

ἡ ὥρα. Nominative subject of ἦλθεν.

ἰδού. See 1:2 (cf. 3:34 on ἴδε).

παραδίδοται. Pres pass ind 3rd sg παραδίδωμι. On the meaning of παραδίδωμι in Mark, see 1:14 and 3:19.

ὁ υἱὸς τοῦ ἀνθρώπου. Nominative subject of παραδίδοται. See also 2:10.

εἰς τὰς χεῖρας. Spatial, in a metaphorical sense.

14:42 ἐγείρεσθε ἄγωμεν· ἰδοὺ ὁ παραδιδούς με ἤγγικεν.

ἐγείρεσθε. Pres mid impv 2nd pl ἐγείρω.

ἄγωμεν. Pres act subj 1st pl ἄγω (hortatory subjunctive). Since ἄγω could be used intransitively as a military term, Cranfield suggests this might be translated, "Let us advance to meet them!" (436). The plural (as all hortatory subjunctives are) suggests that "Jesus' desire [is] that he and his disciples be in readiness to encounter *together* the traitor who is coming" (R. Brown, 1:214).

ἰδού. See 1:2 (cf. 3:34 on ἴδε).

ὁ παραδιδούς. Pres act ptc masc nom sg παραδίδωμι (substantival). Nominative subject of ἤγγικεν. On the meaning and use of παραδίδωμι in Mark, see 1:14 and 3:19.

με. Accusative direct object of παραδιδούς.

ἤγγικεν. Prf act ind 3rd sg ἐγγίζω. This form no more means "is here" in this text than it does in 1:15 (contra Stein 2008, 667). The kingdom was near, but not present in 1:15, and Judas is near, but not yet here in this text; he arrives subsequently (vv. 43, 45).

Mark 14:43-52

[43]Then, while he was still speaking, Judas, one of the Twelve, arrived and with him a crowd armed with swords and clubs, (sent) from the high priests and scribes and elders. [44]Now the one who handed him over had given them a sign, saying, "The one whom I greet with a kiss, he is (the one); seize him and lead (him) away under guard." [45]At once going directly to Jesus he said, "Rabbi," and greeted him with a kiss. [46]So they grabbed Jesus and took him into custody. [47]But a certain one of those standing there, drawing his sword, struck the slave of the high priest and cut off his ear. [48]Jesus said to them, "Have you come with swords and clubs to arrest me as (you would) a revolutionary? [49]I was with you teaching in the temple day after day and you did not seize me, but (this has happened) that the Scriptures might be fulfilled." [50]Then everyone left him and fled.

[51]Now a certain young man, who was wearing (only) a shirt on his naked body, was following Jesus, and they seized him. [52]But he fled naked, leaving his shirt behind.

14:43 Καὶ εὐθὺς ἔτι αὐτοῦ λαλοῦντος παραγίνεται Ἰούδας εἷς τῶν δώδεκα καὶ μετ᾽ αὐτοῦ ὄχλος μετὰ μαχαιρῶν καὶ ξύλων παρὰ τῶν ἀρχιερέων καὶ τῶν γραμματέων καὶ τῶν πρεσβυτέρων.

καὶ εὐθὺς. See 1:10.

αὐτοῦ. Genitive subject of λαλοῦντος.

λαλοῦντος. Pres act ptc masc gen sg λαλέω. Genitive absolute (see 1:32), temporal.

παραγίνεται. Pres mid ind 3rd sg παραγίνομαι. The narrative present tense introduces a new paragraph (see 1:21).

Ἰούδας. Nominative subject of παραγίνεται.

εἷς. Nominative in apposition to Ἰούδας reinforcing the identity of the betrayer as one of the apostles. On the use of εἷς with the partitive genitive (τῶν δώδεκα), *not* as an equivalent to τις in this context, see 10:17 and 14:10. On the use and referent of δώδεκα, see 4:10.

μετ᾽ αὐτοῦ. Accompaniment.

ὄχλος. Part of a compound nominative subject of παραγίνεται (Ἰούδας ... καὶ ... ὄχλος), or the subject of an understood ἐστίν ("and a crowd was with him"; cf. the NIV).

μετὰ μαχαιρῶν καὶ ξύλων. The prepositional phrase indicates the equipment carried by the crowd (BDAG, 637.A.3.c, s.v. μετά; see also v. 48). Along with παραδίδωμι in the next verse, this reinforces the hostile purpose of the crowd. "While it can refer to a large knife, [μάχαιρα] normally means 'sword'" (R. Brown, 1:247).

παρὰ τῶν ἀρχιερέων καὶ τῶν γραμματέων καὶ τῶν πρεσβυτέρων. Source. It was this group of religious leaders who authorized the actions of the armed crowd sent with Judas.

14:44 δεδώκει δὲ ὁ παραδιδοὺς αὐτὸν σύσσημον αὐτοῖς λέγων, Ὃν ἂν φιλήσω αὐτός ἐστιν, κρατήσατε αὐτὸν καὶ ἀπάγετε ἀσφαλῶς.

δεδώκει. Plprf act ind 3rd sg δίδωμι. The pluperfect of δίδωμι does not occur with the augment anywhere in the NT or LXX, though it does in Josephus (ἐδεδώκει, *Ant.* 13:116; 16:135; 20:182) and Philo (*Rewards*, 69). The pluperfect is used to supply background information (off the storyline) regarding Judas' previous arrangements so the reader will understand the significance of the actions in the following verse. The actual storyline focus is on Judas' statement (λέγει, narrative present) and kiss (κατεφίλησεν, aorist) in verse 45.

δὲ. The use of δέ rather than καί may be due to the shift from the general description of Judas and the armed crowd with him to the specifics of the betrayal sign. Alternatively, this might be another instance of the "additive" use (see 7:7).

ὁ παραδιδούς. Pres act ptc masc nom sg παραδίδωμι (substantival). On the meaning and use of παραδίδωμι in Mark, see 1:14 and 3:19.

αὐτόν. Accusative direct object of παραδιδούς.

σύσσημον. Accusative direct object of δεδώκει. The noun σύσσημον refers to "an action or gesture previously agreed upon as a signal, *signal, sign*" (BDAG, 978).

αὐτοῖς. Dative indirect object of δεδώκει.

λέγων. Pres act ptc masc nom sg λέγω (means).

Ὃν ἂν φιλήσω . . . ἀπάγετε ἀσφαλῶς. Clausal complement (direct discourse) of λέγων.

Ὃν ἄν. Accusative direct object of φιλήσω. The addition of ἄν to the relative pronoun gives the expression an indefinite sense ("whomever").

φιλήσω. Aor act subj 1st sg φιλέω. Subjunctive with ὃν ἄν. This is a less common use of φιλέω, meaning "to kiss" (BDAG, 1057.2). The only other NT uses with this sense are ‖ Matt 26:48 and the related passage in Luke 22:47.

αὐτός. Nominative subject of ἐστιν. The pronoun is neither emphatic nor intensive (see 6:17).

ἐστιν. Pres act ind 3rd sg εἰμί.

κρατήσατε. Aor act impv 2nd pl κρατέω.

αὐτόν. Accusative direct object of κρατήσατε.

ἀπάγετε. Pres act impv 2nd pl ἀπάγω. On the meaning, see verse 53.

ἀσφαλῶς. When the referent is to legal or military detention, this adverb is usually translated, "securely, under guard" (BDAG, 147.1). The interest is not in Jesus' safety, "but in his not getting away" (R. Brown, 1:253).

14:45 καὶ ἐλθὼν εὐθὺς προσελθὼν αὐτῷ λέγει, Ῥαββί, καὶ κατεφίλησεν αὐτόν·

ἐλθών. Aor act ptc masc nom sg ἔρχομαι (temporal). The use of both ἐλθών and προσελθών ("coming . . . coming to") seems redundant, though perhaps the addition of the compound form is intended for emphasis (so Doudna, 119: "serves to emphasize the directness with which Judas executed the act of betrayal"), perhaps: "coming (to where they were), he immediately went to him." Or it might simply be an awkward or clumsy statement (Stein 2008,

671); it is stated more simply in || Matt 26:49 (προσελθών only) and worded differently in || Luke 22:49 (ἤγγισεν). For the possibility that the expression is influenced by Semitic style, see Mark 12:12.

εὐθὺς. Adverbial use of εὐθύς, modifying προσελθών ("almost exclusively precedes the verb it modifies," Decker 1997, 88); it describes the rapidity with which an action is performed, "at once" (Decker 1997, 109; cf. Matthew's || use of εὐθέως in 26:49).

προσελθών. Aor act ptc masc nom sg προσέρχομαι (temporal).

αὐτῷ. Dative complement of προσελθών.

λέγει. Pres act ind 3rd sg λέγω.

Ῥαββί. Vocative (indeclinable). Clausal complement (indirect discourse) of λέγει. Although "Rabbi" did not become a regular title in rabbinic literature until after AD 70, there is inscriptional evidence prior to that time (see R. Brown, 1:253–54 n. 18) and the NT itself shows that the title was used before AD 70 and more widely than might otherwise be suspected (see also 9:5).

κατεφίλησεν. Aor act ind 3rd sg καταφιλέω ("to greet with a kiss," synonymous with the simple form φιλέω in the previous verse). The compound form is used in the NT only in this pericope (|| Matt 26:49) and in Luke 7:38, 45; 15:20. That the κατα- prefix implies a kiss on the hand or feet rather than the cheek (so Gundry, 859) seems dubious; such a distinction is not made elsewhere. In the only reference suggested by Gundry with a similar meaning (Luke 7:38, 45), we know that the kiss was on Jesus' feet not because καταφιλέω is used, but because the text explicitly says κατεφίλει τοὺς πόδας αὐτοῦ. R. Brown (1:253) is likely correct that the compound form is simply consistent with "vivid narrative."

αὐτόν. Accusative direct object of κατεφίλησεν.

14:46 οἱ δὲ ἐπέβαλον τὰς χεῖρας αὐτῷ καὶ ἐκράτησαν αὐτόν.

οἱ. Nominative subject of ἐπέβαλον. On the use of οἱ δέ to change subjects, see 1:45. The referent here is the armed crowd (v. 43).

ἐπέβαλον τὰς χεῖρας αὐτῷ. "To lay hands on violently" (cf. BDAG, 367.1.b, s.v. ἐπιβάλλω). This is a common expression in the LXX (e.g., Gen 22:12; 2 Sam 18:12), though it does not always have a negative connotation (e.g., Gen 46:4 is positive).

ἐπέβαλον. Aor act ind 3rd pl ἐπιβάλλω.

τὰς χεῖρας. Accusative direct object of ἐπέβαλον.

αὐτῷ. Dative indirect object of ἐπέβαλον.

ἐκράτησαν. Aor act ind 3rd pl κρατέω. Stein suggests that "the word 'seize' is a more accurate term for describing what happened than the term 'arrest'. . . [since κρατέω] does not involve a modern-day process of arresting someone" (2008, 671 n. 5).

αὐτόν. Accusative direct object of ἐκράτησαν.

14:47 εἷς δέ [τις] τῶν παρεστηκότων σπασάμενος τὴν μάχαιραν ἔπαισεν τὸν δοῦλον τοῦ ἀρχιερέως καὶ ἀφεῖλεν αὐτοῦ τὸ ὠτάριον.

εἷς. . . [τις]. Nominative subject of ἔπαισεν. "It is probable that the numeral is used here, as it is commonly, to call attention to the number, not like the indefinite τις. The probability of this is increased if τις is retained in the text" (Gould, 274). The presence of τις seems secure, since it is supported by both the Alexandrian and Byzantine families (B C W Θ Ψ *f*¹, ¹³ 𝔐; it is likely placed in brackets in the NA²⁷/UBS⁴ due to its absence in ℵ).

δέ. The use of δέ is due to the shift in subjects, from the crowd in verse 46 to the sword-wielding follower in verse 47.

παρεστηκότων. Prf act ptc masc gen pl παρίστημι (substantival). Partitive genitive.

σπασάμενος. Aor mid ptc masc nom sg σπάω ("to draw, pull out," here in reference to drawing a sword from its scabbard; BDAG, 936; see also Acts 16:27).

τὴν μάχαιραν. Accusative direct object of σπασάμενος. The μάχαιρα was a short sword or perhaps a long-bladed knife intended for fighting (in contrast to the ῥομφαία, a long, broad sword; see also v. 43).

ἔπαισεν. Aor act ind 3rd sg παίω (to "attack w. a relatively strong blow, strike," *CL*, 263). This is a general term, more commonly used of striking with a fist, but it can be used of a sword (LXX 2 Sam 20:10; Jos. *Ant.* 5.153) or an arrow (*T. Jud.* 9:3). Both Matt 26:51 and Luke 22:5 use the more specific πατάσσω.

τὸν δοῦλον. Accusative direct object of ἔπαισεν. The reference to τὸν δοῦλον τοῦ ἀρχιερέως may be to the deputy of the high priest, not a slave (Viviano, 71–80; Evans 2001, 425). France suggests that the articular form "may suggest a person of some consequence, perhaps singled out for attack because he was in charge of the arresting party" (593). That is possible, but it may simply indicate the only such δοῦλος of the high priest who was present.

ἀφεῖλεν. Aor act ind 3rd sg ἀφαιρέω. The word here means "to detach someth. by force, *take away, remove, cut off*" (BDAG, 154).

τὸ ὠτάριον. Accusative direct object of ἀφεῖλεν. ὠτάριον is a double diminutive form of οὖς ("ear") with both the older diminutive suffix -ιον and the doubled -αρ -ιον (BDF §111.3). Other accounts have the (single) diminutive form ὠτίον (Matt 26:51; Luke 22:51; John 18:26). A diminutive *meaning* is not intended (see BDAG, 1107; BDF §111.3.3; Petersen, 183). V. Taylor (560) suggests that it refers to the earlobe rather than to the entire outer ear.

14:48 καὶ ἀποκριθεὶς ὁ Ἰησοῦς εἶπεν αὐτοῖς, Ὡς ἐπὶ λῃστὴν ἐξήλθατε μετὰ μαχαιρῶν καὶ ξύλων συλλαβεῖν με;

ἀποκριθεὶς. Aor mid ptc masc nom sg ἀποκρίνομαι (means; Redundant adverbial participle of speaking; see 1:7 and the discussion of this intransitive, "θη middle" form at 3:33).

ὁ Ἰησοῦς. Nominative subject of εἶπεν.

εἶπεν. Aor act ind 3rd sg λέγω.

αὐτοῖς. Dative indirect object of εἶπεν.

Ὡς ἐπὶ λῃστὴν . . . ⁴⁹αἱ γραφαί. Clausal complement (direct discourse) of εἶπεν. Jesus' words in verse 48 "can be read either as a question or as a statement: in either case it is a protest against the manner of his arrest—perhaps rather against the blindness and stupidity that had deemed such force necessary than against the indignity done to himself as such" (Cranfield, 437).

Ὡς. Comparative particle.

ἐπὶ λῃστὴν. Spatial ("against)," suggesting hostile opposition.

λῃστὴν. The word λῃστής can refer either to a "robber, bandit" or a "revolutionary, insurrectionist" (BDAG, 594). The associated description (ἐξήλθατε μετὰ μαχαιρῶν καὶ ξύλων συλλαβεῖν με) would seem to suggest more than just "robber," as would the ultimate charges against Jesus (Evans 2001, 425). NET suggests, however, that the evidence for this usage "generally postdates Jesus' time." This is the same word later used to describe those between whom Jesus is crucified (15:27).

ἐξήλθατε. Aor act ind 2nd pl ἐξέρχομαι.

μετὰ μαχαιρῶν καὶ ξύλων. The preposition μετά indicates the "concrete objects, which serve as equipment" (BDAG, 637.A.3.c, s.v. μετά; see also v. 43).

συλλαβεῖν. Aor act inf συλλαμβάνω (purpose).

14:49 καθ᾽ ἡμέραν ἤμην πρὸς ὑμᾶς ἐν τῷ ἱερῷ διδάσκων καὶ οὐκ ἐκρατήσατέ με· ἀλλ᾽ ἵνα πληρωθῶσιν αἱ γραφαί.

καθ᾽ ἡμέραν. Distributive: "daily, every day, day after day" (BDAG, 437.2.c, s.v. ἡμέρα; on distributive expressions, see 6:7). An alternative explanation, "by day" (i.e., during daylight hours), is

mentioned by BDAG (following Argyle). Stein (2008, 673), one of
the few to embrace this view, appeals to Luke 21:37, perhaps because
of the contrasting phrase "at night" (ESV). The Lukan text, however,
is not parallel to Mark 14:49 and the expression "at night" is not the
same construction.

ἤμην. Impf mid ind 1st sg εἰμί.

πρὸς ὑμᾶς. Association.

ἐν τῷ ἱερῷ. Locative, modifying διδάσκων.

διδάσκων. Pres act ptc masc nom sg διδάσκω (attendant circumstance). Although it might be possible to argue for a periphrastic
construction here (ἤμην . . . διδάσκων, so Stein 2008, 673), that
seems unlikely. If it were a periphrastic, it would indicate that Jesus
was teaching *with his adversaries* (πρὸς ὑμᾶς) in the temple (Green,
120–21).

καὶ. Coordinating conjunction, but here used in an adversative
context ("but, and yet, and in spite of that, nevertheless," Maloney
1981, 69–70; see also BDAG, 1.b.η).

ἐκρατήσατέ. Aor act ind 2nd pl κρατέω.

με. Accusative direct object of ἐκρατήσατε.

ἀλλ᾽ ἵνα. Since ἀλλ᾽ ἵνα can be used elliptically in the sense "(but)
this happened . . . in order that" (BDF §448.7), it seems likely that
Mark intends an historical statement: "it has taken place that . . ." (as
Matthew makes explicit: τοῦτο δὲ ὅλον γέγονεν ἵνα πληρωθῶσιν αἱ
γραφαί; Collins, 686). Alternatively, Anderson (293), Bruce (441),
Voelz (238), and Zerwick (§415), argue for an imperatival ἵνα: "But
let the Scriptures be fulfilled."

πληρωθῶσιν. Aor pass subj 3rd pl πληρόω.

αἱ γραφαί. Nominative subject of πληρωθῶσιν.

14:50 καὶ ἀφέντες αὐτὸν ἔφυγον πάντες.

ἀφέντες. Aor act ptc masc nom pl ἀφίημι (temporal, simultane-
ous with the main verb ἔφυγον). This is probably not to be described
as a participle of attendant circumstance since there are not two
separate actions involved: the leaving and fleeing refer to the same
event. The participle is somewhat superfluous, but this usage of the
participle of ἀφίημι is not uncommon in the Koine (see 12:12 on
ἀφέντες and 15:37 on ἀφείς).

αὐτὸν. Accusative direct object of ἀφέντες.

ἔφυγον. Aor act ind 3rd pl φεύγω. The antecedent is not specified,
but the sense of the context is that it refers to Jesus' disciples.

πάντες. Nominative subject of ἔφυγον.

14:51 Καὶ νεανίσκος τις συνηκολούθει αὐτῷ περιβεβλημένος σινδόνα ἐπὶ γυμνοῦ, καὶ κρατοῦσιν αὐτόν·

νεανίσκος τις. Nominative subject of συνηκολούθει.

συνηκολούθει. Impf act ind 3rd sg συνακολουθέω ("to accompany someone, *to follow*").

αὐτῷ. Dative complement of συνηκολούθει.

περιβεβλημένος. Prf mid ptc masc nom sg περιβάλλω (attributive, modifying νεανίσκος).

σινδόνα. Accusative direct object of περιβεβλημένος. A σινδών was a long-tailed shirt that might have been made of linen or cotton. It was not the usual outer garment (ἱμάτιον).

ἐπὶ γυμνοῦ. Spatial. The adjective γυμνός is here used substantivally ("the naked body," BDAG, 208.1.a). This is "an odd expression, the natural Greek expression for 'over his naked body' being ἐπὶ χρωτός or ἐν χρῷ" (Cranfield, 438). Collins (688) suggests that the phrase ἐπὶ γυμνοῦ could be understood as equivalent to either ἐπὶ γυμνοῦ ἐνδύματος (i.e., "upon the covering of his nakedness" or "upon the garment of his nakedness," meaning that he had a light garment over his underwear) or ἐπὶ γυμνοῦ τοῦ σώματος ("over his naked body").

κρατοῦσιν. Pres act ind 3rd pl κρατέω. The reason for a narrative present at this point is not clear, perhaps due to it being included in a very short (only one sentence), obscure vignette.

αὐτόν. Accusative direct object of κρατοῦσιν.

14:52 ὁ δὲ καταλιπὼν τὴν σινδόνα γυμνὸς ἔφυγεν.

ὁ. Nominative subject of ἔφυγεν. On the use of ὁ δέ to change subjects, see 1:45.

καταλιπὼν. Aor act ptc masc nom sg καταλείπω (temporal).

τὴν σινδόνα. Accusative direct object of καταλιπών (see also v. 51).

γυμνὸς. Complement of ἔφυγεν, describing his condition as he fled/escaped. Syntactically, a nominative adjective is unusual; an adverbial participle of manner might have been expected, but the point is clear. (Had an accusative form been used it would have indicated that from which he fled/escaped.) Although γυμνός can mean "stark naked," it can also mean "poorly dressed" or "lightly clad, without an outer garment" (BDAG, 208.2–3; cf. LN 49.22; see John 21:7).

ἔφυγεν. Aor act ind 3rd sg φεύγω. The verb can mean either "flee" or "escape," and both would make sense here (BDAG, 1052.1, 2).

Mark 14:53-65

⁵³Then they brought Jesus to the high priest and all the chief priests and elders and scribes assembled. ⁵⁴Now Peter followed him at a distance right into the courtyard of the high priest and he was sitting with the guards and warming himself at the fire. ⁵⁵The chief priests and the whole Sanhedrin were seeking evidence against Jesus in order to put him to death, but they were not finding (any), ⁵⁶for many gave false testimony against him, but their testimonies were not consistent. ⁵⁷Now some, having taken their stand (before the court), gave false testimony against him saying, ⁵⁸"We heard him saying, 'I will destroy this handcrafted temple and in the course of three days I will construct another one that is not handcrafted.'" ⁵⁹Yet not even in this way was their testimony consistent. ⁶⁰Standing up in the midst (of the council) the high priest asked Jesus, "Are you not going to answer?! What is this that they are testifying against you?" ⁶¹But Jesus remained silent and answered nothing. So the high priest asked him, "Are you the Messiah, the Son of the Blessed One?" ⁶²Jesus said, "I am, and you will see the Son of Man sitting at the right hand of power and coming with the clouds of heaven." ⁶³Then the high priest, having torn his clothes, said, "What further need do we have for witnesses? ⁶⁴You have heard the blasphemy. What is your decision?" So they all condemned him to be worthy of death. ⁶⁵Then they began to spit on him, to blindfold him, to strike him with their fists, and to say to him, "Prophesy!" And the guards beat him.

14:53 Καὶ ἀπήγαγον τὸν Ἰησοῦν πρὸς τὸν ἀρχιερέα, καὶ συν-έρχονται πάντες οἱ ἀρχιερεῖς καὶ οἱ πρεσβύτεροι καὶ οἱ γραμματεῖς.

ἀπήγαγον. Aor act ind 3rd pl ἀπάγω. This is a legal technical term: "to conduct a pers. from one point to another in a legal process . . . *bring before, lead away*" (BDAG, 95.1). The antecedents are not tightly tracked in this section; the third plural form here goes back to verse 43 (ὄχλος), which continued in verse 46 (οἱ δὲ ἐπέβαλον . . . καὶ ἐκράτησαν) and by the pronoun αὐτοῖς in verse 48.

τὸν Ἰησοῦν. Accusative direct object of ἀπήγαγον.

πρὸς τὸν ἀρχιερέα. Spatial.

συνέρχονται. Pres mid ind 3rd pl συνέρχομαι. The variant reading αὐτῷ (A B Ψ 𝔐) indicates the person (the high priest) or place where they gathered.

Mark 14:53-55 217

πάντες οἱ ἀρχιερεῖς καὶ οἱ πρεσβύτεροι καὶ οἱ γραμματεῖς.
Nominative subject of συνέρχονται. On the significance of πάντες,
see verse 55. "The singular [ἀρχιερεύς] refers to the ruling high
priest, the plural to other chief priests" (Gundry, 896).

14:54 καὶ ὁ Πέτρος ἀπὸ μακρόθεν ἠκολούθησεν αὐτῷ ἕως ἔσω
εἰς τὴν αὐλὴν τοῦ ἀρχιερέως καὶ ἦν συγκαθήμενος μετὰ τῶν
ὑπηρετῶν καὶ θερμαινόμενος πρὸς τὸ φῶς.

ὁ Πέτρος. Nominative subject of ἠκολούθησεν.
ἀπὸ μακρόθεν. Separation ("from a distance," see 5:6).
ἠκολούθησεν. Aor act ind 3rd sg ἀκολουθέω.
αὐτῷ. Dative complement of ἠκολούθησεν.
ἕως ἔσω εἰς. In this seemingly redundant phrase ("until inside
in") ἕως functions as a preposition indicating the limit reached ("as
far as," BDAG, 423.3.b), with an adverb of place (ἔσω is the adverb
form of εἰς) as its object (see also 15:16). Together they may be
translated "right into." The prepositional phrase εἰς τὴν αὐλήν then
specifies the location: "right into the courtyard."
εἰς τὴν αὐλήν. Spatial. On the meaning of αὐλή, see 15:16.
ἦν. Impf act ind 3rd sg εἰμί.
συγκαθήμενος. Pres mid ptc masc nom sg συγκάθημαι (imperfective periphrastic; "to sit with").
μετὰ τῶν ὑπηρετῶν. Association. The word ὑπηρέτης is quite
general ("assistant") and must be defined by the context. Here the
reference is probably to the military people who arrested Jesus and
who had just escorted him to the high priest; thus, "guards" or perhaps "police, deputies" (see also R. Brown, 1:246–52).
θερμαινόμενος. Pres mid ptc masc nom sg θερμαίνω (imperfective periphrastic; "to warm oneself" either with a heat source or with
clothing). The middle voice is appropriate to describe the action
directed toward the subject.
πρὸς τὸ φῶς. Spatial. φῶς can be used synonymously with πῦρ or
πυρά (LN 2.5), as here. Gould suggests that φῶς is used instead of
πῦρ "because it calls attention to the fact that Peter was in sight, not
hid away in the darkness" (278).

14:55 οἱ δὲ ἀρχιερεῖς καὶ ὅλον τὸ συνέδριον ἐζήτουν κατὰ τοῦ
Ἰησοῦ μαρτυρίαν εἰς τὸ θανατῶσαι αὐτόν, καὶ οὐχ ηὕρισκον·

οἱ ... ἀρχιερεῖς καὶ ὅλον τὸ συνέδριον. Nominative subject of
ἐζήτουν. The description ὅλον τὸ συνέδριον does not mandate that

every single member was present (though they may have been). It could be a general statement regarding the majority or most members (cf. R. Brown, 1:401). Evans (444) suggests that this is only a hyperbolic statement of the desire of the Sanhedrin (they all wanted evidence against Jesus) and that there may have been only several members present at the night hearing. Verse 53, however, has already indicated that συνέρχονται πάντες οἱ ἀρχιερεῖς καὶ οἱ πρεσβύτεροι καὶ οἱ γραμματεῖς had gathered.

δέ. The use of δέ is due to the shift in subjects, from Peter in verse 54 to the religious leaders in verse 55.

ἐζήτουν κατὰ τοῦ Ἰησοῦ μαρτυρία. This wording "support[s] the view that this was an inquiry for the purpose of collecting evidence rather than a formal trial" (Cranfield, 441). Note that they are seeking testimony/evidence, not witnesses/people in the middle of the night (R. Brown, 1:433).

ἐζήτουν. Impf act ind 3rd pl ζητέω.

κατὰ τοῦ Ἰησοῦ. Opposition ("against").

μαρτυρίαν. Accusative direct object of ἐζήτουν.

θανατῶσαι. Aor act inf θανατόω. Used with εἰς τό to indicate purpose (only here in Mark).

αὐτόν. Accusative direct object of θανατῶσαι.

ηὕρισκον. Impf act ind 3rd pl εὑρίσκω. This verb does not normally augment with ηυ- (elsewhere in the NT only Acts 7:11).

14:56 πολλοὶ γὰρ ἐψευδομαρτύρουν κατ᾽ αὐτοῦ, καὶ ἴσαι αἱ μαρτυρίαι οὐκ ἦσαν.

πολλοί. Nominative subject of ἐψευδομαρτύρουν.

γάρ. Introduces a subordinate clause explaining why they were not able to find evidence against Jesus.

ἐψευδομαρτύρουν. Impf act ind 3rd pl ψευδομαρτυρέω ("give false testimony," BDAG, 1097).

κατ᾽ αὐτοῦ. Opposition ("against").

καί. Coordinating conjunction, but here used in an adversative context ("but, and yet, and in spite of that, nevertheless," Maloney 1981, 69–70; see also BDAG, 1.b.η). Gundry (898) suggests that this adversative context (ψευδομαρτυρέω used with ἴσαι αἱ μαρτυρίαι οὐκ ἦσαν) may have ecbatic implications: "with the result that."

ἴσαι. Predicate adjective. The context of legal testimony with many false witnesses suggests the translation "consistent."

αἱ μαρτυρίαι. Nominative subject of ἦσαν.

ἦσαν. Impf act ind 3rd pl εἰμί.

14:57 καί τινες ἀναστάντες ἐψευδομαρτύρουν κατ᾽ αὐτοῦ λέγοντες

τινες. Nominative subject of ἐψευδομαρτύρουν.

ἀναστάντες. Aor act ptc masc nom pl ἀνίστημι (temporal or perhaps attendant circumstance). In this context the focus does not seem to be on the physical act of standing up from a sitting position, but should probably be understood in a (semi)legal sense, "to take one's place as a legal witness, to stand before the court" (cf. BDAG, 83.9). The word appears frequently in legal contexts outside the NT. LSJ (144) notes the following forensic uses: "*produce* a witness" (A.1.4, citing Acts 3:22); "μάρτυρα ἀναστής ασθαί τινα 'call him as one's witness,'" (Plato, *Leg.* 937a. [A.3.6]); "of a law-court, rise" (B.2.3, citing Demosthenes, *Mid.*, 21.221, which reads ἐπειδὰν ἀναστῇ τὸ δικαστήριον, "whenever the court of justice should convene" [my translation]).

ἐψευδομαρτύρουν. Impf act ind 3rd pl ψευδομαρτυρέω ("to give false testimony"). On the possibility that this is an inceptive imperfect as in the NASB, see 1:21.

κατ᾽ αὐτοῦ. Opposition ("against").

λέγοντες. Pres act ptc masc nom pl λέγω (means; redundant participle of speaking; see 1:7).

14:58 ὅτι Ἡμεῖς ἠκούσαμεν αὐτοῦ λέγοντος ὅτι Ἐγὼ καταλύσω τὸν ναὸν τοῦτον τὸν χειροποίητον καὶ διὰ τριῶν ἡμερῶν ἄλλον ἀχειροποίητον οἰκοδομήσω

ὅτι. Introduces the clausal complement (direct discourse) of λέγοντες (see 1:15).

Ἡμεῖς. Nominative subject of ἠκούσαμεν. The use of an explicit subject pronoun lends a certain degree of emphasis or focus on the subject's role, understandable here in the context of legal testimony.

ἠκούσαμεν. Aor act ind 1st pl ἀκούω.

αὐτοῦ. Genitive direct object of ἠκούσαμεν.

λέγοντος. Pres act ptc masc gen sg λέγω. Complement in an object-complement double genitive construction (analogous to a double accusative, but in the genitive since ἀκούω takes a genitive object here). On double case constructions, see Culy (2009; this example is discussed on p. 89).

ὅτι. Introduces the clausal complement (direct discourse) of λέγοντος (see 1:15). On the recitative use of ὅτι (twice in this verse), see 1:15.

Ἐγώ. Nominative subject of καταλύσω. On the emphasis implied, see ἡμεῖς above.

καταλύσω. Fut act ind 1st sg καταλύω.

τὸν ναὸν τοῦτον τὸν χειροποίητον. Accusative direct object of καταλύσω. It is often thought that ναός must refer to the building comprised of the Holy Place and the Most Holy Place, which was located at the center of the larger temple complex (ἱερόν), which included the courtyards, walls, and entrances, etc. There are certainly instances where this distinction is valid (e.g., Matt 23:35; Mark 15:38), but ναός can also be used in the wider sense of the temple complex, synonymous with ἱερόν (e.g., Matt 27:5—Judas is certainly not in the Holy Place when he returns the money!). See also BDAG (666.b). The adjective χειροποίητος can mean "man-made" or "made by human hands" (LN 42.32). It is used fourteen times in the LXX, usually as a description of idols and always negative; such connotations may well be intended here.

διὰ τριῶν ἡμερῶν. Temporal. With the genitive in this context the sense is probably "in the course of." This is standard usage in the papyri, but differs from classical usage (Doudna, 29–30).

ἄλλον ἀχειροποίητον. Accusative direct object of οἰκοδομήσω. The adjective ἀχειροποίητος means "*not made by hands* = not of human origin" (*CL*, 65).

οἰκοδομήσω. Fut act ind 1st sg οἰκοδομέω.

14:59 καὶ οὐδὲ οὕτως ἴση ἦν ἡ μαρτυρία αὐτῶν.

οὐδὲ. Here "not even" (BDAG, 734.3) makes the best sense in English.

οὕτως. Adverb modifying ἦν: "thus, in this way/manner."

ἴση. Predicate adjective. When used "of testimony given by witnesses [it may be glossed as] *consistent*" (BDAG, 481).

ἦν. Impf act ind 3rd sg εἰμί.

ἡ μαρτυρία. Nominative subject of ἦν. The article distinguishes the subject from the predicate nominative (adjective) in this instance.

αὐτῶν. Subjective genitive (Wallace 1996, 114).

14:60 καὶ ἀναστὰς ὁ ἀρχιερεὺς εἰς μέσον ἐπηρώτησεν τὸν Ἰησοῦν λέγων, Οὐκ ἀποκρίνῃ οὐδὲν τί οὗτοί σου καταμαρτυροῦσιν;

ἀναστὰς. Aor act ptc masc nom sg ἀνίστημι (temporal).

ὁ ἀρχιερεὺς. Nominative subject of ἐπηρώτησεν.

εἰς μέσον. Locative.

ἐπηρώτησεν. Aor act ind 3rd sg ἐπερωτάω. On ἐπερωτάω versus the simple form ἐρωτάω, see 4:10. In this context it would not be out of place to translate "he interrogated"; at the least it must be recognized that this is not a casual question, but part of a legal proceeding.

τὸν Ἰησοῦν. Accusative direct object of ἐπηρώτησεν.

λέγων. Pres act ptc masc nom sg λέγω (means; redundant participle of speaking; see 1:7 and 3:33).

Οὐκ ἀποκρίνῃ ... καταμαρτυροῦσιν. Clausal complement (indirect discourse) of λέγων. This might be taken as a single statement as in the NA²⁷/UBS⁴, but it is probably best to understand two separate questions here: Οὐκ ἀποκρίνῃ οὐδέν; τί οὗτοί σου καταμαρτυροῦσιν; (so Robertson, 738; Cranfield, 442; cf. WH, UBS³, and most English translations). The use of οὐκ in the first question implies that an affirmative answer is expected. Robertson suggests that here "the use of οὐ may suggest indignation as in οὐκ ἀποκρίνῃ οὐδέν; (Mk. 14:60)" (918). The double negative, οὐκ ... οὐδέν, would reinforce the suggestion of indignation. Although clumsy, perhaps "You're really not going to reply are you?!" catches a bit of the tone. There seems to be a bit of exasperation in the second question as well.

ἀποκρίνῃ. Pres mid ind 2nd sg ἀποκρίνομαι. On this intransitive, "θη middle" form, see 3:33.

οὐδὲν. Accusative direct object of ἀποκρίνῃ.

τί. Accusative direct object of καταμαρτυροῦσιν. Robertson (738) notes that in this statement τί = τί ἐστιν ὅ, i.e., "what is this that they are saying." An alternative analysis, which follows the punctuation of the NA²⁷/UBS⁴ (i.e., a single question rather than two), is possible, but in that case the τί would have to be taken as an indefinite pronoun that is functioning as a relative pronoun (BDF §298.4), "Have you no answer to the accusations that these witnesses bring against you?" A variation of this alternative has been proposed by Buttmann who suggested that a verb was to be supplied between the two parts of the statement: "answerest thou nothing (hearing) what these witness against thee?" (251–52).

οὗτοί. Nominative subject of καταμαρτυροῦσιν.

σου. Genitive of reference: "concerning you."

καταμαρτυροῦσιν. Pres act ind 3rd pl καταμαρτυρέω ("τί τινος *testify someth. against someone*").

14:61 ὁ δὲ ἐσιώπα καὶ οὐκ ἀπεκρίνατο οὐδέν. πάλιν ὁ ἀρχιερεὺς ἐπηρώτα αὐτὸν καὶ λέγει αὐτῷ, Σὺ εἶ ὁ Χριστὸς ὁ υἱὸς τοῦ εὐλογητοῦ;

ὁ. Nominative subject of ἐσιώπα. On the use of ὁ δέ to change subjects, see 1:45. Gundry argues that Mark's use of δέ is concentrated in this section (vv. 53-72) compared with his overall usage. He takes this to be emphasizing "the shifts in actors and speakers" (883). It is true that Mark uses δέ more sparingly than the other Synoptics (157 times or 12 per 1,000 words, compared with Matthew's 494/22 and Luke's 542/23), especially in contrast to καί, which he uses 1,087 times or 81 per 1,000 words (cf. Matthew's 1,194/54 and Luke's 1,483/63). There are other sections of Mark, however, that use an equal or greater frequency of δέ (e.g., 10:36-40 [6 times in 5 verses]; and 15:11-16 [7 times in 6 verses]), also in dialogue. In the present passage δέ occurs four times in four consecutive verses (vv. 61-64). There does not appear to be any particular emphasis here, only typical alternation of speakers in dialogue.

ἐσιώπα. Impf act ind 3rd sg σιωπάω.

οὐκ . . . οὐδέν. The double negative is an emphatic positive statement, "he answered nothing at all."

ἀπεκρίνατο. Aor mid ind 3rd sg ἀποκρίνομαι. Although the aorist -θη- forms of this verb are frequent (see 3:33), the aorist middle form appears to function differently. MM argues that the middle has a "formal and weighty tone," and is used either in solemn statements or in legal proceedings. Uses of the middle in the papyri are "without exception legal reports, in which ἀπεκρίνατο . . . means 'replied,' of an advocate or a party in a suit" (64). Of the exact form ἀπεκρίνατο, MM lists Luke 3:16; John 5:17, 19; and Acts 3:12 as illustrating the "solemn" use, and Matt 27:12; Mark 14:61; and Luke 23:9 as examples of the legal use (so also R. Brown, 1:463–64; Wallace 1996, 421). At the least, the aorist middle appears to have a more formal or solemn force as a less frequently used form.

πάλιν. Probably not "again" in this instance (as if the high priest repeated a question), but rather an inferential conjunction ("further, thereupon," MHT 2:446; see also BDAG, 752.3). Neither gloss functions well in English in this context; the translation above uses "so" as a more natural equivalent.

ὁ ἀρχιερεὺς. Nominative subject of ἐπηρώτα.

ἐπηρώτα αὐτὸν καὶ λέγει αὐτῷ. The use of two linked finite forms of speaking is unusual (cf. John 1:25; T. Sol. A.13:3). The second verb is typically a participle.

ἐπηρώτα. Impf act ind 3rd sg ἐπερωτάω. On ἐπερωτάω versus the simple form ἐρωτάω, see 4:10.

αὐτὸν. Accusative direct object of ἐπηρώτα.

λέγει. Pres act ind 3rd sg λέγω.

αὐτῷ. Dative indirect object of λέγει.

Σὺ εἶ . . . τοῦ εὐλογητοῦ. Clausal complement (direct discourse) of λέγει.

Σὺ. Nominative subject of εἶ. V. Taylor suggests that "σύ is emphatic and contemptuous" (567).

εἶ. Pres act ind 2nd sg εἰμί.

ὁ Χριστὸς. Predicate nominative.

ὁ υἱὸς. Nominative in apposition to ὁ Χριστός.

τοῦ εὐλογητοῦ. This may be a "periphrasis for the name of God, which is not mentioned out of reverence" (BDAG, 408). In the NT εὐλογητός occurs only in reference to God, and only here in an absolute statement. R. Brown, however, comments that "despite the tendency of some to state that *ha-barûk*, the Hebrew equivalent of *ho eulogētos*, was a recognized substitute for the divine name (often citing the much later rabbinic references offered by Dalman or [Strack and Billerbeck]), there is no real evidence of that. 'The Son of the Blessed' is not found elsewhere in either the NT or Jewish literature; *neither is 'the Blessed' as a title for God found*" (1:469). There are, he points out, some adjectival uses that "resemble the general NT use of *eulogētos*, but they do not offer evidence for a substitute divine name." For a discussion of this designation of God in Jewish texts, see Evans (2001, 449).

14:62 ὁ δὲ Ἰησοῦς εἶπεν, Ἐγώ εἰμι, καὶ ὄψεσθε τὸν υἱὸν τοῦ ἀνθρώπου ἐκ δεξιῶν καθήμενον τῆς δυνάμεως καὶ ἐρχόμενον μετὰ τῶν νεφελῶν τοῦ οὐρανοῦ.

ὁ . . . Ἰησοῦς. Nominative subject of εἶπεν. The use of δέ is due to the shift in subjects: the high priest in verse 61b and Jesus in verse 62.

εἶπεν. Aor act ind 3rd sg λέγω.

Ἐγώ. Nominative subject of εἰμί. In contrast to his statement in 15:2, Jesus' Ἐγώ εἰμι is "unambiguously affirmative" (R. Brown, 1:488).

εἰμι. Pres act ind 1st sg εἰμί.

ὄψεσθε. Fut mid ind 2nd pl ὁράω.

τὸν υἱὸν. Accusative direct object of ὄψεσθε. On τὸν υἱὸν τοῦ ἀνθρώπου, see 2:10.

ἐκ δεξιῶν. Source. The expression "καθίσαι ἐκ δ. τινος [means] *sit at someone's right*, i.e. at the place of honor" (BDAG, 218.1.b, s.v. δεξιός). The plural δεξιῶν is idiomatic (see || Matt 26:64; Luke 22:69; also Mark 10:37, 40; 12:36; Matt 22:44; Luke 20:42).

καθήμενον. Pres mid ptc masc acc sg κάθημαι (complement in an object-complement double accusative construction).

τῆς δυνάμεως. Simple common nouns, like δύναμις, are often used as a title for God. For extensive documentation of the usage of this circumlocution in Jewish texts, see Evans (2001, 452).

ἐρχόμενον. Pres mid ptc masc acc sg ἔρχομαι (complement in an object-complement double accusative construction).

μετὰ τῶν νεφελῶν. Spatial. The use of νεφέλη with μετά (instead of the more common ἐπί, ἐν, or εἰς; cf. 13:26; Mt 24:30; 26:64) is found in the Theodotion text of Dan 7:13.

14:63 ὁ δὲ ἀρχιερεὺς διαρρήξας τοὺς χιτῶνας αὐτοῦ λέγει, Τί ἔτι χρείαν ἔχομεν μαρτύρων;

ὁ . . . ἀρχιερεὺς. Nominative subject of λέγει. The use of δέ is due to the shift in subjects: Jesus in verse 62 and the high priest in verse 63.

διαρρήξας. Aor act ptc masc nom sg διαρ(ρ)ήγνυμι/διαρρήσσω ("to tear," BDAG, 235.1.a). Tearing one's garments was a sign of grief or dismay (cf. Acts 14:14). Many of the (fairly frequent) LXX uses of this idiom (e.g., 2 Sam 1:11) are caused by grief at someone's death, suggesting that "tearing one's clothes on hearing something [perceived to be] offensive to God indicates that the grief this causes is as great as or greater than that caused by hearing of death (R. Brown, 1:517; see also V. Taylor, 569).

τοὺς χιτῶνας. Accusative direct object of διαρρήξας. The word χιτών normally refers to the shirt/tunic; here, "the pl. prob. does not mean a number of shirts, but *clothes* gener." (BDAG, 1085; see also BDF §141.8.8).

λέγει. Pres act ind 3rd sg λέγω.

Τί ἔτι χρείαν . . . φαίνεται (v. 64). Clausal complement (direct discourse) of λέγει.

Τί . . . χρείαν. Accusative direct object of ἔχομεν.

ἔχομεν. Pres act ind 1st pl ἔχω.

μαρτύρων. With χρεία, the genitive indicates the nature of the need (BDAG, 1088.1, s.v. χρεία).

14:64 ἠκούσατε τῆς βλασφημίας· τί ὑμῖν φαίνεται; οἱ δὲ πάντες κατέκριναν αὐτὸν ἔνοχον εἶναι θανάτου.

ἠκούσατε τῆς βλασφημίας· The NA²⁷/UBS⁴ punctuates this as a statement, but it could also be taken as a question: "Have you heard the blasphemy?" (cf. WH).

ἠκούσατε. Aor act ind 2nd pl ἀκούω.

τῆς βλασφημίας. Genitive direct object of ἠκούσατε. Usually ἀκούω is followed by an accusative to specify what is heard (the genitive more commonly refers to the person who is heard; BDF §173.1–2), but there are other examples analogous to the usage here (BDAG, 37–38.1.b.γ, s.v. ἀκούω); so the present pattern is neither exceptional nor particularly significant. On the meaning of βλασφημία/βλασφημέω, see Bock (2000).

τί. Nominative subject of φαίνεται.

ὑμῖν. Dative complement of φαίνεται.

φαίνεται. Pres mid ind 3rd sg φαίνω. In this context φαίνω means "to make an impression on the mind, *have the appearance, seem*," and often relates to a decision (BDAG, 1047.5). The clause τί ὑμῖν φαίνεται might be translated, "How does it seem to you?" or "What is your decision?" (BDAG, 1047.5).

οἱ . . . πάντες. Nominative subject of κατέκριναν. The article functions as a nominalizer, indicating that the adjective functions as a noun. "'All' is probably hyperbolic and allows for exceptions such as Joseph of Arimathea and Nicodemus, but apart from such exceptions, Mark wants his readers to understand that the Sanhedrin was united in their condemnation of Jesus" (Stein 2008, 686 n. 15).

κατέκριναν. Aor act ind 3rd pl κατακρίνω.

αὐτὸν. Accusative subject of εἶναι.

ἔνοχον. Predicate accusative of εἶναι.

εἶναι. Pres act inf εἰμί (indirect discourse). "Mark probably uses this form of expression rather than κατέκριναν αὐτὸν θανάτῳ (or ἀποθανεῖν), because he is aware that this was not a formal trial and that they were not pronouncing a sentence but rather giving a legal opinion" (Cranfield, 445).

θανάτου. With ἔνοχος a noun in the genitive may indicate the punishment deserved (as here), the crime, or the person against whom a sin has been committed (BDAG, 338.2.b.α–γ, s.v. ἔνοχος).

14:65 Καὶ ἤρξαντό τινες ἐμπτύειν αὐτῷ καὶ περικαλύπτειν αὐτοῦ τὸ πρόσωπον καὶ κολαφίζειν αὐτὸν καὶ λέγειν αὐτῷ, Προφή-τευσον, καὶ οἱ ὑπηρέται ῥαπίσμασιν αὐτὸν ἔλαβον.

ἤρξαντό. Aor mid ind 3rd pl ἄρχω. The verb ἄρχω is always fol-lowed by a complementary infinitive; here there is a string of four infinitives, each coordinated by καί.

τινες. Nominative subject of ἤρξαντό. The referent of τινες appears to be some members of the Sanhedrin. That it does not refer to the attendants/guards is clear since their actions are introduced with καί at the end of the verse.

ἐμπτύειν. Pres act inf ἐμπτύω (complementary).

αὐτῷ. Dative complement of ἐμπτύειν.

περικαλύπτειν. Pres act inf περικαλύπτω (complementary; "to cover"). Used with αὐτοῦ τὸ πρόσωπον, the expression probably means "to blindfold him."

τὸ πρόσωπον. Accusative direct object of περικαλύπτειν.

κολαφίζειν. Pres act inf κολαφίζω (complementary; "to strike sharply, esp. with the hand, *strike with the fist, beat, cuff* τινά *someone*," BDAG, 555.1). The cognate noun κόλαφος is a vernacular form of κόνδυλος ("knuckle," MHT 2:407).

αὐτὸν. Accusative direct object of κολαφίζειν.

λέγειν. Pres act inf λέγω (complementary).

αὐτῷ. Dative indirect object of λέγειν.

Προφήτευσον. Aor act impv 2nd sg προφητεύω. This verb is the one-word clausal complement (direct discourse) of λέγειν. The parallel in Matt 26:68 fills in the statement, προφήτευσον ἡμῖν, χριστέ, τίς ἐστιν ὁ παίσας σε;

οἱ ὑπηρέται. Nominative subject of ἔλαβον. The referent here is probably the guards who had escorted Jesus from the garden to the hearing before the Sanhedrin (see v. 54).

ῥαπίσμασιν αὐτὸν ἔλαβον. "They received him with blows." ‖ John 19:3 uses δίδωμι: ἐδίδοσαν αὐτῷ ῥαπίσματα. This may be a Latinism: *verberibus eum acceperunt* (BDF §5.3.b; see on 4:21). BDAG says that this expression "does not mean 'the servants took him into custody with blows' (BWeiss, al.), but is a colloquialism . . . *the servants treated him to blows . . . 'worked him over'* . . . the v.l. ἔβαλον is the result of failure to recognize this rare usage" (584.5, s.v. λαμβάνω). The translation above renders the entire phrase, "the guards beat him."

ῥαπίσμασιν. Dative of manner. A ῥάπισμα is probably "a blow inflicted by some instrument such as a club, rod, or whip" (BDAG, 904.1), though it could refer to a face slap with the hand. Describing the force of the dative in this passage, Wallace says that "in this instance a concrete noun is used, but the force is still manner. The violence was not a necessary means of 'welcoming' Jesus, but it depicts the attitude and actions that accompanied this reception" (162).

ἔλαβον. Aor act ind 3rd pl λαμβάνω.

Mark 14:66-72

⁶⁶Now while Peter was below in the courtyard, one of the slave girls of the high priest came by ⁶⁷and having noticed Peter warming himself (by the fire) (and) having looked carefully at him she said, "You also were with the Nazarene Jesus." ⁶⁸But he denied (it) saying, "I neither know him nor know what you are talking about." Then he went out to the gateway [and a rooster crowed]. ⁶⁹The slave girl, seeing him, again began to say to those standing (there), "This man is one of them." ⁷⁰Again he denied it. Then after a little while the ones standing there again said to Peter, "Truly you are one of them, for indeed you are a Galilean." ⁷¹But he began to curse and swear, "I do not know this man whom you are talking about!" ⁷²Immediately a rooster crowed a second time. Then Peter remembered the word that Jesus had spoken to him, "Before a rooster crows twice, you will deny me three times." And going out he wept.

14:66 Καὶ ὄντος τοῦ Πέτρου κάτω ἐν τῇ αὐλῇ ἔρχεται μία τῶν παιδισκῶν τοῦ ἀρχιερέως

ὄντος. Pres act ptc masc gen sg εἰμί. Genitive absolute (see 1:32), temporal.

τοῦ Πέτρου. Genitive subject of ὄντος.

Κάτω. Adverb of place: "below." This may imply that Jesus' interrogation was being conducted in a second floor room above (and perhaps overlooking) the courtyard.

ἐν τῇ αὐλῇ. Locative.

ἔρχεται. Pres mid ind 3rd sg ἔρχομαι. The present tense introduces a new paragraph (see 1:21).

μία. Nominative subject of ἔρχεται.

τῶν παιδισκῶν. Partitive genitive (see 8:8). παιδίσκη is the diminutive form of παῖς, in the NT always with reference to a female slave. It probably does not carry diminutive force.

14:67 καὶ ἰδοῦσα τὸν Πέτρον θερμαινόμενον ἐμβλέψασα αὐτῷ λέγει, Καὶ σὺ μετὰ τοῦ Ναζαρηνοῦ ἦσθα τοῦ Ἰησοῦ.

ἰδοῦσα. Aor act ptc fem nom sg ὁράω (temporal).

τὸν Πέτρον. Accusative direct object of ἰδοῦσα.

θερμαινόμενον. Pres mid ptc masc acc sg θερμαίνω (attributive). On the meaning of the word and the middle voice, see verse 54.

ἐμβλέψασα. Aor act ptc fem nom sg ἐμβλέπω (temporal). The

prefixed form rather than βλέπω in this context probably implies a more careful look than the earlier ἰδοῦσα.

αὐτῷ. Dative complement of ἐμβλέψασα. For ἐμβλέπω with a dative indicating the direction of the gaze, see also 10:21, 27.

λέγει. Pres act ind 3rd sg λέγω.

Καὶ σὺ μετὰ . . . τοῦ Ἰησοῦ. Clausal complement (direct discourse) of λέγει.

σύ. Nominative subject of ἦσθα.

μετὰ τοῦ Ναζαρηνοῦ. Association. On the identification of Jesus as Ναζαρηνός, see 10:47.

ἦσθα. Impf mid ind 2nd sg εἰμί. This is an old form, in Attic it was a perfect, but survives in later Greek as an alternate spelling for ἦς (see MHT 2:203). In the NT it occurs only here and in ‖ Matt 26:69. There are sixteen instances of ἦσθα in the LXX.

τοῦ Ἰησοῦ. Genitive in apposition to τοῦ Ναζαρηνοῦ.

14:68 ὁ δὲ ἠρνήσατο λέγων, Οὔτε οἶδα οὔτε ἐπίσταμαι σὺ τί λέγεις. καὶ ἐξῆλθεν ἔξω εἰς τὸ προαύλιον [καὶ ἀλέκτωρ ἐφώνησεν].

ὁ. Nominative subject of ἠρνήσατο. On the use of ὁ δέ to change subjects, see 1:45.

ἠρνήσατο. Aor mid ind 3rd sg ἀρνέομαι. Jesus' prediction of Peter's denial had used ἀπαρνέομαι (14:30); Mark's description of Peter's first denial (v. 68) uses ἀρνέομαι and the second denial uses ἀπαρνέομαι (v. 70), as does Peter's recollection of Jesus' statement following his third denial (v. 72). The two words are used interchangeably (cf. R. Brown, 1:599).

λέγων. Pres act ptc masc nom sg λέγω (means; redundant participle of speaking; see 1:7).

Οὔτε οἶδα οὔτε ἐπίσταμαι σὺ τί λέγεις. Clausal complement (direct discourse) of λέγων. Most English translations take this as a hendiadys used for emphasis, with σὺ τί λέγεις being taken as the object of both οἶδα and ἐπίσταμαι. Alternatively an object may be supplied from the context, either "him" (see GW and the translation above), or following the sense of the second half of the statement, "I don't know what you're talking about. I don't understand what you're saying" (CEB; cf. CEV). A third alternative is to leave the first verb hanging without an object, suggesting perhaps Peter's confusion and embarrassment: "I don't know . . . I don't understand what you are talking about" (GNB). Another alternative is suggested by the punctuation in WH mg., ἐπίσταμαι· σὺ τί λέγεις ("I don't understand. What are you saying?"), though Evans points out that "it is not likely that Peter would pose a counterquestion, only encouraging the maid servant to pursue the conversation" (2001, 464). V. Taylor comments that "Mark implies that Peter gave in substance a negative answer, but the actual reply is the confused utterance of a man taken suddenly at a loss" (573). This "confused utterance" extends even to "proper" grammatical standards since οὔτε . . . οὔτε is not supposed to be used to connect synonyms (BDF §445.2.2), but in the pressure of the moment it is surely understandable that Peter's reply would not reflect grammatical niceties (see also R. Brown, 1:600).

Οὔτε . . . οὔτε. A correlative construction: "neither . . . nor."

οἶδα. Prf act ind 1st sg οἶδα.

ἐπίσταμαι. Pres mid ind 1st sg ἐπίσταμαι.

σὺ τί λέγεις. Clausal complement of ἐπίσταμαι.

σύ. Nominative subject of λέγεις. "The unusual emphatic position of σύ (σὺ τί λέγεις . . .) admirably reflects affected astonishment" (Bruce, 444).

τί. Accusative direct object of λέγεις.

λέγεις. Pres act ind 2nd sg λέγω.

ἐξῆλθεν. Aor act ind 3rd sg ἐξέρχομαι.

εἰς τὸ προαύλιον. Spatial: "to the gateway."

[καὶ ἀλέκτωρ ἐφώνησεν]. The external evidence appears to favor its omission (א B L W Ψ* 579 892 *pc* it[c] syr[s] sa[mss] bo geo[1]), though there are significant internal considerations that make certainty difficult. Metzger explains that the UBS[4] committee decided that including the phrase in brackets was "the least unsatisfactory solution" (1994, 97).

ἀλέκτωρ. Nominative subject of ἐφώνησεν.

ἐφώνησεν. Aor act ind 3rd sg φωνέω.

14:69 καὶ ἡ παιδίσκη ἰδοῦσα αὐτὸν ἤρξατο πάλιν λέγειν τοῖς παρεστῶσιν ὅτι Οὗτος ἐξ αὐτῶν ἐστιν.

ἡ παιδίσκη. Nominative subject of ἤρξατο. The article may be anaphoric, referring to the same slave girl (Gundry, 920), which seems to be implied by the use of πάλιν later in the clause (but see below on πάλιν). The alternative is to take the article generically, allowing reference to a different person (so Duckwitz, 236, pointing to Matthew's statement, εἶδεν αὐτὸν ἄλλη).

ἰδοῦσα. Aor act ptc fem nom sg ὁράω.

αὐτόν. Accusative direct object of ἰδοῦσα.

ἤρξατο. Aor mid ind 3rd sg ἄρχω.

πάλιν. The adverb ("again") may indicate that this παιδίσκη was the same person as in verse 67 (see above), but it could also mean "in turn" (see BDAG.753.4), which would allow reference to a different person.

λέγειν. Pres act inf λέγω (complementary).

τοῖς παρεστῶσιν. Prf act ptc masc dat pl παρίστημι (substantival). Dative indirect object of λέγειν.

ὅτι. Introduces the clausal complement (direct discourse) of λέγειν (see 1:15).

Οὗτος. Nominative subject of ἐστίν.

ἐξ αὐτῶν. Partitive. ἐκ is "used w. εἶναι *belong to someone or someth.*" (BDAG, 297.4.a.δ); here, "this man is one of them."

ἐστιν. Pres act ind 3rd sg εἰμί.

14:70 ὁ δὲ πάλιν ἠρνεῖτο. καὶ μετὰ μικρὸν πάλιν οἱ παρεστῶτες ἔλεγον τῷ Πέτρῳ, Ἀληθῶς ἐξ αὐτῶν εἶ, καὶ γὰρ Γαλιλαῖος εἶ.

ὁ. Nominative subject of ἠρνεῖτο. On the use of ὁ δέ to change subjects, see 1:45.

πάλιν. The adverb marks Peter's second denial.

ἠρνεῖτο. Impf mid ind 3rd sg ἀρνέομαι. Lane (541 n. 151) thinks that the imperfect "suggests repeated denials," but Gundry counters that "verbs of speaking often take the imperfect tense to express the linearity of a single utterance rather than the iterativeness of multiple utterances" (920). Neither conclusion can be justified by appeal to the tense alone. Gundry's explanation, however, seems to fit better in the context since this is only a summary statement with no description added (contrast the details in both v. 68 and v. 70b).

μετὰ μικρὸν. Temporal: "after a little while" or "a little while later."

πάλιν. The adverb marks the third time that Peter has been challenged.

οἱ παρεστῶτες. Prf act ptc masc nom pl παρίστημι (substantival). Nominative subject of ἔλεγον. The plural indicates that although thus far Peter's accuser had been a παιδίσκη, now a group near the gateway makes the charge.

ἔλεγον. Impf act ind 3rd pl λέγω. On the possibility that this is an inceptive imperfect as in the ISV, see 1:21.

τῷ Πέτρῳ. Dative indirect object of ἔλεγον.

Ἀληθῶς ἐξ αὐτῶν εἶ, καὶ γὰρ Γαλιλαῖος εἶ. Clausal complement (direct discourse) of ἔλεγον.

ἐξ αὐτῶν. Partitive. ἐκ is "used w. εἶναι *belong to someone or someth.*" (BDAG, 297.4.a.δ, s.v. ἐκ); here, "you are one of them."

εἶ. Pres act ind 2nd sg εἰμί.

καὶ. Adverbial: "indeed."

γὰρ. Introduces a clause that explains why the bystanders are sure that Peter must be one of Jesus' followers.

Γαλιλαῖος. Predicate adjective. Matt 26:73 makes it explicit that Peter was recognizable by his dialect (ἀληθῶς καὶ σὺ ἐξ αὐτῶν εἶ, καὶ γὰρ ἡ λαλιά σου δῆλόν σε ποιεῖ), as do later Byzantine mss by adding ἡ λαλιά σου ὁμοιάζει here.

εἶ. Pres act ind 2nd sg εἰμί.

14:71 ὁ δὲ ἤρξατο ἀναθεματίζειν καὶ ὀμνύναι ὅτι Οὐκ οἶδα τὸν ἄνθρωπον τοῦτον ὃν λέγετε.

ὁ. Nominative subject of ἤρξατο. On the use of ὁ δέ to change subjects, see 1:45.

ἤρξατο. Aor mid ind 3rd sg ἄρχω.

ἀναθεματίζειν. Pres act inf ἀναθεματίζω (complementary). BDAG maintains that "ἤρξατο ἀναθεματίζειν καὶ ὀμνύναι means that Peter put himself under curses and took oaths in the course of his denial" (63.b). France (622), however, presents a strong argument that the verb here should be understood to mean that Peter cursed Jesus, not himself. The verb is transitive (BDAG lists only the present instance as intransitive) and means to curse someone else. In the dozen uses in the LXX it is almost always the equivalent of *hērem*, and as a transitive verb is followed by an accusative specifying what is cursed (e.g., Num 21:2, ἀναθεματιῶ αὐτὸν καὶ τὰς πόλεις αὐτοῦ). The only other NT uses (Acts 23:12, 14, 21) add ἑαυτοῦ in each instance to specify that the word is being used reflexively. If this verb is used consistently, then an understood object would need to be supplied in the present passage. "In this context the natural object to be understood is Jesus, so that Mark portrays Peter as voluntarily doing what Pliny was later informed that 'real Christians' could not be compelled to do (Pliny, *Ep.* 10.96.5), cursing Jesus. This understanding of the text, which Christian interpreters naturally find unwelcome (hence translations such as RSV, NIV), is the most probable sense of Marks' words, though he has avoided too blatant offense by leaving the object of the verb unstated" (France, 622).

ὀμνύναι. Pres act inf ὀμνύω (complementary). See also ἀναθεματίζειν above.

ὅτι. Introduces the clausal complement (direct discourse) of ἀναθεματίζειν καὶ ὀμνύναι (see 1:15). Alternatively, this might be understood as two separate statements: "he began to curse" and "he swore, 'I do not know. . . .'"

οἶδα. Prf act ind 1st sg οἶδα.

τὸν ἄνθρωπον τοῦτον. Accusative direct object of οἶδα.

ὄν. Accusative direct object of λέγετε.

λέγετε. Pres act ind 2nd pl λέγω. The accusative relative pronoun indicates what is being talked about. BDAG (588.a.b.β) suggests translating τὸν ἄνθρωπον τοῦτον ὃν λέγετε "this man whom you mean."

14:72 καὶ εὐθὺς ἐκ δευτέρου ἀλέκτωρ ἐφώνησεν. καὶ ἀνεμνήσθη ὁ Πέτρος τὸ ῥῆμα ὡς εἶπεν αὐτῷ ὁ Ἰησοῦς ὅτι Πρὶν ἀλέκτορα φωνῆσαι δὶς τρίς με ἀπαρνήσῃ· καὶ ἐπιβαλὼν ἔκλαιεν.

καὶ εὐθὺς. See 1:10.

ἐκ δευτέρου. Temporal: "a second time." A few mss (ℵ C*vid L 579 pc itᶜ vgᵐˢ) omit this phrase.

ἀλέκτωρ. Nominative subject of ἐφώνησεν.

ἐφώνησεν. Aor act ind 3rd sg φωνέω.

ἀνεμνήσθη. Aor mid ind 3rd sg ἀναμιμνήσκω. This is a "θη middle" form, not passive (see 2:2).

ὁ Πέτρος. Nominative subject of ἀνεμνήσθη.

τὸ ῥῆμα. Accusative direct object of ἀνεμνήσθη.

ὡς. This is not the usual comparative ὡς; rather it is "practically equivalent to ὅ" (BDAG, 1104.1.b.β). Birdsall (272–75; following Kühner's *Grammatik*) has argued in some detail that this is an idiom of long standing (traceable to Homer), "unusual but not unidiomatic" (275), in which ὡς is used rather than the relative when the reference is not just to a statement per se, but an entire situation. "We should then interpret Mk. xiv. 72 to refer not to a simple recollection on Peter's part of the words of a prediction made by Jesus so shortly before, but the flooding back into his mind at the cockcrow, of the whole situation described for us in Mk. xiv. 17-31" (274). This may be valid, but caution should be used to avoid overexegeting the text.

εἶπεν. Aor act ind 3rd sg λέγω.

αὐτῷ. Dative indirect object of εἶπεν.

ὁ Ἰησοῦς. Nominative subject of εἶπεν.

ὅτι. Introduces the clausal complement (direct discourse) of εἶπεν (see 1:15).

ἀλέκτορα. Accusative subject of the infinitive φωνῆσαι.

φωνῆσαι. Aor act inf φωνέω. Used with πρίν the infinitive introduces an event that is subsequent to the action of the main verb (see also on 14:30).

με. Accusative direct object of ἀπαρνήσῃ.

ἀπαρνήσῃ. Fut mid ind 2nd sg ἀπαρνέομαι.

ἐπιβαλών. Aor act ptc masc nom sg ἐπιβάλλω (temporal). Swete concludes that "on the whole it must be confessed that the word remains one of the unsolved enigmas of Mc.'s vocabulary" (366). R. Brown (1:609–10) lists nine proposed solutions. It might be taken as a synonym of ἤρξατο, and so mean "he began to weep" (also LN 68.5). The variant reading ἤρξατο κλαίειν (D Θ 565) makes this meaning explicit. Or it might be a mental term: "and he thought of it," or "when he reflected on it" (Gould, 281; LN 30.7, and HCSB). It has also been equated with ἀποκριθείς; thus perhaps, "responding." All these options are noted in BDAG, though the conclusion given there is that "prob. Mk intends the reader to understand a wild gesture connected with lamentation" (368.1) and that the "NRSV ('he broke down and wept') capture[s] the sense" (cf. NIV, ESV, NET). The translation note in the NET suggests another option: "Grk 'he wept deeply.'" The marginal note in the NASB includes several options: "*Or Thinking of this, he began weeping or Rushing out, he began weeping.*" Moulton (MHT 1:131–32) takes it to mean "he set to" (i.e., "he began") as a description of the "initial paroxysm" of Peter's outburst of grief (see also BDF §308, s.v. βάλλειν). Perhaps we are to think of something to the effect, "throwing up his arms" or even "throwing himself out on the ground." "Mark's choice of idiom must remain obscure, but the essential sense is not in doubt: Peter's bold denials give way to remorse as he realises that he has fallen into precisely the trap of which Jesus had warned him" (France, 623).

ἔκλαιεν. Impf act ind 3rd sg κλαίω. On the possibility that this is an inceptive imperfect as in the NASB and HCSB, see 1:21 (though such a translation has been defended through reference to ἐπιβαλών).

Mark 15:1-5

¹So early in the morning the chief priests, having taken counsel with the elders and scribes and the whole Sanhedrin, (and) having bound Jesus, led (him) out and handed (him) over to Pilate. ²Then Pilate asked him, "Are you the King of the Jews?" And answering,

he said, "(That is what) you say." ³So the chief priests accused him
of many things. ⁴Then Pilate asked him again, "Are you going to
answer nothing? Listen! They are accusing you of many things."
⁵But Jesus made no further reply, so that Pilate was amazed.

**15:1 Καὶ εὐθὺς πρωῒ συμβούλιον ποιήσαντες οἱ ἀρχιερεῖς μετὰ τῶν
πρεσβυτέρων καὶ γραμματέων καὶ ὅλον τὸ συνέδριον, δήσαντες
τὸν Ἰησοῦν ἀπήνεγκαν καὶ παρέδωκαν Πιλάτῳ.**

καὶ εὐθὺς. See 1:10.

πρωῒ. Adverb ("early in the morning") modifying ἀπήνεγκαν καὶ
παρέδωκαν. This adverb also occurs in 1:35; 11:20; 13:35; and 16:2,
about half the NT uses.

συμβούλιον. Accusative direct object of ποιήσαντες.

ποιήσαντες. Aor act ptc masc nom pl ποιέω (temporal, referring
to the decision reached during the night). This statement reca-
pitulates the previous report of the night session, and is necessary
"because Mark interrupted his narrative of the Sanhedrin session to
tell of Peter's denials" (R. Brown, 1:631).

οἱ ἀρχιερεῖς. Nominative subject of ἀπήνεγκαν.

μετὰ τῶν πρεσβυτέρων καὶ γραμματέων καὶ ὅλον τὸ συνέδριον.
Association. The use of μετά may, however, indicate that the priests
are calling the shots (so France, 626). The final καί is ascensive, "*even*
all the Sanhedrin," which was comprised of ἀρχιερεῖς, πρεσβύτεροι,
and γραμματεῖς. The modifier ὅλον cannot be pressed to mean that
every single member was present and agreed with the decision. The
description of Joseph in verse 43 makes it highly unlikely that he
would be party to such an action. More likely, ὅλον refers either to
a substantial majority of the Sanhedrin or to all of those present at
the time.

δήσαντες. Aor act ptc masc nom pl δέω (temporal). Gundry,
suggests that the participle should be understood causatively, since
"the Sanhedrin will have their servants bind Jesus before delivering
him to Pilate themselves" (920). Although that may be the nature of
the case, it cannot be substantiated by the form or lexis (causative
verbs are typically –οω forms) of the participle. Active voice verbs
may be used in contexts in which it is clear that the subject is ultimately responsible, though not necessarily the immediate agent of
the action (Smyth §1711; Wallace 1996, 411), but this is not grammaticalized in the verb form itself.

τὸν Ἰησοῦν. Accusative direct object of δήσαντες.

ἀπήνεγκαν. Aor act ind 3rd pl ἀποφέρω. The use of (ἀπο)φέρω rather than a form of ἄγω may not be "stronger" (contra Gundry, 923), since there is a wide variety of compound forms of ἄγω and φέρω that are often used in similar contexts (note the listings in LN in and near domain 15.177). There are not many instances of ἀποφέρω in the NT (only 6, and only here in Mark), but usage outside the NT evidences a wider range of usage than might be expected from NT usage alone (see BDAG, 124; LSJ, 226).

παρέδωκαν. Aor act ind 3rd pl παραδίδωμι. Jesus was "handed over" as foretold in 9:31 and 10:33 (both texts also use παραδίδωμι); the same word occurs again with reference to Jesus' condemnation and death in 15:10, 15. On the meaning and use of παραδίδωμι in Mark, see 1:14 and 3:19.

Πιλάτῳ. Dative indirect object of παρέδωκαν.

15:2 καὶ ἐπηρώτησεν αὐτὸν ὁ Πιλᾶτος, Σὺ εἶ ὁ βασιλεὺς τῶν Ἰουδαίων; ὁ δὲ ἀποκριθεὶς αὐτῷ λέγει, Σὺ λέγεις.

ἐπηρώτησεν. Aor act ind 3rd sg ἐπερωτάω. On ἐπερωτάω versus the simple form ἐρωτάω, see 4:10.

αὐτὸν. Accusative direct object of ἐπηρώτησεν.

ὁ Πιλᾶτος. Nominative subject of ἐπηρώτησεν.

Σὺ εἶ ὁ βασιλεὺς τῶν Ἰουδαίων. Clausal complement (direct discourse) of ἐπηρώτησεν.

Σὺ. Nominative subject of εἶ. The use of the pronoun σύ with a second singular verb is always emphatic, but the exact nature of the emphasis may vary. It may be that it is "disdainful" (Gould, 283) or reflects "a touch of mockery, perhaps suggesting that Pilate had anticipated meeting someone more impressive" (Evans 2001, 478). Or it may reflect the formal, legal nature of the inquiry. Alternatively, Stein thinks "it is best to interpret this as a straightforward question" (2008, 699). Straightforward it may be, but that does not resolve the question as to why σύ is used in the first place. Stein is correct, however, that any tone of mockery must come from the context, not simply from the presence of σύ.

εἶ. Pres act ind 2nd sg εἰμί.

ὁ βασιλεὺς. Predicate nominative.

τῶν Ἰουδαίων. The genitive indicates the subjects over whom ὁ βασιλεύς reigns.

ὁ. Nominative subject of λέγει. On the use of ὁ δέ to change subjects, see 1:45.

ἀποκριθεὶς. Aor pass ptc masc nom sg ἀποκρίνομαι (means;

redundant participle of speaking; see also 1:7). On this intransitive, "θη middle" form, see 3:33.

αὐτῷ. Dative indirect object of λέγει.

λέγει. Pres act ind 3rd sg λέγω.

Σὺ λέγεις. Clausal complement (direct discourse) of λέγει. The same expression occurs in ‖ Matt 27:11; Luke 23:3 (see also Matt 26:25; Luke 22:70; John 18:37). Whether this is a clear "yes," an intentionally ambiguous reply, or possibly even a denial, is debatable. Collins (713) describes it as ambiguous and evasive. Gundry suggests that Jesus' answer "simultaneously admits 'the king of the Jews' as a given designation . . . and rejects the phrase as a self-designation" (924). Perhaps more satisfactory is R. Brown's explanation: "The connotation is that what has been phrased as a question is true; yet the one who phrased it must take responsibility for it—in this case, must take responsibility for any political interpretation that would have Jesus overthrowing the Roman administration of Judea" (1:733; see Gundry's extended discussion of other interpretations of this phrase (932–33); see also the bibliography in BDAG, 590.2.e, s.v. λέγω; 286.1.a, s.v. εἶπον). The translation above is intended to be noncommittal on this exegetical issue.

Σὺ. Nominative subject of λέγεις.

λέγεις. Pres act ind 2nd sg λέγω. In this idiomatic expression (σὺ λέγεις), λέγω must mean something like "maintain, declare, proclaim," with the idiom meaning "(that is what) you maintain" (BDAG, 590.2.e, s.v. λέγω).

15:3 καὶ κατηγόρουν αὐτοῦ οἱ ἀρχιερεῖς πολλά.

κατηγόρουν. Impf act ind 3rd pl κατηγορέω. This verb is used nearly always as a legal technical term: "bring charges in court" (BDAG, 533.1). On the possibility that this is an inceptive imperfect as in the HCSB and NET, see 1:21. In this instance the imperfect is probably used to give background information explaining why Pilate interrogated Jesus as he did; the initial accusation must have preceded the interrogation to prompt Pilate's opening question (thus making an inceptive statement unlikely). Were it not for πάλιν and πόσα in verse 4 one might be justified in assuming that κατηγόρουν referred only to the initial charges.

αὐτοῦ. Genitive direct object of κατηγόρουν. When both a genitive and an accusative are used with κατηγορέω the genitive denotes the person charged and the accusative the charge that is made. Only here and in verse 4 does κατηγορέω occur in the NT with both, but the pattern is clear when the genitive (e.g., 3:2; Luke 6:7; 23:10; John 5:45 [2×]; Acts 24:8; 25:5, 11) or the accusative occurs alone (e.g., Acts 22:30; 26:19). The only exceptions involve an infinitive (Matt 27:12) and Rev 12:10 (where the person accused occurs in the accusative; the grammatical peculiarities of Revelation may be adequate to explain this instance).

οἱ ἀρχιερεῖς. Nominative subject of κατηγόρουν.

πολλά. Accusative complement of κατηγόρουν (see αὐτοῦ above; R. Brown, 1:734; France, 629 n. 13; Stein 2008, 699–700; contra Gundry, 924, 933; MHT 2:446; and Hawkins, 29, who take πολλά to be adverbial ["accused him much"], which seems to ignore the typical pattern of case usage with κατηγορέω described above).

15:4 ὁ δὲ Πιλᾶτος πάλιν ἐπηρώτα αὐτὸν λέγων, Οὐκ ἀποκρίνῃ οὐδέν; ἴδε πόσα σου κατηγοροῦσιν.

ὁ . . . Πιλᾶτος. Nominative subject of ἐπηρώτα. The use of δέ is due to the change in subjects (Jesus in v. 3, Pilate in v. 4; see 1:45). There is a higher than average concentration of this use in 15:2-16.

πάλιν. The use of πάλιν, followed by Pilate's second question, and the use of πόσα (corresponding to πολλά in v. 3), make it clear that the charges leveled against Jesus were extended after Jesus' initial reply to Pilate.

ἐπηρώτα. Impf act ind 3rd sg ἐπερωτάω. On ἐπερωτάω versus the simple form ἐρωτάω, see 4:10. The verb should not be understood as conative (contra R. Brown, 1:734, "tried to question"), since a question can be asked whether there is a response or not.

αὐτόν. Accusative direct object of ἐπηρώτα.

λέγων. Pres act ptc masc nom sg λέγω (means; redundant participle of speaking; see 1:7 and 3:33).

Οὐκ ἀποκρίνῃ οὐδέν; ἴδε πόσα σου κατηγοροῦσιν. Clausal complement (direct discourse) of ἐπηρώτα . . . λέγων. The second clause of the complement is an indirect question introduced by πόσα.

ἀποκρίνῃ. Pres mid ind 2nd sg ἀποκρίνομαι. On this intransitive, "θη middle" form, see 3:33.

οὐδέν. Accusative direct object of ἀποκρίνῃ.

Ἴδε. See 3:34.

Πόσα. Accusative complement of κατηγοροῦσιν (see v. 3 on αὐτοῦ). πόσος is a correlative interrogative pronoun used in both direct and indirect questions (BDAG, 855–56); here it expresses quantity, "how many things?" (BDAG, 856, 2.b.α), as part of an indirect question.

σου. Genitive direct object of κατηγοροῦσιν (see v. 3 on αὐτοῦ).
κατηγοροῦσιν. Pres act ind 3rd pl κατηγορέω.

15:5 ὁ δὲ Ἰησοῦς οὐκέτι οὐδὲν ἀπεκρίθη, ὥστε θαυμάζειν τὸν Πιλᾶτον.

ὁ . . . Ἰησοῦς. Nominative subject of ἀπεκρίθη. On the use of δέ, see verse 4.

οὐκέτι. The double negative is awkward to put into English; formally it reads, "Jesus no longer answered nothing."

οὐδὲν. Accusative direct object of ἀπεκρίθη.

ἀπεκρίθη. Aor mid ind 3rd sg ἀποκρίνομαι. This is a "θη middle" form, not passive (see 2:2 and 3:33).

θαυμάζειν. Pres act inf θαυμάζω. Used with ὥστε to indicate result. On the semantics of the verb, see also 1:22 on ἐκπλήσσω.

τὸν Πιλᾶτον. Accusative subject of θαυμάζειν.

Mark 15:6-15

[6]Now at the feast (Pilate) would release one prisoner for them whom they requested. [7]But the one called Barabbas was imprisoned with the rebels who had committed murder during the riot. [8]And coming up, the crowd began to ask (that he should do) as he customarily did for them. [9]So Pilate answered them, "Do you want me to release the King of the Jews for you?" [10]For he knew that the chief priests had handed him over because of envy. [11]But the chief priests incited the crowd that he should rather release Barabbas for them. [12]So Pilate responded to them again, "What, then, do you want me to do with [the one whom you call] 'The King of the Jews'?" [13]But they cried out again, "Crucify him!" [14]Then Pilate said to them, "Why? What crime has he committed?" But they cried even louder, "Crucify him!" [15]So Pilate, because he wanted to satisfy the crowd, released Barabbas to them and handed over Jesus, having flogged (him), to be crucified.

15:6 Κατὰ δὲ ἑορτὴν ἀπέλυεν αὐτοῖς ἕνα δέσμιον ὃν παρῃτοῦντο.

Κατὰ δέ ἑορτὴν. Distributive, "at each celebration of this festival" (Gundry, 925). Here, ἑορτήν refers to the Passover and/or Feast of Unleavened Bread. The use of δέ reflects the shift in topic at this point; the narrative moves from Pilate's interrogation of Jesus to the sentencing.

ἀπέλυεν. Impf act ind 3rd sg ἀπολύω. The imperfect once again sets up the scene about to unfold beginning in verse 8 by providing explanatory background information to enable the reader to understand the request presented to Pilate by the crowd in verse 7. The statement may be customary, but that is based largely on the distributive sense of κατά along with the context.

αὐτοῖς. Dative indirect object of ἀπέλυεν. The referent of the pronoun is not explicit, though it becomes clear in verse 8 that it refers to ὁ ὄχλος.

ἕνα δέσμιον. Accusative direct object of ἀπέλυεν.

ὅν. Accusative direct object of παρῃτοῦντο.

παρῃτοῦντο. Impf mid ind 3rd pl παραιτέομαι.

15:7 ἦν δὲ ὁ λεγόμενος Βαραββᾶς μετὰ τῶν στασιαστῶν δεδεμένος οἵτινες ἐν τῇ στάσει φόνον πεποιήκεισαν.

Verse 7 is somewhat parenthetical, since it interrupts the flow of antecedents from verse 6 to verse 8. Pilate is the referent in verses 6 and 8 despite the mention of Barabbas in verse 7.

ἦν. Impf act ind 3rd sg εἰμί.

δέ. The conjunction δέ moves from the general (prisoners, v. 6) to the specific (Barabbas).

ὁ λεγόμενος. Pres pass ptc masc nom sg λέγω (substantival). Nominative subject of the periphrastic ἦν . . . δεδεμένος. Cranfield (449–50) suggests that "the only other place in the N.T. where ὁ λεγόμενος is used in an exactly analogous way seems to be Lk. xxii. 47. Elsewhere it is used to attach a title or alternative name to a personal name already mentioned (e.g. Mt. xxvii. 22) or to attach a name to a common name or equivalent (e.g. Mt. xxvi. 3, Jn ix. 11). So while (in view of Lk. xxii. 47) this expression cannot be called impossible, it is certainly unusual."

Βαραββᾶς. Complement in a subject-complement double nominative construction. The name Barabbas is Aramaic, "son of the father."

μετὰ τῶν στασιαστῶν. Association.

στασιαστῶν. The term στασιαστής refers to "a factious pers. who causes public discord, *rebel, revolutionary*" (BDAG, 940); only here in the NT, and not at all in the LXX. It is quite common, however, in Josephus (more than 70 times). Barabbas is also called a λῃστής in John 18:40, as are the two men crucified with Jesus in Mark 15:27. Neither στασιαστής nor λῃστής are to be identified with the Zealots or Sicarii or other revolutionary groups (see R. Brown, 1:688–92).

δεδεμένος. Prf pass ptc masc nom sg δέω (stative periphrastic with ἦν, functionally equivalent to a pluperfect finite form).

οἵτινες. Nominative subject of πεποιήκεισαν. The plural οἵτινες and πεποιήκεισαν refer to the group of rebels (τῶν στασιαστῶν) with whom Barabbas was associated.

ἐν τῇ στάσει. Temporal. Although στάσις can be used positively to refer to either "standing, existence, occurrence" or negatively to "uprising, revolt, riot," the related verb στασιάζω has only the negative sense "to rebel," as does the noun στασιαστής used just above.

φόνον. Accusative direct object of πεποιήκεισαν.

πεποιήκεισαν. Plprf act ind 3rd pl ποιέω. The augment has dropped off the pluperfect form as is common in Koine usage.

15:8 καὶ ἀναβὰς ὁ ὄχλος ἤρξατο αἰτεῖσθαι καθὼς ἐποίει αὐτοῖς.

ἀναβὰς. Aor act ptc masc nom sg ἀναβαίνω (temporal or perhaps attendant circumstance). The prefixed ἀνά might refer to Pilate's location as geographically elevated, but it may be that ἀναβαίνω means simply "to arrive" (France, 631; cf. BDAG, 58.1.a.α, "of movement in a direction without special focus on making an ascent").

ὁ ὄχλος. Nominative subject of ἤρξατο.

ἤρξατο. Aor mid ind 3rd sg ἄρχω.

αἰτεῖσθαι. Pres mid inf αἰτέω (complementary).

καθὼς ἐποίει αὐτοῖς. Clausal complement (indirect discourse) of αἰτεῖσθαι. As BDAG explains, "the accompanying clause is somet[imes] to be supplied fr[om] the context: . . . ἤρξατο αἰτεῖσθαι (ἵνα ποιήσῃ αὐτοῖς) κ. ἐποίει αὐτοῖς *as he was accustomed to do for them* Mk 15:8" (493.1, s.v. καθώς). Or as France suggests, "in Mark's compressed syntax the imperfect ἐποίει of the subordinate clause does duty also for the object of the request: 'to do as he always did for them'" (632).

ἐποίει. Impf act ind 3rd sg ποιέω. Mark has already told his readers that the crowd presented such a request every year at Passover (v. 6; see also Matt 27:15). An imperfect verb is common in such statements of customary activity (cf. Matt 26:55, ἐκαθεζόμην; John 21:18, ἐζώννυες; Acts 3:2, ἐτίθουν).

αὐτοῖς. Dative of advantage.

15:9 ὁ δὲ Πιλᾶτος ἀπεκρίθη αὐτοῖς λέγων, Θέλετε ἀπολύσω ὑμῖν τὸν βασιλέα τῶν Ἰουδαίων;

ὁ . . . Πιλᾶτος. Nominative subject of ἀπεκρίθη. On the use of δέ, see verse 4.

ἀπεκρίθη. Aor mid ind 3rd sg ἀποκρίνομαι. On this intransitive, "θη middle" form, see 3:33.

αὐτοῖς. Dative indirect object of ἀπεκρίθη.

λέγων. Pres act ptc masc nom sg λέγω (means; redundant participle of speaking; see 1:7).

Θέλετε ἀπολύσω . . . τῶν Ἰουδαίων. Clausal complement (direct discourse) of λέγων.

θέλετε. Pres act ind 2nd pl θέλω. One might expect the following subjunctive clause to be introduced by ἵνα, but a recognized pattern was to omit the conjunction when θέλω is second person and the following subjunctive is first person, i.e., "when the relations of the verbs are such as to make a Deliberative Subjunctive probable" (Burton §171; see also MHT 2:421.4.b.β). This pattern is consistent in the NT: Matt 13:28; 20:32; 26:17; 27:17, 21; Mark 10:36, 51; 14:12; 15:9, 12; Luke 9:54; 18:41; 22:9. The use of ἵνα is not unknown, but it is rare in this situation (e.g., *Hist. Rech.* 7:13, τί θέλεις ἵνα ποιήσωμέν σοι).

ἀπολύσω ὑμῖν τὸν βασιλέα τῶν Ἰουδαίων. An embedded indirect question functioning as the clausal complement of θέλετε: "Do you want (that) I should release . . . ?"

ἀπολύσω. Aor act subj 1st sg ἀπολύω (deliberative subjunctive in an indirect question).

ὑμῖν. Dative of advantage.

τὸν βασιλέα. Accusative direct object of ἀπολύσω.

τῶν Ἰουδαίων. The genitive indicates the subjects over whom ὁ βασιλεύς reigns.

15:10 ἐγίνωσκεν γὰρ ὅτι διὰ φθόνον παραδεδώκεισαν αὐτὸν οἱ ἀρχιερεῖς.

ἐγίνωσκεν. Impf act ind 3rd sg γινώσκω. Imperfect verbs are often used in explanatory statements that are off the storyline; the tense here does not suggest that "it gradually dawned on [Pilate]" (Bruce, 447) nor that "Pilate had the knowledge for a while" (R. Brown, 1:801).

γὰρ. The subordinating conjunction introduces a clause that explains why Pilate asked the preceding question.

ὅτι. Introduces the clausal complement (indirect discourse) of a verb of mental perception (ἐγίνωσκεν).

διὰ φθόνον. Causal.

παραδεδώκεισαν. Plprf act ind 3rd pl παραδίδωμι. The augment has dropped off as is common in Koine usage. The more remote pluperfect is used instead of the perfect because it occurs in an explanatory statement. Normally the tense of the original is retained in indirect discourse, but McKay (1981, 323 n. 84; 306 n. 31) suggests that this is an instance in which the tense is shifted from perfect to pluperfect. This is an instance in which the subject is responsible for the state or condition described by a transitive, active verb (see McKay 1994 §3.4.5; 1981, 296–97; and *TDM*, 110, 232–33 n. 109). On the meaning and use of παραδίδωμι in Mark, see 1:14 and 3:19.

αὐτόν. Accusative direct object of παραδεδώκεισαν.

οἱ ἀρχιερεῖς. Nominative subject of παραδεδώκεισαν.

15:11 οἱ δὲ ἀρχιερεῖς ἀνέσεισαν τὸν ὄχλον ἵνα μᾶλλον τὸν Βαραββᾶν ἀπολύσῃ αὐτοῖς.

οἱ ... ἀρχιερεῖς. Nominative subject of ἀνέσεισαν. On the use of δέ, see verse 4.

ἀνέσεισαν. Aor act ind 3rd pl ἀνασείω ("to stir up, incite," BDAG, 71).

τὸν ὄχλον. Accusative direct object of ἀνέσεισαν.

ἵνα. Introduces a content clause indicating what it was that the chief priests were inciting the crowd to demand.

ἀπολύσῃ. Aor act subj 3rd sg ἀπολύω. Subjunctive with ἵνα.

αὐτοῖς. Dative of advantage. On the use of plural forms with ὄχλος in Mark, see 5:21.

15:12 ὁ δὲ Πιλᾶτος πάλιν ἀποκριθεὶς ἔλεγεν αὐτοῖς, Τί οὖν [θέλετε] ποιήσω [ὃν λέγετε] τὸν βασιλέα τῶν Ἰουδαίων;

ὁ ... Πιλᾶτος. Nominative subject of ἔλεγεν. On the use of δέ, see verse 4.

πάλιν. "Again" because Pilate has already addressed them in this regard (v. 9).

ἀποκριθεὶς. Aor mid ptc masc nom sg ἀποκρίνομαι (means; redundant participle of speaking; see 1:7). On this intransitive, "θη middle" form, see 3:33.

ἔλεγεν. Impf act ind 3rd sg λέγω.

αὐτοῖς. Dative indirect object of ἔλεγεν. The antecedent is apparently the crowd (τὸν ὄχλον in v. 11), not the chief priests.

Τί οὖν [θέλετε] ... τῶν Ἰουδαίων. Clausal complement (direct discourse) of ἔλεγεν.

Τί. Accusative direct object of ποιήσω.

θέλετε. Pres act ind 2nd pl θέλω.

ποιήσω [ὃν λέγετε] τὸν βασιλέα τῶν Ἰουδαίων. Clausal complement of θέλετε.

ποιήσω. Aor act subj 1st sg ποιέω (deliberative subjunctive). Here the sense is "to do to/with" (BDAG, 841.4). On the lack of a ἵνα, see the discussion of the syntactical pattern in 15:9.

[ὃν λέγετε] τὸν βασιλέα τῶν Ἰουδαίων. Clausal complement of ποιήσω with ὃν λέγετε.

ὅν. Accusative direct object of λέγετε. Matthew's construction (27:22) is similar, though substituting the name for the pronoun and a synonymous expression for the complement: Τί οὖν ποιήσω Ἰησοῦν τὸν λεγόμενον Χριστόν.

λέγετε. Pres act ind 2nd pl λέγω. In this context the verb means "to call, name" (BDAG, 590.4). In placing these words in the mouth of the crowd (second person), Pilate does not say that Jesus is such a king, but only that they have used that appellation. He may, in doing so, be mocking them. In Mark's account neither the crowd nor the chief priests have so designated Jesus, but that the religious leaders have accused him of claiming to be a king is implied in Pilate's question in 15:2. Luke 23:2 confirms that this was, indeed, one of the charges leveled against Jesus.

τὸν βασιλέα τῶν Ἰουδαίων. Accusative complement in an object-complement double accusative construction with ὃν λέγετε, or accusative of respect without ὃν λέγετε.

τῶν Ἰουδαίων. The genitive indicates those over whom the king reigns.

15:13 οἱ δὲ πάλιν ἔκραξαν, Σταύρωσον αὐτόν.

οἱ. Nominative subject of ἔκραξαν. On the use of οἱ δέ to change subjects, see 1:45.

πάλιν. BDAG notes that "a special difficulty is presented by Mk 15:13, where the first outcry of the crowd is reported w. the words οἱ δὲ πάλιν ἔκραξεν" (753.5). Five possible explanations are discussed in BDAG: (1) δὲ πάλιν may be a connective [perhaps "then"]; (2) a different source was used; (3) πάλιν may mean "back," i.e., they shouted back to Pilate (so R. Brown, 1:824); (4) it is, indeed, a second cry, the first being reflected in verse 8 (ὁ ὄχλος ἤρξατο αἰτεῖσθαι); or (5) πάλιν might mean "in turn" (BDAG's meaning #4; also Cranfield, 451, "thereupon"). Since alternative 4 allows πάλιν to be taken in its usual sense of "again," and there is insufficient data to make the alternatives more plausible, I am inclined to say that Mark does, indeed, refer to a second cry even though a preceding cry has not been explicitly mentioned. Gundry comments that "'But again they yelled' implies that the crowd's previous request for Pilate to release Barabbas took the form of yelling . . . not that they have previously yelled for Jesus' crucifixion as now they do" (928). This also has the effect of clarifying that the antecedent of οἱ δέ is the crowd, not the chief priests (so Gundry, 938).

ἔκραξαν. Aor act ind 3rd pl κράζω.

Σταύρωσον αὐτόν. Clausal complement (direct discourse) of ἔκραξαν.

σταύρωσον. Aor act impv 2nd sg σταυρόω. Stein (2008, 701) points out that this is the first specific reference to the form of Jesus' death as crucifixion, with previous references using ἀπόλλυμι (e.g., 3:6), ἀποκτείνω (8:31), κατακρίνω θανάτῳ (10:33), and θανατόω (14:55).

αὐτόν. Accusative direct object of σταύρωσον.

15:14 ὁ δὲ Πιλᾶτος ἔλεγεν αὐτοῖς, Τί γὰρ ἐποίησεν κακόν; οἱ δὲ περισσῶς ἔκραξαν, Σταύρωσον αὐτόν.

ὁ . . . Πιλᾶτος. Nominative subject of ἔλεγεν. On the use of δέ, see verse 4.

ἔλεγεν. Impf act ind 3rd sg λέγω. There is no indication in the context that Pilate was "continually saying . . . [revealing] a sustained effort on his part to release Jesus" (Stein 2008, 702). To base this simply on a claim that ἔλεγεν is an inceptive imperfect (as does Stein) is unjustified.

αὐτοῖς. Dative indirect object of ἔλεγεν. The referent is the crowd (οἱ δέ, v. 13, refers back to αὐτοῖς in v. 12 and to τὸν ὄχλον in v. 11), not the chief priests.

Τί γὰρ ἐποίησεν κακόν. Clausal complement (direct discourse) of ἔλεγεν.

Τί γάρ. This expression, "often in questions, where the English idiom leaves the word untranslated, adds *then, pray,* or prefixes *what!* or *why!* to the question . . . Esp. τίς γάρ; τί γάρ; in direct questions" (BDAG, 189.1.f, s.v. γάρ). The translation suggested for this text is "Why, what crime has he committed?"

Τί . . . κακόν. Accusative direct object of ἐποίησεν.

ἐποίησεν. Aor act ind 3rd sg ποιέω.

οἱ. Nominative subject of ἔκραξαν. On the use of οἱ δέ, see 1:45.

περισσῶς. The adverb is used as a comparative; with κράζω, "even louder" (BDAG, 806).

ἔκραξαν. Aor act ind 3rd pl κράζω.

σταύρωσον. Aor act impv 2nd sg σταυρόω.

αὐτόν. Accusative direct object of σταύρωσον.

15:15 ὁ δὲ Πιλᾶτος βουλόμενος τῷ ὄχλῳ τὸ ἱκανὸν ποιῆσαι ἀπέλυσεν αὐτοῖς τὸν Βαραββᾶν, καὶ παρέδωκεν τὸν Ἰησοῦν φραγελλώσας ἵνα σταυρωθῇ.

ὁ . . . Πιλᾶτος. Nominative subject of ἀπέλυσεν. On the use of δέ, see verse 4.

βουλόμενος. Pres mid ptc masc nom sg βούλομαι (causal).

τῷ ὄχλῳ. Dative of advantage with τὸ ἱκανὸν ποιῆσαι.

τὸ ἱκανὸν ποιῆσαι. On the possible use of a Latin idiom, *satisfacere alicui*, "to satisfy," see 4:21 and BDAG (472.1, s.v. ἱκανόν), BDF (§5.3.b), and Gundry (938). MHT (1:20–21) give the general form of the idiom as ποιεῖν τὸ ἱκανόν, clarifying that the article goes with ἱκανόν, not the infinitive. Formally, "to do/make the sufficiency," thus, "to satisfy," "to do someone a favor," or "to grant the request," with the dative indicating who is satisfied/favored/granted.

τὸ ἱκανὸν. Accusative direct object of ποιῆσαι.

ποιῆσαι. Aor act inf ποιέω (complementary).

ἀπέλυσεν. Aor act ind 3rd sg ἀπολύω.

αὐτοῖς. Dative of advantage.

τὸν Βαραββᾶν. Accusative direct object of ἀπέλυσεν.

παρέδωκεν. Aor act ind 3rd sg παραδίδωμι. On the meaning and use of παραδίδωμι in Mark, see 1:14 and 3:19 (see also 15:1).

τὸν Ἰησοῦν. Accusative direct object of παρέδωκεν.

φραγελλώσας. Aor act ptc masc nom sg φραγελλόω (temporal; "to flog, scourge, whip"). This is a Latin loanword (see 4:21 on ὑπὸ τὸν μόδιον . . . ἢ ὑπὸ τὴν κλίνην) from *flagello* (BDAG, 1064). See the extensive list of references to the practice in Gundry (938). In Jesus' third passion prediction the synonymous Greek term μαστιγόω is used (10:34). Gundry points out that "the switch to a Latinism is probably due to the Semitic character of the dominical saying [10:34] on the one hand and the Roman setting of the present episode" (929). The more general term παιδεύω occurs in Luke 23:16, 22 which, in the context, implies φραγελλόω/μαστιγόω, but is not an explicit reference to that form of punishment. The related noun φραγέλλιον is used in John 2:15, but there it is only a whip made of rope or cord, not the penal *flagellum* used in this instance.

ἵνα. Introduces a purpose clause.

σταυρωθῇ. Aor pass subj 3rd sg σταυρόω. Subjunctive with ἵνα.

Mark 15:16-20

[16]Then the soldiers led him into the palace — that is, the Praetorium — and they called together the whole cohort. [17]They dressed him in a purple garment and placed on him, having twisted (it) together, a thorny crown. [18]And they began to call out to him, "Hail! King of the Jews!" [19]They beat his head with a reed, spit on him, and kneeling down, they (pretended to) pay him homage. [20]When they had mocked him they stripped him of the purple garment and dressed him in his own clothes. Then they led him out to crucify him.

15:16 Οἱ δὲ στρατιῶται ἀπήγαγον αὐτὸν ἔσω τῆς αὐλῆς, ὅ ἐστιν πραιτώριον, καὶ συγκαλοῦσιν ὅλην τὴν σπεῖραν.

Οἱ ... στρατιῶται. Nominative subject of ἀπήγαγον. On the use of δέ, see verse 4.

ἀπήγαγον. Aor act ind 3rd pl ἀπάγω.

αὐτὸν. Accusative direct object of ἀπήγαγον.

ἔσω τῆς αὐλῆς. Adverb of place, used as a preposition (Robertson, 643.20) with the genitive to indicate the place (see also 14:54 on ἔσω). BDF (§184) suggests a partitive genitive ("farther into the palace"), but Gundry is more likely correct that ἔσω indicates that "Jesus' Jewish accusers have not entered Pilate's court (lest they defile themselves and not be fit to eat the Passover . . .)" (940). An αὐλή is generally an "enclosed open space, courtyard" (BDAG, 150.1), but came to be used of more specific locations such as a sheep pen, farm yard, or of a royal courtyard and the surrounding buildings (thus "palace"; note that αὐλή is equivalent to the πραιτώριον here).

ὅ ἐστιν. On this formulaic phrase, see 3:17. "The noun which forms the predicate in a relative sentence, annexed for the purpose of explanation (ὅς—ἐστί), sometimes gives its own gender and number to the relative, by a kind of attraction" (Winer 1882, 206.3; see also Robertson, 712.4; Wallace 1996, 338); that is, ὅ agrees with the neuter πραιτώριον rather than its feminine antecedent αὐλῆς.

ὅ. Nominative subject of ἐστιν.

ἐστιν. Pres act ind 3rd sg εἰμί.

πραιτώριον. Predicate nominative. This is a Latin loanword (see 4:21). The πραιτώριον was originally a reference to the "praetor's tent in camp, w. its surroundings" (BDAG, 859; the praetor was a high-ranking Roman official). In this context it refers to the Roman governor's official residence (LN 7.7).

συγκαλοῦσιν. Pres act ind 3rd pl συγκαλέω.

ὅλην τὴν σπεῖραν. Accusative direct object of συγκαλοῦσιν. A σπεῖρα ("cohort") was a tenth of a legion, or about 600 men.

15:17 καὶ ἐνδιδύσκουσιν αὐτὸν πορφύραν καὶ περιτιθέασιν αὐτῷ πλέξαντες ἀκάνθινον στέφανον·

ἐνδιδύσκουσιν. Pres act ind 3rd pl ἐνδιδύσκω ("to put on clothing, dress," synonymous with the older form ἐνδύω in v. 20). When the active voice is used, a double accusative construction typically indicates the person who is dressed and with what they are dressed. On the high concentration of narrative present forms in 15:17-27 (the highest in Mark), see C. Campbell (70–71; see also 14:32).

αὐτὸν. Accusative direct object of ἐνδιδύσκουσιν.

πορφύραν. Complement in an object-complement double accusative construction. πορφύρα refers to "purple cloth/garment," or perhaps "*a red-coloured cloak*, such as common soldiers wore" (Souter, 211, citing this text; cf. BDAG, 855). Matt 27:28 refers to the garment as a χλαμύδα κοκκίνην ("scarlet robe").

περιτιθέασιν. Pres act ind 3rd pl περιτίθημι.

αὐτῷ. Dative complement of περιτιθέασιν.

πλέξαντες. Aor act ptc masc nom pl πλέκω (temporal; "to weave, braid, plait, twist together," LN 49.27; BDAG, 824). Note that the plural participle clearly modifies περιτιθέασιν, not the singular στέφανον.

ἀκάνθινον. The adjective ἀκάνθινος means "thorny, made of thorns/thorn branches" (BDAG, 34).

στέφανον. Accusative direct object of περιτιθέασιν.

15:18 καὶ ἤρξαντο ἀσπάζεσθαι αὐτόν, Χαῖρε, βασιλεῦ τῶν Ἰουδαίων·

ἤρξαντο. Aor mid ind 3rd pl ἄρχω.

ἀσπάζεσθαι. Pres mid inf ἀσπάζομαι (complementary). Although ἀσπάζομαι is usually a friendly, complementary greeting, it can be used to mock as it is here. "Mark's salutation makes it likely that he intends the scene as a burlesque of the 'Ave Caesar' acclamation of the emperor" (R. Brown, 1:868).

αὐτόν. Accusative direct object of ἀσπάζεσθαι.

χαῖρε. Pres act impv 2nd sg χαίρω. The mocking tone of this greeting might be expressed as "Hey! King of the Jews!" (CEB), or perhaps with a more traditional, but in this context of crucifixion, a very sarcastic, English expression, "Long live the king" (GW).

βασιλεῦ. Vocative.

τῶν Ἰουδαίων. The genitive indicates those over whom the king rules.

15:19 καὶ ἔτυπτον αὐτοῦ τὴν κεφαλὴν καλάμῳ καὶ ἐνέπτυον αὐτῷ καὶ τιθέντες τὰ γόνατα προσεκύνουν αὐτῷ.

ἔτυπτον. Impf act ind 3rd pl τύπτω. This imperfect verb is often translated as "again and again they struck" (NIV, NET) or "they kept hitting" (HCSB) in an attempt to express what is viewed as an iterative imperfect. Such ideas can be expressed explicitly in Greek, but it is questionable if this ought to be based only on a tense form. The imperfect is likely used here as part of a summary and is adequately expressed with a simple tense in English as it is, e.g., in the NRSV, NJB, REB, and NLT. That these actions were likely repeated is not in question, but that comes, not from the tense, but from the tenor of the entire passage. An English reader assumes this just as well from a simpler translation that is not as likely to be abused or over-emphasized.

τὴν κεφαλὴν. Accusative direct object of ἔτυπτον.

καλάμῳ. Dative of means.

ἐνέπτυον. Impf act ind 3rd pl ἐμπτύω. On the use of the imperfect, see above on ἔτυπτον.

αὐτῷ. Dative complement of ἐνέπτυον.

τιθέντες τὰ γόνατα. On the possible Latinism, *genua ponere/ponentes*, see 4:21 and BDAG (1003.1.b.γ, s.v. τίθημι; 205, s.v. γόνυ).

τιθέντες. Pres act ptc masc nom pl τίθημι (temporal or perhaps manner).

τὰ γόνατα. Accusative direct object of τιθέντες.

προσεκύνουν. Impf act ind 3rd pl προσκυνέω. On the use of the imperfect, see ἔτυπτον above. Since the context makes it clear that this is mockery, the NLT does well in saying, "dropped to their knees in mock worship."

αὐτῷ. Dative complement of προσεκύνουν.

15:20 καὶ ὅτε ἐνέπαιξαν αὐτῷ, ἐξέδυσαν αὐτὸν τὴν πορφύραν καὶ ἐνέδυσαν αὐτὸν τὰ ἱμάτια αὐτοῦ. καὶ ἐξάγουσιν αὐτὸν ἵνα σταυρώσωσιν αὐτόν.

ὅτε. On ὅτε with an aorist, see *TDM* (83, 214 n. 139).

ἐνέπαιξαν. Aor act ind 3rd pl ἐμπαίζω. The passion prediction in 10:34 also used ἐμπαίζω.

αὐτῷ. Dative complement of ἐνέπαιξαν.

ἐξέδυσαν. Aor act ind 3rd pl ἐκδύω. As Jesus was dressed (ἐνδιδύσκω) in verse 17, he is now stripped (ἐκδύω) of his garments of mockery. In a double accusative construction the direct object typically indicates the person who is stripped/undressed and the complement indicates what is stripped from them.

αὐτὸν. Accusative direct object of ἐξέδυσαν.

τὴν πορφύραν. Complement in an object-complement double accusative construction ("purple garment," see also v. 17).

ἐνέδυσαν. Aor act ind 3rd pl ἐνδύω. In a double accusative construction the direct object typically indicates the person who is dressed and the complement indicates with what they are dressed.

αὐτὸν. Accusative direct object of ἐνέδυσαν.

τὰ ἱμάτια. Complement in an object-complement double accusative construction.

ἐξάγουσιν. Pres act ind 3rd pl ἐξάγω.

ἵνα. Introduces a purpose clause.

σταυρώσωσιν. Aor act subj 3rd pl σταυρόω. Subjunctive with ἵνα.

αὐτὸν. Accusative direct object of σταυρώσωσιν.

Mark 15:21-32

[21]They conscripted a passerby, a certain Simon of Cyrene, who was coming from the country—the father of Alexander and Rufus—in order that he should carry (Jesus') cross. [22]And they led him to the place Golgotha, which being translated is, "Place of the Skull." [23]They offered him wine flavored with myrrh, but he did not take it. [24]And so they crucified him and divided his garments by casting lots for them (to determine) what each one would take. [25]Now it was the third hour when they crucified him. [26]The superscription specifying his charge was inscribed, "The King of the Jews."

[27]They crucified two robbers with him, one on the right and one on his left. [29]Those who passed by jeered at him, shaking their heads and saying, "So! The one who destroys the temple and builds it in three days! [30]Save yourself by coming down from the cross." [31]Likewise also the chief priests together with the scribes, mocking among themselves, said, "Others he saved, himself he is not able to save. Let the Messiah—this King of Israel—come down now from the cross so that we may see and believe." Those crucified with him (also) heaped insults on him.

15:21 Καὶ ἀγγαρεύουσιν παράγοντά τινα Σίμωνα Κυρηναῖον ἐρχόμενον ἀπ' ἀγροῦ, τὸν πατέρα Ἀλεξάνδρου καὶ Ῥούφου, ἵνα ἄρῃ τὸν σταυρὸν αὐτοῦ.

ἀγγαρεύουσιν. Pres act ind 3rd pl ἀγγαρεύω ("*requisition . . . press into service*, and *so force, compel*," BDAG, 7). The word was used "in reference to compulsory service of any kind" (Swete, 378).

παράγοντά. Pres act ptc masc acc sg παράγω (substantival, "one who was passing by"). Accusative direct object of ἀγγαρεύουσιν. The second accent comes from the enclitic τινα.

τινα Σίμωνα Κυρηναῖον. Accusative in apposition to παράγοντα.

ἐρχόμενον. Pres mid ptc masc acc sg ἔρχομαι (attributive).

ἀπ' ἀγροῦ. Source.

τὸν πατέρα. Accusative in apposition to τινα Σίμωνα Κυρηναῖον.

Ἀλεξάνδρου καὶ Ῥούφου. All three names in this verse were very common names in the first century, Simon being a classic Jewish name (though also used by Gentiles), and Alexander and Rufus being Greco-Roman in origin (though also popular among Jews; see Hengel 1979, 72; *New Docs*, 1.120 §77).

ἵνα. Introduces a purpose clause.

ἄρῃ. Aor act subj 3rd sg αἴρω. Subjunctive with ἵνα.

τὸν σταυρὸν. Accusative direct object of ἄρῃ. This was probably only the cross member, not the entire cross. The vertical portion was likely a permanent structure at the execution site.

15:22 καὶ φέρουσιν αὐτὸν ἐπὶ τὸν Γολγοθᾶν τόπον, ὅ ἐστιν μεθερμηνευόμενον Κρανίου Τόπος.

φέρουσιν. Pres act ind 3rd pl φέρω. The verb is probably best understood as "led" here (BDAG, 1051.2.b.β; cf. 7:32; 8:22; 11:2, 7), rather than "carried" (contra Bruce, 449; cf. Swete, 379; France, 641), though the conscription of Simon (v. 21) suggests that he was too weak to carry the cross, likely the result of having been flogged (φραγελλώσας, v. 15).

αὐτὸν. Accusative direct object of φέρουσιν.

ἐπὶ τὸν Γολγοθᾶν τόπον. Spatial. The grammar is very awkward here. The object of the preposition is τόν . . . τόπον. The feminine word in attributive position, Γολγοθᾶν, apparently functions adjectivally, despite the mismatch of gender. It might be described as apposition, but if so, the word order seems odd. Γολγοθᾶν is a Greek transliteration of the Aramaic word *gulĕgōlta'* meaning "the place of the skull." Matt 27:33 smooths the phrase nicely: εἰς τόπον λεγόμενον Γολγοθᾶ. The English word "Calvary" comes from the Latin word for skull: *calva/calvaria*.

ὅ ἐστιν μεθερμηνευόμενον. On this translation formula, see 3:17.

ὅ. Nominative subject of ἐστιν. The mismatch of gender is due to the use of a stereotyped phrase used for translation equivalents (see 3:17). It does not agree with Γολγοθᾶν (contra Gundry, 955), since that word is feminine (BDAG, 205).

ἐστιν. Pres act ind 3rd sg εἰμί.

μεθερμηνευόμενον. Pres pass ptc neut nom sg μεθερμηνεύω (means). Some would class ἐστιν μεθερμηνευόμενον as a periphrastic (so Green, 282–83).

Τόπος. Predicate nominative.

15:23 καὶ ἐδίδουν αὐτῷ ἐσμυρνισμένον οἶνον· ὃς δὲ οὐκ ἔλαβεν.

ἐδίδουν. Impf act ind 3rd pl δίδωμι. The third plural subject would, in the flow of the context, refer to the soldiers as those who offered Jesus wine (note the preceding and following phrases: ἀγγαρεύουσιν παράγοντά, v. 21; φέρουσιν αὐτόν, v. 22; σταυροῦσιν αὐτὸν καὶ διαμερίζονται τὰ ἱμάτια αὐτοῦ, v. 24; and ἐσταύρωσαν αὐτόν, v. 25). The imperfect is used in a conative statement of attempted action (it is the statement that is conative, not the tense). As the subsequent statement makes clear, δίδωμι can only have the sense of "offer" (cf. BDAG, 243.16, though not citing this text), since Jesus did not accept or drink the proffered wine.

αὐτῷ. Dative indirect object of ἐδίδουν.

ἐσμυρνισμένον. Prf pass ptc masc acc sg σμυρνίζω (attributive; "flavored with myrrh" (BDAG, 934; only here in the NT).

οἶνον. Accusative direct object of ἐδίδουν.

ὅς. Nominative subject of ἔλαβεν. The relative pronoun can be used as a demonstrative or personal pronoun (BDAG, 727.2.a; Robertson, 695.d). This is more common in a correlative type construction (ὃς μέν ... ὃς δέ, BDAG, 727.2.b; BDF §249–50) than is ὃς δέ alone.

δέ. The conjunction introduces a contrast between Jesus being given wine and his refusal to drink it.

ἔλαβεν. Aor act ind 3rd sg λαμβάνω.

15:24 καὶ σταυροῦσιν αὐτὸν καὶ διαμερίζονται τὰ ἱμάτια αὐτοῦ, βάλλοντες κλῆρον ἐπ᾽ αὐτὰ τίς τί ἄρῃ.

σταυροῦσιν. Pres act ind 3rd pl σταυρόω. A narrative present tense that functions to highlight the transition to the crucial event of the pericope, indeed, of the entire book (see also 1:21 on εἰσπορεύονται).

αὐτόν. Accusative direct object of σταυροῦσιν.

διαμερίζονται. Pres mid ind 3rd pl διαμερίζω. The middle is used with the plural subject to indicate that they divided them among themselves (V. Taylor, 589; BDAG, 233.2).

τὰ ἱμάτια. Accusative direct object of διαμερίζονται.

βάλλοντες. Pres act ptc masc nom pl βάλλω (means).

κλῆρον. Accusative direct object of βάλλοντες. "Casting lots" may not have been a dice game (see Evans 2001, 502).

ἐπ' αὐτά. Reference, indicating for what something is done (BDAG, 366.14.b.α).

τίς τί ἄρῃ. An indirect question with two interrogative pronouns (formally, "who should take what") has a distributive sense, "what each one would take" (BDF §298.5). This is "a blending of two interrogative sentences (τίς ἄρῃ; τί ἄρῃ;) familiar in class. Gk., but rare in the N.T." (Swete, 380).

τίς. Nominative subject of ἄρῃ.

τί. Accusative direct object of ἄρῃ.

ἄρῃ. Aor act subj 3rd sg αἴρω. As BDAG (28.2.a) phrases it, the verb refers to taking "a gambler's winnings."

15:25 ἦν δὲ ὥρα τρίτη καὶ ἐσταύρωσαν αὐτόν.

ἦν. Impf act ind 3rd sg εἰμί. The imperfect serves to supply background information.

δέ. The conjunction δέ is used rather than καί since the grammatical subject changes as Mark shifts from a report of the crucifixion event to a background statement of the time of that event.

ὥρα τρίτη. Predicate nominative. The third hour was 9 a.m.

καί. BDAG notes that "it is also coordination rather than subordination when [καί] connects an expr[ession] of time with that which occurs in the time" (494.1.b.γ). Thus, "it was the third hour when they crucified him" (BDF §442.4).

ἐσταύρωσαν. Aor act ind 3rd pl σταυρόω.

αὐτόν. Accusative direct object of ἐσταύρωσαν.

15:26 καὶ ἦν ἡ ἐπιγραφὴ τῆς αἰτίας αὐτοῦ ἐπιγεγραμμένη, Ὁ βασιλεὺς τῶν Ἰουδαίων.

ἦν . . . ἐπιγεγραμμένη. Periphrastic. (See an alternative evaluation below on ἐπιγεγραμμένη.)

Mark 15:24-27   253

ἦν. Impf act ind 3rd sg εἰμί.

ἡ ἐπιγραφὴ. Nominative subject of ἦν. An ἐπιγραφή was "ordinarily of a document incised on stone, but also of identifying notices on any kind of material: *inscription, superscription* of the 'titulus' fastened to a cross" (BDAG, 369). The other NT uses include || Luke 23:38 and three uses in Jesus' query regarding the inscription on a δηνάριον in Mark 12:16 || Matt 22:20 and Luke 20:24. The technical Latin term *titulus* is transliterated as τίτλος in || John 19:19.

τῆς αἰτίας αὐτοῦ. Genitive of description, "the inscription describing/specifying his charge." An αἰτία was a legal technical term referring to the basis for legal action, *charge, ground for* [legal] *complaint*" (BDAG, 31.3.a).

ἐπιγεγραμμένη. Prf pass ptc fem nom sg ἐπιγράφω ("to form letters or words on any kind of surface, BDAG, 369–70; cognate with ἐπιγραφή). Despite the intervening subject, this should be viewed as a stative periphrastic construction with ἦν (Wallace 1996, 583 n. 33; Green, 434) that is functionally equivalent to a pluperfect finite form. It would also be possible to view it as an attributive participle (cf. BDAG's, 370, "identifying notice").

Ὁ βασιλεὺς τῶν Ἰουδαίων. Clausal complement (direct discourse) of ἦν ... ἐπιγεγραμμένη. This was a foreign/Roman title (see, e.g., Matt 2:2; Josephus, *J.W.* 1.282, 388), also used frequently by Josephus who wrote in a Roman context; the Jewish title was "King of Israel" (see v. 32).

15:27 Καὶ σὺν αὐτῷ σταυροῦσιν δύο λῃστάς, ἕνα ἐκ δεξιῶν καὶ ἕνα ἐξ εὐωνύμων αὐτοῦ.

σὺν αὐτῷ. Association.

σταυροῦσιν. Pres act ind 3rd pl σταυρόω. The narrative present tense marks the beginning of a new paragraph and also by means of the direct object introduces two new participants in the narrative: δύο λῃστάς (see 1:21 on εἰσπορεύονται). The subject is the same as the preceding paragraph: the soldiers.

δύο λῃστάς. Accusative direct object of σταυροῦσιν. On the meaning of λῃστής, see 15:7 on στασιαστής.

ἕνα ... καὶ ἕνα. Accusative in apposition to δύο λῃστάς, indicating each of the two respectively.

ἐκ δεξιῶν. "On the right." This is a common expression (see, e.g., Matt 25:33; Mark 16:5; Luke 1:11; Acts 2:25).

ἐξ εὐωνύμων αὐτοῦ. "At his left" (see Matt 25:41; Mark 10:40).

15:28 καὶ ἐπληρώθη ἡ γραφὴ ἡ λέγουσα, Καὶ μετὰ ἀνόμων ἐλογίσθη.

This verse has been inserted by later scribes (L Θ 083 0250 *f*[1, 13] 33 𝔐); it is not found in ℵ A B C D Ψ *pc*.

15:29 Καὶ οἱ παραπορευόμενοι ἐβλασφήμουν αὐτὸν κινοῦντες τὰς κεφαλὰς αὐτῶν καὶ λέγοντες, Οὐὰ ὁ καταλύων τὸν ναὸν καὶ οἰκοδομῶν ἐν τρισὶν ἡμέραις,

οἱ παραπορευόμενοι. Pres mid ptc masc nom pl παραπορεύομαι (substantival; "to go or pass by," BDAG, 770). The description is apt since the Romans typically performed crucifixions near main roads to provide public exposure.

ἐβλασφήμουν. Impf act ind 3rd pl βλασφημέω. Here, "'to demean through speech,' an esp. sensitive matter in an honor-shame oriented society" (BDAG, 178). In this context the imperfect likely does refer to a situation in which variations of the statement given were repeated multiple times, though that should not be based on the imperfect tense (though the imperfective aspect is appropriate in such cases), but on the general tenor of the scenario depicted. The same is true of ἔλεγον (v. 31) and ὠνείδιζον (v. 32).

αὐτὸν. Accusative direct object of ἐβλασφήμουν.

κινοῦντες τὰς κεφαλὰς. "Shake the head to and fro as a sign of scorn and derision" (BDAG, 545.2.a, s.v. κινέω; see also LN 16.2). This may be a Koine idiom since LSJ (952) does not list a gloss for κινέω that communicates this nuance.

κινοῦντες. Pres act ptc masc nom pl κινέω ("to move, set in motion"). Although taking the participle as manner might make sense for κινοῦντες, the parallel with the conjoined λέγοντες suggests that means is the better explanation.

τὰς κεφαλὰς. Accusative direct object of κινοῦντες.

λέγοντες. Pres act ptc masc nom pl λέγω (means).

Οὐὰ. An "interjection denoting amazement" (BDAG, 734), which may be either negative, as here (it is part of the expression of ἐβλασφήμουν), or positive. The parallel in Matt 27:40 does not include οὐά or any other interjection at this point. The word occurs nowhere else in the NT or LXX, though BDAG (734) provides a few extrabiblical references. It is probably onomatopoetic (so Gould, 292). LSJ (1268) notes that it is the equivalent of the Latin vah! an exclamation "of admiration, or of astonishment." It "gains its sense from the tone of voice rather than from a lexical meaning" and here "the following words suggest that it conveys vindictive sarcasm" (France, 647).

ὁ καταλύων. Pres act ptc masc nom sg καταλύω (substantival). This is a pendant nominative, which is picked up by the resumptive σεαυτόν in verse 30.

τὸν ναὸν. Accusative direct object of καταλύων.

οἰκοδομῶν. Pres act ptc masc nom sg οἰκοδομέω (substantival; parallel with καταλύων and governed by the same article).

ἐν τρισὶν ἡμέραις. Temporal.

15:30 σῶσον σεαυτὸν καταβὰς ἀπὸ τοῦ σταυροῦ.

σῶσον. Aor act impv 2nd sg σῴζω.

σεαυτὸν. Accusative direct object of σῶσον.

καταβὰς. Aor act ptc masc nom sg καταβαίνω (means; Bruce, 449, suggests temporal, "having descended," but acknowledges that "by descending" is also viable).

ἀπὸ τοῦ σταυροῦ. Source.

15:31 ὁμοίως καὶ οἱ ἀρχιερεῖς ἐμπαίζοντες πρὸς ἀλλήλους μετὰ τῶν γραμματέων ἔλεγον, Ἄλλους ἔσωσεν, ἑαυτὸν οὐ δύναται σῶσαι·

ὁμοίως. The adverb modifies ἔλεγον.

καὶ. Adverbial: "also."

οἱ ἀρχιερεῖς. Nominative subject of ἔλεγον.

ἐμπαίζοντες. Pres act ptc masc nom pl ἐμπαίζω ("to subject to derision, *ridicule, make fun of, mock* (in word and deed)," BDAG, 323.1). The participle is perhaps to be viewed as one of manner, since it reflects the attitude with which they spoke.

πρὸς ἀλλήλους. BDAG notes "πρὸς ἀλλήλους *to one another, with each other, among themselves*" (874.3.a.ε).

μετὰ τῶν γραμματέων. Association.

ἔλεγον. Impf act ind 3rd pl λέγω. On the use of the imperfect tense, see verse 29 on ἐβλασφήμουν.

Ἄλλους ἔσωσεν, ἑαυτὸν οὐ δύναται σῶσαι. This was likely a recognized expression at the time (see line 9 of the text cited in *New Docs* 4.20–21 §5).

Ἄλλους. Accusative direct object of ἔσωσεν.

ἔσωσεν. Aor act ind 3rd sg σῴζω.

ἑαυτὸν. Accusative direct object of σῶσαι.

δύναται. Pres mid ind 3rd sg δύναμαι.

σῶσαι. Aor act inf σῴζω (complementary).

15:32 ὁ Χριστὸς ὁ βασιλεὺς Ἰσραὴλ καταβάτω νῦν ἀπὸ τοῦ σταυροῦ, ἵνα ἴδωμεν καὶ πιστεύσωμεν. καὶ οἱ συνεσταυρωμένοι σὺν αὐτῷ ὠνείδιζον αὐτόν.

ὁ Χριστὸς. Nominative subject of καταβάτω.

ὁ βασιλεὺς. Nominative in apposition to ὁ Χριστός. The statement, ὁ Χριστὸς ὁ βασιλεὺς Ἰσραήλ, conveys sarcasm and mockery.

καταβάτω. Aor act impv 3rd sg καταβαίνω. The third person is probably used because they were speaking to themselves rather than addressing Jesus directly. It could, however, be viewed as an indirect command that is functionally equivalent to a second person imperative; such use, however, is normally for purposes of politeness, which is not at all the case here.

ἵνα. Introduces a (sarcastic) purpose clause.

ἴδωμεν. Aor act subj 1st pl ὁράω. Subjunctive with ἵνα.

πιστεύσωμεν. Aor act subj 1st pl πιστεύω. Subjunctive with ἵνα. See also 1:15.

οἱ συνεσταυρωμένοι. Prf pass ptc masc nom pl συσταυρόω (substantival; "to crucify together with," BDAG, 978). This word is not attested earlier than the NT, and all 300 instances in TLG are Christian writers. The perfect tense refers to those in the same condition as Jesus. The plural refers to the words of both criminals, though Luke's account apparently depicts a later stage in which one of them repents of his earlier belligerence (see Luke 23:39-43).

σὺν αὐτῷ. Association. The preposition σύν matches the prefix in the preceding compound verb, a common stylistic feature in Koine.

ὠνείδιζον. Impf act ind 3rd pl ὀνειδίζω. On the use of the imperfect tense, see verse 29 on ἐβλασφήμουν. It says too much to appeal to the "continuous force" of the imperfect to mean that "even the co-crucified kept on reviling Jesus" (R. Brown, 2:999); imperfective aspect does portray the situation as a process, but this is not necessarily the same as a "continuous force" and "keeping on" which are too easily overread in English.

αὐτόν. Accusative direct object of ὠνείδιζον.

Mark 15:33-41

[33]At noon darkness came on all the land until 3 p.m. [34]Then at 3 p.m. Jesus cried out with a loud voice, "*Eloi, Eloi! Lama sabachthani?*" which being translated is, "My God, My God! Why have you forsaken me?" [35]Some of those standing (there), when they heard

(him cry out) said, "Listen! He's calling Elijah." ³⁶But someone, running and filling a sponge with cheap wine and placing it on a reed,
gave him a drink saying, "Leave him alone. Let's see if Elijah comes
to take him down." ³⁷But Jesus, giving a loud cry, breathed his last.
³⁸Then the curtain of the temple was torn in two from top to bottom. ³⁹Now the centurion who was standing in front of him, seeing
that he died in this way, said, "This man truly was the Son of God."
⁴⁰There were also women observing from a distance among whom
were Mary Magdalene, Mary the mother of James the Younger and
of Joses, Salome — ⁴¹(these women) followed him and ministered to
him when they were in Galilee — and many others who had accompanied him to Jerusalem.

**15:33 Καὶ γενομένης ὥρας ἕκτης σκότος ἐγένετο ἐφ᾽ ὅλην τὴν
γῆν ἕως ὥρας ἐνάτης.**

γενομένης. Aor mid ptc fem gen sg γίνομαι. Genitive absolute
(1:32), temporal.
ὥρας ἕκτης. Genitive subject of γενομένης ("the sixth hour," i.e.,
noon).
σκότος. Nominative subject of ἐγένετο.
ἐγένετο. Aor mid ind 3rd sg γίνομαι.
ἐφ᾽ ὅλην τὴν γῆν. Spatial. The adjective ὅλος always occurs in
predicate position, though it functions attributively. The extent of
"the land" (τὴν γῆν) that was darkened cannot be determined since
γῆ has a very wide range of reference and there are no contextual
indicators in this instance.
ἕως ὥρας ἐνάτης. Improper preposition with the genitive, indicating extent of time until something happens. The "ninth hour" is
3 p.m.

**15:34 καὶ τῇ ἐνάτῃ ὥρᾳ ἐβόησεν ὁ Ἰησοῦς φωνῇ μεγάλῃ, Ελωι
ελωι λεμα σαβαχθανι; ὅ ἐστιν μεθερμηνευόμενον Ὁ θεός μου ὁ
θεός μου, εἰς τί ἐγκατέλιπές με;**

τῇ ἐνάτῃ ὥρᾳ. Dative of time (point of time at which something
happens; here "at the ninth hour," i.e., "at 3 p.m.").
ἐβόησεν. Aor act ind 3rd sg βοάω. Mark is the only gospel writer
to use this verb in describing any of Jesus' utterances from the
cross (though Matt 27:46 has ἀναβοάω). Most use the simple λέγω
(John exclusively so); φωνέω (Luke 23:46), κράζω (Matt 27:50), and
Mark's ἀφίημι φωνήν (15:37) are also used.

ὁ Ἰησοῦς. Nominative subject of ἐβόησεν.

φωνῇ μεγάλῃ. Dative of means.

Ελωι ελωι λεμα σαβαχθανι. The entire clause functions as the clausal complement (direct discourse) of ἐβόησεν. This is an Aramaic transliteration (thus no diacritics are used). ελωι occurs only here in the NT; the parallel in Matt 27:46 uses ἠλι. For an extensive consideration of the Aramaic expression and the textual variants in the manuscript tradition, see P. Williams (2004, 2–12), who concludes that the variation between Matthew and Mark may simply be "independent transcriptions of the same utterance" (8; see also R. Brown, 2:1051–55).

ὅ ἐστιν μεθερμηνευόμενον. On this translation formula, see 3:17.

ὅ. Nominative subject of ἐστιν.

ἐστιν. Pres act ind 3rd sg εἰμί.

μεθερμηνευόμενον. Pres mid ptc neut nom sg μεθερμηνεύω (means). Some would class ἐστιν μεθερμηνευόμενον as a periphrastic (so Green, 282–83).

Ὁ θεός μου ὁ θεός μου, εἰς τί ἐγκατέλιπές με. Clausal predicate nominative of ἐστιν (or clausal complement of a periphrastic ἐστιν μεθερμηνευόμενον).

Ὁ θεός ... ὁ θεός. Nominatives of address. The articles make it clear that the forms are nominative rather than vocative.

εἰς τί. "Why?" (BDAG, 290.4.f, s.v., εἰς, "for what purpose?"). See also 14:4.

ἐγκατέλιπές. Aor act ind 2nd sg ἐγκαταλείπω.

με. Accusative direct object of ἐγκατέλιπές.

15:35 καί τινες τῶν παρεστηκότων ἀκούσαντες ἔλεγον, Ἴδε Ἠλίαν φωνεῖ.

τινες. Nominative subject of ἔλεγον.

τῶν παρεστηκότων. Prf act ptc masc gen pl παρίστημι (substantival). Partitive genitive (see 8:8; 9:17).

ἀκούσαντες. Aor act ptc masc nom pl ἀκούω (temporal).

ἔλεγον. Impf act ind 3rd pl λέγω.

Ἴδε Ἠλίαν φωνεῖ. Clausal complement (direct discourse) of ἔλεγον.

Ἴδε. See 3:34.

Ἠλίαν. Accusative direct object of φωνεῖ.

φωνεῖ. Pres act ind 3rd sg φωνέω. On the use of φωνέω meaning, "to invite, summon," see 9:35 and 10:49.

15:36 δραμὼν δέ τις [καὶ] γεμίσας σπόγγον ὄξους περιθεὶς καλάμῳ ἐπότιζεν αὐτὸν λέγων, Ἄφετε ἴδωμεν εἰ ἔρχεται Ἠλίας καθελεῖν αὐτόν.

δραμὼν. Aor act ptc masc nom sg τρέχω. The first of a string of three attendant circumstance participles (γεμίσας, περιθείς), unusual in modifying an imperfect rather than the more common aorist verb. They are, however, "used to introduce a new action or a shift in the narrative" (Wallace 1996, 642). The main statement is τις . . . ἐπότιζεν and the three participles describe parallel, but subordinate events.

δέ. The conjunction δέ is probably used because there is a more narrow subject than the preceding statement: the plural τινες in verse 35, but the singular τις here.

τις. Nominative subject of ἐπότιζεν.

[καὶ]. Although καί seems awkward and unnecessary here (why link the first two of three parallel participles?), the external support is fairly broad (א A C 059 083 *f*¹ 33 𝔐) and could be judged the more difficult reading. The shorter, simpler reading that omits the article has relatively less external support, but it includes a significant witness, Vaticanus (which may account for its omission in the WH text): B L Ψ *f*¹³ 2542 ℓ⁸⁴⁴ *pc*. I am inclined to omit καί in this instance, though for purposes of English style all three participles are linked with *and*.

γεμίσας. Aor act ptc masc nom sg γεμίζω (attendant circumstance; see δραμών above).

σπόγγον. Accusative direct object of γεμίσας ("sponge").

ὄξους. Genitive of content. Though often glossed as "*sour* wine," LSJ suggests "poor wine, '*vin ordinaire*'" (1234) for ὄξος. In this context it was not what we know as vinegar, though vinegar could be made from it and in an appropriate context ὄξος may refer to such wine vinegar. Rather, it was a poor quality wine that "relieved thirst more effectively than water and, being cheaper than regular wine, it was a favorite beverage of the lower ranks of society and of those in moderate circumstances" (BDAG, 715; see also Collins, 756–57, for an extended summary of ὄξος in the ancient world).

περιθεὶς. Aor act ptc masc nom sg περιτίθημι (attendant circumstance; see δραμών above). Here, the verb may be translated "to place on," though it technically means "to place around."

καλάμῳ. Locative.

ἐπότιζεν. Impf act ind 3rd sg ποτίζω. Although often translated, "offered him a drink," there is no indication that this is part of a tendential statement (as was the similar statement in v. 23). If this is the same event as recorded in John 19:28-30 (and that cannot be determined with confidence, though it seems possible), then Jesus may well have accepted this drink.

αὐτόν. Accusative direct object of ἐπότιζεν.

λέγων. Pres act ptc masc nom sg λέγω (temporal). As a singular adverbial participle, λέγων places the following words in the mouth of the one who gave him the drink. By contrast, Matt 27:46 says οἱ δὲ λοιποὶ ἔλεγον, Ἄφες ἴδωμεν, with the singular imperative addressed to the person giving Jesus the drink.

Ἄφετε ἴδωμεν. The pattern of an imperative form (often verbs of movement such as ἐγείρω, ἀφίημι, φέρω, ἀνίστημι, ἔρχομαι, or συνάγω, though sometimes words exhorting courage such as ἀνδρίζομαι or θαρσέω) followed by a hortatory subjunctive is not uncommon (see Matt 26:46; 27:49; Mark 14:42; John 14:31; and more than more than a dozen times in the LXX).

Ἄφετε. Aor act impv 2nd pl ἀφίημι. BDAG (5.b) translates ἄφετε ἴδωμεν "let us see." It might be possible to understand ἄφετε as "wait" (so RSV, followed by NRSV, ESV; see also NJB, NLT), but that is a sense that appears possible elsewhere only in Herm. *Sim.* 67.4. It is not listed with this meaning in BDAG, LN, LEH, or LSJ. R. Brown suggests that it might be simply an intensive, "Do let us see . . ." (2:1064–65).

ἴδωμεν. Aor act subj 1st pl ὁράω (deliberative subjunctive).

εἰ. Introduces an indirect question.

ἔρχεται. Pres mid ind 3rd sg ἔρχομαι. The time reference is future.

Ἠλίας. Nominative subject of ἔρχεται.

καθελεῖν. Aor act inf καθαιρέω (purpose). Most nonmetaphorical uses of this word with the meaning "to take down" (it can also mean "to destroy") are with reference to Jesus' body being taken down from the cross (15:46; Luke 23:53; Acts 13:29).

αὐτόν. Accusative direct object of καθελεῖν.

15:37 ὁ δὲ Ἰησοῦς ἀφεὶς φωνὴν μεγάλην ἐξέπνευσεν.

ὁ . . . Ἰησοῦς. Nominative subject of ἐξέπνευσεν.

ἀφεὶς. Aor act ptc masc nom sg ἀφίημι. In the present context with an impersonal object this word, which has a wide semantic range ("to let go, divorce; cancel, pardon; leave; leave standing; tolerate," etc.), means "to give up, emit" (BDAG, 156.1.b). Matthew uses it to describe Jesus giving up his spirit (27:50, a fairly common expression in Greek literature). The adverbial nuance of the participle is debated. Gundry (948; followed by Evans 2001, 508) argues that it is to be equated with the main verb (i.e., ἐξέπνευσεν) such that emitting a loud cry is a description of his dying ("his shout of superhuman strength was his last breath") because "everywhere else in Mark the aorist circumstantial participle of ἀφίημι equates with the main verb of the clause." There are nine such participles (1:18, 20; 4:36; 7:8; 8:13; 12:12; 13:34; 14:50; 15:37). As discussed at 12:12, some of these may be considered redundant when they occur with an aorist verb of motion (8:13; 12:12; 14:50 are the most likely instances). In these cases, the participle does refer essentially to the same action as the main verb. In other instances, however, the participle likely refers to sequential actions (13:34 is the clearest such example; 1:18, 20; 4:36 [narrative present] are probable). There are two instances with present tense verbs (4:36; 7:8) and two aorists that are not verbs of movement (13:34; 15:37). Usage cannot therefore decide 15:37; though the participle and verb are both aorist, the finite form is not a verb of movement. Although it is grammatically *possible* that emitting a loud cry (ἀφεὶς φωνὴν μεγάλην) and expiring (ἐξέπνευσεν) are to be equated, it is not mandated by grammar and usage (Gundry has overstated the grammatical evidence). If this verse refers to the same incident as recorded in John 19:30, which is possible, but not certain, then there are distinct verbal referents involved. It is also possible that this is a recapitulative statement and refers back to the previous cry of verse 34, resuming the narrative after the report of Jesus being offered a drink (so R. Brown, 2:1079).

φωνὴν μεγάλην. Accusative direct object of ἀφείς.

ἐξέπνευσεν. Aor act ind 3rd sg ἐκπνέω ("breathe out one's life/soul, *expire*, euphem[ism] for *die*" (BDAG, 308).

15:38 Καὶ τὸ καταπέτασμα τοῦ ναοῦ ἐσχίσθη εἰς δύο ἀπ᾽ ἄνωθεν ἕως κάτω.

Καὶ. Gundry (950) reads this conjunction as ecbatic (i.e., result), making Jesus' forceful exhalation of the "wind of the Spirit" the force that tore the curtain. Given the probable distance involved (even if Gundry, 970, were right that the actual crucifixion site was on the Mount of Olives and much closer to the temple than tradition recalls), that would surely have been a mighty blast of wind. Were that Mark's intention (or that of any of the other gospel writers), one would have expected a much clearer indication of such a miracle.

τὸ καταπέτασμα. Nominative subject of ἐσχίσθη. This "curtain of the temple" probably refers to the large curtain in Herod's temple that divided the two rooms of the sanctuary proper (see Evans 2001, 510; R. Brown, 2:1098–1118).

ἐσχίσθη. Aor pass ind 3rd sg σχίζω. Although often cited as a "divine passive"—it is obvious that the veil did not tear on its own accord—that is a questionable grammatical category.

εἰς δύο. Spatial: into two pieces.

ἀπ' ἄνωθεν ἕως κάτω. "From top to bottom." The preposition ἀπό indicates the source (i.e., the beginning of the tear) and ἕως (here used as a preposition with the genitive) indicates the limit reached (i.e., how far the tear extended).

15:39 Ἰδὼν δὲ ὁ κεντυρίων ὁ παρεστηκὼς ἐξ ἐναντίας αὐτοῦ ὅτι οὕτως ἐξέπνευσεν εἶπεν, Ἀληθῶς οὗτος ὁ ἄνθρωπος υἱὸς θεοῦ ἦν.

Ἰδών. Aor act ptc masc nom sg ὁράω (temporal).

δέ. The conjunction is used due to the change in subjects.

ὁ κεντυρίων. Nominative subject of εἶπεν. κεντυρίων ("centurion"), a Latin loanword from *centurio* (see 4:21), is a uniquely Markan word in the NT (see also vv. 44, 45). Elsewhere in the NT the word ἑκατόνταρχος is used.

παρεστηκώς. Prf act ptc masc nom sg παρίστημι (attributive).

ἐξ ἐναντίας αὐτοῦ. This expression ("in front of him") is a long-standing idiom that at one time likely contained a recognized ellipsis, the feminine genitive singular noun with which the adjective ἐναντίας agreed having long since been dropped (see BDF §241.1.1).

ὅτι. Introduces the clausal complement (indirect discourse) of ἰδών.

οὕτως. The adverb makes it clear that the centurion did not just observe *that* Jesus died, but rather the *manner* in which he died. The view that this refers to the centurion seeing Jesus' last breath tear the curtain of the temple from a distance (Gundry, 950; Evans 2001, 510) not only falters on the unlikelihood of such an event but, more importantly, it must change the force of οὕτως from a statement of manner modifying ἐξέπνευσεν (i.e., "saw how he died"), to a statement referring back to verse 38 indicating the result of the veil being torn. The placement of οὕτως following ὅτι stands strongly against such a conclusion. R. Brown (2:1145) also thinks that Mark intends his readers to think of the centurion seeing the veil being torn, but he avoids the logistical problems by denying historicity and classing that event as apocalyptic. Another alternative that seems less likely is that οὕτως has only a resumptive force here: "in other words, the purpose of the adverb is simply to take up the thread of the narrative again after the brief digression of v. 38" (Collins, 766). BDAG, however, has no such usage listed and I am unaware of other any clear examples of such.

ἐξέπνευσεν. Aor act ind 3rd sg ἐκπνέω (see v. 37).

εἶπεν. Aor act ind 3rd sg λέγω.

Ἀληθῶς οὗτος ὁ ἄνθρωπος υἱὸς θεοῦ ἦν. Clausal complement (direct discourse) of εἶπεν.

οὗτος ὁ ἄνθρωπος. Nominative subject of ἦν.

υἱὸς θεοῦ. Predicate nominative. "Anarthrous predicate nouns preceding the verb may function primarily to express the nature or character of the subject" (Harner, 75; see the extended discussion of this text on 79–81). An appeal to Colwell's Rule to establish definiteness rather than indefiniteness (as does Stein 2008, 718) is ineffective since Colwell only addressed the question of word order and articularity when a definite noun was involved; he *assumed* definiteness on other grounds as a presupposition to his rule. The rule states that "in sentences in which the copula is expressed, a definite predicate nominative has the article when it follows the verb; it does not have the article when it precedes the verb" (Colwell, 13). The converse of the rule may not be assumed; i.e., it is not true that because a predicate noun precedes a copulative verb, it is therefore definite (see Wallace 1996, 256–69; Harris, 301–13). The verbal link with Mark's introduction appears to be intentional, thus 1:1 and 15:39 form the "theological bookends" of the Gospel.

ἦν. Impf act ind 3rd sg εἰμί.

15:40 Ἦσαν δὲ καὶ γυναῖκες ἀπὸ μακρόθεν θεωροῦσαι, ἐν αἷς καὶ Μαρία ἡ Μαγδαληνὴ καὶ Μαρία ἡ Ἰακώβου τοῦ μικροῦ καὶ Ἰωσῆτος μήτηρ καὶ Σαλώμη,

Ἦσαν. Impf act ind 3rd pl εἰμί.

δέ. The use of δέ rather than καί reflects the new subject and topic.

γυναῖκες. Nominative subject of ἦσαν . . . θεωροῦσαι.

ἀπὸ μακρόθεν. Source. The prepositional phrase modifies ἦσαν θεωροῦσαι to indicate the location from which the women were watching, rather than indicating that the women had come from a distance, which would normally require an article with the prepositional phrase.

θεωροῦσαι. Pres act ptc fem nom pl θεωρέω (imperfect periphrastic, see Green, 199–201; alternatively, the participle could be viewed as attributive: "there were women who were watching from a distance").

ἐν αἷς. Association (with a plural object ἐν is typically equivalent to "among").

Μαρία . . . καὶ Μαρία . . . καὶ Σαλώμη . . . ⁴¹καὶ ἄλλαι πολλαὶ αἱ συναναβᾶσαι. Nominative subject of αν implied form of εἰμί. Μαρία and Σαλώμη were the most common women's names at this time (Ilan, 192–93).

Μαρία ἡ Μαγδαληνὴ καὶ Μαρία ἡ Ἰακώβου τοῦ μικροῦ καὶ Ἰωσῆτος μήτηρ. To distinguish the two women named Mary, a description is appended to each with an article (nominative in apposition). The first Mary is identified through a reference to her home town of Magdala (ἡ Μαγδαληνή, "the Magdalene"); the second as "the mother (ἡ . . . μήτηρ) of James and Joses (Ἰακώβου . . . καὶ Ἰωσῆτος)." In turn James is identified as "the younger" (τοῦ μικροῦ, genitive in apposition to Ἰακώβου; or perhaps "shorter," see BDAG, 651.1.a, b). Μαρία ἡ Ἰακώβου τοῦ μικροῦ μήτηρ also occurs in verse 47 and in 16:1.

15:41 αἳ ὅτε ἦν ἐν τῇ Γαλιλαίᾳ ἠκολούθουν αὐτῷ καὶ διηκόνουν αὐτῷ, καὶ ἄλλαι πολλαὶ αἱ συναναβᾶσαι αὐτῷ εἰς Ἱεροσόλυμα.

αἳ. Nominative subject of ἠκολούθουν . . . καὶ διηκόνουν. Although almost all English versions (REB is an exception) begin a new sentence at this point due to exigencies of English style, the long Greek sentence continues with a relative clause that explains these women's association with Jesus.

ὅτε. Introduces a temporal clause.

ἦν. Impf act ind 3rd sg εἰμί.

ἐν τῇ Γαλιλαίᾳ. Locative.

ἠκολούθουν. Impf act ind 3rd pl ἀκολουθέω. The two imperfect forms in this verse, occurring in a subordinate, relative clause, introduce background information to fill in the reader as to the identity of the women mentioned.

αὐτῷ. Dative complement of ἠκολούθουν.

διηκόνουν. Impf act ind 3rd pl διακονέω.

αὐτῷ. Dative complement of διηκόνουν.

ἄλλαι πολλαὶ. See verse 40 on Μαρία . . . καὶ Μαρία . . . καὶ Σαλώμη . . . καὶ ἄλλαι πολλαὶ αἱ συναναβᾶσαι.

συναναβᾶσαι. Aor act ptc fem nom pl συναναβαίνω (attributive; "to come/go up with," BDAG, 965).

αὐτῷ. Dative of association with a σύν– compound verb.

εἰς Ἱεροσόλυμα. Spatial. On the form of Ἱεροσόλυμα, see 3:8.

Mark 15:42-47

⁴²And with evening already approaching, since it was Preparation Day — that is, the day before the Sabbath — ⁴³Joseph of Arimathea, a prominent member of the council, who himself was also awaiting the kingdom of God, came (and) boldly went to Pilate and asked for the body of Jesus. ⁴⁴Now Pilate was amazed that he was already dead and, having summoned the centurion, he asked him if Jesus had already died. ⁴⁵Having learned (this) from the centurion, he released the corpse to Joseph. ⁴⁶Having bought a length of linen (and) taken down (the corpse), he wrapped him in the linen cloth and placed him in a tomb which was hewn out of rock and he rolled a stone across the entrance of the tomb. ⁴⁷Now Mary Magdalene and Mary the mother of Joses were watching where he was laid.

15:42 Καὶ ἤδη ὀψίας γενομένης, ἐπεὶ ἦν παρασκευὴ ὅ ἐστιν προσάββατον,

ὀψίας. Genitive subject of γενομένης. Although the substantival adjective ὀψία often means "evening," the word only requires that it be late in the day, whether late afternoon or evening (see BDAG, 746.2). The somewhat vague nature of the time reference is illustrated in Matt 14:15, 23 where ὄψιος occurs twice (ὀψίας δὲ γενομένης in both instances), but the two references are separated by what is probably several hours.

γενομένης. Aor mid ptc fem gen sg γίνομαι. Genitive absolute (1:32), temporal.

ἐπεί. The conjunction explains the statement in the following verse: since it was the day before the Sabbath, Joseph presents his request to Pilate.

ἦν. Impf act ind 3rd sg εἰμί.

παρασκευή. In the NT, παρασκευή ("preparation") is always used as a designation of the day preceding the Sabbath or another feast day on which work was not permitted. All NT references are in the context of the Passion and refer to the day of Jesus' crucifixion, which preceded the Passover Feast (Matt 27:62; Mark 15:42; Luke 23:54; John 19:14, 31, 42). Traditionally this was viewed as Friday (and later παρασκευή came to be a Christian designation of the sixth day of the week), though with alternate chronologies of the Passion (e.g., a Wednesday crucifixion) the reference would be to an earlier day.

ὅ. Nominative subject of ἐστιν. The neuter is used as part of a set phrase that provides an explanation of what precedes. Mark apparently assumes that many of his readers would not otherwise understand the designation παρασκευή (feminine).

ἐστιν. Pres act ind 3rd sg εἰμί.

προσάββατον. Predicate nominative. This noun refers to the "day before the Sabbath" (BDAG, 875; only here in the NT; see also LXX Ps 92:1 v.l.; Jdt 8:6).

15:43 ἐλθὼν Ἰωσὴφ [ὁ] ἀπὸ Ἁριμαθαίας εὐσχήμων βουλευτής, ὃς καὶ αὐτὸς ἦν προσδεχόμενος τὴν βασιλείαν τοῦ θεοῦ, τολμήσας εἰσῆλθεν πρὸς τὸν Πιλᾶτον καὶ ᾐτήσατο τὸ σῶμα τοῦ Ἰησοῦ.

ἐλθών. Aor act ptc masc nom sg ἔρχομαι (temporal).

Ἰωσήφ. Nominative subject of εἰσῆλθεν.

[ὁ] ἀπὸ Ἁριμαθαίας. Source (ἀπό is beginning to replace ἐκ in this sense in the Koine; BDF §209.3). The article functions as a nominalizer, changing the prepositional phrase into a nominative in apposition to Ἰωσήφ. For similar uses of ἀπό, see Matt 21:11; John 1:45; Acts 6:9; 10:38; 21:27.

εὐσχήμων βουλευτής. Nominative in apposition to Ἰωσήφ. The adjective εὐσχήμων means "considered especially worthy of public admiration, *prominent, of high standing/repute, nobl*e" (BDAG, 414.2; see also Acts 13:50; 17:12). This is a third declension adjective whose stem ends in -ον, with the *omicron* lengthening to *omega* since there is no case ending in the nominative. A βουλευτής was "a member of an advisory or legislative body," (BDAG, 181). The LXX uses this term in parallel with kings (μετὰ βασιλέων βουλευτῶν γῆς, Job 3:14; see also 12:17) and Josephus uses it of Jewish authorities in parallel with "rulers" (οἵ τε ἄρχοντες καὶ βουλευταί, *J.W.* 2.204). Although V. Taylor says that βουλευτής "was not a technical expression current among the Jews, and appears to be used in Mk and Lk for Gentile readers to describe a member of the Sanhedrin" (600), R. Brown (1:342–48) has plausibly argued that συνέδριον (Sanhedrin), γερουσία (Council of Elders), and βουλή (Council, Senate) refer to the same institution in the first century prior to AD 70 and were used interchangeably. Though the evidence is limited (βουλευτής occurs only here and ‖ Luke 23:50), "no NT author ever uses a denominative from *synedrion* to describe a Sanhedrin member, e.g., *synedros* or *synedriakos*" (R. Brown, 2:1214 n. 21); Brown wonders if βουλευτής were not considered (by Mark at least) to be the standard term for such an individual.

ὅς. Nominative subject of ἦν προσδεχόμενος.

αὐτός. Adjectival intensive modifying ὅς.

ἦν. Impf act ind 3rd sg εἰμί.

προσδεχόμενος. Pres mid ptc masc nom sg προσδέχομαι (imperfective periphrastic). The periphrastic does not "lend force to the verb" (contra R. Brown, 2:1214 n. 22), but is simply a substitute form for stylistic purposes (Green, 331–32).

τὴν βασιλείαν. Accusative direct object of ἦν προσδεχόμενος.

τοῦ θεοῦ. The genitive indicates the regent of the kingdom: the kingdom over which God reigns.

τολμήσας. Aor act ptc masc nom sg τολμάω (manner; the ptc "has almost the force of an adv.," Swete, 392).

εἰσῆλθεν. Aor act ind 3rd sg εἰσέρχομαι.

πρὸς τὸν Πιλᾶτον. Spatial.

ᾐτήσατο. Aor mid ind 3rd sg αἰτέω.

τὸ σῶμα. Accusative direct object of ᾐτήσατο.

15:44 ὁ δὲ Πιλᾶτος ἐθαύμασεν εἰ ἤδη τέθνηκεν καὶ προσκαλεσάμενος τὸν κεντυρίωνα ἐπηρώτησεν αὐτὸν εἰ πάλαι ἀπέθανεν·

δὲ. The use of δέ is due to the change of subjects (Joseph in v. 43, Pilate in v. 44).

ὁ . . . Πιλᾶτος. Nominative subject of ἐθαύμασεν.

ἐθαύμασεν. Aor act ind 3rd sg θαυμάζω (see 1:22 on ἐκπλήσσω). More commonly θαυμάζω would be followed by ὅτι (BDF §454.1.1; e.g., John 3:7) or ἐπί (though only in the sense, "to be surprised at X," e.g., Luke 2:33), but see 1 John 3:13 for the only other NT use with εἰ. Mark most often uses θαυμάζω absolutely, though it is followed by διά in 6:6.

εἰ. Introduces an indirect question (the direct question would have been, "Is he already dead?"). The use of εἰ rather than ὅτι (see above) "introduces an element of doubt" (Gundry, 985) or astonishment (Zerwick §404).

τέθνηκεν. Prf act ind 3rd sg θνῄσκω. The perfect asks regarding Jesus' condition "Is he dead?" not "Did he die?"(contrast the question put to the centurion later in the verse in which an aorist; see also Robertson, 845). In the NT θνῄσκω occurs only in the perfect tense (9 times); the more common term is ἀποθνῄσκω, which occurs primarily in the aorist (85 times) and present (21 times), and never in the perfect in either the NT or LXX.

προσκαλεσάμενος. Aor mid ptc masc nom sg προσκαλέομαι (temporal).

τὸν κεντυρίωνα. Accusative direct object of προσκαλεσάμενος. See also verse 39.

ἐπηρώτησεν. Aor act ind 3rd sg ἐπερωτάω. On ἐπερωτάω versus the simple form ἐρωτάω, see 4:10.

αὐτὸν. Accusative direct object of ἐπηρώτησεν.

εἰ. Introduces an indirect question.

πάλαι. Although this adverb may imply that it was "somewhat longer than the time span suggested by the use of ἤδη" (BDAG, 751.3), in practical terms the time span is essentially the same as that asked shortly before using ἤδη. Bock (2005, 551) proposes that it means, "if [he had been dead] long," but BDAG translates, "whether he was already dead" (751.3). The textual variant at this point harmonizes the two questions by replacing πάλαι (ℵ A C L Y 0233 *f*[1, 13] 28 33 𝔐) with ἤδη (B D W Q). "Although the reading πάλαι may perhaps have arisen through a desire to avoid the repetition of ἤδη in the sentence, it is more probable that copyists, feeling that πάλαι was somehow inappropriate in the context, sought to ameliorate the passage by replacing it with ἤδη" (Metzger 1994, 101).

ἀπέθανεν. Aor act ind 3rd sg ἀποθνῄσκω.

15:45 καὶ γνοὺς ἀπὸ τοῦ κεντυρίωνος ἐδωρήσατο τὸ πτῶμα τῷ Ἰωσήφ.

γνοὺς. Aor act ptc masc nom sg γινώσκω (temporal).

ἀπὸ τοῦ κεντυρίωνος. Source. On κεντυρίων, see verses 39, 44.

ἐδωρήσατο. Aor mid ind 3rd sg δωρέομαι. The verb means "to present someth. as a gift or confer a benefit, prob. with some suggestion of formality . . . present, bestow" (BDAG, 266); the translation uses a functional equivalent. Swete (392) suggests that it sounds like language of "an official character," perhaps even the equivalent of the Latin *donavit corpus*. Gundry (981) suggests a contrast between παραδίδωμι describing Jesus being given over to the authorities (14:10, 11, 18, 21, 41, 42, 44; 15:1, 10, 15) and δωρέομαι which connotes "a formal donation of [the] corpse."

τὸ πτῶμα. Accusative direct object of ἐδωρήσατο. This noun is formed from πίπτω ("that which is fallen," *CL*, 310). "When employed for the dead body of a human being it carries a tone of contempt" (Swete, 392). The variant reading σῶμα (A C W Ψ 083 *f*[1, 13] 33 𝔐) is "a more dignified word" (BDAG, 895).

τῷ Ἰωσήφ. Dative indirect object of ἐδωρήσατο.

15:46 καὶ ἀγοράσας σινδόνα καθελὼν αὐτὸν ἐνείλησεν τῇ σινδόνι καὶ ἔθηκεν αὐτὸν ἐν μνημείῳ ὃ ἦν λελατομημένον ἐκ πέτρας καὶ προσεκύλισεν λίθον ἐπὶ τὴν θύραν τοῦ μνημείου.

ἀγοράσας. Aor act ptc masc nom sg ἀγοράζω (temporal).

σινδόνα. Accusative direct object of ἀγοράσας. σινδών refers to "linen cloth" (BDAG, 924). This was "a piece of new linen, not a garment" (V. Taylor, 601). Although the cloth was used as a burial shroud, translating it as such (e.g., RSV, ESV, NJB) makes a very general term into a technical one.

καθελών. Aor act ptc masc nom sg καθαιρέω (temporal). This verb uses the root *αιρε in the present, future, and imperfect, but *ϝελ in the aorist and perfect (*MBG*, 319 n. 1). Though calling this a "technical term" (Bruce, 452) may be overstated, it is at least the normal term used to describe removing a body after crucifixion (BDAG, 487.1, cites Polybius 1.86.6; Philo, *Flaccus*, 83; Josephus, *J.W.* 4.317; and Josh 8:29; 10:27).

αὐτόν. Accusative direct object of ἐνείλησεν. The use of a masculine rather than neuter form with τὸ πτῶμα is probably due to agreement "in sense" (the reference is to Jesus).

ἐνείλησεν. Aor act ind 3rd sg ἐνειλέω ("to envelop an object by wrapping it in someth., *wrap (up) in* τινί *someth.*," BDAG, 334). There is only an implicit augment with this form, since the stem begins with ει (ἐν + εἰλέω). The implied subject of the verb is Joseph. Joseph was responsible for the action described, but it was likely performed by servants. This is probably also true of the preceding καθελών and perhaps even ἀγοράσας, as well as ἔθηκεν and προσεκύλισεν, which follow.

τῇ σινδόνι. The dative indicates the material in which the body was wrapped.

ἔθηκεν. Aor act ind 3rd sg τίθημι.

αὐτόν. Accusative direct object of ἔθηκεν.

ἐν μνημείῳ. Locative.

ὅ. Nominative subject of ἦν.

ἦν. Impf act ind 3rd sg εἰμί.

λελατομημένον. Prf pass ptc neut nom sg λατομέω (stative periphrastic, functionally equivalent to a pluperfect finite form). The word means "to form a cavity or chamber by cutting away rock," (BDAG, 587; only here and ‖ Matt 27:60).

ἐκ πέτρας. Source. In contrast to the individual pieces (λίθος) made of rock, πέτρα normally (as here) refers to "bedrock or massive rock formations" (BDAG, 809.1).

προσεκύλισεν. Aor act ind 3rd sg προσκυλίω ("*roll [up to]* τι *someth.* λίθον τῇ θύρᾳ *a stone to the opening*," BDAG, 882; only here and ‖ Matt 27:60). The choice of this verb implies a horizontal entry to the tomb rather than the vertical shaft that was more common for private burials at the time (R. Brown, 2:1247).

λίθον. Accusative direct object of προσεκύλισεν.

ἐπὶ τὴν θύραν. Spatial. Here θύρα is not the door per se, but the *doorway*, i.e., the entrance or opening into the tomb (see BDAG, 462.2.a).

15:47 ἡ δὲ Μαρία ἡ Μαγδαληνὴ καὶ Μαρία ἡ Ἰωσῆτος ἐθεώρουν ποῦ τέθειται.

ἡ ... Μαρία ἡ Μαγδαληνὴ καὶ Μαρία. Nominative subject of ἐθεώρουν.

ἡ Ἰωσῆτος. The article functions as a nominalizer changing the genitive noun Ἰωσῆτος into a nominative in apposition to Μαρία ("mother of" is assumed from the context).

ἐθεώρουν. Impf act ind 3rd pl θεωρέω. Although they likely observed the entire proceedings, the imperfect tense cannot be pressed to mean that "the women were there for a time, and thus probably throughout the brief burial" (R. Brown, 2:1251).

ποῦ. Introduces an indirect question: "where?"

τέθειται. Prf pass ind 3rd sg τίθημι.

Mark 16:1-8

[1]Now when the Sabbath had passed, Mary Magdalene, Mary the (mother) of James, and Salome bought spices that they might go and anoint him. [2]Very early in the morning of the first day of the week they came to the tomb, the sun having risen. [3]They said to each other, "Who will roll away the stone from the entrance of the tomb for us?" [4]Looking up they saw that the stone was rolled away, for it was very large. [5]Entering the tomb they saw a young man seated on the right side, clothed in a white garment, and they were alarmed. [6]But he said to them, "Do not be alarmed; you are seeking Jesus the Nazarene—the Crucified One. He has risen; he is not here. Here is the place where they laid him. [7]But go say to his disciples and to Peter, 'He is going ahead of you to Galilee; you will see him there just as he told you.'" [8]Going out, they fled from the tomb, for trembling and astonishment had taken hold of them, and they said nothing to anyone, for they were awed.

16:1 Καὶ διαγενομένου τοῦ σαββάτου Μαρία ἡ Μαγδαληνὴ καὶ Μαρία ἡ [τοῦ] Ἰακώβου καὶ Σαλώμη ἠγόρασαν ἀρώματα ἵνα ἐλθοῦσαι ἀλείψωσιν αὐτόν.

διαγενομένου. Aor mid ptc neut gen sg διαγίνομαι (genitive absolute, temporal; "to mark the passage of time," LN 67.84).

τοῦ σαββάτου. Genitive subject of διαγενομένου.

Μαρία ἡ Μαγδαληνὴ καὶ Μαρία … καὶ Σαλώμη. Nominative subject of ἠγόρασαν.

ἡ τοῦ Ἰακώβου. The article functions as a nominalizer changing the genitive noun τοῦ Ἰακώβου into a nominative in apposition to Μαρία ("mother of" is assumed from the context; see also 1:19).

ἠγόρασαν. Aor act ind 3rd pl ἀγοράζω.

ἀρώματα. Accusative direct object of ἠγόρασαν. ἄρωμα refers to "any kind of *fragrant substance, fragrant spice/salve/oil/perfume,* esp. used in embalming the dead" (BDAG, 141).

ἐλθοῦσαι. Aor act ptc fem nom pl ἔρχομαι (probably attendant circumstance, though that is less common with a subjunctive verb).

ἵνα. Introduces a purpose clause.

ἀλείψωσιν. Aor act subj 3rd pl ἀλείφω. Subjunctive with ἵνα.

αὐτόν. Accusative direct object of ἀλείψωσιν.

16:2 καὶ λίαν πρωῒ τῇ μιᾷ τῶν σαββάτων ἔρχονται ἐπὶ τὸ μνημεῖον ἀνατείλαντος τοῦ ἡλίου.

λίαν πρωῒ. The two adverbs used together mean "very early in the morning." The following dative specifies the day involved. Evans (2001, 534) thinks that λίαν πρωῒ contradicts ἀνατείλαντος τοῦ ἡλίου, but there is no reason why sunrise may not be described as very early. Stein rightly cautions against giving these terms "greater temporal precision than Mark intended" (2008, 729).

τῇ μιᾷ τῶν σαββάτων. The use of the cardinal number μιᾷ (εἷς) in place of the ordinal πρῶτος in the sense "the first day" is an idiomatic, fixed phrase in Hellenistic Greek, perhaps due to Hebraistic influences (BDAG, 293.4.a, s.v. εἷς; Doudna, 92–96; for a counter-view, see MHT 1:95–96; 2:439). The feminine μιᾷ likely reflects an implied ἡμέρα. See similar expressions in Matt 28:1; Luke 24:1; John 20:1, 19; Acts 20:7; and 1 Cor 16:2 (all with σάββατον). On the plural of σαββάτων, here meaning "week" rather than "Sabbath," see 1:21.

ἔρχονται. Pres mid ind 3rd pl ἔρχομαι. The narrative present (see 1:21 on εἰσπορεύονται) is part of the storyline, parallel with ἠγόρασαν (v. 1), and is perhaps used due to the geographic shift in location.

ἐπὶ τὸ μνημεῖον. Spatial.

ἀνατείλαντος. Aor act ptc masc gen sg ἀνατέλλω. Genitive absolute (see 1:32), temporal. This is the only genitive absolute in

Mark that concludes a sentence, the more common position being sentence initial (Fuller, 164). "The use of a second genitive absolute (ἀνατείλαντος ἡλίου) is unusual so deeply embedded in the paragraph, but is used here to close off the introductory material with a temporal reference that establishes the time of the events that are being recounted. The use of the genitive absolute helps to clarify the action that follows by establishing that it was dawn, and that the events that follow are not those of mistaken identity or misdirection on the basis of it being dark" (Porter 2008, 128).

τοῦ ἡλίου. Genitive subject of ἀνατείλαντος.

16:3 καὶ ἔλεγον πρὸς ἑαυτάς, Τίς ἀποκυλίσει ἡμῖν τὸν λίθον ἐκ τῆς θύρας τοῦ μνημείου;

ἔλεγον. Impf act ind 3rd pl λέγω. The imperfect is used to introduce discourse.

πρὸς ἑαυτάς. Association. The form ἑαυτάς is seldom seen in the NT (only here and 1 Tim 2:9); it is the third person plural form of the reflexive pronoun ἑαυτοῦ.

Τίς ἀποκυλίσει . . . τοῦ μνημείου. Clausal complement (direct discourse) of ἔλεγον.

Τίς. Nominative subject of ἀποκυλίσει.

ἀποκυλίσει. Fut act ind 3rd sg ἀποκυλίω ("to roll away," BDAG, 114).

ἡμῖν. Dative of advantage.

τὸν λίθον. Accusative direct object of ἀποκυλίσει.

ἐκ τῆς θύρας. Separation.

16:4 καὶ ἀναβλέψασαι θεωροῦσιν ὅτι ἀποκεκύλισται ὁ λίθος· ἦν γὰρ μέγας σφόδρα.

ἀναβλέψασαι. Aor act ptc fem nom pl ἀναβλέπω (temporal). The prefixed ἀνά need not imply that the tomb was geographically higher, only that they "looked up from their path to see the tomb when it came into view" (Gundry, 999).

θεωροῦσιν. Pres act ind 3rd pl θεωρέω. This is a narrative present. When this verb is followed by ὅτι the meaning is often "to recognize, realize" (cf. BDF §397.1).

ὅτι. Introduces the clausal complement (indirect discourse with a verb of perception) of θεωροῦσιν.

ἀποκεκύλισται. Prf pass ind 3rd sg ἀποκυλίω ("to roll away," see v. 3). The perfect describes the already existing condition of the

stone. "The emphasis is upon the fact that the stone is simply standing there, removed" (Porter 2008, 130). That the statement is passive
rather than middle seems obvious from the context despite the lack
of an explicit agent marker.

ὁ λίθος. Nominative subject of ἀποκεκύλισται.

ἦν. Impf act ind 3rd sg εἰμί.

γὰρ. Introduces a subordinate, explanatory clause that almost
seems out of place, since it does not explain the preceding statement
(that the stone was rolled away), but rather the question recorded in
the previous verse, "Who will roll the stone away?" "Its extremely
large size [μέγας σφόδρα] would rather explain why they should *not*
have found it already rolled away" (Gundry, 990). Mark's emphasis,
as Gundry goes on to point out, is on the fact that the stone has been
rolled away, "so he puts it before his explanation of the reason for
the women's question." The syntax thus reinforces the grammatical
emphasis of the perfect verb. "Writers who use γάρ frequently, as
Mark does, are not always logical thinkers who develop an argument
stage by stage, representing each further statement as the necessary
deduction from the previous one, or who tell a story in strict chronological sequence, with every detail in its logical position in the narrative. . . . In narrative they mention first the important or striking
points in the story, and then fit in the explanatory details afterwards
by using γάρ, whether or not these details should logically precede
the main points. . . . The mention of the size of the stone should logically precede the women's question, or at any rate the statement that
the stone had been moved. But since, on the one hand, the interest at
the beginning of the story is focused upon the actions of the women,
and, on the other hand, the really striking point in the narrative is
the fact of the stone's removal, these elements are recorded first.
Then the evangelist remembers that he should have mentioned the
size of the stone in order to account for the women's anxiety about
moving it, and this is added last of all in a γάρ-clause which bears no
logical relation to the immediately preceding sentence but which is
nevertheless genuinely explanatory" (Thrall, 47–48).

μέγας. Predicate adjective.

σφόδρα. Adverb modifying μέγας.

**16:5 καὶ εἰσελθοῦσαι εἰς τὸ μνημεῖον εἶδον νεανίσκον καθή-
μενον ἐν τοῖς δεξιοῖς περιβεβλημένον στολὴν λευκήν, καὶ ἐξεθαμβήθησαν.**

εἰσελθοῦσαι. Aor act ptc fem nom pl εἰσέρχομαι (temporal).

εἰς τὸ μνημεῖον. Spatial. On the repeated preposition, see 1:21.

εἶδον. Aor act ind 3rd pl ὁράω.

νεανίσκον. Accusative direct object of εἶδον.

καθήμενον. Pres mid ptc masc acc sg κάθημαι (complement in an object-complement double accusative construction).

ἐν τοῖς δεξιοῖς. Locative, i.e., on the right side of the tomb area.

περιβεβλημένον. Prf mid ptc masc acc sg περιβάλλω (attributive).

στολὴν λευκήν. Accusative direct object of περιβεβλημένον. Although the young man is not specifically identified as such, the emphasis of his description as being dressed in white certainly suggests an angelic or heavenly messenger of some sort (see Lane, 587; cf. Acts 1:10; Rev 4:4; 7:9; 19:14). Matt 28:2-3 makes the identification explicit (cf. John 20:12).

ἐξεθαμβήθησαν. Aor mid ind 3rd pl ἐκθαμβέω. This is a "θη middle" form. On the meaning of ἐκθαμβέω ("to be alarmed"), a word that occurs in the NT only in Mark, see 9:15.

16:6 ὁ δὲ λέγει αὐταῖς, Μὴ ἐκθαμβεῖσθε· Ἰησοῦν ζητεῖτε τὸν Ναζαρηνὸν τὸν ἐσταυρωμένον· ἠγέρθη, οὐκ ἔστιν ὧδε· ἴδε ὁ τόπος ὅπου ἔθηκαν αὐτόν.

ὁ. Nominative subject of λέγει. On the use of ὁ δέ to change subjects, see 1:45.

λέγει. Pres act ind 3rd sg λέγω.

αὐταῖς. Dative indirect object of λέγει.

Μὴ ἐκθαμβεῖσθε . . . ⁷καθὼς εἶπεν ὑμῖν. Clausal complement (direct discourse) of λέγει.

ἐκθαμβεῖσθε. Pres mid impv 2nd pl ἐκθαμβέω ("to be alarmed," see v. 5 and 9:15). The young man uses the same verb as was used in the previous description of the women's reaction (v. 5).

ζητεῖτε. Pres act ind 2nd pl ζητέω.

Ἰησοῦν . . . τὸν Ναζαρηνὸν. Accusative direct object of ζητεῖτε. The discontinuous syntax, with Ἰησοῦν separated from τὸν Ναζαρηνὸν τὸν ἐσταυρωμένον by the main verb, is unusual and may "[draw] attention to the one being sought, who is characterized as the one in the crucified state" (Porter 2008, 134). On the identification of Jesus as Ναζαρηνός, see 10:47. For a similar combination of descriptions, see Acts 4:10 (though Luke uses Ναζωραῖος rather than Ναζαρηνός).

τὸν ἐσταυρωμένον. Prf pass ptc masc acc sg σταυρόω, either substantival, "Jesus of Nazareth, the Crucified One," or (perhaps more likely) attributive, "Jesus the crucified Nazarene." The perfect tense describes Jesus in the state in which the women expected to find him: crucified, i.e., lying dead in the tomb. Alternatively, Porter (2008, 134–35) suggests that the perfect tense pictures Jesus in keeping with the Markan emphasis on the crucifixion and the early church's similar description (e.g., 1 Cor 1:23; 2:2; Gal 3:1; Acts 4:10). Although both explanations for the use of the perfect reflect true statements, I think it is more likely that the women's viewpoint is primary here rather than the later theological descriptions.

ἠγέρθη. Aor mid ind 3rd sg ἐγείρω. This is a "θη middle" intransitive form, not passive (see 2:2). Pascut, however, suggests that ἠγέρθη should be viewed as a passive, but "used because it emphasizes the action whose doer is irrelevant for the present context. . . . One of the main functions of the passive voice is agent defocusing" (322).

ἔστιν. Pres act ind 3rd sg εἰμί. On the accent, see 12:32.

Ἴδε. See 3:34. This interjection might have a verbal flavor, "Look!" or "See!" (so most English translations), or it may mean simply "here," i.e., "Here is the place" (BDAG, 466.3).

ὁ τόπος. Predicate nominative of an implied ἐστίν: "Here is the place." Alternatively this could be explained as a "parenthetical nominative" used with a frozen or stereotyped form, the particle ἴδε, originally an imperative of εἶδον (so BDF §144; BDAG, 466). As such, even though the original form was a singular, it is used with both singular (e.g., 11:21) and plural (e.g., 13:1) nominative forms following. The referent of τόπος is not the tomb, but more specifically the niche or shelf within the tomb where the body had been placed (V. Taylor, 607). This should not be claimed as an instance in which Mark's incorrect grammar is corrected by Matthew (contra Stein 1987, 53–54). Matthew 28:6 does use an alternative construction, δεῦτε ἴδετε τὸν τόπον, in which the accusative is used as the direct object of the verb ἴδετε, but either statement is acceptable. It may be true that this is a less polished statement; it occurs in the NT only in Mark and John, both of which are among the simpler, less sophisticated Greek NT writers. If so, then it would be better to say that Matthew, if he reflects knowledge of Mark (as seems likely), may have used a more polished statement.

ἔθηκαν. Aor act ind 3rd pl τίθημι.

αὐτόν. Accusative direct object of ἔθηκαν.

16:7 ἀλλὰ ὑπάγετε εἴπατε τοῖς μαθηταῖς αὐτοῦ καὶ τῷ Πέτρῳ ὅτι Προάγει ὑμᾶς εἰς τὴν Γαλιλαίαν· ἐκεῖ αὐτὸν ὄψεσθε, καθὼς εἶπεν ὑμῖν.

ὑπάγετε. Pres act impv 2nd pl ὑπάγω. The use of two imperatives back to back, one a present and the other aorist, is interesting. The difference is probably not great, though the present may be used for what is the most urgent of the two commands (the aorist imperative is generally the unmarked imperative form); they will never be able to tell the disciples the news until they have first gone. Duckwitz says that "ὑπάγετε is usually found in asyndeton when followed by another imperative" (253). This is true in the NT, though there are only four instances of the exact construction (Matt 27:65; 28:10; Mark 6:38; 16:7). If the data is widened to include singular forms of ὑπάγω, the following instances of the pattern are also found: Matt 5:24; 8:4a; Mark 1:44a; John 4:16a; 9:7; and Rev 10:8. Instances not following the pattern are Mark 5:19, 34; John 9:11; and Rev 16:1. The pattern breaks down in the AF where the two imperatives are always joined by καί (Herm. *Vis.* 9:7; 23:5; *Sim.* 77:1; 87:1).

εἴπατε. Aor act impv 2nd pl λέγω.

τοῖς μαθηταῖς . . . καὶ τῷ Πέτρῳ. Dative indirect object of εἴπατε.

ὅτι. Introduces the clausal complement (direct discourse) of εἴπατε (see 1:15).

Προάγει. Pres act ind 3rd sg προάγω. The sense is probably best understood with future reference, though that cannot be determined from Mark's account alone. It seems to be an overstatement to insist that "the pres. is not a virtual fut., but gives the assurance that Jesus is on the way to Galilee *now*" (contra V. Taylor, 608, emphasis original). Likewise Gundry tries to make room for a present time reference by saying that Jesus' "going ahead has not yet taken him far enough from the tomb to prevent his appearance. Since he has already started by leaving the tomb, the present tense . . . replaces the future tense" (992). Though harmonizing the sequence of Jesus' post-resurrection appearances is not easy (due primarily to insufficient information), it would seem that the appearances in Galilee took place after Jesus' appearances to the disciples on the road to Emmaus, his appearance to Peter, and his initial appearance to the disciples in the Upper Room. Alternatively, Evans understands the reference to be not to the journey to Galilee, but to Jesus' leadership in ministry once they are in Galilee, "the ministry of proclaiming and advancing the kingdom, broken off for a short time in order to make the fateful journey to Jerusalem, will now resume" (2001, 537–38).

ὑμᾶς. Accusative direct object of προάγει. The plural forms ὑμᾶς, ὄψεσθε, and ὑμῖν make it clear that the message is for all the disciples, not just Peter.

εἰς τὴν Γαλιλαίαν. Spatial.

αὐτὸν. Accusative direct object of ὄψεσθε.

ὄψεσθε. Fut mid ind 2nd pl ὁράω. For an extensive critique of attempts to differentiate the post-resurrection appearances of Jesus from his second coming on the basis of the tenses of ὁράω, see Gundry (1007–8).

καθὼς. Though classed as a comparative adverb, καθώς does not suggest a similarity, but introduces a statement of identity: "just as" (see 14:28).

εἶπεν. Aor act ind 3rd sg λέγω.

ὑμῖν. Dative indirect object of εἶπεν.

16:8 καὶ ἐξελθοῦσαι ἔφυγον ἀπὸ τοῦ μνημείου, εἶχεν γὰρ αὐτὰς τρόμος καὶ ἔκστασις· καὶ οὐδενὶ οὐδὲν εἶπαν· ἐφοβοῦντο γάρ.

ἐξελθοῦσαι. Aor act ptc fem nom pl ἐξέρχομαι (temporal or attendant circumstance).

ἔφυγον. Aor act ind 3rd pl φεύγω.

ἀπὸ τοῦ μνημείου. Separation.

εἶχεν. Impf act ind 3rd sg ἔχω. The sense here is, "had taken hold of, gripped." The singular verb agrees with the closest subject (τρόμος) in the compound construction.

γὰρ. Introduces a clause that explains why the women fled from the tomb.

αὐτὰς. Accusative direct object of εἶχεν.

τρόμος καὶ ἔκστασις. Nominative subject of εἶχεν. The impersonal characteristics are personified (Duckwitz, 253). For τρόμος καὶ ἔκστασις, see 1:22 on ἐκπλήσσω. The duality might suggest hendiadys, "tremulous astonishment" (so Gundry, 1012). "They are so excited by what they have seen and heard that their bodies begin to shake" (Evans 2001, 538). τρόμος refers to "trembling" (BDAG, 1016), while ἔκστασις should be understood here as "amazement, astonishment" rather than a "trance" (see BDAG, 309).

οὐδενὶ οὐδὲν εἶπαν. Though I would not use the word "terrified" as the primary description, Moule's (1965, 133) comments are appropriate: "That the women are described as saying nothing to anybody (verse 8) clearly does not mean that they did not tell their experience to their close friends [i.e., the apostles and other followers of Jesus]. It probably means no more than that they were too terrified and in too much of a hurry to stop and speak to anybody they chanced to meet between the tomb and wherever they were staying" (cf. Cranfield, 469; Gundry, 1009). To read this as disobedience in which the women never obeyed the young man's command (see Evans 2001, 538 and Edwards 2002, 496 as recent examples of this conclusion) is reading far more into the text than is stated or implied despite the double negative.

οὐδενί. Dative indirect object of εἶπαν.

οὐδὲν. Accusative direct object of εἶπαν.

εἶπαν. Aor act ind 3rd pl λέγω.

ἐφοβοῦντο. Impf mid ind 3rd pl φοβέομαι. Wallace (2008, 38) suggests that the "open-ended" nature of the imperfect is well suited to Mark's purpose of leaving the reader hanging at the end of his book to ponder the significance of these events. Though often read as if the women were "scared silly," that is probably the wrong impression. φοβέομαι can refer to being "scared," but it can also have connotations of "the fear of the Lord" (cf. τὸν φόβον τοῦ κυρίου, Acts 9:31; 2 Cor 5:11). In the LXX this concept is usually expressed as φόβος κυρίου (e.g., 2 Chr 19:7; Ps 18:10; Prov 1:7), though ἔκστασις, εὐσέβεια, and θεοσέβειά are occasionally used. One indication of this association is the word pair earlier in the verse: τρόμος καὶ ἔκστασις. Although τρόμος can be paired with φοβέομαι in contexts where "trembling and afraid" are probably negative descriptions (e.g., 2 Cor 7:15), the connotations may also be positive (e.g., Phil 2:12); here the paired word is ἔκστασις ("astonishment"). A similar, positive association is found with ἔκστασις and θάμβος in Acts 3:10. In Mark 5:33, a woman similarly responds to a miracle with fear and trembling (φοβηθεῖσα καὶ τρέμουσα). Overall, these statements are more likely to be taken in a positive sense, reflecting the women's awe in light of the resurrection they had just discovered. Of course confrontation with the supernatural will have some element of fear, but the motivation and nature of that fear is quite different from the "Scooby Doo" type of fear. Luke appears to have understood the situation this way for he describes the women as κλινουσῶν τὰ πρόσωπα εἰς τὴν γῆν (24:7), which would seem to indicate reverence here (cf. LN 17.21), an appropriate response if they recognized the messenger as an angel. The idiom in Luke appears to be similar to a common expression in the LXX: ἔκυψεν Δαυιδ ἐπὶ πρόσωπον αὐτοῦ ἐπὶ τὴν γῆν καὶ προσεκύνησεν αὐτῷ (1 Sam 24:9), though this uses κύπτω rather than κλίνω. Though Luke's account should not be used to "prove" one's exegesis of an earlier text, it may serve to indicate how someone much closer to the situation understood the same event. See also Matthew's account (with the same qualification): ἀπελθοῦσαι ταχὺ ἀπὸ τοῦ μνημείου μετὰ φόβου καὶ χαρᾶς μεγάλης ἔδραμον ἀπαγγεῖλαι τοῖς μαθηταῖς αὐτοῦ (28:8). For a similar assessment of the women's fear, see Cranfield (470; "Mark's account . . . underlines the mystery and awe-fulness of the Resurrection"), Lane (590–92), and Magness (98–102). For one of the better defenses of the opposing analysis, see Lincoln (286–87).

γάρ. Introduces a statement that explains why they said nothing to anyone as they fled back to the city. Much ink has been spilled over Mark's Gospel apparently abruptly ending with γάρ. Though it may seem odd to an English reader that a book would end with the equivalent of "for," that is not at all the case in Greek, since γάρ is a postpositive conjunction. In a two word clause containing γάρ it *must* be the last word. "It should be noted that γάρ w. a verb (and nothing else) can form a sentence" (BDAG, 189.1.a, citing 10 examples). Another NT instance is found in John 13:13 (ὑμεῖς φωνεῖτέ με Ὁ διδάσκαλος καί Ὁ κύριος, καὶ καλῶς λέγετε, εἰμὶ γάρ). An interesting parallel is Gen 18:15, which not only ends a sentence with γάρ, but is a two-word clause using the same verb: ἠρνήσατο δὲ Σαρρα λέγουσα Οὐκ ἐγέλασα· ἐφοβήθη γάρ (see also Gen 45:3, where a paragraph ends with a very similar statement: ἐταράχθησαν γάρ). BDAG also lists five examples in which a letter, story, introduction, or entire book end with γάρ. For examples of books ending with γάρ, see Plotinus's *32nd Treatise* (τελειότερον γάρ, referenced in Van der Horst, 121–24; Enn. 5.5.38 in TLG) and Gaius Musonius Rufus' *Twelfth Tractate* (referenced in Iverson, 79–80, 94), which is also a short, two-word sentence (γνώριμον γάρ, *Diss.* 12.48 in TLG). The example from Musonius should be used cautiously given the fragmentary nature of these texts—they are extracts of his lectures compiled by his students, though Greek-speaking students had no hesitation to end their compilation with γάρ. Iverson (93) clearly demonstrates that although such statements "are extremely, extremely rare at all times and in all genres," they *are* attested. He (82 n. 12) gives figures from the complete TLG database of 1,884 sentences ending with γάρ followed by a period plus another 786 where it is followed by a question mark. If limited to the 3rd century BC through the 2nd century AD, there are 272 instances of γάρ followed by a period (Iverson, 82 n. 12). See also BDAG's discussion, (1061.1.a, s.v. φοβέω) with extensive bibliography, and Van der

Horst (121–22 n. 3), who has an extensive bibliography focusing especially on earlier journal articles.

Brief γάρ clauses are characteristic of Mark (e.g., 1:16; 3:21; 9:6; 10:22; 16:4) and Mark uses φοβέω absolutely (without any explanatory words or phrases) five times (5:15, 33, 36; 6:50; 10:32). Croy (50–51) argues that the absolute use of φοβέω is most common in the aorist, but rare in the imperfect. This does not reflect Markan usage, however, since the six instances in Mark include two aorist forms (5:15, 33), two imperfects (10:32; 16:8), and two present forms (5:36; 6:50). Though such an abrupt ending has been declared impossible (or at least highly unlikely) for an ancient writer (it supposedly reflects modern literary style), it should be noted that Luke's ending of Acts is no less abrupt (see Wallace 2008, 34–35). Magness (25–47) points to similar examples of such "suspended" endings in the ancient world, in the OT (49–63), and in the NT itself (65–85).

APPENDIX

Ancient Christian Writings Related to the Ending of the Gospel of Mark

The Issues Related to the Ending of Mark

It is no secret that there is uncertainty as to the ending of Mark's Gospel. All critical commentaries on this book include a discussion of the issues, but it is not a modern question; even in the early centuries such discussions are attested. It is not the place of a grammatical handbook to attempt the resolution of such a textual question, though a brief summary of the question is included along with a more detailed discussion of relevant grammatical issues. A judgment regarding the originality of the ending of Mark should not be based only or even primarily on internal issues of style. The question must be considered on a holistic basis, beginning with external evidence. Questions of style, despite the brevity of the sample available, are important as a second step in such an evaluation. Without plausible external evidence the appeal to internal considerations is no more than conjecture. In the case of Mark 16:9-20, both forms of evidence are present. Since the external evidence is not discussed here in detail, the following grammatical discussion must be supplemented with other studies that focus specifically on the external evidence (see esp. D. Black, 2008, for essays defending four views on the subject, chapter 1 of which provides the most detailed discussion of external evidence; Waterman, 52–83, for a wide-ranging survey of various views since 1980; and Hort's classic discussion of the issues in WH, 2:28–51).

There are actually many possible endings to Mark's Gospel. Depending on how the tally is made, there could be ten or more endings evident in the manuscript tradition, though there are only a few viable alternatives. The majority of the manuscripts include what has been known traditionally as Mark 16:9-20 or the "Long Ending." There is both a shorter version (the "Short Ending") and a longer version of the Long Ending (the "Long-Long Ending"). Of these, only the "Long Ending" has garnered some support, albeit slight, among contemporary NT scholars as being the original ending of the Gospel. (Historically, the Long Ending was viewed much more favorably.)

There are two major positions reflected in twentieth- and twenty-first-century NT scholarship. Some have concluded that Mark ended deliberately with what we today know as 16:8. Others suggest that the original ending has been lost. Although a lost ending is still a popular opinion (see, e.g., Edwards 2002; Evans 2001; France 2002; Gundry 1993), I conclude that Mark deliberately and abruptly ended with verse 8. Indeed, it is the apparent abruptness of this ending (though it is no more abrupt than his introduction) that has occasioned the proliferation of alternative endings. Since Mark is different from the other Gospels in his conclusion, it is natural that some thought it necessary to assimilate Mark's work to match the general style of the others. With only a brief account of the resurrection, no record whatsoever of Jesus' post-resurrection ministry, and no final words of "Great Commission," it may have seemed unfinished. Although the various endings that originated in the early church (and they go back to the second century) do give Mark's account a "feel" like the others, they lose Mark's sharp focus on the empty tomb, interpreted by God as a resurrection.

Once a well-meaning writer penned one of the new endings and it entered the transmission process, it is evident why we have such a proliferation of endings. Most scribes were cautious, conservative guardians of the biblical text and thus felt it was better to include one (or more) of the alternatives (even if the text of the Gospel was also known to end at verse 8 in other manuscripts) than to omit what they thought could have been original. Their motivation was not a great deal different than Bible publishers today, all of whom include at least one alternative ending and some two (NLT gives the most complete list, citing the short and long endings as well as the Freer Logion), even though they also follow the scribes' example by including a note indicating that the various alternate endings may not be original.

Extant Texts Purporting to Be the Ending of Mark

In the texts given below a full grammatical commentary has not been given, though a translation has been included (except for the traditional "long ending," since it is familiar) with a list of glosses for less common vocabulary. The textual evidence for the various endings is not given, but is readily available elsewhere.

A. *The So-Called "Short Ending" of Mark*

The following summary statement appears in some manuscripts of Mark, sometimes following 16:8a (omitting 8b, καὶ οὐδενὶ οὐδὲν εἶπαν, ἐφοβοῦντο γάρ), other times preceding or following the "Long Ending": Πάντα δὲ τὰ παρηγγελμένα τοῖς περὶ τὸν Πέτρον συντόμως ἐξήγγειλαν. Μετὰ δὲ ταῦτα καὶ αὐτὸς ὁ Ἰησοῦς ἀπὸ ἀνατολῆς καὶ ἄχρι δύσεως ἐξαπέστειλεν δι᾽ αὐτῶν τὸ ἱερὸν καὶ ἄφθαρτον κήρυγμα τῆς αἰωνίου σωτηρίας. ἀμήν ("All these instructions they quickly reported to those with Peter. After these things Jesus himself also sent out through them from east to west the sacred and imperishable proclamation of eternal salvation. Amen").

Less common vocabulary in this ending includes δύσις ("west"), ἐξαγγέλλω ("to proclaim, report"), ἱερός ("pertaining to being of transcendent purity," *holy*, BDAG, 470), and συντόμως ("in a short time," *promptly, readily*, BDAG, 976).

In manuscripts that have the "Short Ending" followed by the "Long Ending," the following note often appears between them: ἐστὶ καὶ ταῦτα φερόμενα ("These [words] are also found").

B. *The So-Called "Long Ending" of Mark (Traditionally Identified as Mark 16:9-20)*

[9]Ἀναστὰς δὲ πρωῒ πρώτῃ σαββάτου ἐφάνη πρῶτον Μαρίᾳ τῇ Μαγδαληνῇ, παρ᾽ ἧς ἐκβεβλήκει ἑπτὰ δαιμόνια. [10]ἐκείνη πορευθεῖσα ἀπήγγειλεν τοῖς μετ᾽ αὐτοῦ γενομένοις πενθοῦσι καὶ κλαίουσιν· [11]κἀκεῖνοι ἀκούσαντες ὅτι ζῇ καὶ ἐθεάθη ὑπ᾽ αὐτῆς ἠπίστησαν.

[12]Μετὰ δὲ ταῦτα δυσὶν ἐξ αὐτῶν περιπατοῦσιν ἐφανερώθη ἐν ἑτέρᾳ μορφῇ πορευομένοις εἰς ἀγρόν· [13]κἀκεῖνοι ἀπελθόντες ἀπήγγειλαν τοῖς λοιποῖς· οὐδὲ ἐκείνοις ἐπίστευσαν.

[14]Ὕστερον [δὲ] ἀνακειμένοις αὐτοῖς τοῖς ἕνδεκα ἐφανερώθη καὶ ὠνείδισεν τὴν ἀπιστίαν αὐτῶν καὶ σκληροκαρδίαν ὅτι τοῖς θεασαμένοις αὐτὸν ἐγηγερμένον οὐκ ἐπίστευσαν. [15]καὶ εἶπεν αὐτοῖς, Πορευθέντες εἰς τὸν κόσμον ἅπαντα κηρύξατε τὸ εὐαγγέλιον πάσῃ τῇ κτίσει. [16]ὁ πιστεύσας καὶ βαπτισθεὶς σωθήσεται, ὁ δὲ ἀπιστήσας κατακριθήσεται. [17]σημεῖα δὲ τοῖς πιστεύσασιν ταῦτα παρακολουθήσει· ἐν τῷ ὀνόματί μου δαιμόνια ἐκβαλοῦσιν, γλώσσαις λαλήσουσιν καιναῖς, [18][καὶ ἐν ταῖς χερσὶν] ὄφεις ἀροῦσιν κἂν θανάσιμόν τι πίωσιν οὐ μὴ αὐτοὺς βλάψῃ, ἐπὶ ἀρρώστους χεῖρας ἐπιθήσουσιν καὶ καλῶς ἕξουσιν.

[19]Ὁ μὲν οὖν κύριος Ἰησοῦς μετὰ τὸ λαλῆσαι αὐτοῖς ἀνελήμφθη εἰς τὸν οὐρανὸν καὶ ἐκάθισεν ἐκ δεξιῶν τοῦ θεοῦ. [20]ἐκεῖνοι δὲ

284 Appendix

ἐξελθόντες ἐκήρυξαν πανταχοῦ, τοῦ κυρίου συνεργοῦντος καὶ τὸν λόγον βεβαιοῦντος διὰ τῶν ἐπακολουθούντων σημείων.

The adjective ἄρρωστος means "sick, ill," βλάπτω means "to harm, injure" (BDAG, 177), ἐπακολουθέω means "to happen as a result or appropriate event in connection with someth[ing], *follow*" and perhaps also *authenticating* (BDAG, 358), θανάσιμος means "deadly," μορφή means "form, outward appearance, shape" (BDAG, 659), παρακολουθέω means "to follow, accompany, attend" (BDAG, 767), σκληροκαρδία refers to "an unyielding frame of mind, *hardness of heart, coldness, obstinacy, stubbornness*" (BDAG, 930), and συνεργέω means "to engage in cooperative endeavor, *work together with, assist, help*" (BDAG, 969). See also "Grammatical Issues in the Long Ending of Mark" below.

In some manuscripts this ending is introduced with an obelus and a critical note (the one cited here is found in MS 1) to the effect that ἐν τισὶ μὲν τῶν ἀντιγραφῶν ἕως ὧδε πληροῦται ὁ εὐαγγελιστὴς ἕως οὗ καὶ Εὐσέβιος ὁ Παμφίλου ἐκανόνισεν· ἐν πολλοῖς δὲ καὶ ταῦτα φέρεται ("On the one hand, in some of the copies the Evangelist ends at this point as Eusebius of Pamphilus also judges; but in many [copies] these [words] also are included").

The noun ἀντίγραφον refers to "a copy of a book" (BDAG, 88), a εὐαγγελιστής, is a "*proclaimer of the gospel, evangelist*" (BDAG, 403), and the verb κανονίζω means "*to measure; to judge*" (LSJ, 875)

C. The "Long-Long Ending" of Mark

The following "Freer Logion" is inserted in some manuscripts between verses 14 and 15 of the "Long Ending." It is characterized by "florid" phrasing unlike anything else in the Gospels (Holmes 2001, 22): . . . ἐπίστευσαν.] κἀκεῖνοι ἀπελογοῦντο λέγοντες ὅτι ὁ αἰὼν οὗτος τῆς ἀνομίας καὶ τῆς ἀπιστίας ὑπὸ τὸν Σατανᾶν ἐστιν, ὁ μὴ ἐῶν τὰ ὑπὸ τῶν πνευμάτων ἀκάθαρτα τὴν ἀλήθειαν τοῦ θεοῦ καταλαβέσθαι δύναμιν· διὰ τοῦτο ἀποκάλυψον σοῦ τὴν δικαιοσύνην ἤδη. ἐκεῖνοι ἔλεγον τῷ Χριστῷ, καὶ ὁ Χριστὸς ἐκείνοις προσέλεγεν ὅτι πεπλήρωται ὁ ὅρος τῶν ἐτῶν τῆς ἐξουσίας τοῦ Σατανᾶ, ἀλλὰ ἐγγίζει ἄλλα δεινὰ καὶ ὑπὲρ ὧν ἐγὼ ἁμαρτησάντων παρεδόθην εἰς θάνατον ἵνα ὑποστρέψωσιν εἰς τὴν ἀλήθειαν καὶ μηκέτι ἁμαρτήσωσιν· ἵνα τὴν ἐν τῷ οὐρανῷ πνευματικὴν καὶ ἄφθαρτον τῆς δικαιοσύνης δόξαν κληρονομήσωσιν. ἀλλὰ [εἶπεν αὐτοῖς . . . ("They excused themselves saying, 'This age of lawlessness and unbelief is under Satan, who does not allow the truth and power of God to overcome the unclean things of the spirits. Therefore reveal your righteousness now.' They spoke (this) to the Messiah. And the Messiah replied to them, 'The limits of the years of Satan's power is fulfilled, but other terrible things are near. And for those who have sinned I was delivered over to death, that they should return to the truth and sin no more, in order that they should inherit the spiritual and incorruptible glory of righteousness which is in heaven.' But [he said to them. . . .'"

The verb ἀπολογέομαι means "to speak in one's own defense against charges presumed to be false, defend oneself" (BDAG, 117), δεινός means "pertaining to causing or being likely to cause fear, fearful, terrible" (BDAG, 215), ἐάω means "to allow someone to do something, let, permit" (BDAG, 269), ὅρος refers to a "boundary, limit" (BDAG, 725), and προσλέγω means "to answer, reply" (BDAG, 883).

Grammatical and Vocabulary Issues in the Long Ending of Mark

Some of the grammatical considerations that impinge on the question of Mark's ending are discussed below (ending a book with γάρ has already been discussed at 16:8). Literary matters beyond the level of grammar and syntax are not discussed here, but worth noting in that regard is the article by J. Williams (1999).

Vocabulary statistics have sometimes been employed in arguing against the originality of 16:9-20. A convenient summary of such statistics is provided by Danove (1993, 122–24; see also Danove 2001, 70–71). There are sixteen words in 16:9-20 that do not appear elsewhere in the Gospel, several of which occur multiple times in verses 9-20: πορεύομαι, πενθέω, θεάομαι, ἀπιστέω, ἔτερος, μορφή, ὕστερος, ἕνδεκα, παρακολουθέω, ὄφις, θανάσιμος, βλάπτω, ἀναλαμβάνω, συνεργέω, βεβαιόω, and ἐπακολουθέω. There are also five words the usage of which is not characteristic of Mark's Gospel: ἐκεῖνος as a pronoun (see qualification below), ἐπιτίθημι with ἐπί, κτίσις meaning "all humankind" (BDAG, 573.2.b, contra Danove's definition), κἄν meaning "and if," and κύριος as a title of Jesus. Four phrases do not appear elsewhere in Mark's Gospel: τοῖς μετ᾽ αὐτοῦ γενομένοις, μετὰ ταῦτα, καλῶς ἕξουσιν, and μὲν οὖν. There are other phrases that could potentially be added, such as γλώσσαις λαλήσουσιν καιναῖς.

Such arguments must, however, be used with caution due to the brevity of the material in question (see O'Donnell), especially when single words are involved. Statistical arguments for authorship, even based on words occurring only once in the questioned text, prove very little on their own since there is no law forbidding any writer from using a word only once. It is true that δύσις occurs in the NT only in the Short Ending and θανάσιμος occurs only in the Long Ending (v. 18), but both are common outside the NT (see BDAG). Although πενθέω occurs only here in Mark, it also occurs only once in Luke, twice in Matthew, and not at all in John, so such usage is average, not unusual. Indeed, there are 72 *hapax legomena* in Mark 1:1–16:8. Another factor bearing on a vocabulary argument is the degree of specificity: Are the words involved common words that any writer would use frequently (especially structural words such as particles and conjunctions), or are they words that would only be used in very specific contexts? Though ὄφις occurs only in the Long Ending (v. 18), as T. Williams points out, "there is hardly another instance in the story [i.e., Mark's Gospel] in which the word could have been employed" (405). But even with these cautions it may be significant that there are sixteen such words in only twelve verses (and verses regarding which there is textual question); the concentration may give greater weight.

More significant are the *repeated* occurrence of unique words in this limited section of text. Although verses 9-20 uses πορεύομαι three times to indicate physical movement of people (vv. 10, 12, 15), Mark uses it nowhere else, yet it is a very common word for travel in Greek generally and in the Gospels in particular. He normally uses ἔρχομαι (85 times + compounds: ἐκ–, 38; εἰς–, 30; ἀπό–, 22, etc.) or less commonly ἄγω and its compounds (37 times total). There are four compound forms of πορεύομαι, which appear a total of fourteen times (εἰς–, 8; παρά–, 4; πρός– and σύν– once each), but no simple form. Matthew and Luke both have a higher frequency of πορεύομαι, whereas Mark has a higher frequency of ἔρχομαι and its compounds. If compound forms of πορεύομαι are included, Mark and Matthew are closer, but Luke is distinctively higher. This suggests that three uses of πορεύομαι in six verses is at the least unusual for Mark; Gould (306) calls it a "striking anomaly." It is also worth noting that Mark's compound forms of πορεύομαι are always present tense. When an aorist verb of movement is involved, it is always ἔρχομαι or one of its compounds; yet in the long ending two of the three instances of πορεύομαι are aorist (Elliott 1971, 259). Burgon counters that such arguments must show "*which* of the ordinary compounds of πορεύομαι S. Mark could *possibly* have employed for the uncompounded verb, in the three places which have suggested the present inquiry," arguing that these three instances "admit of no substitute in the places where they severally occur" (234–35). The answer does not appear to be exceptionally difficult, for parallels can be found for each one, though part of the reply must be that Mark more commonly uses ἔρχομαι where other writers use πορεύομαι. Mark could have used a form of ἔρχομαι in 16:10 (cf. 10:1), παραπορεύομαι in 16:12 (cf. 2:23), and εἰσέρχομαι in 16:15 (cf. 13:15). Broadus had earlier posed the same question and offers the same conclusion that Burgon picks up, but neither addresses the alternate use of ἔρχομαι nor the possibility of παραπορεύομαι. Broadus does claim that εἰσέρχομαι "would be quite out of place," but his only reason is that it would be "less terse and vigorous than the simple [πορεύομαι]" (358).

The data for θεάομαι is similar: two uses in verses 9-20 in contrast to Mark's usual choice of βλέπω (15 times + 17 compound forms) and ὁράω (50 times), neither of which occur in the Long Ending. Farmer acknowledges that this "points away from Marcan composition" (89). Likewise with ἀπιστέω: twice in verses 9-20, rather than πιστεύω with a negative (e.g., οὐκ ἐπιστεύσατε, 11:31; μὴ πιστεύετε, 13:21). The word ἀπιστέω does occur in Luke (24:11, 41) and Acts (28:24), but it is not otherwise used in any of the Gospels. Related forms do occur: ἀπιστία (Mark 6:6; 9:24; and in the Long Ending at 16:14) and ἄπιστος (9:19). The significance of the use of ἀπιστέω twice in verses 9-20 (and not elsewhere in Mark) can only be mitigated if the evidence is lumped together with all other privative forms of the noun and adjective (which is what Farmer, 89–90, does).

Usage arguments are trickier. Though Danove lists ἐκεῖνος as a pronoun as not characteristic of Mark, he acknowledges in a footnote that of the nineteen instances of ἐκεῖνος prior to 16:9, three *are* pronouns. (Danove's list leaves out two additional instances of κἀκεῖνον as a pronoun in 12:4, 5.) His point may be that it *usually* functions as an adjective, but that it is never used as an adjective in 9-20. The point is moot, however, since this argument could be used of Mark 7 in which the same is true. On the other hand, there are five uses of ἐκεῖνος in one short pericope; so the frequency could be significant. Farmer's discussion (86) of ἐκείνη in verse 10 is limited to the feminine form and as a result does not include all the relevant data. In his separate discussion of the crasis form κἀκεῖνοι in verse 11, he argues that this form introduces a subordinate clause in both instances in the Long Ending (vv. 11, 13a) as it does in 12:4, 5, thus demonstrating Markan style since this occurs nowhere else in the NT.

The use of ἐπιτίθημι with ἐπί may be significant. Mark's usual pattern is the dative in healing contexts (5:23; 6:5; 7:32; 8:23), but he does use a cognate prepositional phrase in 8:25 (ἐπέθηκεν τὰς χεῖρας ἐπὶ τοὺς ὀφθαλμοὺς αὐτοῦ). Though this might appear to override the objection, there is a bit more to this usage than initially apparent. In Mark ἐπιτίθημι is typically accompanied by a dative indirect object when an animate being is involved (3:16-17; 5:23; 6:5; 7:32; 8:23), but when an inanimate object is involved the same idea is expressed by a prepositional phrase using ἐπί (8:25). (In this case "animate" is a reference to a person as a whole, not to a particular body part, which, though "living," is not an animate entity.) This pattern is consistent in Mark, but violated in the Long Ending. Though this may seem like a small sample with only one prepositional example, ἐπιτίθημι functions consistently with a group of verbs having the same constraints (ἀπαγγέλλω, ἀποστέλλω, βάλλω, παραδίδωμι, προσπίπτω). As such it "constitutes a strong grammatical argument against Markan composition" (Danove 2001, 74).

As for κτίσις, this noun only occurs three times in Mark. In the two occurrences prior to 16:9 it is part of a set phrase, ἀπ᾽ ἀρχῆς κτίσεως (10:6; 13:19; alluding to Genesis 1), in which κτίσις refers to "the sum total of everything created" (BDAG, 573.2.b). In 16:15 it has a more limited referent: all the people who live in the created world (cf. Col 1:21). Given the limited use in Mark, I find the minor semantic difference unpersuasive one way or the other. Likewise with κἄν the frequency is low (only 3 uses total in Mark including vv. 9-20) and the difference in meaning slight. The use of κύριος in verses 9-20 appears to be a more secure argument. The references to Jesus in the Gospels are more restrained than later writers. There are only two possible uses of κύριος earlier in Mark as a christological title (5:19; 11:3), but both are debatable (see the discussion at 11:3).

The absence of exact phrases elsewhere in Mark is not necessarily proof in itself given the enormous flexibility of language in constructing sentences. If there are particular collocations involved, there may, however, be greater significance. The exact four phrases Danove cites do not occur earlier in the book, but parallel constructions can be cited. For τοῖς μετ᾽ αὐτοῦ γενομένοις there are numerous grammatical parallels, e.g., τοῖς σὺν αὐτῷ οὖσιν (2:26); οἱ ἀπὸ Ἱεροσολύμων καταβάντες (3:22); and τοὺς περὶ αὐτὸν κύκλῳ καθημένους (3:34). To argue that such a construction (a substantival participle with an embedded prepositional modifier) only refers to the disciples in 16:10 seems to be stretching the point (contra Danove 1993, 123 n. 21), since it refers to a wide range of referents in Mark (see also 4:16, 18; 7:15, 20; 13:17) and since the example in 3:34 likely includes the disciples. There is no reason why Mark could not have written this phrase.

The simple phrase μετὰ ταῦτα initially seems so obvious an expression that it would be useless for the present purposes, but it may have some legitimacy here. The phrase is not used in Mark prior to 16:9, nor in Matthew, though it is a common expression in Luke and John. (It also occurs in the Short Ending of Mark.) None of the Lukan or Johannine uses have an equivalent expression in Matthew or Mark; either there is no parallel account or the equivalent statement is missing altogether. Though this does not mean that Mark could not have written this (as an isolated instance, any word or phrase could occur once), the likelihood of his doing so seems less than might be assumed.

A similar conclusion seems justified for καλῶς ἕξουσιν (v. 18). Though it cannot be said that Mark could not have written it, it is an unusual phrase to express physical healing. Mark typically uses θεραπεύω (1:34; 3:2, 10; 6:5, 13) or σῴζω (5:23, 28; 6:56; 10:52) for this purpose, or occasionally ἰάομαι (5:29), or εἶναι ὑγιῆ (5:34). (Some such statements are probably idiolectal; John, e.g., is the only NT writer to use the expression γίνομαι + ὑγιής.) Nowhere else in the NT does a writer use ἔχω + substantival καλός regardless of the meaning, though there are similar idioms with the opposite meaning: κακῶς + participle of ἔχω = "the sick (person), those who are sick" (1:32, 34; 2:17; 6:55) and εἶχον μάστιγας, "to have physical troubles" (3:10). Again, this does not prove that Mark could not have written καλῶς ἕξουσιν, but it appears to be the less likely option.

The combination μὲν οὖν deserves a similar assessment. It is an expression characteristic of Acts (27 of 39 NT instances), though rarely elsewhere in the NT (once in Luke, twice in John, 5 times in Paul, 3 times in Hebrews). By itself, οὖν is relatively rare in Mark, occurring only five times (4 in the words of Jesus, once by Pilate), always in discourse, but here it occurs in narrative. Likewise, μέν by itself is only used five times in Mark, always in discourse (see 4:4 on ὃ μὲν), but in 16:19 it is in narrative; it "differs markedly from that elsewhere in the Gospel" (Lee, 6).

There are some other similar expressions that deserve attention. In 16:9 Mary Magdalene is described with the unique (in NT Greek) expression παρ' ἧς ἐκβεβλήκει ἑπτὰ δαιμόνια. Nowhere else is ἐκβάλλω used with the preposition παρά in reference to exorcism. Normally ἐκβάλλω is used alone with no preposition (1:34, 39; 3:15, 22; 6:13; 9:38; the pattern is the same in the other Gospels). Only once is a preposition used and that is ἐκ (7:26, and nowhere else in the Gospels). There are similar phrases with a preposition followed by a relative pronoun in an exorcistic context, but they use ἀπό + ἐξέρχομαι (Luke 8:2, 35, 38). Even in contexts other than exorcisms ἐκβάλλω is never used in the NT with παρά; most commonly the preposition is ἐκ or εἰς. As Gould concludes, "this is the only case of the use of this prep. in describing the casting out of demons, and it is as strange as it is unexplained" (305).

The "extended genitive absolute" in verse 20 (τοῦ κυρίου συνεργοῦντος καί ... βεβαιοῦντος) has sometimes been cited as evidence against the authenticity of the Long Ending (Elliott 1971, 261). Although genitive absolutes with two participles are not common in the NT, Mark uses the construction in 6:22 and a compound periphrastic in 8:1.

The phrase πρώτῃ σαββάτου (v. 9) occurs nowhere else in the NT, but a similar construction (τῇ πρώτῃ ἡμέρᾳ τῶν ἀζύμων) occurs in 14:12. It might be wondered, however, if such a reference in regards to the first day of the week is not part of "standard usage," and in that case the standard collocation with σάββατον seems to be μία σαββάτων (an elliptical expression for μία ἡμέρα σαββάτων; see Matt 28:1; Mark 16:2; Luke 24:1; John 20:1, 19; Acts 20:7; 1 Cor 16:2; see also the superscription of LXX Ps 23). LXX usage typically employs πρώτη ἡμέρα in regard to a feast (e.g., Exod 12:15) or of a month (e.g., Ezra 10:17). The superscription to Ps 47 uses δευτέρᾳ σαββάτου, "the second day of the week" (as does *Did.* 8.1). The Pseudepigrapha uses πρώτη ἡμέρα, "on the first day" (*Jub.* 2:2) and τῇ πρώτῃ ἡμέρᾳ ἑβδομάδος, "on the first day of the week" (*Jub.* 3:1). Josephus typically uses πρώτη ἡμέρα (*Ant.* 1.29), or in the similar construction, τῇ πρώτῃ τῆς ἑορτῆς ἡμέρᾳ (*Ant.* 5.22). Philo likewise uses πρώτην ἡμέραν (*Spec. Laws* 2.162, in regard to a feast). Later usage continues the same pattern (texts from TLG). Justin Martyr refers to the resurrection of Jesus τῇ μιᾷ τῶν σαββάτων ἡμέρᾳ (*Dial.* 41.4). Origen has μίαν σαββάτων (though in a quote from Matt 28:1; *Cels.* 2.70). Gregory of Nyssa refers to ἡ μία τῶν σαββάτων ἡμέρα (*Trid. Mort.*) and μία σαββάτων (*Inscr. Psal.*; TLG cites both from *Gregorii Nysseni opera*, vol. 9.1, p. 289, l. 9 and vol. 5, p. 71, l. 14 respectively). Eusebius cites Mark 16:2, τῇ μιᾷ τῶν Σαββάτων (*Quaest. evangel.*; Migne [MPG], vol. 22, p. 937, l. 18). I have not extended the search into later centuries as the usage is clear and consistent.

It appears that the normal pattern is to use the ordinal (πρώτη) with ἡμέρα, but the cardinal (μία) in the elliptical expression μία [ἡμέρα] σαββάτων, though the use with σαββάτων appears in our literature almost exclusively in the NT; the OT and related texts are more concerned with the seventh day, typically ἡ ἡμέρα ἡ ἑβδόμη (e.g., Exod 16:26, 27), also an ordinal. Also of note is the use of the singular σαββάτου; the only other NT uses of the singular in a temporal sense of "week" are δὶς τοῦ σαββάτου (Luke 18:12, "twice a week") and κατὰ μίαν σαββάτου (1 Cor 16:2, "on the first day of the week"). In the LXX we find τὸ σάββατον ("the Sabbath," usually genitive or accusative, e.g., 2 Kgs 11:5; Neh 13:19), but almost never in the sense of "week" (the superscription to Psalm 47 is the only exception). The use of the singular by Josephus and Philo is the same, as it is in the Pseudepigrapha and the Apostolic Fathers. Farmer (84) admits that the use of the singular "remains unexplained."

There are two contrasting uses here: τῇ μιᾷ τῶν σαββάτων in 16:2 and πρώτῃ σαββάτου in 16:9—odd for being used divergently only a few verses apart, if Mark were the author of both, when usage almost everywhere else is so consistent. These differences in themselves are not adequate to prove a difference of authorship between the Long Ending and Mark (i.e., between 16:9-20 and 1:1–16:8), but it does suggest that this is very unusual usage since πρώτῃ σαββάτου cannot be paralleled, so far as I can determine, except in one other similar expression (δευτέρᾳ σαββάτου). Farmer (84) attempts to side-step this evidence by appealing to different sources used by Mark, but given the almost total lack of any other texts that have an expression like πρώτῃ σαββάτου, that seems improbable.

Another syntactical pattern that is relevant is the clause ordering of verses 9-20 contrasted with Mark 1:1–16:8. Porter's study of thematization in Mark suggests that the normal ordering of clauses is Predicator – Adjunct – Subject – Complement. "By contrast . . . the ordering of Mark 16:9-20 . . . is: Adjunct – Subject – and then Predicator or Complement the same number of times. . . . This is a distinctly different thematization pattern than is found in the rest of the Gospel and would seem to be in clear support of the longer ending of Mark being inconsistent in at least this linguistic feature with the rest of the Gospel" (Porter 2011, 114).

Although the individual examples cited above can sometimes be countered with parallels elsewhere or other explanations, it is the cumulative effect of these data in one textually disputed passage that is significant. As Wallace concludes, "there is not a single passage in Mark 1:1–16:8 comparable to the stylistic, grammatical, and lexical anomalies that we find clustered in verses 9-20. Although one might be able to parry off individual pieces of evidence, the cumulative effect is devastating for authenticity. Further, if the text is already suspicious because of external data, then these linguistic peculiarities are strong evidence of the spurious nature of the [Long Ending]" (2008, 30–31).

GLOSSARY

ad sensum—Latin, "according to sense." This phrase is most often used in the expression, *constructio ad sensum*, a usage in which a more natural construction is used instead of strict grammatical agreement.

Adjectivizer—In Greek syntax, this term refers to an article that is used to change a non-adjective into an adjectival modifier. Thus, in the phrase, ἀπὸ παντὸς ἔθνους τῶν ὑπὸ τὸν οὐρανόν, the article τῶν changes the prepositional phrase, ὑπὸ τὸν οὐρανόν, into an attributive modifier of παντὸς ἔθνους.

Aktionsart—A description of the actional features ascribed to the verbal referent as to the way in which it happens or exists. It is not a grammatical category based on the form of the verb, but is a pragmatic category based on the meaning of the word (lexis) as it is used in a particular context. Descriptions such as iterative, punctiliar, ingressive, etc. describe phrases or statements not the tense alone, though it involves the lexical meaning of the verb involved.

Anacoluthon—A construction involving some sort of break in grammatical sequence.

Anaphoric—Referring back to, i.e., coreferential with, a preceding word or group of words. Thus, pronouns are anaphoric references to participants that have already been introduced into the discourse.

Anarthrous—Lacking an article.

Antecedent—An element that is referred to by another expression that follows it. Thus, the antecedent of a relative pronoun is that element in the preceding context for which the relative clause provides additional information.

Apocrypha—Those books found in the LXX but not in the MT are called collectively the Apocrypha. These works, some originally written in a Semitic language (Hebrew or Aramaic) and later translated into Greek, and some composed in Greek, were not accepted as canonical by the Jews and they are not accepted today by Protestants, though they do have status in Roman Catholicism and the Orthodox churches.

Apodosis—The "then" clause in a conditional construction; may occur as either the first or second clause. See also *protasis*.

Apollonius' Canon—The second-century-AD grammarian, Apollonius Dyscolus, set out the rule that when one noun (usually in genitive case) modifies another noun, both will be articular or both will be anarthrous.

Aposiopesis—A sudden break in the midst of a sentence, often implying an inability or unwillingness to proceed. "A conscious suppression of part of a sentence under the influence of a strong emotion like anger, fear, pity" (Robertson, 1203).

Apostolic Fathers—About a dozen of the earliest post–NT writings from the early church are conventionally designated as the Apostolic Fathers.

Apposition—When two nouns occur together in the same case and they explain each other, they are said to be in apposition.

Aramaism—See *Semitism*.

Arthrous/Articular—Including an article.

Ascensive—The adverbial use of καί which is typically translated "even" or "also" is designated as ascensive in contrast to its more customary function as a coordinating conjunction. It is usually identified by the lack of two grammatically equal elements on either side of the καί.

Aspect—The semantic category by which a speaker or writer grammaticalizes a view of the situation by the selection of a particular verb form in the verbal system. This is a grammatical category expressed by the form of the verb. The view is either perfective, imperfective, or stative and is expressed by the aorist, present/ imperfect, and perfect/pluperfect forms respectively (in contrast to *Aktionsart*). See the Introduction.

Asyndeton—Linking clauses without the use of a conjunction; also called *parataxis*.

Attraction—Relative pronouns at times take on or are "attracted" to the case of their antecedent. For example, in the text, τῇ παραδόσει ὑμῶν ᾗ παρεδώκατε ("by your traditions which you pass on," Mark 7:13), the expected case for the relative pronoun would be accusative since it functions as the direct object of παρεδώκατε. Instead, it has been attracted to the dative case of its antecedent (παραδόσει). See also *inverse attraction*.

Auxiliary verb—See *copula*.

Background (discourse structure)—This term is used to refer to information that is off the storyline (event line), i.e., those events or material that do not move the narrative forward. Instead, background information explains other statements (either storyline or foreground) or fills in information that readers need in order to understand the storyline. In the narrative genre of the NT, this is often expressed with imperfect or pluperfect tense forms. (There are multiple variations of this terminology among scholars, some of whom reverse the terminology used here.)

Causative—Causative verbs or constructions denote that a new state of affairs is brought about or "caused" by the action of the verb or construction (e.g., ποιήσω ὑμᾶς γενέσθαι ἁλιεῖς, 1:17; "I will cause you to be fishers"). Although some verbs ending in –οω tend to have causative meaning in many contexts, other verbs can be used in statements that clearly imply a causative idea. At times a distinction in voice is involved.

Clausal complement—This type of complement is structurally a direct object, but since it is a clause rather than a noun phrase scholars often use the language of "complement" rather than "direct object." Verbs introducing direct or indirect discourse form the largest number of examples in Mark, e.g., λέγει τῷ παραλυτικῷ, Τέκνον, ἀφίενταί σου αἱ ἁμαρτίαι ("he said to the paralytic, 'Son, your sins are forgiven'"). In this example the last five words are the clausal complement.

Clitic—A word that is written as a separate word in the syntax but is pronounced and accented as if it were part of another word. There are two types. Enclitics give their accent to the preceding word; proclitics shift the accent to the following word.

Collocation—The conventional association of two or more words that produces a particular nuance is termed a collocation. In Mark 5:41-42, the collocation of ἐγείρω, which can mean either "wake up" or "arise," with ἀνέστη . . . καὶ περιεπάτει clarifies that the meaning in this context is "arise."

Comparative adjectives—Some adjectives (and adverbs) can compare more than one instance of an item. There are four degrees possible: positive, comparative, superlative, and elative. English examples of these four are, *big*, *bigger*, *biggest*, and *very big*. In Greek the distinctions are blurring and comparative forms often have superlative meaning and superlatives sometimes are used as elatives (see ch. 6 of Decker 2014).

Complement—In the handbook, this term is used in two ways in addition to its use in the phrase, "clausal complement": (1) A constituent, other than an accusative direct object, that is required to complete a verb phrase. Verbs that include a prepositional prefix often take a complement whose case is determined by the prefix. For example, verbs with the prefix συν- characteristically take a dative complement. (2) The second element in a double case construction (usually accusative, sometimes genitive), which completes the verbal idea.

Conditional statement—A statement consisting of two clauses, the truth (or falsity) of the main statement (apodosis) being conditioned by the dependent clause (protasis). This is typically expressed by means of formal syntactical criteria (first, second, third, and fourth-class conditions), but may also be expressed informally by other constructions. See *informal conditions*.

Constructio ad sensum—"Construction according to sense." A construction that follows the sense of the expression rather than strict grammatical rules, e.g., the use of a plural verb with a subject that is syntactically singular but refers to a group of people (e.g., ὄχλος).

Copula—A linking verb (εἰμί, γίνομαι, or ὑπάρχω) that joins a subject and predicate (normally both in nominative case) into an equative clause.

Crasis—The merging of two words through the use of contraction, e.g., κἀμοί for καὶ ἐμοί.

Ecbatic (clause)—An older term for result; it may also be applied to the function of individual elements such as the infinitive or participle.

Elative—See *comparative adjectives*.

Enclitic—See *clitic*.

Equative verb/clause—See *copula*.

External evidence—In textual criticism the evidence available from manuscripts and versions is described as external evidence. See also *internal evidence*.

Final (clause)—An older term for a purpose clause; it may also be applied to the function of individual elements such as the infinitive or participle.

Form marker—A morpheme appended to the verb stem preceding the personal ending (if there is one) to indicate the tense (and sometimes voice); e.g., the morpheme -σα- marks the form as aorist, -θησ- as future passive, etc. Also known as a "tense suffix," "tense formative," or "tense morpheme."

Formal equivalence—When translating from one language to another the attempt to reproduce the formal features (part of speech, word order, etc.) of the source language as closely as possible in the receptor language is described as formal equivalence. Sometimes called "literal" translation. See also *functional equivalence.*

Functional equivalence—When translating from one language to another the attempt to reproduce the meaning of the source language in the receptor language without being bound to use the same formal features is described as functional equivalence (formerly called dynamic equivalence). See also *formal equivalence.*

Hapax legomenon—A word that occurs only one time in the NT or in a designated body of literature.

Headless relative clause—A relative clause with no expressed antecedent, e.g., "He is doing that which is not lawful."

Hebraism—See *Semitism.*

Hendiadys—The use of two words to express a single idea; e.g., ἐκεφαλίωσαν καὶ ἠτίμασαν, "give a shameful beating" in Mark 12:4. Sometimes referred to as a doublet.

Historical present (tense)—See *narrative present.*

Hyperbole—A figure of speech in which there is intentional use of overstatement for emphasis.

Idiolectal—Pertaining to an individual's distinct use of language.

Imperfective (aspect)—The semantic value of the present and imperfect tenses that indicates that the writer/speaker is portraying the situation as a process.

Indefinite plural—Writers sometimes use a plural verb with no explicit antecedent in the context. In so doing they are making an indefinite statement that "they," unspecified people in general, are doing something; the specific identity of the people involved is not important to the narrative. See Mark 1:22 and the Introduction.

Informal condition—The expression of a conditional meaning apart from the formal syntactical constructions often described as first, second, third, and fourth-class conditions. This may be expressed in multiple ways including adverbial participles, infinitives, indefinite relative clauses, etc. See Mark 8:36.

Internal evidence—In textual criticism the evidence for a variant reading that is based on consideration of what the author is most likely to have written (intrinsic probability) or what a scribe may have changed (transcriptional probability) is described as internal evidence. See also *external evidence.*

Intransitive—A type of verb that does not require a direct object. Some verbs may be either transitive or intransitive depending on the statement in which they are used.

Inverse attraction—Inverse attraction occurs when the antecedent takes on the case of the relative pronoun that follows. This is far less common than *attraction.*

Latinism—In Markan studies this term refers to loan words or phrases brought into Greek from Latin.

Lexis—The lexical meaning of a word.

Linking verb—See *copula*.

Litotes—A figure of speech in which a statement is made by negating the opposite idea; it is a form of understatement. See Mark 12:34.

Marked—Departing from the normal or neutral pattern, or having additive features. At various levels of grammar, speakers/writers have a choice between various options. One option will typically be viewed as the "default" or "unmarked" member of the set. The other members are "marked." Something that is "marked" may be more prominent, in focus, emphatic, etc.

Metonymy—A figure of speech in which one term is used in place of another with which it is associated. In the expression, "in Isaiah the prophet" (Mark 1:2), the writer (the prophet Isaiah) is used in metonymy for his writings (the book that the prophet Isaiah wrote).

Narrative present (tense)—Authors may use a present tense verb in the storyline of a narrative (normally aorist is used) to serve as a narrative marker for the beginning of a paragraph, to introduce new participants, or to note a geographic shift in the story. This usage has traditionally been called the *historical present* (i.e., a present tense that makes a past/historical reference) by those who have assumed that, with a few exceptions, the present tense always refers to present time.

Nominal (clause)—A noun or something that functions like a noun. In a nominal clause, a nominative noun stands alone in the clause without a verb, and sometimes without any other elements.

Nominalizer—In Greek syntax, this term refers to an article that is used to change a word, phrase, or clause into a substantive. Most commonly, nominalizers are used to make an adjective, participle, or prepositional phrase function as a substantive.

Objective genitive—See *verbal genitive*.

Parataxis—Syntactical linkage of clauses without the use of coordinating or subordinating conjunctions (in contrast to *hypotaxis*). Also called *asyndeton*.

Partitive genitive—The use of a genitive modifier to indicate the whole of which the head word is a part.

Perfective (aspect)—The semantic value of the aorist tense that indicates that the writer/speaker is portraying the situation in summary as a whole with no reference to any process that might be involved. See also *imperfective aspect* and *stative aspect*.

Perfective (prefix)—The use of a prepositional prefix to intensify the meaning of the verb to which it is attached.

Performative—A statement that accomplishes the intended act by its very utterance, e.g., Jesus' statement in Mark 2:5, ἀφίενταί σου αἱ ἁμαρτίαι.

Periphrastic—The combination of a linking verb and an anarthrous, nominative case participle which together express a single idea. This construction is used in place of a single verb. See the Introduction.

Postcedent—When the "antecedent" of a pronoun *follows* the pronoun, it may be called a postcedent. See also *internally headed relative clause*, which uses one form of a postcedent.

Proclitic—See *clitic*.

Prolepsis—The transfer of the subject of the subordinate clause to the main clause as an accusative object, reference being resumed in the subordinate clause with a pronoun, either explicitly or by the inherent subject of the verb.

Proleptic—Traditionally used to describe instances where verb tenses other than the future tense refer to a future event.

Protasis—The "if" clause in a conditional construction; it may occur before or after the apodosis.

Pseudepigrapha—A collection of noncanonical Jewish writings that originated in the Second Temple period. Some were originally written in a Semitic language (Hebrew or Aramaic) and later translated into Greek, and some were composed in Greek. In most cases we have only the Greek version.

Recitative ὅτι—The use of ὅτι to introduce direct discourse.

Referent—The person, thing, or situation to which a statement refers. This is not the same as an antecedent, which is a grammatical relationship. E.g., in Mark 1:7, the grammatical antecedent of οὗ is ὁ ἰσχυρότερος, but the referent of both is Jesus.

Semitism—The influence of a Semitic language (Hebrew or Aramaic) on a Greek writer sometimes produces a form of expression that is atypical of a native Greek speaker. Sometimes this influence is indirect, mediated through the Septuagint (thus a Septuagintism).

Stative (aspect)— The semantic value of the perfect and pluperfect tenses that indicates that the writer/speaker is portraying a situation as a state or condition with no reference to any process or expenditure of energy. See also *imperfective aspect* and *perfective aspect*.

Stative (*Aktionsart*)—Some verbs do not express action lexically; the most common example is εἰμί. In terms of *Aktionsart*, these verbs are described as stative verbs.

Storyline (discourse structure)—This term is used to refer to information that moves the narrative forward. In the narrative genre of the NT this is most commonly expressed with aorist tense forms or sometimes narrative presents.

Subjective genitive—See *verbal genitive*.

Superlative adjective—See *comparative adjectives*.

Synecdoche—A figure of speech in which the part is used to refer to the whole.

Tendential—This is an *Aktionsart* statement that refers to an event that is intended or about to occur. It should be used as a description of a statement, not a tense.

Tense—A morphological category of the Greek verb that expresses aspect. Although Greek tenses often have a conventional association of time with particular tenses (e.g., aorist is predominantly used of past time), this is a pragmatic value due to use in particular contexts (e.g., narrative storyline typically employs the aorist tense to record in summary a series of past events). See *aspect*.

Transcriptional probability—In textual criticism the evaluation of internal evidence often considers the likelihood of what a scribe may have written, either as an accidental, unintentional mistake, or as an intentional change or correction.

Transitive—A type of verb that requires a direct object. Some verbs may be either transitive or intransitive depending on the statement in which they are used.

Unmarked—The default option among two or more grammatical choices. See also *marked*.

Verbal aspect—See *aspect*.

Verbal genitive—When a genitive noun modifies a headword that is a noun of action (most easily identified by that word having a cognate verbal form), the genitive modifier may be either a subjective or objective genitive. In the case of a subjective genitive, the genitive modifier identifies the subject responsible for performing the action implied by the head word. An objective genitive, by contrast, identifies the object which receives the action implied by the head word.

BIBLIOGRAPHY

The various ancient sources and translations cited throughout the handbook are cited primarily from the digital editions in Accordance; they are not listed separately here.

Abbott-Smith, G. *A Manual Lexicon of the New Testament.* 3rd ed. Edinburgh: T&T Clark, 1936.

Anderson, Hugh. *The Gospel of Mark.* New Century Bible. London: Oliphants, 1976.

Aland, Kurt, and Barbara Aland. *The Text of the New Testament.* 2nd ed. Grand Rapids: Eerdmans, 1995.

Argyle, A. W. "The Meaning of *kath' hēmeran* in Mark xiv.49." *Expository Times* 63 (1951): 354.

Bakker, Egbert J. "Voice, Aspect and *Aktionsart*: Middle and Passive in Ancient Greek." Pages 23–47 in *Voice: Form and Function.* Edited by B. Fox and P. Hopper. Typological Studies in Language 27. Philadelphia: Benjamins, 1994.

Balz, Horst, and Gerhard Schneider, eds. *Exegetical Dictionary of the New Testament.* 3 vols. Edinburgh: T&T Clark, 1978–1980.

Barton, George A. "The Use of ἐπετιμᾶν in Mark 8:30 and 3:12." *Journal of Biblical Literature* 41 (1922): 233–36.

Bauer, Walter. "The 'Colt' of Palm Sunday (Der Palmesel)." *Journal of Biblical Literature* 72 (1953): 220–29.

Beyer, Klaus. *Semitische Syntax im Neuen Testament.* Studien zur Umwelt des Neuen Testaments, Band 1: Satzlehre Teil 1. Göttingen: Vandenhoeck & Ruprecht, 1962.

Birdsall, J. Neville. "τὸ ῥῆμα ὡς εἶπεν αὐτῷ ὁ Ἰησοῦς: Mk xiv.72." *Novum Testamentum* 2 (1958): 272–75.

Black, David Alan. "Discourse Analysis, Synoptic Criticism, and Markan Grammar: Some Methodological Considerations." Pages 90–98 in *Linguistics and New Testament Interpretation: Essays on Discourse Analysis*. Edited by D. A. Black, K. Barnwell, and S. Levinsohn. Nashville: Broadman, 1992.

Black, David Alan, ed. *Perspectives on the Ending of Mark: 4 Views*. Nashville: Broadman & Holman, 2008.

Black, Stephanie L. *Sentence Conjunctions in the Gospel of Matthew: καί, δέ, τότε, γάρ, σύν and Asyndeton in Narrative Discourse*. Journal for the Study of the New Testament Supplement Series 216. Studies in New Testament Greek 9. London: Sheffield, 2002.

Blass, F., and A. Debrunner. *A Greek Grammar of the New Testament and Other Early Christian Literature*. Translated and revised by Robert W. Funk. Chicago: University of Chicago Press, 1961.

Bock, Darrell L. *Blasphemy and Exaltation in Judaism: The Charge against Jesus in Mark 14:53-65*. Wissenschaftliche Untersuchungen zum Neuen Testament 2.106. Tübingen: Mohr Siebeck, 1998. Reprint. Grand Rapids: Baker, 2000.

———. *The Gospel of Mark*. Pages 391–560 in vol. 11 of Cornerstone Biblical Commentary. Carol Stream, Ill.: Tyndale, 2005.

Bolt, Peter G. *The Cross from a Distance: Atonement in Mark's Gospel*. New Studies in Biblical Theology 18. Downers Grove, Ill.: InterVarsity, 2004.

Boyer, James L. "The Classification of Infinitives: A Statistical Study." *Grace Theological Journal* 6 (1985): 3–27.

Bratcher, Robert G., and Eugene A. Nida. *A Translator's Handbook on the Gospel of Mark*. Helps for Translators. London: United Bible Societies, 1961.

Broadus, John A. "Exegetical Studies: Style of Mark xvi.9-20, As Bearing upon the Question of Genuineness." *The Baptist Quarterly* 3 (1869): 355–62.

Brown, Colin, ed. *New International Dictionary of New Testament Theology*. 4 vols. Grand Rapids: Zondervan, 1986.

Brown, Raymond E. *The Death of the Messiah: From Gethsemane to the Grave. A Commentary on the Passion Narratives in the Four Gospels*. 2 vols. Anchor Bible Reference Library. New York: Doubleday, 1994.

Brown, F., S. R. Driver, and C. A. Briggs. *A Hebrew and English Lexicon of the Old Testament*. Oxford: Clarendon, 1907.

Bruce, Alexander Balmain. "The Synoptic Gospels." Pages 1–651 in vol. 1 of *The Expositor's Greek Testament*. Edited by W. Robertson Nicoll. London: Hodder & Stoughton, 1897. Reprint. Grand Rapids: Eerdmans, 1967.

Brugmann, Karl. *Griechische Grammatik*. 3rd ed. Munich: C. H. Beck, 1900.

Burgon, John. *The Last Twelve Verses of Mark*. Oxford: Parker, 1871. Reprint. NP: Sovereign Grace Book Club, 1959.

Burk, Denny. *Articular Infinitives in the Greek of the New Testament: On the Exegetical Benefit of Grammatical Precision*. Sheffield: Sheffield Phoenix, 2006.

Burkitt, F. Crawford. *Evangelion da-Mepharreshe*. 2 vols. Cambridge: Cambridge University Press, 1904.

Burton, Ernest De Witt. *Syntax of the Moods and Tenses in New Testament Greek*. 3rd ed. Edinburgh: T&T Clark, 1898.

Buttmann, Alexander. *A Grammar of the New Testament Greek*. Translated by J. H. Thayer. Andover, Mass.: Draper, 1891.

Cadbury, Henry J. *The Style and Literary Method of Luke*. Harvard Theological Studies 6. Cambridge, Mass.: Harvard University Press, 1920.

———. *The Making of Luke-Acts*. 2nd ed., 1958. Reprint. Peabody, Mass.: Hendrickson, 1999.

Calvin, John. *A Harmony of the Gospels Matthew, Mark and Luke*. 3 vols. Calvin's Commentaries. Edited by David and Thomas Torrance. Grand Rapids: Eerdmans, 1972.

Campbell, Constantine R. *Verbal Aspect, the Indicative Mood, and Narrative: Soundings in the Greek of the New Testament*. Studies in Biblical Greek 13. New York: Peter Lang, 2007.

Campbell, Ken. "What Was Jesus' Occupation?" *Journal of the Evangelical Theological Society* 48 (2005): 501–19.

Caragounis, Chrys C. *The Development of Greek and the New Testament: Morphology, Syntax, Phonology, and Textual Transmission*. Grand Rapids: Baker Academic, 2006.

Carson, D. A. *Greek Accents: A Student's Manual*. Grand Rapids: Baker, 1985.

Charlesworth, James H., ed. *The Old Testament Pseudepigrapha*. 2 vols. Anchor Bible Reference Library. New York: Doubleday, 1983–1985.

Collins, Adela Yarbro. *Mark: A Commentary*. Hermeneia. Minneapolis: Fortress, 2007.

Colwell, E. C. "A Definite Rule for the Use of the Article in the Greek New Testament." *Journal of Biblical Literature* 52 (1933): 12–21.

Conrad, Carl. "New Observations on Voice in the Ancient Greek Verb." November 19, 2002. http://www.ioa.com/~cwconrad/Docs/NewObsAncGrkVc.pdf. Accessed April 22, 2004.

———. "Propositions Concerning Ancient Greek Voice." 2005. <http://www.artsci.wustl.edu/~cwconrad/GrkVc.html>. Accessed 2005–.

———. "A Brief Commentary on the Gospel of Mark." 2004. <http://www.ioa.com/~cwconrad/Mark/>. Accessed 2007–.

Conybeare, F. C., and George Stock. *Grammar of Septuagint Greek*. Boston: Ginn., 1905.

Cranfield, C. E. B. *The Gospel According to St. Mark*. Cambridge Greek Testament. Cambridge: Cambridge University Press, 1959.

Croy, N. Clayton. *The Mutilation of Mark's Gospel*. Nashville: Abingdon, 2003.

Culy, Martin M. "Would Jesus Exaggerate? Rethinking Matthew 26.38//Mark 14.34." *The Bible Translator* 57 (2006): 105–9.

———. "Double Case Constructions in Koine Greek." *Journal of Greco-Roman Christianity and Judaism* 6 (2009): 82–106.

Curtius, Georg. *The Greek Verb*. London: John Murray, 1883.

Cushman, Neal D. "A Critique of Rikk E. Watts' Isaianic New Exodus in the Markan Prologue." Ph.D. diss., Baptist Bible Seminary, 2012.

Dana, H. E., and Julius R. Mantey. *A Manual Grammar of the Greek New Testament*. New York: Macmillan, 1955.

Danker, Frederick William. *A Greek-English Lexicon of the New Testament and Other Early Christian Literature*. 3rd ed. Based on Walter Bauer's *Griechisch-deutsches Wörterbuch zu den Schriften des Neuen Testaments und der frühchristlichen Literatur*, 6th ed., ed. Kurt Aland and Barbara Aland, with Viktor Reichmann and on previous English editions by W. F. Arndt, F. W. Gingrich, and F. W. Danker. Chicago: University of Chicago Press, 2000.

———. *The Concise Greek-English Lexicon of the New Testament*. Chicago: University of Chicago Press, 2009.

Danove, Paul L. *The End of Mark's Story: A Methodological Study*. Biblical Interpretation Series 3. Leiden: Brill, 1993.

———. *Linguistics and Exegesis in the Gospel of Mark: Applications of a Case Frame Analysis and Lexicon*. Journal for the Study of the New Testament Supplement 218. Sheffield: Sheffield Academic Press, 2001.

Decker, Rodney J. "The Use of εὐθύς ('immediately') in Mark." *Journal of Ministry and Theology* 1 (1997): 90–121.

———. *Temporal Deixis of the Greek Verb in the Gospel of Mark with Reference to Verbal Aspect*. Studies in Biblical Greek 10. New York: Peter Lang, 2001.

———. "The Function of the Imperfect Tense in Mark's Gospel." Pages 347–64 in *The Language of the New Testament: Context, History, and Development*. Edited by S. E. Porter and A. W. Pitts. Leiden: Brill, 2013a.

———. "Markan Ideolect in the Study of the Greek of the New Testament." Pages 43–66 in *The Language of the New Testament: Context, History, and Development*. Edited by S. E. Porter and A. W. Pitts. Leiden: Brill, 2013b.

———. *Reading Koine Greek: An Introduction and Integrated Workbook*. Grand Rapids: Baker, 2014.

Deissmann, Adolf. *Bible Studies*. Translated by A. Grieve. Edinburgh: T&T Clark, 1901.

———. *Light from the Ancient East*. 4th ed. New York: Doran, 1927. Reprint. Peabody, Mass.: Hendrickson, 1995.

Derrett, J. Duncan M. *Midrash in Action and as a Literary Device*. Vol. 2 of *Studies in the New Testament*. Leiden: Brill, 1978.

Doudna, John Charles. *The Greek of the Gospel of Mark*. Journal of Biblical Literature Monograph Series 12. Philadelphia: Society of Biblical Literature, 1961.

Duckwitz, Norbert H. O. *Reading the Gospel of St. Mark in Greek: A Beginning, with Introduction, Notes, Vocabulary, and Grammatical Appendix*. Mundelein, Ill.: Bolchazy-Carducci, 2011.

Edwards, James R. "Markan Sandwich Stories: The Significance of Interpolations in Markan Narratives." *Novum Testamentum* 31 (1989): 193–216.

———. *The Gospel According to Mark*. Pillar New Testament Commentary. Grand Rapids: Eerdmans, 2002.

Ehrman, Bart. "A Leper in the Hands of an Angry Jesus." Pages 77–98 in *New Testament Greek and Exegesis: Essays in Honor of Gerald F. Hawthorne*. Edited by A. Donaldson and T. Sailors. Grand Rapids: Eerdmans, 2003.

———. *Misquoting Jesus*. San Francisco: HarperSanFrancisco, 2005.

Ellingworth, Paul. "The Dog in the Night: A Note on Mark's Non-Use of *kai*." *Bible Translator* 46 (1995): 125–28.

Elliott, J. K. "The Text and Language of the Endings to Mark's Gospel." *Theologische Zeitschrift* 27 (1971): 255–62.

———. "An Eclectic Textual Commentary on the Greek Text of Mark's Gospel" and "The Text and Language of the Endings to Mark's Gospel." Pages 189–211 in *The Language and Style of the Gospel of Mark*. Edited by J. K. Elliott. Novum Testamentum Supplement 71. Leiden: Brill, 1993.

———. "Mark 1.1-3: A Later Addition to the Gospel?" *New Testament Studies* 46 (2000): 584–88.

Evans, Craig A. "Mark's Incipit and the Priene Calendar Inscription: From Jewish Gospel to Greco-Roman Gospel." *Journal of Greco-Roman Christianity and Judaism* 1 (2000): 67–81.

———. *Mark 8:27–16:20*. Word Biblical Commentary 34B. Nashville, Nelson, 2001.

Fanning, Buist M. *Verbal Aspect in New Testament Greek*. Oxford Theological Monographs. Oxford: Clarendon, 1990.

Farmer, William R. *The Last Twelve Verses of Mark*. Cambridge: Cambridge University Press, 1974.

Field, Frederick. *Notes on the Translation of the New Testament*. Cambridge: Cambridge University Press, 1899. Reprint. Peabody, Mass.: Hendrickson, 1994.

Fitzmyer, Joseph A. "The Aramaic Qorbān Inscription from Jebel Ḥallet Eṭ-Ṭûri and Mark 7:11/Matt 15:5." *Journal of Biblical Literature* 78 (1959): 60–65.

Fohrer, Georg, and Eduard Lohse. "Σιών, Ἰερουσαλήμ, Ἰεροσόλυμα, Ἰεροσολυμίτης." Pages 292–338 in vol. 7 of *Theological Dictionary of the New Testament*. Edited by G. Kittel and G. Friedrich. Translated by G. Bromiley. 10 vols. Grand Rapids: Eerdmans, 1964–1976.

France, R. T. *The Gospel of Mark: A Commentary on the Greek Text*. New International Greek Testament Commentary. Grand Rapids: Eerdmans, 2002.

Fuller, Lois K. "The 'Genitive Absolute' in New Testament/ Hellenistic Greek: A Proposal for Clearer Understanding." *Journal of Greco-Roman Christianity and Judaism* 3 (2006): 142–67.

Funk, Robert W. *A Beginning-Intermediate Grammar of Hellenistic Greek*. 3 vols. 2nd ed. Missoula, Mont.: Scholars Press, 1973.

Garland, David E. *Mark*. NIV Application Commentary. Grand Rapids: Zondervan, 1996.

Gould, Ezra P. *A Critical and Exegetical Commentary on the Gospel According to St. Mark*. International Critical Commentary. Edinburgh: T&T Clark, 1896.

The Greek New Testament. Edited by Barbara Aland, Kurt Aland, Johannes Karavidopoulos, Carlo M. Martini, and Bruce Metzger. 4th ed. United Bible Societies. Peabody, Mass.: Hendrickson, 2001.

Green, Robert E. "Criteria for the Periphrastic in the Greek of the New Testament." Ph.D. diss., Baptist Bible Seminary, 2012.

Guelich, Robert A. *Mark 1–8:26*. Word Biblical Commentary 34A. Dallas: Word, 1989.

Gundry, Robert H. *Mark: A Commentary on His Apology for the Cross*. Grand Rapids: Eerdmans, 1993.

Harner, Philip B. "Qualitative Anarthrous Predicate Nouns: Mark 15:39 and John 1:1." *Journal of Biblical Literature* 92 (1973): 75–87.

Harris, Murray J. "The Definite Article in the Greek New Testament." Appendix I (pp. 301–13) of *Jesus as God: The New Testament Use of Theos in Reference to Jesus*. Grand Rapids: Baker, 1992.

Hartley, Donald E. "The Congenitally Hard-Hearted: Key to Understanding the Assertion and Use of Isaiah 6:9-10." Ph.D. diss., Dallas Theological Seminary, 2005.

Hartman, Lars. *Mark for the Nations: A Text- and Reader-Oriented Commentary*. Eugene, Ore.: Pickwick, 2010.

Hawkins, John C. *Horae Synopticae*. Oxford: Clarendon, 1899.

Hengel, Martin. *Acts and the History of Earliest Christianity*. Translated by J. Bowden. Philadelphia: Fortress, 1979.

———. *Studies in the Gospel of Mark*. Translated by J. Bowden. London: SCM Press, 1985.

Holmes, Michael W. "To Be Continued . . . The Many Endings of the Gospel of Mark." *Bible Review* 17 (2001): 12–23, 48–50.

Hooker, Morna D. *The Gospel According to Saint Mark*. Black's New Testament Commentary. London: A. & C. Black. Reprint, Peabody, Mass.: Hendrickson, 1991.

Hort, F. J. A. *The Gospel According to St Mark: The Greek Text Edited with Introduction and Notes*. Cambridge: Cambridge University Press, 1902. Reprinted in *Expository and Exegetical Studies* by F. J. A. Hort. Minneapolis: Klock & Klock, 1980.

Hurtado, Larry, and Paul Owen. *Who Is This Son of Man? The Latest Scholarship on a Puzzling Expression of the Historical Jesus*. London: T&T Clark, 2011.

Incigneri, Brian J. *The Gospel to the Romans: The Setting and Rhetoric of Mark's Gospel*. Biblical Interpretation 65. Leiden: Brill, 2003.

Ilan, Tal. "Notes on the Distribution of Jewish Women's Names in Palestine in the Second Temple and Mishnaic Periods." *Journal of Jewish Studies* 40 (1989): 186–200.

Iverson, Kelly R. "A Further Word of Final Γάρ (Mark 16:8)." *Catholic Biblical Quarterly* 68 (2006): 79–94.

Jeremias, Joachim. "λίθος, λίθινος." Pages 268–80 in vol. 4 of *Theological Dictionary of the New Testament*. Edited by G. Kittel and G. Friedrich. Translated by G. Bromiley. 10 vols. Grand Rapids: Eerdmans, 1964–1976.

———. "πολλοί." Pages 536–45 in vol. 6 of *Theological Dictionary of the New Testament*. Edited by G. Kittel and G. Friedrich. Translated by G. Bromiley. 10 vols. Grand Rapids: Eerdmans, 1964–1976.

———. *The Parables of Jesus*. Translated by S. H. Hooke. 2nd English ed. London: SCM Press, 1963.

———. *The Eucharistic Words of Jesus.* Translated by N. Perrin. London: SCM Press, 1966.

Jobes, Karen, and Moisés Silva. *An Invitation to the Septuagint.* Grand Rapids: Baker, 2000.

Johansson, Daniel. "Κύριος in the Gospel of Mark." *Journal for the Study of the New Testament* 33 (2010): 101–24.

Kemmer, Suzanne. *The Middle Voice.* Philadelphia: Benjamins, 1993.

Kilpatrick, G. D. "Some Notes on Marcan Usage" [and several related studies]. Pages 151–84 in *The Language and Style of the Gospel of Mark.* Edited by J. K. Elliott. Novum Testamentum Supplement 71. Leiden: Brill, 1993.

Koehler, Ludwig, and Walter Baumgartner, eds. *The Hebrew and Aramaic Lexicon of the Old Testament.* Translated and edited by M. E. J. Richardson. 2 vols. Leiden: Brill, 2002.

Lane, William L. *The Gospel of Mark.* New International Commentary on the New Testament. Grand Rapids: Eerdmans, 1974.

Lee, J. A. L. "Some Features of the Speech of Jesus in Mark's Gospel." *Novum Testamentum* 27 (1985): 1–26.

Legg, S. C. E. *Novum Testamentum Graece, Euangelium Secundum Marcum.* Oxford: Clarendon, 1935.

Liddell, Henry George, and Robert Scott. *A Greek-English Lexicon.* Revised and augmented by Sir Henry Stuart Jones and Roderick McKenzie. 9th edition with a revised supplement. New York: Oxford University Press, 1996.

Lincoln, Andrew T. "The Promise and the Failure: Mark 16:7, 8." *Journal of Biblical Literature* 108 (1989): 283–300.

Louw, Johannes P., and Eugene A. Nida, eds. *Greek-English Lexicon of the New Testament Based on Semantic Domains.* 2nd ed. New York: United Bible Societies, 1989.

Magness, J. Lee. *Marking the End: Sense and Absence in the Gospel of Mark.* Atlanta: Scholars Press, 1986. Reprint. Eugene, Ore.: Wipf & Stock, 2002.

Makujina, John. "'Till Death Do Us Part,' Or the Continuation of Marriage in the Eschaton? Answering Recent Objections to the Traditional Reading of Γαμέω-Γαμίζω in the Synoptic Gospels." *Filologia Neotestamentaria* 25 (2012): 57–74.

Maloney, Elliott C. *Semitic Interference in Marcan Syntax.* SBL Dissertation Series 51. Chico, Calif.: Scholars Press, 1981.

———. "The 'Impersonal' Plural Active of the Verb in the Synoptic Gospels and Acts: Semitic Interference?" Pages 138–62 in *Studies in the Greek Bible: Essays in Honor of Francis T. Gignac, S.J.* Edited by J. Corley and V. Skemp. Catholic Biblical Quarterly

Monograph Series 44. Washington D.C.: Catholic Biblical Association of America, 2008.

Mann, C. S. *Mark*. Anchor Bible 27. New York: Doubleday, 1986.

Manson, T. W. *The Teaching of Jesus: Studies of Its Form and Content*. 2nd ed. Cambridge: Cambridge University Press, 1935.

Marcus, Joel. *Mark*. 2 vols. Anchor Bible 27. New York: Doubleday, 2000, 2009.

Martin, Troy W. "Watch During the Watches (Mark 13:35)." *Journal of Biblical Literature* 120 (2001): 685–701.

McKay, K. L. "On the Perfect and Other Aspects in New Testament Greek." *Novum Testamentum* 23 (1981): 289–329.

———. *A New Syntax of the Verb in New Testament Greek*. Studies in Biblical Greek 5. New York: Peter Lang, 1994.

McKnight, Scot. "A Generation Who Knew Not Streeter." Pages 65–95 in *Rethinking the Synoptic Problem*. Edited by D. A. Black and D. R. Beck. Grand Rapids: Baker, 2001.

Metzger, Bruce M. *Lexical Aids for Students of New Testament Greek*. Princeton: By the author, 1969.

———. *A Textual Commentary on the Greek New Testament*. 2nd ed. New York: United Bible Societies, 1994.

Meyer, Heinrich A. W. *Critical and Exegetical Hand-Book to the Gospels of Mark and Luke*. Translated by R. Wallis. Edited by W. Dickson and M. Riddle. Vol. 2 of *Meyer's Commentary on the New Testament*. [New York]: Funk & Wagnalls, 1884. Reprint. Winona Lake, Ind.: Alpha, 1979.

Michel, Otto. "οἶκος, οἰκία, et al." Pages 119–59 in vol. 5 of *Theological Dictionary of the New Testament*. Edited by G. Kittel and G. Friedrich. Translated by G. Bromiley. 10 vols. Grand Rapids: Eerdmans, 1964–1976.

Miller, Neva F. "Appendix 2: A Theory of Deponent Verbs." Pages 423–30 in *Analytical Lexicon of the Greek New Testament*. Edited by T. Friberg, B. Friberg, and N. Miller. Grand Rapids: Baker, 2000.

Moule, C. F. D. *An Idiom-Book of New Testament Greek*. 2nd ed. Cambridge University Press, 1959.

———. *The Gospel According to Mark*. Cambridge: Cambridge University Press, 1965.

Moulton, James Hope, Wilbert Francis Howard, and Nigel Turner. *A Grammar of New Testament Greek*. 4 vols. Edinburgh: T&T Clark, 1908–1976.

Moulton, James Hope, and George Milligan. *Vocabulary of the Greek New Testament*. London: Hodder & Stoughton, 1930. Reprint. Peabody, Mass.: Hendrickson, 1997.

Mounce, William D. *The Morphology of Biblical Greek*. Grand Rapids: Zondervan, 1994.

Muraoka, T. *A Greek-English Lexicon of the Septuagint*. Louvain, Belgium: Peeters, 2009.

Neirynck, F. *Duality in Mark: Contributions to the Study of the Markan Redaction*. Bibliotheca ephemeridum theologicarum lovaniensium 31. Leuven, Belgium: Leuven University Press, 1972.

New Documents Illustrating Early Christianity: A Review of Greek Inscriptions and Papyri. Edited by G. H. R. Horsley (vols. 1–5) and S. R. Llewelyn (vols. 6–9). Macquarie University: The Ancient History Documentary Research Centre, 1981–2002.

Novum Testamentum Graece. Edited by Barbara and Kurt Aland, Johannes Karavidopoulos, Carlo M. Martini, and Bruce Metzger. 27th ed. Stuttgart: Deutsche Bibelgesellschaft, 1993.

O'Donnell, Matthew Brook. "Linguistic Fingerprints or Style by Numbers? The Use of Statistics in the Discussion of Authorship of New Testament Documents." Pages 206–62 in *Linguistics and the New Testament: Critical Junctures*. Edited by S. E. Porter and D. A. Carson. Sheffield: Sheffield Academic, 1999.

Pascut, Beniamin. "The So-Called *Passivum Divinum* in Mark's Gospel." *Novum Testamentum* 54 (2012): 313–33.

Pennington, Jonathan T. "Deponency in Koine Greek: The Grammatical Question and the Lexicographical Dilemma." *Trinity Journal* 24 (2003): 55–76.

———. "Test Driving the Theory: Middle Voice Forms in Matthew." Paper presented at the annual meeting of the SBL, Atlanta, Ga., 2010.

Pernot, Hubert. "Greek and the Gospels." *Expository Times* 38 (1927): 103–8.

Petersen, Walter. *Diminutives in -ION: A Study in Semantics*. Weimar, Germany: R. Wagner Sohn, 1910.

Plummer, Alfred. *The Gospel According to St. Mark*. Cambridge Greek Testament. Cambridge: Cambridge University Press, 1914. Reprint. Grand Rapids: Baker, 1982.

Porter, Stanley E. "'In the Vicinity of Jericho': Luke 18:35 in the Light of Its Synoptic Parallels." *Bulletin of Biblical Research* 2 (1992): 91–104.

———. *Verbal Aspect in the Greek of the New Testament, with Reference to Tense and Mood*. Studies in Biblical Greek 1. 2nd ed. New York: Peter Lang, 1993.

———. *Idioms of the Greek New Testament*. Sheffield: JSOT Press, 1994.

————. "The Greek Language of the New Testament." Pages 99–130 in *A Handbook to the Exegesis of the New Testament*. Edited by S. E. Porter. New Testament Tools and Studies 25. Leiden: Brill, 1997.

————. "Verbal Aspect and Discourse Function in Mark 16:1-8." Pages 123–37 in *Studies in the Greek Bible: Essays in Honor of Francis T. Gignac, S.J.* Edited by J. Corley and V. Skemp. Catholic Biblical Quarterly Monographs 44. Washington D.C.: Catholic Biblical Association, 2008.

————. "Matthew and Mark: The Contribution of Recent Linguistic Thought." Pages 97–119 in *Mark and Matthew I: Comparative Readings: Understanding the Earliest Gospels in Their First-Century Settings*. Edited by E.-M. Becker and A. Runesson. Wissenschaftliche Untersuchungen zum Neuen Testament 271. Tübingen: Mohr Siebeck, 2011.

Proctor, M. A. "The 'Western' Text of Mark 1:41: A Case for the Angry Jesus." Ph.D. diss., Baylor University, 1999.

Rahlfs, Alfred. *Septuaginta*. Revised by Robert Hanhart. Stuttgart: Deutsche Bibelgesellschaft, 2006.

Reiser, Marius. *Syntax und Stil des Markusevangeliums im Licht der hellenistischen Volkliteratur*. Wissenschaftliche Untersuchungen zum Neuen Testament 2.11. Tübingen: J. C. B. Mohr, 1984.

Robertson, A. T. *A Grammar of the Greek New Testament in the Light of Historical Research*. 4th ed. Nashville: Broadman, 1923.

Robertson, A. T., and W. Hersey Davis. *A New Short Grammar of the Greek Testament*. 10th ed. New York: Harper & Brothers, 1933. Reprint. Grand Rapids: Baker, 1977.

Rosenthal, Franz. *Grammar of Biblical Aramaic*. Wiesbaden: Harrassowitz, 1963.

Schlier, Heinrich. "ἀμήν." Pages 335–38 in vol. 1 of *Theological Dictionary of the New Testament*. Edited by G. Kittel and G. Friedrich. Translated by G. Bromiley. 10 vols. Grand Rapids: Eerdmans, 1964–1976.

Schrage, Wolfgang. "συναγωγή, ἐπισυναγωγή, ἀρχισυνάγωγος, ἀποσυνάγωγος." Pages 798–852 in vol. 7 of *Theological Dictionary of the New Testament*. Edited by G. Kittel and G. Friedrich. Translated by G. Bromiley. 10 vols. Grand Rapids: Eerdmans, 1964–1976.

Schultz, Helmut. "Jerusalem." Pages 324–29 in vol. 2 of *New International Dictionary of New Testament Theology*. Edited by Colin Brown. 3 vols. Grand Rapids: Zondervan, 1975–1985.

Seesemann, Heinrich. "ὀπίσω, ὄπισθεν." Pages 289–92 in vol. 5 of *Theological Dictionary of the New Testament*. Edited by G. Kittel and G. Friedrich. Translated by G. Bromiley. 10 vols. Grand Rapids: Eerdmans, 1964–1976.

Sherwin-White, A. N. *Roman Society and Roman Law in the New Testament*. Oxford: Oxford University Press, 1963. Reprint. Grand Rapids: Baker, 1978.

Silva, Moisés. *God, Language and Scripture: Reading the Bible in the Light of General Linguistics*. Foundations of Contemporary Interpretation 4. Grand Rapids: Zondervan, 1990.

Sim, Margaret Gavin. *Marking Thought and Talk in New Testament Greek: New Light from Linguistics on the Particle ἵνα and ὅτι*. Eugene, Ore.: Pickwick, 2010.

Smith, Barry D. *Introducing the New Testament: A Workbook*. Moncton, NB, Canada: Crandall University, 2010. <http://www.abu.nb.ca/courses/NTIntro/PDFFiles.htm>, part 5, <http://www.abu.nb.ca/courses/NTIntro/PDF/5_Mark.pdf>. Accessed May 28, 2011.

Smyth, Herbert Weir. *Greek Grammar*. Revised by Gordon M. Messing. Cambridge, Mass.: Harvard University Press, 1956.

Souter, Alexander. *A Pocket Lexicon to the Greek New Testament*. Oxford: Clarendon, 1916.

Stein, Robert H. *The Synoptic Problem: An Introduction*. Grand Rapids: Baker, 1987.

———. *Studying the Synoptic Gospels: Origin and Interpretation*. 2nd ed. [of The Synoptic Problem]. Grand Rapids: Baker, 2001.

———. *Mark*. Baker Exegetical Commentary on the New Testament. Grand Rapids: Baker, 2008.

Steyn, Gert J. "Which 'LXX' Are We Talking about in NT Scholarship?" Pages 697–707 in *Die Septuaginta: Text, Kontexte, Lebenswelton*. Edited by M. Karrer and W. Kraus. Wissenschaftliche Untersuchungen zum Neuen Testament 219. Tübingen: Mohr Siebeck, 2008.

Strathmann, H. "μάρτυς, μαρτυρέω, μαρτυρία, μαρτύριον, et al." Pages 474–514 in vol. 4 of *Theological Dictionary of the New Testament*. Edited by G. Kittel and G. Friedrich. Ttranslated by G. Bromiley. 10 vols. Grand Rapids: Eerdmans, 1964–1976.

Swete, Henry Barclay. *The Gospel According to St Mark: The Greek Text with Introduction Notes and Indices*. 3rd ed. London: Macmillan, 1909.

Taylor, Bernard A. "Deponency and Greek Lexicography." Pages 167–76 in *Biblical Greek Language and Lexicography: Essays in Honor of Frederick W. Danker*. Edited by B. Taylor, J. A. L. Lee, P. R. Burton, and R. E. Whitaker. Grand Rapids: Eerdmans, 2004.

Taylor, Vincent. *The Gospel According to St. Mark.* 2nd ed. [London]: Macmillan, 1966. Reprint. Grand Rapids: Baker, 1981.

Thesaurus Linguae Graecae: A Digital Library of Greek Literature. University of California, Irvine, 2009. (Web-based edition, post-TLG E, accessible at <www.tlg.uci.edu>, most recent database update: 25 May 2013.)

Thrall, Margaret E. *Greek Particles in the New Testament: Linguistic and Exegetical Studies.* New Testament Tools and Studies 3. Grand Rapids: Eerdmans, 1962.

Tischendorf, Constantine. *Novum Testamentum Graece.* 2 vols. 8th ed. Leipzig: Giesecke & Devrient, 1899.

Titrud, Kermit. "The Function of καί in the Greek New Testament and an Application to 2 Peter." Pages 240–70 in *Linguistics and New Testament Interpretation: Essays on Discourse Analysis.* Edited by D. A. Black. Nashville: Broadman, 1992.

Turner, C. H. "Marcan Usage: Notes, Critical and Exegetical on the Second Gospel." Pages 3–146 in *The Language and Style of the Gospel of Mark.* Edited by J. K. Elliott. Novum Testamentum Supplement 71. Leiden: Brill, 1993.

Turner, Nigel. *Syntax.* Vol. 3 of *A Grammar of New Testament Greek.* Edited by J. Moulton. Edinburgh: T&T Clark, 1963.

———. "The Style of Mark." Pages 11–30 in *Style.* Vol. 4 of *A Grammar of New Testament Greek.* Edited by J. Moulton. Edinburgh: T&T Clark, 1976.

Van der Horst, P. W. "Can a Book End with a ΓΑΡ? A Note on Mark XVI.8." *Journal of Theological Studies* 23 (1972): 121–24.

Viviano, B. T. "The High Priest's Servant's Ear: Mark 14:47." *Revue Biblique* 96 (1989): 71–80.

Voelz, James W. "The Greek of Codex Vaticanus in the Second Gospel and Marcan Greek." *Novum Testamentum* 47 (2005): 209–49.

Wackernagel, Jacob. *Lectures on Syntax with Special Reference to Greek, Latin, and Germanic.* Translated and edited by D. Langslow. Oxford: Oxford University Press, 2009.

Wallace, Daniel B. *Greek Grammar Beyond the Basics: An Exegetical Syntax of the New Testament.* Grand Rapids: Zondervan, 1996.

———. "Mark 16:8 as the Conclusion to the Second Gospel." Pages 1–39 in *Perspectives on the Ending of Mark: 4 Views.* Edited by D. A. Black. Nashville: Broadman & Holman, 2008.

Waltke, Bruce K., and M. O'Connor. *An Introduction to Biblical Hebrew Syntax.* Winona Lake, Ind.: Eisenbrauns, 1990.

Wasserman, Tommy. "The 'Son Of God' Was in The Beginning (Mark 1:1)." *Journal of Theological Studies*, n.s. 62.1 (2011): 20–50.

Waterman, Mark M. W. *The Empty Tomb Tradition of Mark: Text, History, and Theological Studies*. Los Angeles: Agathos, 2006.

Westcott, B. F., and F. J. A. Hort. *Introduction to the New Testament in the Original Greek and Introduction to the New Testament in the Original Greek with Notes on Selected Readings*. 2 vols. New York: Harper & Brothers, 1882.

Wikgren, Allen. "ΑΡΧΗ ΤΟΥ ΕΥΑΓΓΕΛΙΟΝ." *Journal of Biblical Literature* 61 (1942): 11–20.

Williams, Joel F. "Literary Approaches to the End of Mark's Gospel." *Journal of the Evangelical Theological Society* 42 (1999): 21–35.

Williams, Peter J. "The Linguistic Background to Jesus' Dereliction Cry (Matthew 27:46; Mark 15:34)." Pages 1–12 in *The New Testament in Its First Century Setting: Essays on Context and Background in Honour of B. W. Winter on His 65th Birthday*. Edited by P. J. Williams, A. D. Clarke, P. M. Head, and D. I. Brewer. Grand Rapids: Eerdmans, 2004.

———. "An Examination of Ehrman's Case for ὀργισθείς in Mark 1:41." *Novum Testamentum* 54 (2012): 1–12.

Williams, Travis B. "Bringing Method to the Madness: Examining the Style of the Longer Ending of Mark." *Bulletin of Biblical Research* 20.3 (2010): 397–418.

Winer, George Benedict. *A Grammar of the Idiom of the New Testament*. Edited by G. Lünemann. Translated by J. H. Thayer. Andover, Mass.: Draper, 1866; 2nd printing with corrections, 1874.

———. *A Grammar of the Idiom of the New Testament*. Translated by W. F. Moulton. Edinburgh: T&T Clark, 1882.

Young, Richard A. *Intermediate New Testament Greek*. Nashville: Broadman & Holman, 1994.

Zerwick, Maximilian. *Biblical Greek Illustrated by Examples*. Rome: Scripta Pontificii Instituti Biblici, 1963.

GRAMMAR INDEX

315

AUTHOR INDEX

Lightning Source UK Ltd.
Milton Keynes UK
UKHW012252080721
386851UK00003B/131

9 781481 302395